The Life and Death
HAROLD
HOLT

The Life and Death of

HAROLD
HOLT

TOM FRAME

ALLEN&UNWIN

In association with the National Archives of Australia

Allen & Unwin
83 Alexander Street
Crows Nest NSW 2065
Australia
Phone: (61 2) 8425 0100
Fax: (61 2) 9906 2218
Email: info@allenandunwin.com
Web: www.allenandunwin.com

National Archives of Australia
PO Box 7425
Canberra Business Centre ACT 2610
Australia
Phone: (61 2) 6212 3609
Fax: (61 2) 6212 3914
Email: archives@naa.gov.au
Web: www.naa.gov.au

The National Library of Australia
Cataloguing-in-Publication entry:

Frame, T.R. (Thomas R.), 1962 –.
    The life and death of Harold Holt.

    Includes index.
    ISBN 1 74114 672 0.

    1. Holt, Harold, 1908–1967. 2. Prime ministers – Australia
    – Biography. 3. Australia – Politics and government
    1965–1972. I. Title.

994.06

Index compiled by Helen Frame
Set in 11.5/14 pt Bembo by Midland Typesetters, Maryborough, Victoria
Printed by Griffin Press, Netley, South Australia

10 9 8 7 6 5 4 3 2 1

Harold Holt's philosophy of life

'If'

Rudyard Kipling

If you can keep your head when all about you
Are losing theirs and blaming it on you,
If you can trust yourself when all men doubt you,
But make allowance for their doubting too;
If you can wait, and not be tired by waiting,
Or, being lied about, don't deal in lies,
Or, being hated, don't give way to hating,
And yet don't look too good, nor talk too wise.
If you can dream—and not make dreams your master;
If you can think—and not make thoughts your aim,
If you can meet with Triumph and Disaster
And treat those two impostors just the same;
If you can bear to hear the truth you've spoken
Twisted by knaves to make a trap for fools,
Or watch the things you gave your life to, broken,
And stoop and build 'em up with worn-out tools;
If you can make one heap of all your winnings
And risk it on one turn of pitch-and-toss,
And lose, and start again at your beginnings
And never breathe a word about your loss:
If you can force your heart and nerve and sinew
To serve your turn long after they are gone,
And so hold on when there is nothing in you
Except the Will which says to them: 'Hold on'
If you can talk with crowds and keep your virtue,
Or walk with Kings—nor lose the common touch,
If neither foes nor loving friends can hurt you,
If all men count with you, but none too much:
If you can fill the unforgiving minute
With sixty seconds' worth of distance run,
Yours is the Earth and everything that's in it,
And—which is more—you'll be a Man, my son!

Contents

Foreword   The Honourable Peter Costello, MP   ix

Introduction: A life that should have overshadowed a death   xi
Acknowledgments   xviii

The Life

1   A lonely life, 1908–40   3
2   The early years   9
3   Laying the foundations, 1940–49   20
4   Halcyon days, 1950–58   41
5   Heir apparent   54
6   Immigration, 1950–56   64
7   Labour and National Service, 1950–58   76
8   Patience and persistence, 1958–65   99
9   The bloodless succession, January–February 1966   131

And Death

10   From good to better, March–December 1966   157
11   'All the Way': External Affairs, 1966–67   174
12   From bad to worse, January–October 1967   204
13   Controversy and complaint, November–14 December 1967   225
14   Fate and destiny, 15 December 1967–12 March 1968   246
15   Myths and mysteries?, 1968–2005   272
16   The legacy   296

Appendix 1: Milestones in Harold Holt's career   309
Appendix 2: Holt ministries   313
Note on sources   317
Notes   319
Index   357

Foreword

I REMEMBER THE DAY THAT Harold Holt disappeared in the surf off Portsea as my first clear memory of an Australian political event. It was the first time I had ever seen a news flash on TV.

At first the reports were of confusion. The Prime Minister was missing. There was general horror that such a thing could occur. Then over subsequent hours and days the television screen played out the real life drama of the search. Ultimately there was no satisfactory explanation of what had happened or how, and a sense of hollow loss gathered over the mystery.

Up until now too little serious work has been published on the career and the times of Harold Holt, as the circumstances of his death came to overshadow the achievements of his life. In the sweep of history where we like to remember a leader or his term by a particular incident, Holt's disappearance became the defining event of his Prime Ministership.

As Tom Frame shows in this thoughtful and insightful account, Holt was a substantive politician who changed and modernised Australia in important ways. This book paints a picture of Harold Holt the man and his engagement in contemporaneous events that led to great policy changes in Australia.

Harold Holt was the Prime Minister who dismantled one of the most significant founding policies of the Federation: the 'White Australia' policy. And it was Harold Holt who brought on the historic referendum that belatedly allowed for the counting of Aboriginal people in the Census, and empowered the federal government to legislate for all Australians.

Australia's serious engagement with Asia began with Harold Holt, who in less than two years as Prime Minister visited Singapore, Malaysia, Thailand, Vietnam, Cambodia, Hong Kong, Laos, Taiwan and South Korea.

The conversion from imperial to decimal currency, which had far-reaching implications for every Australian, was planned by Holt as Treasurer before he oversaw the changeover as Prime Minister.

Harold Holt was the first Member for Higgins in the House of Representatives. He is remembered most visibly in the electorate of Higgins through, of all things, the Harold Holt Memorial Swimming Pool. This has always seemed to me to be a slightly disturbing memorial.

But apart from the visible memorial is the living memory of friends, supporters and family. Through his sons, Sam and Nick Holt, I have heard a lot of the colour and the personal aspects of Harold and Zara and their family life. Of course, many of the campaign workers who served on Harold's Electorate Committee and in the Liberal Party branches in Higgins have also worked with me. All of them tell stories of someone universally liked, unfailingly polite and widely respected.

It is now nearly 40 years since the untimely end of Holt's Prime Ministership. With the advantage of that period to assess the outcome of many of the changes to policy Holt initiated or supervised, Tom Frame has brought us an important study of the man and his times.

The Honourable Peter Costello, MP
Federal Member for Higgins,
Deputy Leader of the Liberal Party,
Treasurer of the Commonwealth of Australia

Introduction

A life that should have overshadowed a death

MANY BIOGRAPHERS FIND THAT a sympathetic relationship develops between them and their subject. The American Anglican priest and journalist, William Bayard, whose biography of Woodrow Wilson was published just before Wilson was elected President of the United States, argued that every biographer projects 'his own prepossessions and desires into his conception of the career of his hero'. Although this is perhaps overstating the case, a biography usually requires an empathetic author. But the biographer's opinion of the subject is unlikely to remain unchanged throughout the research and writing of the biography. As the subject's character and motivations are gradually unravelled, revealed and understood, the subject becomes the focus of either more or less esteem, respect and admiration. The biographer also develops a greater appreciation of the context of the subject's life and the material and emotional circumstances influencing their actions and attitudes. Some suggest that significant times produce significant individuals. Others claim that forceful individuals change the outcome of events or the direction of public life. A third group says that neither mortals nor time controls what happens in history but rather providence, destiny, fate or even chance. For me, all three are represented and present in history, and reflected in the life and times of Harold Edward Holt.

As a small boy Harold never received the parental affection he appeared to crave. As an adult he sought affirmation and acclamation from a range of personal challenges and professional achievements. He brought to public office humility and humanity, during a parliamentary career that spanned more than three decades. Holt was strengthened, toughened and chastened by politics and government. His initiative, energy and determination would have a long and abiding impact on parliamentary processes and everyday life. He changed the character of existing institutions and created new ones.

Despite this, Harold Holt has frequently been portrayed as a victim of circumstances in which he could exert little influence and over which he certainly could not exercise control. In a 1973 *Meanjin* article, Manning Clark thought that Holt was not the right man for the times when he became Prime Minister in January 1966.

> Holt stood for something: he wanted to break down Australia's reputation as one of the last-ditch defenders of the white man's supremacy. But almost before he began his work he was sucked into the maelstrom of Vietnam. So a man who had a desperate drive to love and be loved found himself in partnership with all those societies in the world which were about to be swept into the dust-bin of human history. But before he was engulfed by the progressive forces the sea took him and he was seen no more. His funeral in Melbourne became a requiem for a dying culture.[1]

Geoffrey Bolton pointed to the circumstances of his becoming Prime Minister as a fatal legacy: '[Holt] suffered from the expectation that, like Anthony Eden after Churchill, he would prove to have been too long the crown prince to develop a style and politics of his own'.[2] Don Whitington also thought that Holt's long wait for leadership had dire consequences: 'Although he became Prime Minister eventually, he had served too long in subordinate roles, been too loyal to too many other men and causes, seen the big prizes carried off by too many others too often, to be capable of handling supreme authority with the flair and élan, the dignity and authority the Australian public had come to expect after men like Curtin and Menzies'.[3] Craig McGregor argues that 'after Menzies, the Liberal Party found itself saddled with three nondescript Prime Ministers, each successively worse than the one before. The first was . . . a smiling, dapper, plasticine man who was by instinct much more of a consensus politician than Menzies'.[4] Social commentator Ronald Conway saw Holt as an 'intelligent, decent man [but] . . . also a garrulous public bore—yet another bookkeeper thrust upon high'.[5]

Having come to know Harold Holt over the last decade through reading his words, listening to his voice on audiotapes and watching television footage of interviews, I would take issue with these descriptions as being inaccurate and, perhaps, politically biased. I will leave the reader to determine which. But what prompted me to embark on a biography of Harold Holt? My interest in Holt started in the early 1990s while researching my doctoral thesis on the loss of the destroyer HMAS *Voyager* after its collision with the aircraft carrier HMAS *Melbourne* on 10 February 1964. The thesis was published in 1992 with the title *Where Fate Calls: The HMAS* Voyager *Tragedy.*[6] I was struck by the extent to which Holt misjudged a looming public controversy and the backbench revolt his mismanagement prompted. The decision to hold an unprecedented second Royal Commission into the loss of *Voyager* wounded Holt's government and weakened his leadership. Yet when I started some research into Australia's conversion to decimal currency in February 1966, Holt's active role in planning for decimalisation contributed substantially to the efficiency and effectiveness of its implementation.

My decision to write a biography was, ultimately, provoked by what I considered unfair personal and professional denigration of the late Prime Minister. This took two forms. For almost 40 years, Holt has been castigated for an off-the-cuff remark at the White House in June 1966, when he pledged that Australia would be 'All the Way with LBJ' in South Vietnam. Holt is not the only Australian Prime Minister to make fulsome public statements about the trans-Pacific relationship. John Gorton promised to go 'Waltzing Matilda' with the United States in South-east Asia; William McMahon spoke of 'a time in the life of a man' to suggest that Australia was conscience-bound to support the United States in South Vietnam; Bob Hawke said that 'Australia and the United States would be together forever'; and John Howard has told President George W. Bush that America has 'no closer friend anywhere in the world' than Australia.

The second was the hullabaloo surrounding his 'mysterious' disappearance off Cheviot Beach in December 1967 and the malicious rumours and controversy it prompted. Some claim that Holt either committed suicide or sought asylum with the Chinese after years of espionage. Such claims are easy to make, difficult to dissect and almost impossible to refute, but I hope to show that those who make them have not provided sufficient evidence to warrant their allegations even being taken seriously. And yet, the force and effect of their imputations has remained.

But can a book be sustained solely by a desire to challenge misinformed opinion or malicious deception? Holt's political career contained important contributions to Australian political, social and economic life that have not been adequately recognised. Although he is not usually numbered among the great Prime Ministers of Australia, how he achieved and exercised national leadership is itself worthy of analysis. I began the research for this book in 1993 but was distracted along the way by other writing projects. This explains why some of the personal interviews were conducted in the mid-1990s and others more recently.

Surprisingly little has been written about Harold Holt. Zara Holt's light and breezy semi-autobiographical *My Life and Harry*,[7] published within a year of her husband's disappearance, is one of only three extended treatments. It offers some detail on Holt's early life, insights into his character and personal recollections of her travels with him. The narrative is, however, quite disjointed and she is, possibly deliberately, vague on the circumstances surrounding the end of their courtship in 1935, her subsequent marriage to James Fell, the birth of her three children, and her divorce and marriage to Harold Holt. Zara's intention naturally is to paint the most flattering portrait of her husband and to display the best picture of their relationship. She makes no mention of Harold's infidelity nor of her sadness at his indifference to some of her needs.

The second account of Holt's life is Anthony Grey's *The Prime Minister Was a Spy*,[8] published in 1983. Quite apart from its sensational allegations that Holt was a long-time spy for the Nationalist and Communist governments of China and that he was whisked away from Cheviot Beach in a Chinese submarine (both of which are dealt with in Chapter 13), it contains a large amount of material that cannot be verified from extant primary sources. There are no footnotes or references to official sources or documents, and Grey's principal source of verbal information, Lieutenant Commander Ronald Titcombe MBE RAN Ret'd, died in January 2001. I interviewed both Grey and Titcombe in September and October 2000 but could not establish where they had obtained the personal details concerning Holt's life in the period 1927–34, nor was I able to obtain any documents relating to the book's sensational claims. I do not know whether Titcombe left any personal papers and Grey has been negotiating for some years over the sale of his papers to any Australian archival institution prepared to buy them. These documents remain in his possession.

The third is Lloyd Broderick's Honours thesis, 'Transition and tragedy: The Prime Ministership of Harold Holt, 1966–67'.[9] It is based primarily on *Hansard*, newspaper and magazine articles, and published secondary works but does include some valuable insights drawn from interviews he

conducted with Holt's colleagues. Of greatest interest to me is his disagreement with the widely held view that the so-called "'Menzies Era"
did not end until the day of Holt's death'. I share Broderick's view that
1966–67 was 'indeed a time of transition' that must be assessed separately
from the Menzies years, a view also shared by Ian Hancock in his excellent
essay in John Nethercote's edited collection, *Liberalism and the Australian
Federation*.[10]

In addition to these three works, short and uneven biographies of Holt
appear in the many compendiums on Australia's prime ministers. The best
is clearly Ian Hancock's chapter in *Australian Prime Ministers*.[11] Although it
runs to only 5000 words it is accurate and fair. This cannot be said for Paul
Hasluck's extended contemporary portrait of Holt in *The Chance of
Politics*, published by his son Nicholas Hasluck after his death.[12]

Almost everything Hasluck has to say about Holt is either critical or
dismissive. He clearly had little respect for Holt's intelligence and scant
regard for his abilities. When Hasluck mentions that Holt communicated
well with people 'at his level', the reader is left in no doubt that this 'level'
was clearly far below Hasluck's own. By way of example, Hasluck states
that although Holt was his 'inferior in intellectual grasp, understanding,
knowledge and powers of analysis, [he] was a far better politician than I
could ever be'. While he does laud the qualities of colleagues such as
Richard Casey, Shane Paltridge and Allen Fairhall, Hasluck seems unable
to bring himself to praise Holt, who is portrayed as superficial, shallow and
simple. Holt succeeded only by personal charm and the mediocrity of his
colleagues. Despite several factual inaccuracies in his account, Hasluck
claims an intimate personal knowledge of Holt and the attitudes of others
towards him, while professing to know the mind of everyone whose
opinion mattered in Canberra. Zara is deemed 'vulgar' and without 'style',
and her daughters-in-law denounced for exposing their 'naked bodies' to
photographers. (Holt did receive a number of letters condemning him
for being photographed with his bikini-clad daughters-in-law. Mrs A.
Blamirer said that 'the representative of this nation cannot afford to lose
dignity and smudge his image be permitting overzealous camera men to
take offensive Hollywood style pictures'.)[13] While Hasluck offers some
rare personal insights into the Liberal Party between 1949 and 1967, *The
Chance of Politics* says a great deal more about the author than those he
claimed to know so well.

In terms of its size and the sources from which it draws, this is the
first comprehensive treatment of Australia's seventeenth prime minister.[14]

There are, however, two deficiencies in this account that I readily acknowledge. The first is the absence of narrative drawing on private diaries and personal correspondence. Harold Holt never kept a private diary, nor did he write many private letters in which he expressed personal thoughts or aspirations. He kept his feelings and opinions largely to himself. There is no record, for instance, of when he thought Menzies would actually retire and how this made him feel. Paul Hasluck's private opinion of Holt has been published, but there is no record of Holt's assessment of Hasluck's performance or suitability for prime ministerial office. Holt kept silent on the strengths and weaknesses of both allies and adversaries. Holt was not a great reader and showed little interest in history, so it is not surprising that there is no evidence Holt ever planned to write memoirs or an autobiography. Not long after he became Prime Minister he received a letter from Lord (Stanley Melbourne) Bruce concerning how he might treat would-be biographers. Bruce suggested that he might grant a biographer access to his papers but retain a right of veto over what might be drawn from them.[15] Holt's reply bordered on indifference. Beyond diligently keeping an extensive scrapbook of press cuttings covering his public life from his first election campaign in 1934, he appeared largely unconcerned with how history would view him or his government.

The second deficiency relates to details about Holt's life before 1949. Other than a broad outline, not a great deal is known about his childhood or adolescence. We know practically nothing of his mother or even the cause of her early death. He never mentioned her or his parents' divorce in any public forum. There are contrasting accounts of Harold's sometimes turbulent relationship with his father, Tom Holt, but his brother Cliff predeceased him and did not leave any recollections of these matters. Harold never commented on his tumultuous relationship with Zara during the 1930s nor on his romance with Lola Thring and the birth of her daughter Frances after she married Harold's father in 1936. It is not clear when he and Zara decided to resume their relationship and whether the birth of Zara's twins had any bearing on their subsequent decision to marry. I suspect it did but cannot prove it.

Holt was almost silent about his brief time in the Army, his reasons for declining commissions in both the Australian Imperial Force and the Royal Australian Air Force, and whether he seriously considered returning to uniformed life after he lost his Cabinet position in 1941. We do not know precisely why he withdrew his support for embattled Prime Minister

Robert Menzies in 1941 and whether the two men ever spoke at length about the matter. Holt did not reflect on the demise of the United Australia Party (UAP) in 1944 nor explain why he did not play a leading role in the establishment of its successor—the Liberal Party. There are few references to personal friendships or political affiliations, religious beliefs or private ambitions. Other than his contributions to parliamentary debates and public speeches, there are very few details of his life outside parliament.

Most of this changed in December 1949 when the Liberals won office and Holt was given a senior portfolio. Thereafter, it is possible to determine his whereabouts almost every day of every year and what he was doing—at least as far as his public duties were concerned.

While I have endeavoured to obtain private material about personal matters, the information is sparse and uneven. This biography is, therefore, unavoidably more about Harold Holt the politician and less about Harold Holt as son, brother, husband, father, grandfather and friend. Similarly, a number of interviewees told me that Holt had intimate relationships with women before and after he married Zara. In endeavouring to offer an accurate and insightful portrait of a man, I do not wish him or his reputation any harm. Because some aspects of his private life found expression in his public duties they are legitimately the subject of comment and critique. I have not included the names of women with whom Holt allegedly had a sexual relationship because I was unable to confirm or deny that most of these relationships took place. By their very nature they were always illicit and Holt was very 'discreet'. Holt's former colleagues assumed rather than knew he was seeing other women although Zara confirmed his frequent infidelities with some bitterness shortly before her death. The sole exception is Marjorie Gillespie, who identified herself publicly as Holt's last lover. I am not concerned with the details of her relationship with Holt; only that he was intimate with a woman other than his wife. Holt's extramarital affairs are relevant only because they reveal a side of Holt's character that hints at its essence—a need for affection and an essentially selfish desire to be loved. I have no doubt that Zara was right when she insisted that Harold never seriously contemplated leaving her for another woman. Had he not disappeared off Cheviot Beach in December 1967, I am sure that he and Zara would have grown old together in retirement on the North Queensland coast. While I have not attempted to censure Holt for his behaviour, I am nonetheless able to record my sympathy for Zara who felt betrayed and diminished by her husband's behaviour.

Acknowledgments

THIS BOOK WAS WRITTEN with the goodwill of Harold Holt's family who made material available and answered specific questions but is in no sense an 'authorised' or 'commissioned' biography. It is neither an apology nor a eulogy. As I was five years old when Holt disappeared, my impressions of this man and his life have been informed entirely by photographs and films, documents and papers, and the recollections of his family and friends. I am not a member of any political party nor am I affiliated with any organisation whose aims or objectives are of a party political nature. I have not received any money from any organisation to assist with the research or publication of this book. The opinions expressed are, therefore, entirely my own.

A great many people have contributed to this work in many different ways. The staff at the Lyndon Baines Johnson Presidential Library in Austin, Texas know their collection intimately and were generous with their assistance; Brian Loughnane, the Federal Director of the Liberal Party, granted me access to the Liberal Party's records in the National Library of Australia. The names of those who gave of their time in granting an interview or in answering my correspondence are listed in the bibliography and include: Professor Peter Bailey, Sir Nigel Bowen, Sir John Bunting, Dr Jim Cairns, Clyde Cameron, Sir John Carrick, Ian Castles, Sir Fred Chaney, Don Chipp, Sergeant David Dimsey (Victorian State Coroner's Assistants Unit), Dr Jim Forbes, Sir John Gorton, Sir Clarrie Harders, Peter Howson, John Jess, Sir James Killen, Terry Larkin, Sir Peter Lawler, the Reverend Dr Malcolm Mackay, Dr A. W. Martin, Dame Pattie Menzies, Sir Hubert Opperman, Frederick Osborne, Andrew Peacock,

Keith Pearson, Sir James Scholtens, Ian Sinclair, Commander John Smith RAN Rtd, Edward St John, Reg Withers and Gough Whitlam. Tony Eggleton, former Prime Ministerial Press Secretary, was most helpful. Jim Short, Noel Flanagan, Terry Larkin, Professor Peter Bailey, Pat De Lacy, Mary Newport, Peter Kelly and John Farquharson read and commented upon earlier drafts. Malcolm Fraser read sections of the penultimate draft. Although not identifying any errors of fact, he declined to make any comment, stating that: 'This should not be construed as expressing any agreement or disagreement towards the book'.[1] John Nethercote, who by chance was on board the P&O liner RMS *Iberia* as it sailed past Cheviot Beach *en route* from Melbourne to Sydney just twelve hours before Harold Holt went for his fateful swim, read the entire manuscript and made many invaluable comments. His knowledge of people and events associated with Federal Parliament and the Commonwealth Public Service is extraordinary and I am most appreciative of his advice.

I owe a particular debt of gratitude to Nick and Sam Holt for their generous assistance and support. At Allen & Unwin, Rebecca Kaiser believed in this project from the outset and was a vigorous advocate of its merits. Emma Cotter was, once again, a very sensitive and insightful editor. Gabrielle Hyslop, Angela McAdam, Alex Bellis, Lenore Coltheart and David Bell from the National Archives of Australia were superb. I am grateful for their daily enthusiasm for my project, the ready provision of assistance from staff familiar with the collection, for maintaining a research room that was conducive to research and note-taking, and for the illustrative material in this book. Rosa Ferranda, the Director of Legislation and Documents at the Senate Table Office, arranged for me to examine the RAAF Flight Authorisation Books and Passenger Manifests that were at the centre of the 1967 VIP airline scandal; Murray Bragge supplied me with original copies of the *Australian* the day before and after Holt's drowning; Terry and Eleanor Holt provided some invaluable Holt family history.

I especially want to thank the Honourable Peter Costello MP— Federal Treasurer, Deputy Leader of the Liberal Party and Member for Higgins—for contributing the Foreword. Mr Costello has followed in several of Harold Holt's footsteps. Both he and Harold Holt held the Treasury portfolio and were deputy party leader for a considerable period. Holt was the first member for Higgins after its creation in 1949 and served the electorate for eighteen years. At the time of writing, Mr Costello has held the seat for fifteen years.

Finally I would like to thank my wife Helen and daughters Megan and Kelly for their interest in my work and their loving encouragement. It is only because they provide such a happy home environment that I can find the enthusiasm to research and the energy to write. There is something of Helen, Megan and Kelly in all my books.

Dr Tom Frame
Canberra, ACT
Australia Day 2005

PART 1
The Life

CHAPTER 1
A lonely life
1908–40

FAMILIES IMPART TO THEIR members a sense of identity, continuity, even destiny. It is in families that values are taught and virtues acquired, where expectations are conveyed and privileges conferred. Those born into affluent or influential families soon recognise that they are being encouraged to live in a certain way because it exploits the advantages endowed upon the whole family. Other children grow up in social settings that are free from any sense of inheritance or transcendent duty. The Holt family was an example of the latter.

The surname 'Holt' has an English local origin derived from the place where an individual once lived or held land. A 'holt' was a 'wood' or a 'grove'. Early instances of the surname are frequently preceded by the words 'de' or 'del' which translates literally as 'man from'. A 'Hugh de Holte' of Kent was recorded in the *Templars Records* of 1185. Simon del Holt was recorded in the *Pipe Rolls* of Warwickshire. Only one branch of the family became prominent, through their possession of Ashton Hall in Birmingham during the sixteenth century.[1] The family coat of arms carries the motto *exaltavit humiles*, which is usually translated as 'He hath exalted the humble'.

James Holt, a shoemaker from a poorer Birmingham branch of the family, emigrated to Australia with his wife Mary-Ann in 1829. Their eldest son, Henry, was aged three when they arrived in Sydney. After trying his hand at the gold diggings, Henry began the first bullock cart service from the Canberra district to Sydney. He married Ann Lemon on 26 January 1858 at St Peter's Anglican Church at Campbelltown. They had six sons and six daughters. The eldest, Thomas, was born at Campbelltown in 1858. In 1874 the Holts arrived at Nubba in the Harden-Murrumbur-rah district west of Canberra where they obtained a 1040-acre property at Sherlock Creek, later known as 'Sunnyside', by government grant. Henry died in 1903 and is buried in Murrumburrah cemetery. 'Sunnyside' was then managed by his four surviving sons—Tom, Bill, Harry and Jack— who ran sheep and cattle, and grew wheat and oats. Tom Holt married Mary Ann Worner at St Barnabas' Anglican Church, Broadway in 1882, and was elected Mayor of Wallendbeen Shire in 1917 and 1924. The couple had six children. Thomas ('Tom') James, their first son, was born in 1886.

As the farm was not big enough to support a family, young Tom became a schoolteacher and was eventually employed as sports master at Cleveland Street School in Sydney where he reputedly taught Australian test representative Alan Kippax the basics of cricket. Not far from the Cleveland Street school was a hotel on George Street run by the Pearce family. It was there that Tom met Olive May Pearce (formerly Williams— her mother had remarried after the death of her first husband).[2] Olive had a sister, Ethel (who later went blind), a half-sister named Vera and a half-brother called Harold. Tom and Olive were married on 7 January 1908 in Newtown. Their first son, Harold Edward, was born at the family home, 58 Cavendish Street, Stanmore (an inner-western suburb of Sydney) on 5 August 1908. As there is nothing to suggest that Harold was born prematurely, Olive must have been pregnant at the time of her wedding. Harold's younger brother, Clifford Thomas (usually known as 'Cliffie'), arrived eighteen months later. The two boys, both of whom were baptised Anglicans, had very similar facial features and physical builds.

Tom Holt left teaching in 1914 after he purchased the licence of the Duke of Wellington Hotel in Payneham, South Australia. The move to South Australia may have been linked to Olive's family connections as she was born at Eudunda. Harold and Cliff remained behind in Sydney with their uncle Harold Martin and his wife Ethel. Young Harold attended Randwick State School until 24 September 1916. He was then enrolled at Nubba Public School from 9 October 1916 until the end of the year. This may have coincided with the breakdown of his parents' marriage. He then went to Abbottsholme College in the northern Sydney suburb of Killara where he first met a young William McMahon. His parents divorced when Harold was just ten years old. In what may seem a surprising career move, Tom Holt then joined Hugh D. McIntosh, manager of the Tivoli Circuit, and managed the renowned singer Ada Reeve's triumphal 'Spangles' world tour before becoming the Tivoli–J.C. Williamson travelling representative in London and New York. Tom had good connections in the world of variety entertainment—Harold's aunt Vera Pearce (Olive's half-sister) was a well-known movie actress, first in Australia and later in London, while his uncle Harold Martin was editor of *Everyone's Variety: Devoted to the Moving Picture Industry, Vaudeville, Drama, Carnival, Circus and Kindred Entertainment.* With their father in well-paid employment, early in 1920 Harold persuaded Tom to enrol him and Cliff as boarders at Melbourne's prestigious Wesley College after a young friend told Harold how good a school it was. Harold was then aged eleven. Whereas Harold would spend the next seven years at Wesley, Cliff left school after his fifteenth birthday. Sharing his father's interest in theatrical entertainment, Cliff got a job with 'Uncle Marty' as a journalist on *Everyone's Variety*. In later life the Holt boys would care for their uncle who suffered various sicknesses in addition to battling an alcohol addiction. This may have accounted for their own abstemious habits.

Harold thoroughly enjoyed Wesley, where he formed many close friendships. He earned the nickname 'Puss', apparently because the broad grin that readily crossed his face made him resemble a cat. His Aunt Vera told him to 'do some acting. You've got the figure, voice and looks'.[3] Although he appeared in an amateur season of A.P. Herbert's *The Man in the Bowler Hat*, he never seriously considered the stage. In his matriculation year, Harold was second in his class. Third was Reginald 'Spot' Turnbull, later Labor Treasurer of Tasmania and an Independent Senator, who was appointed a senior prefect ahead of Holt. Harold excelled in debates and took part in the Wesley versus Geelong College Annual Debate in 1926 on the question: 'That government ownership is preferable to private enterprise'. During school holidays Harold went to the homes of relatives or college friends. He also visited Nubba and enjoyed riding horses, catching rabbits and playing tennis. Other than when he was with his uncles, aunts and cousins, Harold did not experience the joys of close family life in a loving home. His mother died when he was sixteen and he did not attend her funeral.

In his final year at Wesley, Harold was awarded the Alexander Wawm Scholarship for academic and sporting prowess and qualities of character. He had studied English, Algebra, Trigonometry, Physics, Chemistry, History and Civics. An interesting coincidence is that one R.G. Menzies was also a star pupil at Wesley College. In receiving the award, Harold was given the privilege of singing a special school leaving song at the annual

Speech Night in December 1926. This was the proudest moment of his young life, but not one relative was in the hall. He would never forget how utterly alone he felt that night.[4]

After winning a scholarship to Queen's College, Harold began his law studies at Melbourne University in 1927. He won College 'Blues' for cricket and Australian Rules football and was a keen tennis player. He won the College Oratory Medal and Essay Prize, and became President of the College's Sports and Social Club. He was selected for the Melbourne Inter-University Debating Team. He was also a member of the United Australia Organisation 'A' Grade debating team and President of the Law Students' Society. By this time, Harold had met Zara Kate Dickens, and an instant mutual attraction would develop into an always close but frequently tumultuous relationship. Zara recalled 'jealousies and arguments . . . quarrelling, beguiling, passionate, deep affection and clashing of wills'. She conceded that they 'had completely different personalities and outlooks. Harold was very organised and strong-minded, tidy and hard-working, while I was vague, dreamy, always running behind time and away with the pixies'.[5] However, they became constant companions after Harold graduated from Melbourne University with a Bachelor of Laws in 1930. Harold was admitted to the Victorian Bar on 10 November 1932 and did his articles with the Melbourne firm of Fink, Best & Miller. In 1933 the paucity of work led him to practise as a solicitor rather than a barrister. Harold moved into a boarding house while he and Zara talked about marriage. Tom Holt, who was then in London, wanted Harold to join him in England and continue his education at a British university, but the Depression forced Tom to return to Australia and put an end to any prospect of Harold studying overseas.

Harold and Zara started looking at small houses in which to live after they were married although Harold's legal practice barely covered his board and lodgings. To make some money, Zara opened a dress shop in Melbourne's Little Collins Street with her friend Betty James (later Lady Bettine Grounds, wife of the architect Sir Roy Grounds). When the business was dissolved (probably in 1934) and the profits distributed, Zara cleared £1500. This was a substantial sum of money that she believed would allow her and Harold to get married. But her success prompted what Zara referred to as a 'violent row'. In her account of what followed, Harold was adamant that he would not marry her until he was earning sufficient money to support them both. He instructed her to go overseas and to spend the money. This was strange advice given Harold's thrifty attitudes and frugal habits. He lived in a bed-sit and frequently relied on the hospitality of friends to avoid the cost of preparing food. She interpreted this to mean that 'I wasn't good enough for him and I was simply furious'.[6]

Piqued, Zara bought a ticket on a passenger ship bound for the United States. She then went on to Britain where she met Captain (later Major) James Heydon Fell, who was preparing to rejoin his regiment, the 15th Lancers, in India. She accepted his invitation to spend some time in Poona on the way back to Australia. When Zara returned from India, Harold told her his financial prospects had improved and resumed talk of marriage. But as he had not formally proposed, Zara was apparently far from convinced that Harold was seriously contemplating marriage. She continued to think about James Fell, who was planning a visit to Australia. On the night before James' ship was due to arrive in Melbourne from India, Harold produced a diamond and sapphire engagement ring. We do not know why Zara did not accept the ring but having had his hand forced, Harold duly reciprocated. He told Zara that if she met that 'Indian type' the next morning, she would never see him again'.[7] In what appears to have been an impulsive act, Zara married James Fell in Melbourne on 2 March 1935. A week later they sailed for India and Fell rejoined his regiment in Jubbulpore. Curiously, Harold kept several clippings reporting the event from Melbourne newspapers.

There is a plausible alternative to Zara's version. Her decision to leave was, in fact, a furious response to learning that Harold had formed a close relationship with one of their mutual friends. Tom Holt had established a business partnership with Francis Thring, proprietor of Efftee Productions (and later Radio 3XY) and father of the flamboyant Australian actor Frank Thring. Although he was still fond of Zara, Harold had turned his affections towards Thring's daughter Viola Margaret, known to everyone as 'Lola'. To Harold's disgust, Lola was also being wooed by Tom Holt, 25 years her senior. Three years younger than Harold, Lola became his stepmother in 1936.[8] In the late 1930s Tom Holt lost a small fortune in failed theatrical ventures and he retired early in 1941 because of ill-health—possibly Parkinson's disease. He died at Melbourne on 10 October 1945 almost broke.[9]

After Lola shifted her affections to his father, Harold read in the newspapers that Zara was returning to Australia for the birth of her first child, Nicholas. He kept the press report in his scrapbook. Nicholas was born at Melbourne on 15 September 1937. Despite Zara's claim that Harold told her he would never see her again if she continued with Fell, she and Harold met soon after her arrival in Victoria. They spent a great deal of time together before James Fell came to Australia to see his son. Not long after the Fells returned to India, Zara announced that she was pregnant again—with twins, conceived in August 1938. Sam and Andrew were born in Melbourne on 23 May 1939. James Fell came to Australia for several months afterwards but returned to India alone. Zara offers no explanation as to why their marriage failed. According to Zara, she and Harold were soon back together again and thinking of marriage because Harold was now in receipt of a reasonable income.

It appears that Zara had forgiven Harold for his infidelity with Lola, while Harold realised that he could not live without Zara. But what prevented them from marrying immediately? It was largely a question of appearances and the law. In the 1930s, the end of a marriage attracted considerable social stigma. To ensure that Harold was not implicated in the collapse of Zara's marriage, a decent interval needed to elapse before they could make their relationship public. There was also the long-standing Holt family 'secret' that Harold was the twins' father. There is no shortage of evidence attesting to their blood tie. There is an uncanny physical similarity between Andrew, Sam and Harold, and Sam, in particular, has many of Harold's mannerisms. Harold and Zara would not marry until 1946.

CHAPTER 2

The early years

IN ADDITION TO HIS everyday legal practice, in 1935 Holt accepted an offer made through connections of his father and brother (now publicity director of Hoyts Theatres) to become Secretary of the Victorian Cinematograph Exhibitors' Association—the industry lobby group for cinema proprietors, which also brought lucrative work in the Commonwealth Arbitration Court. He was also developing his interest in politics. Holt had attended a meeting of the Young Nationalists at Healesville outside Melbourne in 1933 addressed by the organisation's founders, Wilfred Kent Hughes and Robert Gordon Menzies. Together with John Spicer (later Commonwealth Attorney-General) and Richard Casey (a future British peer and Governor-General) Holt decided to join the Prahran branch. On 15 September 1934, Holt contested the Federal seat of Yarra for the United Australia Party (UAP). The sitting member was the Leader of the Opposition and former Labor Prime Minister, James Scullin. A correspondent for the *Australasian* newspaper predicted that this could 'mark the beginning of a brilliant career . . . He possesses, in addition to his talents as a speaker and debater, a pleasant personality, a keen brain, and abundant energy and enthusiasm. He is, in short, just the type of young man we want in politics'.[1]

At his campaign launch, Holt was heckled from the floor for half an hour before a policeman managed to restore order. He warned the electorate against supporting political control of financial institutions, such as nationalisation of banks, and said that 'socialism did not mean in the hands of Mr Lang [the New South Wales State Labor leader] or Mr Scullin an equal distribution of national property. It meant government by a strong body of officials'. Holt was trying to portray Jack Lang as an autocratic

9

figure behind Federal Labor. He argued that the community was well represented on the Commonwealth Bank Board, and that the Lyons Government (which had been elected in 1931 with a commanding majority) had helped men back into employment and reduced unemployment despite the bleak years of the Depression. Holt spoke at street rallies, on the back of trucks and in halls throughout the electorate. One press report said his 'voice was drowned in a veritable deluge of hostile interjections, questions, ironical cheers, rumblings of passing trams and the backfiring of motorcycles'.[2] As Yarra was a strong Labor seat, Holt was heckled wherever he went, but his courage in standing against the former prime minister was admired.

When the election result was declared, the UAP won 28 seats to Labor's 18. The Country Party won 14 seats and Lang Labor 9. South Australia's Liberal and Country League won five seats. In the Senate, the UAP won 16 seats and the Country Party 2. The result in Yarra was no surprise. Scullin received 25 601 first preferences; Holt 10 741; the Communist candidate Ernie Thornton polled 3072 votes, up from 1095 in the previous ballot. Holt praised Scullin for his 'personal integrity and political ability'. The UAP thanked Holt for his efforts: 'Although you did not win Yarra you put up a great fight and scored a very satisfactory result'.[3] The Party Executive believed he was a hard-working candidate who ought to be encouraged further.

At the state election held on 2 March 1935, Holt was a candidate in the safe Labor seat of Clifton Hill. A drunken heckler interrupted his campaign launch at the Masonic Hall. A policeman had to remonstrate with a heckler who disrupted another rally. But Holt was not fazed. In his campaign speeches he concentrated on unemployment and industrial relations. He proposed housing projects to alleviate unemployment. As expected, he was again unsuccessful. The sitting member, John Cremean, who was also the Labor Leader in the Victorian Legislative Assembly, polled 13 636 votes to Holt's 8531. A few days after the election, Cremean wrote a generous personal note to Holt: 'It is not often that one has an opponent as able, as courteous and as decent as you were, and I wish you well in the future'.[4] Not daunted by his defeat, Holt continued to expand his social and political contacts. He became honorary secretary of the Royal Empire Society and cultivated an acquaintance with Dame Mabel Brookes (wife of Sir Norman Brookes—the first non-Briton to win the Wimbledon tennis championship) and her politically influential mother, Alice Mabel Maud Emmerton. He participated in tea parties and tennis afternoons arranged by Dame Mabel at 'Cliff House' in Mount Eliza. Dame Mabel was one of Melbourne's leading socialites and charity workers. Holt squired one of her daughters to various functions. In some respects, they became Holt's substitute family. Dame Mabel would later remark: 'Once, talking seriously to me, he said that politics was all he had. Nothing he would do must interfere with it'.[5] Through Dame Mabel and Mrs Emmerton, Holt was also closely associated with the Australian Women's National League (AWNL), the most influential women's organisation in the country. Robert Menzies, who had won the seat of Kooyong in 1934, allied with Mrs Emmerton and moved swiftly to secure Holt's preselection to the Federal seat of Fawkner after the death of George Maxwell KC, the blind barrister who had been the member since 1917.

Holt received more votes than the other six candidates combined. One of the unsuccessful candidates, Councillor A.H. Woodfull, said that Holt 'did not have the maturity which was needed' and that he would stand as the 'Independent' United Australia candidate. But Woodfull later withdrew claiming ill-health. Another failed candidate, C.J. Crowley, claimed that Holt had been 'foisted upon the UAP voters' and announced that he would stand as an Independent. He also later withdrew. This left Holt, who turned 27 during the campaign, to contest the seat with the Labor Party's Donald Cameron, the Acting Secretary of the Victorian Trades Hall Council.

When Holt was endorsed, the headline in *Smith's Weekly* was 'Political Godmothers Rule United Australia'. It noted the 'petticoat control' of the electorate exerted by the AWNL and particularly by its Vice President, Mrs H.A.A. Embling (the wife of a former Mayor of Prahran). The report was accurate inasmuch as the League provided half of the delegates to the preselection committee and the electoral roll in Fawkner consisted of 29 644 women and only 20 191 men but it also repeated the rumour that Holt was secretly engaged to the daughter of a League official. In the ensuing election campaign, Holt tried to ally himself with the former member and told the electorate that his first appearance at the Bar had been as Maxwell's junior. In his campaign speeches, Holt praised the efforts of the Lyons Government (now a coalition of the UAP and the Country Party) and advocated support for housing–unemployment schemes, slum reclamation and a national unemployment insurance scheme. Holt adopted what would become a characteristically 'Deakinite' position. He thought that poverty existed because 'the problem of production had been solved but distribution was still a difficulty'. As for the philosophical differences between the UAP and Labor, Holt told the electorate that: 'We must endeavour to find the relationship which lay somewhere between the complete non-interference of the last century and the complete interference of the Socialist State'. He said 'it was to be hoped that when the balance has been struck, a plan of economy would be attained without depriving man of his personal freedom, initiative, enterprise or the opportunities of his own development'.

When asked to describe his political outlook, Holt said:

My own interest in politics arises from the conviction that this is a political age, whereas the nineteenth century, occupied with problems of industrial production and expansion, was a scientific age. Today the problems are social and political—securing an effective use of those productive forces which a century of scientific endeavour produced and the equitable distribution of their product. My support for this particular party arises from the conviction that it is the one party which does aim at legislating for the community as a whole and not for one particular class.[6]

On election day, 17 August 1935, Holt said: 'In no period of Australia's history has it been more necessary for young men to take an interest in political affairs than now'. In Fawkner, despite predictions that Maxwell's majority of 14 922 would be cut to 5000, Holt had done well, polling 24 594 votes to Cameron's 16 433. Holt's majority was 8151. Despite the customary swing away from the government party in a by-election, Holt had managed to maintain much of the UAP's majority with commentators agreeing that the by-election did not reveal any appreciable swing away (it was 6.6 per cent) from the Lyons Government. The Party was pleased with its newest and youngest parliamentarian, whose electorate took in the prestigious Melbourne suburbs of South Yarra, Toorak, Prahran, Armadale and Windsor.

In his maiden speech in the House of Representatives, delivered on 23 September 1935 as part of a condolence motion for his late predecessor, Holt said 'my earnest wish is to conduct myself in this house in a manner of which [Maxwell] would approve'.[7] The rest of his speech focused on youth unemployment, foreign affairs and the importance of physical fitness for military recruitment. He claimed that younger educated men did not want Australia to break away from the Empire, that Australia had a duty to stand by Britain at all times, and the League of Nations represented an ideal worth fighting for. In a later debate on the

Italo-Abyssinian Dispute, he would argue that 'Australia as a signatory to the Covenant of the League must do its part to ensure that international law and order will triumph over international anarchy'.[8] As a 'Coronation plan', Holt also advocated 'work and technical training for unemployed youths, occupational centres for young men out of work and Government control of all labour bureaus to facilitate transfer of unemployed from one area to another where work was available'. It was not a profound address nor was its delivery outstanding. But he was young and nervous. Holt's public speeches were solid and workmanlike. Only once would he ever say anything really memorable—and even then it was when he uttered some-one else's words. Holt had no grand vision for Australia or its people. There was no 'New Deal' or 'Great Society' that he longed to create. He believed in the virtue of hard work and discipline; the importance of expanding opportunity for individuals and business; and avoiding the over-regulation of the economy or social life. After delivering his maiden speech, Holt wrote a short article for a Melbourne newspaper outlining his impressions of Canberra and parliamentary life.

> Private members now receive a parliamentary allowance of £850 pa, which amount, owing to Financial Emergency legislation, remains £150 below the normal allowance of £1000. Out of his annual allowance, the private member may have to provide for the maintenance of a home in his own State, pay incidental travel expenses to and from Canberra, and while carrying out his parliamentary duties in his own electorate, and also meet the cost of the meals and accommodation while in Canberra. In addition to these expenses, a member finds that he has many calls in his electorate upon his private charity.

After his first month, he advocated shorter parliamentary speeches but longer parliamentary terms, selective broadcasting of parliamentary debate, the provision of air travel for all parliamentarians, the establishment of 'special quarters' attached to Parliament House, and the party desegre-gation of the parliamentary dining hall and billiard tables. He was critical of the lack of parliamentary and party discipline, and Cabinet's reluctance to share information and insight with the backbench.

Holt's life had quickly become hectic. He had established an office in Melbourne's legal precinct (the western end of Collins Street) with Jack Graham. Although they were partners in the firm that was to become Holt, Graham & Newman, Graham was paid to maintain Holt's legal practice and cinema work while the new Member for Fawkner attended to his parliamentary and electorate duties. If Holt did not succeed in politics or came to tire of the lifestyle, he could always return to the law and build up his practice. It was an arrangement that would continue for nearly 30 years, despite occasional practical problems such as the difficulty of parking his car. The Melbourne newspapers reported that the Victorian District Court fined Holt 30 shillings in May 1936 for leaving his car unattended in George Parade in Melbourne's city where it obstructed traffic. Holt replied: 'There is one law for the rich, one for the poor, and a thousand for the motorist'.

As the youngest parliamentarian in Canberra, Holt represented the concerns of the nation's youth and sought to bring his youthful perspective to whatever Parliament was debating. He was well liked by his political colleagues who appreciated his reserves of energy, attention to detail, loyalty, amiable nature and complete lack of pretension. Enid Lyons admitted:

> I expected not to like him, but from the beginning I saw in him qualities that suggested far greater depths of character than appeared on the glossy surface. Of his mental capacity there was ample evidence in his scholastic attainments and in the substance of his speeches. His style as a speaker was not particularly attractive, but there was sincerity of feeling discernable in all he said. In the party room, when discussion turned to social questions, the man-about-town, the young sophisticate, disappeared, and the man who knew and sympathised with the problems of people less favoured than himself took his place. Although he was a businessman, 'Big Business' (if I may use the jargon of politics) had no appeal for him.[9]

Perhaps Holt had already recognised that consistency and reliability rather than charisma or creativity eventually would bring him ministerial office.

Holt also had to become accustomed to lonely hotel rooms in Canberra and a boarding house in Melbourne. While he did not suffer from a want of human contact, he lived alone and had few close relationships. But as the most eligible bachelor in Parliament, the press sought his views on women and fashion.

> I don't like women to dress so conspicuously that they make a man feel hot under the collar to be seen with them but on the other hand, they should not be too inconspicuous. Women seem to be most charming in summer frocks,

plain, cool linens, prints and all that sort of thing. Perhaps it's the prettier colours that appeal to me. I like pastel shades very much and all the 'off' colours, dusty pinks, blues, greens and so on. They are more subtle.[10]

He concluded that most women 'dress to make their sisters sit up and take notice'. The women's gossip columnist in the *Australasian* remarked that Holt had 'all his father's charm; and another thing, besides being a ripping ballroom dancer he plays an intelligent game of bridge. As if this was not enough he looks fine on horseback; plays a good game of tennis, and, girls, he's single'.[11]

With the rise of fascism in Europe and Asia, Holt was troubled by developments in those countries that had 'cast aside democracy and resorted to dictatorships. This was largely due to their geographical position, which created a military caste concerned with national defence rather than the rights of individuals'.[12] In February 1936, Holt supported the introduction of compulsory military training (in the belief that voluntary training was ineffective and inadequate, and that a National Register was necessary) but opposed overseas borrowing for defence purposes. Holt thought the Government was over-reliant on air defence and argued that Australia did not have the capacity to replace the aircraft that would be lost in defending Australia's coastal and overseas shipping. Noting the desire of many nations for more land to cope with overcrowding, Holt advocated a substantial increase in population 'either by an increase of births over deaths, or by the infusion of healthy stock from the white races abroad'. The Australian population had, surprisingly, decreased between 1930 and 1934. Holt argued for changing Australia's immigration laws to grant equal opportunities for women to become citizens, for more women to enter Parliament and for divorce law reform that was more favourable to women. Holt also lobbied for the National Fitness Campaign advocated by the *Age* newspaper, pointing out to Prime Minister Lyons that the British government had invested in the program, and he was appointed to the Coordinating Council for Physical Fitness. It was becoming clear that Holt had strong views and would be prepared to express them. For example, he voted with the Opposition when the Government attempted to avoid answering a question on the consequences for Australia of the constitutional crisis created by King Edward VIII's decision to marry the American divorcée, Wallis Simpson. Holt felt the matter needed to be discussed and drafted his own question for Parliament calling on support for the king the next day.

When the Federal electoral boundaries were changed in 1937, the member for Bendigo, Eric Fairweather Harrison, floated the idea of challenging Holt for preselection in Fawkner but it quickly became clear that the preselectors in Fawkner were not going to abandon their rising star after just one term. As a relatively safe UAP seat, it was expected that Holt would retain Fawkner and, on 23 October 1937, Holt recorded a convincing win. He gained 33 277 votes to defeat the ALP's William Doran (17 124 votes) and the Independent William Bottomley (9941). When the election result was declared, the Lyons Government was returned to office. The UAP had won 27 seats and the Country Party 16. The Labor Opposition, now led by John Curtin, had won 29 seats. Labor had won 16 Senate seats to the UAP's 3. But as the European crisis headed inexorably towards another world war, in February 1939 Holt enlisted in the 4th Field Brigade Artillery, based at Prahran. He was not a stranger to uniformed service. For three years he had been a member of the Wesley College Cadet Corps and the Melbourne University Rifles under a scheme where young men aged between 18–21 received military training before they started their career. Holt had not joined the Citizens Militia after leaving university because he 'did not think it advisable to take men for training from the professions or responsible positions',[13] but when a special part-time unit was established for business and professional men, he joined under Lieutenant Colonel David Fraser and learned to operate an 18-pounder gun.

When Prime Minister Joseph Lyons died on 7 April 1939, the Country Party leader, Dr Earle Page, was appointed Prime Minister. On 18 April the UAP elected Robert Gordon Menzies, who had resigned from the Government early in March, as leader. Before surrendering office, Page launched a savage public attack on Menzies for undermining Lyon's leadership and withdrew the Country Party from the Coalition. Menzies was invited to form a Government but had to do so without the Country Party. The Cabinet of twelve ministers, drawn entirely from the UAP, was sworn in on 26 April. Another four UAP members, including the 30-year-old Harold Holt, were appointed 'Ministers without Portfolio'. Holt's task was to assist Richard Casey in the new Department of Supply and Development. The *News Chronicle* described him as 'the youngest Cabinet minister Australia has ever had'.[14] He was actually the third youngest. Letters and congratulatory telegrams flooded in from the Prahran Council, the Australian Natives Association, the Limbless Soldiers' Association of New South Wales, the Victorian Debaters' Association, businesses, the film industry, legal colleagues, his old school and members of the public. Archie Michaelis of the Victorian Legislative Assembly wrote: 'I hope it will prove not to be a temporary one, but that it will be the start of a long career of office'.[15] His friend Keith Allen said: 'It really is time that younger men were given a chance to show their ability in the political world'.[16] He hoped that ministerial rank would allow him to further some of his pet ideas. He advised Councillor F.H. Buss of the National Fitness Campaign that he would remain a member because 'the new Cabinet is likely to be far more sympathetic than the last'.[17] But other activities had to be reduced. He wrote to Lieutenant Colonel Fraser: 'I regret the fact that this new appointment will interfere considerably with my training with the 12th Battery. Until the present session of Parliament ceases, I do not expect to be in Melbourne on any Wednesday night'. Fraser arranged for Holt to have indefinite leave.[18]

With war imminent, the newly formed Department of Supply and Development was responsible for the manufacture and supply of war munitions and aircraft, and the establishment and expansion of vital defence industries. There was little that was actually new in the department. It had assumed responsibility for 6000 Defence Department staff and was largely a coordinating body for existing activities. Holt's duties were initially *ad hoc*—essentially the overflow from Casey's in-tray. On 7 August 1939, Casey asked Holt to 'take over the overseeing of the work of the factories and of the Contracts Board by acting as President of the Principal Supply Officers' [PSO] Committee'.[19] Holt administered science and technology matters during Casey's absences overseas on ministerial duties, although the Council for Scientific and Industrial Research (CSIR) was nominally under the control of the prime minister. On 18 October 1939, authority was delegated to him formally under the *Science & Industry Research Act 1920–1939* and he became 'Minister in Charge of Scientific and Industrial Research acting for and on behalf of the Prime Minister'.[20] Holt enjoyed a good relationship with Sir David Rivett, the CSIR's Chief Executive Officer, although Rivett complained to Holt on 30 January 1940 that 'someone or other in Canberra seems to know a great deal more about the CSIR work than anyone else'. A series of press reports claimed to reveal work in which the CSIR was not actually engaged or inaccurately reported on work that was being done, especially in relation to flax. He asked Holt for his assistance in identifying the person who was 'adopting unsuccessfully the prophetic role in connection with our work'.[21] They were never named in public.

When Sir Frederick Stewart replaced Casey in early 1940, there was an attempt to formalise the division of departmental responsibilities between the two ministers. Holt was given 'those matters coming under the administration of the Prime Minister's Department [and delegated by Casey before he went to Washington] . . . namely the Council for Scientific and Industrial Research [CSIR], North Australia Survey Act and the National Oil Pty Ltd Agreement . . . technical training of artisans for our Defence needs and the Standing Committee on Liquid Fuels . . . and the Civil Supply Section'.[22] Holt was to concentrate on administration while Stewart would be devoted to policy matters. Stewart suggested that Holt be co-opted to the Economic Cabinet as his responsibilities 'come properly under the heading of "Development" and have an economic bearing'.[23]

On 13 March 1940 Holt would bring a submission to the Economic Cabinet seeking approval for the establishment of a CSIR Division of Industrial Chemistry for civilian and military work. He also recognised the need to advance the work of the radiophysics laboratory. Holt would bring to Cabinet a range of submissions from the CSIR concerning mining, agriculture, security arrangements at CSIR facilities, the strength of woven paper yarn bags compared with bags made from jute, and the manufacture of spectacle frames. The CSIR would ask him to consider urgent war matters such as equipment for calibrating 'gauges and other standard workshop tools in secondary industry'.[24] This work would bring Holt into contact with a number of departments and agencies and with senators and members bearing suggestions or petitions for possible consideration by the CSIR.

The Menzies Government met in the House of Representatives for the first time on 3 May 1939. Several items of legislation from the Lyons Government were introduced into the House and passed into law. Holt's primary efforts were directed at preparing for the mobilisation of the Australian workforce in the event of war. The National Register Act obliged all working men and women to complete registration cards indicating their occupations and skills. Holt would use this information as the basis of a national system of manpower mobilisation he had initiated.[25] Parliamentary sittings ended on 16 June. When Parliament resumed on 6 September, Menzies had already announced that Australia was at war with Germany. Over the next six months, Holt deputised for a number of his ministerial colleagues in the portfolios of Trade and Customs, a ministry held by the Prime Minister after the resignation of James Lawson, and Civil Aviation and Air while James Fairbairn was overseas negotiating Australia's contribution to the Empire Air Training Scheme. By March 1940, Menzies had come to an agreement with the Country Party whereby it would join a Coalition. Five of its members were to be offered portfolios. As the most junior UAP minister, Holt lost his place in the ministry to Arthur Fadden. He understood and accepted Menzies' decision and carried no grudge. In a press statement issued on 13 March 1940, Holt said:

> I have very natural regrets at writing 'Finish' to a period of work with the Menzies Government which has been full of interest and I hope even of some value. I regret having to sever the very happy associations I have enjoyed with my former colleagues in the Government. Those regrets will however be amply compensated if the two parties who have now come together can display a spirit of unity to evoke this country's most determined energies and develop the strength nationally to make a generous contribution to the Empire war effort.

For the first time in six years, he could start to think about matters beyond politics.

CHAPTER 3

Laying the foundations

1940–49

WHEN HOLT LOST HIS place in the Menzies Government, Germany was poised to invade the Netherlands, Belgium and France, having already occupied much of Poland and also Norway. The Allied position was becoming desperate. Holt, along with fellow parliamentarian William Hutchinson and Senator Keith Wilson, decided to volunteer for full-time military service. Liberal colleague Tom White had already joined the Royal Australian Air Force (RAAF) and was a Squadron Leader. Although as a former Acting Minister for Air he was offered a senior commission in the Air Force, Holt sought no favours and decided to become a private soldier. His enlistment date in the Second Australian Imperial Force (AIF) is recorded as 22 May 1940. Parliamentarians who enlisted received their military pay in addition to their parliamentary allowance and would be given 'a pair' during parliamentary divisions. If they were sent overseas, they could be nominated for the next election prior to their departure.[1] Holt explained his decision to join the Army:

> no one who has read the accounts of the fighting in the past few days can fail to be impressed by the seriousness of the threat against the Allies and thereby against the institutions we cherish. The Government has made a call to the young men of Australia to serve with its overseas forces. As the youngest member of the House, I could not feel happy in my position if I were not prepared to make some sacrifice and take an active part.

A distinguished soldier and parliamentary colleague in later years, H.B.S. 'Jo' Gullett, saw Holt in a Melbourne pub after he enlisted in the

AIF: '[Holt] was posted to our brigade's artillery regiment. He had no
military experience and was a corporal, or bombardier as junior non-
commissioned officers are called in the artillery. We were pleased to see
each other and it was clear to me that Harold liked army life well enough,
and was looking forward to serving abroad'.[2] Richard Casey wrote to Holt
on 22 June 1940 congratulating him on enlisting in the AIF and explaining his frustrations with the American system of government and public
administration, and his efforts to provoke their involvement in the
European war against Hitler. In reply, Holt told Casey he was looking
forward to proceeding overseas and serving for the duration of the war.[3]

Holt was given leave from the 7th Battery, 2/4th Field Regiment at
Puckapunyal to contest the Federal election of 21 September 1940. He
was not allowed to wear uniform but could use his military rank. The press
clearly enjoyed referring to 'Gunner Holt'. As Fawkner had 7000 financial
UAP members, there was no shortage of volunteers to manage the
campaign while their local member was distracted by military life. At his
launch at the Malvern Town Hall, Holt said: 'We can make the best war
effort as a nation by strengthening the Menzies Government with a
popular mandate and additional parliamentary support . . . a polyglot of
elements would lead Australia if the Government was defeated'. He argued
that the election's 'paramount issue is Australia's position in the great world
conflict and how best not only to protect herself but to give the fullest
measure of assistance to the Empire as a whole in the titanic struggle'.[4]
Holt called on the Labor Party to participate in an All-Party National
Government but Opposition Leader John Curtin was not interested in the
suggestion. Holt's other policy commitments were to 'One Australian
Army, "Pay as you Go" taxation with post-war credits, destruction of the
noxious "isms"—Communism, Fascism, Wardism and Dedmanism,
abolition of irresponsible Trades Hall control and the preservation of our
British liberties'.

By this time Holt had nearly completed his artillery training at Pucka-
punyal and was preparing for deployment overseas, probably to North
Africa or Palestine. It was not to be. At 8 a.m. on 13 August 1940 a RAAF
Lockheed Hudson light bomber carrying the Minister for the Army,
Brigadier Geoffrey Street, his secretary, R.E. Elford, the Vice-President of
the Executive Council, Sir Henry Gullett, the Minister for Civil Aviation
and Air, James Fairbairn, the Chief of General Staff, Lieutenant General
Sir Brudenell White, and his Chief of Staff, Lieutenant Colonel Francis
Thornwaite, took off from Laverton in Victoria. On arrival above

Canberra at 10 a.m., according to a contemporary newspaper account, the Hudson

> wobbled in the air, then spiral-dived into a hillside two miles from the Canberra aerodrome. When it hit the ground eyewitnesses more than a mile away saw a vivid flash a fraction before the noise of the crash. The wrecked machine burst into flames. The victims were incinerated. RAAF men who ran across paddocks to the spot were beaten back by the heat. They had to stand by for half an hour until the flames subsided.[5]

All the passengers were killed, as were Flight Lieutenants Richard Hitchcock and Richard Weisner, Corporal John Palmer and Aircraftsman Charles Crosdale. This was a tragedy for the Air Force, the Army, the Commonwealth Government and the country. In his official statement Menzies said: 'This is a shocking piece of news. It is a great calamity, the full significance of which even yet is not fully realised, and in addition to that it is a most grievous personal loss'.[6] In his official history of the war effort, Paul Hasluck remarked that 'the loss of any of these men alone would have weakened the Ministry and Parliament. The loss of the three together tore a great hole in the fabric of government'.[7] Senator Philip McBride and the Country Party's rising star, Arthur Fadden, were selected to replace Street and Fairbairn. They were sworn in immediately. Allan Dawes, a distinguished journalist who had been press secretary to Geoffrey Street, was sent to see Holt with a message: the Prime Minister wanted confirmation of his willingness to return to the Government after the election. This Holt readily gave.

Although a member of the armed forces, Holt provided a commentary on progress in the tally room for a commercial radio station as polling booth figures confirmed his re-election. In fact, his share of the primary vote in Fawkner increased. Holt polled 38 387 votes to the ALP's Arthur Fraser (22 538) and Independent Alexander Mills (12 677). Holt was now confident of a consistent margin in excess of 12 000. The UAP had won only 23 seats (reduced by one when Arthur Coles declared himself Independent) and the Country Party 14. There were 32 Labor members. The cross bench consisted of four Lang Labor members and one Independent. In the Senate, the UAP and the Country Party won 16 seats to Labor's 3. The Government was re-elected but without a majority. Its hold on office depended on the support of the two Independents. Unaware that Menzies already had him in mind for a portfolio, the press regarded Holt's recall to

Cabinet as being highly likely. He was said to be popular personally while his contributions as the Assistant Minister for Supply had been widely praised. It was rumoured that Holt would become Minister for Air (as he had dealings with aircraft during his time in the Supply portfolio) or Minister for Customs. These were considered the most likely options as Sir Earle Page had expressed an interest in the proposed new portfolio of Labour and National Service.

On 28 October 1940 Holt was formally offered a portfolio and agreed to leave the Army. More than one colleague believed this was a mistake. 'Jo' Gullett thought that Holt later lacked the kind of authority and decisiveness that he might have acquired in the Army. Holt was 'just another professional politician. And he could so easily have been "Digger Holt"'.[8] Or given he was artillery rather than infantry corps—'Gunner Holt'. Menzies decided to appoint Holt to the newly formed Department of Labour and National Service. The press reported that Holt was chosen because of his success in negotiating the Dilution of Labour Agreement with the Amalgamated Engineering Union when Assistant Minister for Supply. Menzies said: 'It is appropriate that a younger man should be dealing with a problem that is almost essentially a young man's problem'.[9] As Holt explained:

> The Government believes that the Department will become an instrument for cooperation through which representatives of State governments and employers and employees will be able to throw their full weight behind the war machine. It should be possible in this way to get practical results without the establishment of a new and unwieldy bureaucracy. The research and analysis of questions of manpower, while possibly less spectacular, should comprise some of the most profitable work for the Department.[10]

He was once again the Minister in Charge of Scientific and Industrial Research and ranked eleventh in a Cabinet of fifteen members.

Holt returned to the Cabinet and immediately took a hands-on approach to his portfolio, visiting government and commercial factories and industries. He met personally with union leaders and secured their support for streamlined arbitration and conciliation processes to expedite settlement of industrial disputes, particularly in sensitive war-related industries. These measures were agreed by the Advisory War Council. Holt very soon enjoyed the confidence of both employer groups and the trade unions.

With the German Army enjoying a series of military successes, it was vital to maximise Australia's contribution to the war. Holt established the Commonwealth Manpower Committee and the Manpower Priorities Board. In June 1940, BHP's Managing Director, Essington Lewis, had been appointed Director-General of Munitions. He was given the task of organising a Department of Munitions that would have responsibility for the manufacture and procurement of all ordnance, small arms, explosives, ammunition and other war material. Ben Chifley had been appointed to the new post of Director of Labour Supply. When Holt's department was created in October 1940, one of his first ministerial actions was to invite Chifley to continue in a similar role. The all-party Advisory War Council, formed on 28 October 1940, supported unanimously the quest for more adequate and prompt industrial conciliation procedures and Chifley contributed significantly to the evolution of these procedures.[11] Holt recognised the importance of bipartisan support and displayed considerable ability in bringing together individuals and groups with different ideological outlooks and political aspirations.

Recognising his inexperience, Holt assembled a capable and creative team to coordinate the many facets of the department's work. The Secretary of the Department was 36-year-old Dr Roland Wilson, a Rhodes and Harkness Fellow with doctorates from Oxford and Chicago, who was considered the rising public servant of the time. From a building and construction family, Wilson had been Commonwealth Statistician for the previous four years and had a capacity for negotiation and a good sense of industrial relations. They would prove a formidable team. The chairman of the New South Wales Public Service Board, Wallace Wurth (later Director-General of Manpower), joined as Deputy in the department. The new Minister's responsibilities included labour policy, determining manpower priorities, allocating labour to war industries, workforce training and planning for the post-war rehabilitation of the labour force.[12] A post-reconstruction division was also established and a number of bright young graduates recruited to develop policy options for the post-war world. They included civil servants such as John Burton, Arthur Tange, Fin Crisp, Pierce Curtin, Percy Judd, Phil Dorrian, Gerald Firth and Dick Heyward, all of whom went on to become important public figures. But as Dr H.C. 'Nugget' Coombs noted:

> Their Minister, Harold Holt, although proving a successful and congenial minister in his dealings with trade unions, had neither the seniority nor the

political clout to assert their claims against the established bureaucrats whose prevailing attitude seemed to be that post-war problems could wait until those responsible had the time to attend to them. Accordingly, the aspirations of these young academics were largely ignored or dismissed and their sense of frustration mounted.[13]

Holt's foremost challenge was to prevent strikes and industrial unrest from impeding the war effort.

> Recognising the influence which the labour potential can exert the Commonwealth Government has decided to establish a central organisation that will make the most effective practical use of man-power and women-power. The marshalling of those resources in order to obtain the maximum war effort for Australia, and a maximum degree of help and cooperation for Great Britain and the sister Dominions, is the primary objective of the new Department.[14]

But the most lasting of Holt's achievements in his first portfolio was the introduction of universal child endowment. In January 1941, while Menzies was abroad, Cabinet decided to introduce child endowment of five shillings per week for each child under 16 years after the first, regardless of family income. This was a means of assisting families at a time when the wartime adjustment of award wages threatened to fall with undeserved severity on family groups. Although it was customary for legislation of such significance to be introduced by the Prime Minister or a senior Cabinet Minister, the Treasurer, Arthur Fadden, 'passed the responsibility to Harold as I felt it would be to his great advantage to be associated at this stage of his career with such a major measure'.[15] Holt, who had lobbied for universal child endowment since he first entered Parliament, promoted the scheme as a 'foretaste and pledge of the full reconstruction that will be possible when we can again turn our surplus productive forces to the purposes of peace'.[16] Holt told the readers of the *Australian Women's Weekly*:

> I don't need to tell any housewife coping with her household budget these days how much that extra £1 [for five children] a week will be. We are determined that this endowment money will be spent expressly on the maintenance and upbringing of the child. For this reason payments will be made to the mother or to the person directly responsible for the child's care.[17]

The *Child Endowment Act* was passed in April 1941. The press praised Holt's initiative and noted he was 'the only bachelor in Federal Parliament'. He was referred to as the 'Godfather to 1,000,000 Australian children'. Labor Opposition leader John Curtin said in the House of Representatives: 'I am sure that the House would like some expression of appreciation, and, indeed, of admiration for the Minister for the labour he has expended on this Bill and for the notable place which this monumental legislation will give him in the annals of this federation'.[18] Holt was rightly proud of his achievement.

Despite the war and the need for government unity, there was growing antagonism towards Menzies and opposition to his leadership within the UAP. When Menzies consulted with a few of his ministers on 26 August 1941 about the possibility of a National Government headed by Curtin with an equal number of ministers from both sides of the Parliament, they were frank in their opinion that Menzies was electorally unpopular and needed to make way for a new Prime Minister. Holt, expressing his embarrassment, said a National Government might be more likely if the conservative forces had a new leader, and suggested Fadden. Menzies replied that he 'was not taking anything that was being said as a personal attack, but that all I wanted to get at was the truth of their political views'.[19] Menzies made up his mind to resign. At a Party meeting on 28 August, William McCall and William Hutchinson spoke against Menzies and demanded a change of Prime Minister. They claimed he had lost the confidence of the Parliament, the people and his own party. Holt did not know what to do. Menzies was a friend and colleague to whom he owed much. Holt believed deeply in loyalty but he also believed that Menzies was no longer the man to lead the nation. Holt did not rise to support his leader. In all, six ministers (Eric Spooner, Billy Hughes, Earle Page, John McEwen, H.L. Anthony and Harold Holt) withheld their support although Holt was the last of them to do so. Menzies told Cabinet that he would resign. When the ever-loyal Eric John Harrison (the UAP member for Wentworth in New South Wales) urged him to stand fast and demand loyalty from his detractors, he said his mind was made up. After the Cabinet meeting, Menzies' secretary, Cecil Looker, recorded his boss as saying: 'I have been done . . . I'll lie down and bleed awhile'.[20]

Holt was conscious that he had walked away from the small group of Menzies' most resolute supporters and agonised over his decision at a number of levels: 'We were devoted to him and gave him the same honest advice that we always did. But the fact was that divisions had developed within the party and it was felt unity could only be restored under Fadden'.[21] In any event, Labor declined the invitation to join a National Government with or without Menzies as Prime Minister. Holt would later remark to his colleague, Howard Beale:

> 'No one can possibly understand it who was not there living in the climate of that time. Bob was very difficult, there was a deep resentment towards him within our party, and it seemed to many of us that any sort of national unity was impossible whilst he was leader. I simply did what I thought was best for the country and the party at that time'. I believed him, and I am sure Menzies came to believe him, too; but some he never forgave, even though they later became his ministers again.[22]

Holt had been honest with his leader and acted in the public interest. Menzies recognised that Holt's decision was not motivated by any sense of personal gain or political ambition, and respected him for it. Menzies 'was not a forgiving man, although he did forgive Harold Holt for having stood out against him during the war'.[23] Within a few years, Menzies would publicly praise Holt for his great abilities and boundless zeal.

When the prime ministership passed to the Country Party leader, Arthur Fadden, Holt retained the portfolio of Labour and National Service. But the fate of the Fadden Government would be largely determined by the actions of the two Victorian Independents: Arthur Coles, founder of G.J. Coles retail stores, and Alex Wilson, who described himself as 'Independent Country Party'. They had decided to support the Labor Party, now fully reunited in the Parliament as Opposition after the internal factional splits of the 1930s, in a vote against the Budget.

When Parliament resumed, Coles said that in deciding to vote against the Government he was not challenging the principles of the Budget but trying to bring stability to government. This gave Holt the opportunity to make the most effective speech of the debate. He recalled that Coles had been elected with UAP cooperation and entered Parliament as the advocate of a National Government. He had even tried to form a new party designed to absorb other parties or impose its own policy on existing parties. His vote would now displace a Ministry which had worked for his own objective—a National Government. When the Opposition had refused to enter into a National Government Coles, by this time a member of the UAP, deserted the Party again after a change of leadership had raised the prospect of achieving political stability. Holt said: 'I question whether members on this side of the committee have ever come into contact with a more unbalanced and irresponsible political mind than that of the member for Henty'.[24] In his speech, Holt also dealt with the disruptions that would be associated with a general election and the consequences of the divisions that Coles was creating by his actions and statements. Holt argued that stability could be achieved without an election if Coles stood loyally and constantly behind the members he had been elected to support. Menzies, still Leader of the UAP and now Minister for Defence Co-ordination, remained silent throughout the debate. When the two Independents crossed the floor to join with the Opposition on 7 October 1941, the Fadden Government was no more. Fadden returned his commission to the Governor-General and Labor Leader John Curtin was invited to form a government. Menzies resigned as UAP Leader on 8 October after Fadden was chosen as Leader of the Opposition. Billy Hughes, approaching 80 years of age, became UAP Leader and Deputy Leader of the Opposition.

The next two years in Holt's life were marked by an element of uncertainty although his place in the House was never in danger. But he was unsure about the direction of his life. He resumed his legal work in Melbourne and was active in the Arbitration Courts. He continued to represent theatrical employers while serving as the Opposition's spokesman on industrial relations. Although he considered returning to the Army, Alexander Downer (Senior) thought Holt 'showed good judgement in not re-enlisting' after the Government fell in 1941.[25] But this would remain a sensitive subject. In a speech on the militia in 1942, Eddie Ward said that Holt should return to the Army as he was no longer needed in the Cabinet. A newspaper reported that 'as soon as the House adjourned, Mr Holt walked across to Mr Ward. There was a discussion during which Mr Holt was heard to ask Mr Ward to come outside'. Although some observers thought the two would come to blows, they were later seen in deep discussion outside the entrance to the House of Representatives.

Over the next few years, Holt's contributions to parliamentary life were limited mainly to industrial matters. He was able to score points against the Curtin Government but the UAP's overall political fortunes remained weak and it soon became apparent to Holt that the UAP's electoral organisation was beyond reform. As early as November 1941, only weeks after Menzies' humiliating resignation and the defeat of the Federal Coalition, the Victorian UAP Leader, Tom Hollway, became involved in 'a public wrangle with the party's organisational wing. Menzies joined

Hollway in a press statement'.[26] The *Argus* reported on 25 November 1941 that the two leaders advocated 'a rigorous reconstruction of the party's organisation'. Federal Parliamentarians Rupert Ryan (Richard Casey's brother-in-law), Senator John Spicer and Harold Holt supported the call. On 1 December 1941, Holt addressed the Australian Women's National League. He suggested that to match 'the highly efficient political machine of the Labor Party, with its hundreds of branches and tightly knit Federal organisation', the UAP would also have to create 'an effective Federal organisation of its own with a uniform policy'.[27] By 1943, with Billy Hughes retaining the leadership by refusing to hold a Party meeting, the UAP was in terminal decline. The impetus for change had to come from the Parliamentary Party. Holt 'argued that a revival of the party should be inspired by the federal parliamentary party by means of a conference of delegates from supporting organisations from all states. It was still too early for such action, however, as internecine warfare between those organisations—LDP, UAP, Nationalists and CP—suggested that their differences were still of more significance to them than their mutual interests'.[28] In his 1943 election campaign speech, Holt said the seventeenth Parliament 'would go down in history as the worst Parliament Australia had ever had'. He complained that Australia was 'the highest taxed country in the world' and lamented the 'degree of industrial unrest [which was] unrivalled in any other part of the globe'. He went on to highlight Communist control of trade unions and their funds for the purpose of political agitation. Labor was, he said, 'a defeatist party with an outmoded ideology'.[29]

But Holt himself was vulnerable. There were rumours that he was being pressured to stand aside from his seat of Fawkner to make way for Sir Keith Murdoch. The Sydney *Telegraph* said that Holt, 'who has fundamentally liberal instincts, has been spoiled and has mentally run to fat'.[30] Murdoch then published a newspaper article declaring his intention of supporting an Independent candidate in the seat of Fawkner and encouraging others to join the fray. Brigadier William Cremor was a militia officer and a past president of the Victorian Teachers' Union and the Legacy Club. Holt was concerned about the wealth and power of those supporting Cremor. In the end, six candidates contested the 21 August 1943 election. The result was a little surprising. Cremor gained 15 958 votes, mostly at Holt's expense. Holt's primary vote was reduced to 23 931, only 423 ahead of his Labor rival Thomas Jude. The Communist candidate, Malcolm Good, polled 3300 first preferences. After the distribution of preferences, Holt had 41 602 votes and Jude 30 109—a majority of 11 493, similar to those he had achieved in the three previous elections. He breathed a sigh of relief but realised the folly of taking preselection or the people of Fawkner for granted. Menzies wrote to Holt on 30 August 1943:

> Congratulations on your win in Fawkner. Having regard to the powerful organisation which was set up behind the third candidate [Cremor] and the general swing to Labour [sic], you must regard your vote as a distinct personal triumph. We shall be a relatively small band in the new Parliament but there will be plenty of good work for us to do.[31]

As expected, the Curtin Government was returned to office and the UAP's parliamentary ranks were devastated. Labor had won 49 seats and commanded a substantial majority. The UAP won just 12 of the 74 House of Representative seats and had lost its majority in the Senate where Labor had won all nineteen seats contested. Holt, in a defiant mood, said at the Prahran Town Hall when the poll was declared that the election result was a 'death blow to the die-hard Tories'. The Melbourne press reported Holt's claim that:

> it has also been a UAP Dunkirk but if due heed were taken of the lessons it taught, the setback would be in the interests of the party. It is only by a revolutionary change in outlook and the adjustment of policies to the great problems of today that the party can give the people effective leadership . . . there are some elements of good in Labor's policy, and the UAP answer must not be die-hard Toryism; it needs liberalism in its spirit and democracy in its organisation.[32]

Menzies regained the UAP leadership on 23 September 1943. There were three candidates for the position of Deputy Leader—Percy Spender, William Hutchinson and Holt—then Billy Hughes announced that he would contest the position. Nearing his 80th birthday and being the most strident of all Menzies' critics, Hughes' decision surprised many in the Party room. Holt and Hutchinson immediately withdrew. After considering his position, Spender also withdrew and Hughes was elected. But Menzies had already started to think about building a new political organisation. At a conference held in Canberra between 13–16 October 1943, a decision in principle was made to form a new party.

On 29 November 1943, Holt issued a statement on the future of the UAP: 'At present we have no Federal organisation. We cannot match the highly efficient political machine of the ALP with its hundreds of branches and tightly knit Federal organisation until we have created an effective Federal body'. He thought the necessary 'revival must be inspired, and to a large degree directed, by the Federal Parliamentary Party. Organisation without a policy is obviously ineffective'. When Billy Hughes was expelled from the UAP in April 1944 for rejoining the Advisory War Council against the Party's wishes, many tipped Holt to be his replacement. But as Menzies was from Victoria, it was thought preferable to have a member from another state as deputy. The member for Wentworth, Eric Harrison, was elected as Deputy Leader. One newspaper remarked that Holt's 'stocks have slumped. He is never mentioned now as a [possible prime minister], seems to have slipped into the background where he is reasonably important but not dominating. He seems to have everything except that special something that goes to make a leader'.[33]

The reality was that Holt's public profile had slipped. He issued few public statements and did not play a prominent role in the creation of the new political party. Holt's only official position was membership of the Parliamentary Joint Committee on War Expenditure from October 1943 until August 1946. But his philosophical inclinations remained clear: 'Experience has taught me Socialism cannot be applied without regimenting and bludgeoning the individual. I believe in the individual's right to live his own life in his own way, without being pushed around by someone in authority'.[34] In his public speeches, Holt railed against what he regarded as covert attempts at compulsory unionism and radio broadcasts of parliamentary proceedings. Introduced in 1942 and made mandatory for the Australian Broadcasting Commission in 1946 after the proclamation of the *Parliamentary Proceedings Broadcasting Act*, Holt claimed the broadcasts would encourage politicians to grandstand and prolong parliamentary proceedings. He felt so strongly about the matter that between July 1946 and October 1949, he served on the Joint Committee on Broadcasting Parliamentary Proceedings. He also saw the need for more opportunities to help demobilised service personnel. He supported changes to calculating the basic wage but criticised Labor for transferring power from the Parliament to the Executive in the Banking Bill. Holt said that 'no country which claimed to retain any vestige of freedom for the individual would give to its executive power, not only to direct the channels along which credit should flow, but attempt to specify how it should be done'.[35]

His contributions to parliamentary debate were, however, piecemeal and sporadic. He looked forward to the creation of a new party to provide a holistic ideological approach to Australia's post-war problems.

A conference held in Albury from 14–16 December 1944 settled the principles upon which the new political organisation would be founded. Holt was not a major practical contributor to the formation of the Party but he was the first to join the Prahran branch of the Liberal Party after its formation on 8 February 1945. Menzies announced in the House of Representatives on 21 February 1945 that the main Opposition party would from henceforth be known as the Liberal Party. At the inaugural meeting of the Party in northern Tasmania one month later, Holt spoke of a rift between the Government and the non-Labor forces:

> between the ideals of a Government which sought to drug the nation with talk of social service and the ideals of all those who still believe in personal initiative, in individual risk-taking for the sake of the commensurate rewards and in the principles of private enterprise . . . It is because that cleavage is so plain that we must sink our party and personal differences and unite the people who think as we do.[36]

The outlook of the new party was an attempt at genuine liberalism. Holt said:

> We share the broad policy objectives of Labor—a steadily rising standard of living, encouragement and development of effort by the individual. However, the Socialist approach will impede rather than assist those objectives. Actually between Labor and my party there is a difference of method, not of objective. The difference is between the regimented State and the State in which the emphasis rests on the individual.

In a speech delivered during the August 1945 by-election for the seat of Fremantle made vacant by John Curtin's death, Holt said the Liberal Party policy stands for 'the "four decencies": a good job, a home, adequate social security and an expanded educational service'.[37] The first meeting of the Federal Council of the Liberal Party was held over four days at the end of the month.

With a new party emerging as a viable alternative to Labor, the Melbourne *Herald* noted that at 37 years of age, Holt is 'mature, individualistic and hostile to party rigidities. His counsel carries a lot of weight with his colleagues. He is considered a certain successor to Robert Gordon Menzies, and a potential Prime Minister'.[38] The *Sunday Telegraph* remarked: 'His voice is clear and mellow, he refrains from gibes, gets on amiably with most of the Opposition . . . he speaks neither with Menzies' brilliance nor his scholarship, isn't much of a one for a quip or an epigram; and, sometimes fluffs his points a little'.[39] By this time, Holt had been in Parliament for more than a decade. Although he maintained an interest in a new legal partnership he had formed with Maurice Sloman, he had committed himself completely to politics. He was now a full-time parliamentarian and was in line for a senior ministerial post when the Liberal Party was eventually returned to government. Holt faced the electors of Fawkner again on 28 September 1946 and was confident of retaining his seat. Mrs Coralie Brown, an independent and somewhat eccentric candidate, made the campaign more colourful. She was a grandmother at the age of 41 and advocated free education from kindergarten to university. Holt met Mrs Brown for the first time at the Malvern Town Hall on Monday 26 August 1946 and invited her to the stage after she asked him to outline what, other than child endowment, he had done for the electorate since being elected in 1935. She told a member of the audience that 'Mr Holt told me that he has had strong opposition before, but he has always won. I told him he had never met me before'.[40] He need not have been too worried. She polled 2121 votes to Holt's 39 047. The Labor candidate, William Bourke, did well, receiving 30 835 first preferences.

But the election was a disappointment for the new party. Labor, under Ben Chifley, had won 43 seats; the Liberals 17. The Country Party won 12 seats (including one Liberal Country). The non-Labor side of politics had recovered a few seats in the House but was down to just three seats in the Senate. Labor had 33. Holt's attention returned to personal matters and Zara Fell. On her return to Australia in late 1940, Zara and the three boys lived in a house at 50 Washington Street in Toorak. Zara rented the property and there was an understanding that she would make an offer if it became available for purchase. It was not until Zara was divorced and James Fell remarried that Harold persuaded her to marry him. They were finally wed on 8 October 1946 in the front room of Zara's parents' home (110 St Georges Road, Toorak) by a Presbyterian minister, the Reverend Jeffrey Brown. The best man was Brian 'Barney' Connolly, later Australian Trade Commissioner in Trinidad, New York, San Francisco and Athens. Robert Menzies was at the wedding, which was followed by a reception for 150 guests at the Hotel Australia. After their marriage, the Holts bought the Washington Road house, where they would remain until 1954 when they moved to St Georges Road.[41]

Harold legally adopted the three small boys and was a father to them in every respect. They changed their name to Holt by deed poll in 1957, loved him and always called him 'Dad' or, later, 'Pop'. Zara started calling him 'Harry'. Mrs Edith Mary 'Tiny' Lawless had come to live with the Holts as a combination nanny–housekeeper. Zara then established a 'fashion boutique' in Toorak Village known as 'Magg' which catered for a wealthy clientele. Although she would employ 20 people in the back workroom and another two or three sales assistants, Zara's business would always be subordinate to Harold's political career. He told her: 'you must never do anything that interferes with my political life. If you have to come abroad with me you have to come, and you'll just have to leave your business'.[42] Zara proved to be a shrewd businesswoman although she seemed flighty to some and flamboyant to many.

With the war over and the Liberal Party attempting to consolidate, Holt became the Opposition spokesman on Immigration and Industrial Relations. He attempted to embrace a genuinely liberal attitude towards both portfolios and appeared to have a sound grasp of the defining issues. Holt conceded that 'some unrest in industry is a continuing condition just as it is in human beings and in human affairs . . . unrest in industry has redressed many an evil and produced a progressive improvement in working conditions'. He distinguished between strikes and lockouts and good and bad workers and bosses. But he felt industrial relations' greatest problem was the politicisation of the trade union movement, and that many strikes were not about wages or conditions but a wider attack on society by Communists. 'Their aggressiveness is accentuated in Australia by their Communist leadership of the coalmining, stevedoring and seamen's unions'. He quoted from Communist union leader (and former Fawkner electoral foe) Ernie Thornton and 'Comrade L. Sharkey', President of the Communist Party, in claiming that Communist dominance of trade unions was assisted by rank and file apathy, and the exploitation of mateship—'one of the virtues in our national character'.

Holt feared that Australia was drifting towards a ' "New Anarchy" resulting from an inadequate political expression of the economic basis of our society'. He said: 'Australian politicians fall into two broad groups, one comprising the members of the Labor Party pledged to a socialist program, and the other comprising non-Labor parties advocating private enterprise'. There was also dissent and in-fighting within trade unions between Communist and non-Communist factions. And yet, the politicisation of the trade union movement meant that political power rested in the hands of those who were not accountable to the electorate. This was particularly evident in relation to foreign affairs. In 1945 Australian maritime unions boycotted ships from the Netherlands bound for the Dutch East Indies, in support of the Indonesian anti-Imperial struggle. Holt noted that 'the Government opposes the bans, the ACTU disapproves of them but the ships are not loaded'. The question facing the nation, he said, was 'whether the Government can and should regulate the activities of trade unions or allow them to operate as an irresistible pressure group'. Admitting that Australia has a 'strongly entrenched tradition against the use by governments of military forces to break a strike', he attempted to articulate a moderate view: 'The employer must foster a sense of purpose and pride of achievement in his worker. The worker must recognise the unceasing difficulties of conducting a business on a profitable basis in a competitive world'. This meant 'exploding the doctrine of the class war. We must reveal the baselessness of a so-called "right to strike"'.[43]

Country-wide industrial disputes were directly affecting the nation's economic performance while the Chifley Government seemed incapable of curbing militant unionism. But Holt concentrated on what he regarded as Labor's socialist agenda. In 1948 he attacked, in Parliament, the Shipping Bill which proposed establishing a Commonwealth shipping line and developing an Australian shipbuilding industry, although he was critical of the Australian Shipping Board's poor performance and the domination of the waterfront by the Communist-led Waterside Workers Federation. He claimed the Banking Bill, which would empower the Commonwealth Bank to lay down policy on trading bank credit advances, was actually an attack on private enterprise. In a pamphlet produced by the Liberal Party, Holt argued that excessive government participation and regulation of industry and manufacturing would lead to diminished private investment, inflation and recession. He said that 'small businesses are the large companies of the future. They need not only profits that can be ploughed back, but if they are to grow they will require additional capital. Their need is not for government loans but venture capital that enters the business as a partner for profit or loss'.[44] He argued that the Government's role was to promote:

political stability, confidence in the policies of the administration, a tax-scale which gives incentives for risk-taking, an acceptable industrial code which will ensure continuity of work and will be applied with authority, and a minimum of government interference in industry. Public works may have a limited usefulness as a stop-gap programme while production arising from private investment is being developed.[45]

Holt was also critical of the persistent shortage of basic goods, particularly petrol, the continuation of rationing and what he saw as the over-extension of government activity. He claimed that 30 per cent of the total national production was passing through the hands of the Chifley Government for activities that had no useful purpose in peacetime. He accused Labor of deliberately working to reduce the prestige and authority of Parliament by transferring critical financial functions to a supreme economic council that had 'become a mere recording instrument for the one man who dominated it—Mr Chifley'.[46] Holt also attempted to make political capital from his other area of responsibility—Immigration.

While Arthur Calwell's administration of the new Immigration Department was earning him deserved praise, Holt managed to score a number of points from the Minister's alleged inflexibility and lack of compassion. The case of Annie O'Keefe, an Indonesian widow with eight children, was one such instance. She had fled to Australia in 1942 after her Indonesian husband was killed while serving with Dutch forces against the Japanese. After several years in Australia, Annie received a marriage proposal from 67-year-old bachelor John O'Keefe and applied for permanent resident status. The Immigration Department considered the case and resolved that Mrs O'Keefe should be deported. Calwell said: 'If we let these people stay we have got to let the flood gates open to anyone to come in. You can have a White Australia and you can have a Black Australia but a mongrel Australia is impossible'. Holt accused Calwell of doing more 'to promote resentment and hatred than any other minister in the history of this administration . . . The White Australia Policy is supported by every political party . . . [but is] under challenge because of the heavy-handed, harsh, rigid application of the policy in particular cases by the Minister'.[47] Holt told the Melbourne *Herald* that 'it was inevitable that the resentment aroused throughout Asia by the harsh administration of our immigration policy would bring reprisals'.[48] In 1947 the High Court overturned the Immigration Department's decision on the grounds that Mrs O'Keefe was not a prohibited migrant.

Holt could make his own judgments about international attitudes towards Australian policies when he travelled abroad for the first time in August 1948 to attend the Empire (later Commonwealth) Parliamentary Association meeting in London as a member of the Australian delegation (with Dorothy Tangney and John Howse). This was the first post-war Association gathering and the only time he would travel abroad without Zara. He saw it as a great adventure and the fulfilment of a long-held aspiration, later commenting:

> in the early years I spent in politics, governments, ministers and the community as a whole had their gaze directed to the extent that it went outside Australia to the British Isles, with perhaps one journey in a lifetime to Europe. This was the sort of dream that people who were able to accumulate rather more wealth than savings build up in their minds, to get back to what was then described as 'home', to the British Isles . . . that was about as good as anybody would hope for.[49]

While in Europe, Holt visited the British sector in Germany and attended the meetings of the United Nations in Paris. By the time he returned, the Country Party had agreed to a joint electoral campaign with the Liberal Party in order to exploit the Labor Government's unpopularity.

The Chifley Government announced a Federal Election for 10 December 1949. To counter the continuation of wartime rationing, plans to nationalise the banks and the health service, and increasing Communist infiltration of the trade union movement, Menzies made three pledges: to assist free enterprise, to protect States' rights and to put value back into the pound. Holt prepared a series of commissioned articles for the Melbourne *Herald*, the theme of which was: 'the big issue of the election is now crystal clear. Australia stands at the crossroads with a clear choice between Socialism and liberalism'.[50] The Liberals, he claimed,

> accept the responsibility to maintain full employment. We would establish the conditions necessary to encourage private investment. We would remove the threat of Socialism which stifles expansion and risk-taking. Our tax scale would give incentive. We would use suitable budgetary and financial measures, including government borrowing, to stimulate investment and maintain demand. We would regard public works as a useful adjunct. But our emphasis on increased production from mine, farm and factory, we could stimulate exports to other countries. Confidence still possesses a magic in the

creation of prosperity. Contrast the practical, realistic Liberal programme, which still guarantees freedom of choice of work, with the doctrinaire regimented blue-print of the Chifley Socialists.[51]

At a political rally in the Melbourne Town Hall, Holt told the audience not to 'be misled by Ben Chifley's Irish charm and humour, because there is no more fanatical Socialist in the Federal Cabinet'.[52] Holt attacked Labor for raising taxes and big government spending and said the Liberals would 'repeal the 1947 *Bank Nationalisation Act* and seek to include in the Constitution a provision making such a Socialist monopoly impossible without the approval of the people expressed by referendum'.[53] He criticised the Labor Party for not putting Communists last on their 'How to Vote' cards in some electorates but even giving Communists their preferences ahead of all other non-Labor parties, asserting that the Coalition had 'undertaken to deal with Communism as an enemy within our gates. To do so [we] will need the backing of every loyal Australian'.[54] Holt also warned his own party that:

> the next three years might be the Liberal Party's last real chance to establish itself as the alternative to Labor . . . There is a serious danger of Liberalism being forced to [the] extreme right and the political contest of the future resolving itself into a struggle between the right and left wings of labour. English Liberalism—a driving force a generation ago—is virtually extinct.[55]

Holt was adamant that more than just 'a swing of the pendulum is needed to place the Party in power'.

In his own electorate, Holt faced another new challenge. At the 1949 election, the Senate would be enlarged from the original 36 to 60 Senators (ten from each State) and election would henceforth be on a proportional representation basis. At the same time, the House of Representatives was increased from 75 to 121 members (including a non-voting member for the Australian Capital Territory). As a result of boundary changes, Fawkner became potentially marginal. Indeed, the candidate Holt easily defeated in 1946, William Bourke, would win the seat of Fawkner in 1949 with a slim majority. In May 1948, Holt had said he thought that Labor's intention to increase the size of Parliament was 'a hasty, clumsy, slip-shod plan inspired not by statesmanship but by self-preservation'. He now decided to stand in the seat of Higgins which had been detached from his old electorate and incorporated the Melbourne suburbs of Armadale, Caulfield, Darling and Malvern. It was a mere eight square miles in area. There was only one other candidate for him to face in 1949, Labor's Jules Meltzer. Holt polled 26 018 votes or 66.8 per cent of the primary vote and Higgins became (and remains) one of the safest Liberal seats in the country. To the great surprise of many in the Government, the Liberal Party won 55 seats and the Country Party 19 to Labor's 47. In the Senate, although the Coalition won 23 of the contested seats to Labor's 19, it was still in a minority of 8 because of Labor's 15–3 legacy from 1946.

The Governor-General, William (later Sir William) McKell, swore in the new Menzies Ministry on 19 December 1949. Menzies and three of his ministers, including Holt, wore formal short black coats and striped trousers. As expected, Holt was given the senior portfolios of Labour and National Service and Immigration. The 'twinning' of the two departments under one Minister highlighted the connection between the needs of the labour market and immigration. The President of the Australian Council of Trade Unions (ACTU), Albert Monk, had earlier urged Menzies to put the two portfolios together and even suggested Holt for the Labour and National Service job. Menzies would later decide to give Holt responsibility for handling all the Government's industrial questions. Calwell had also hoped that Holt would succeed him at Immigration. Holt's departmental head at Labour and National Service was William Funnell. He had been in the post since 1946 but would be succeeded by Harry (later Sir Henry) Bland in January 1952.[56] The Secretary of the Immigration Department was Sir Tasman Heyes, who would serve throughout Holt's tenure before retiring in 1961. Funnell's office was in Melbourne while Heyes was based in Canberra. Holt's private secretary in the Immigration portfolio was Noel Flanagan, a very able and promising public servant who was the main point of contact between the Minister and his department. Holt's private secretary at Labour and National Service was Wal Talbot. Although he had two private secretaries, Flanagan rather than Talbot accompanied Holt whenever he travelled, including visits to coal fields or industrial facilities. Holt and Flanagan were also keen tennis partners with Holt frequently asking Flanagan to book the Parliament House lawn tennis court and acquire four new tennis balls for an early afternoon match.

The influential *Smith's Weekly* remarked that 'no man in the whole Cabinet team is better suited than Holt to the task allotted him'.[57] Holt now ranked fourth in Cabinet, beneath Menzies, Fadden, the Leader of the Country Party and Treasurer, and Harrison, the Liberal Party Deputy

Leader and Defence Minister. As Harrison was 57 years old, it was clear that Holt was Menzies' heir apparent. Holt was riding high. In a public Christmas message, he claimed that:

> a decisive political battle has been fought and won, and we can feel justly proud, as a people, of the good humour and calm consideration that was given, with few exceptions, so generally displayed on the great issues of the campaign. But that now lies behind us, and part of the responsibility of the new Government is to weld the Australian people more closely together.[58]

It was now time for Holt's considerable political potential to be translated into a solid parliamentary and ministerial performance.

CHAPTER 4

Halcyon days

1950–58

AFTER ENDURING SO MUCH social disruption and official regulation between 1939 and 1945, most Australians wanted a minimum of government interference in their lives. There was, not surprisingly, a narrowing of popular political vision, with the focus turning to civic and domestic issues, and material security. The family and the home were to be the secure centres and refuge from an uncertain world in which ideological conflict had the potential to unleash a global war involving nuclear weapons. Australians demanded jobs that paid them enough to cover mortgage repayments, purchase household goods and provide for the daily necessities of life. Few people realised the country was on the verge of an unprecedented economic boom. Although the unemployment rate was only 1.7 per cent when the Coalition Government was elected, there were insufficient houses for newly married couples, prices were unstable although wartime controls persisted, and inflation was not yet under control.

Harold Holt, himself a 'family man' with a wife and three young children to house, clothe and feed, held the two portfolios that touched most directly on the kind of society Australia was and wanted to become. Immigration (see Chapter 6) was changing Australian culture by introducing new values and customs. Industrial relations (see Chapter 7) had become an ideological battleground. Why were two such challenging portfolios combined under one minister? The Menzies Government had adopted the development thrust of Labor's economic policy which was based on a high rate of immigration to provide both a large labour force and a potential reservoir of sailors, soldiers and airmen.[1] The Cabinet acknowledged that such a policy would strain the nation's production capacity and place substantial pressure on domestic savings, but it was prepared to accept the economic and political stresses created by a widening gap between demand and supply. The Commonwealth Bank, then the central bank as well as a major trading bank, advised the Government that such a high rate of immigration would be inflationary. To counter this, the Government would need to increase spending on its public works program or reduce immigration levels. Neither was an attractive option.

In the 1951 election campaign, Holt rejected Labor's allegation that the Government was responsible for inflation and uncontrolled prices:

> The Menzies Government believes that rising prices must be dealt with from two broad directions. We must take measures to check the amount of spending power in the community and thus relieve the pressure of demand. At the same time we must expand essential production, this being in the long run, the best answer to the shortage of goods.[2]

He lashed out at the Labor Party's claim that Australia was slipping towards a depression—prices for primary exports remained high; Australia had well-developed secondary industries which were better served in equipment and manpower; production outputs in coal, steel, timber and building materials were increasing steadily; the high birth rate and immigration levels were stimulating the economy; central banking was more highly developed than in the 1930s; and the Commonwealth Government had greater discretion in adjusting fiscal and credit policies.

By 1952 some feared that the economy was inflationary while others thought it was heading for a depression. National development supported by a high intake of migrants was to drive the economy. But the infrastructure needed to support a rapidly growing population—housing, public transport, electricity and water supplies, education and health—was lagging behind while there was a chronic shortage of investment capital. The Treasurer, Arthur Fadden, pleaded with Cabinet to remain firm and persevere with existing policies but, by the end of 1952, Holt had emerged as the leader of 'elements demanding drastic changes in existing policy'. Holt's chief concern was unemployment and the need to keep the figure below 2 per cent. There was, he said, uncertainty in the labour market and the prospect that jobs would be in short supply. BHP had 'no real demand' for some products, there was too much coal on the market, manufacturers reported decreases in new orders and there were signs of a slump in the building industry. Fadden argued that business was prone to nervousness and panic which should not cause the Government to alter policy. In July Cabinet agreed to the immigration intake for 1953 being reduced from 160 000 to 80 000. In the meantime, Holt was 'invited' to reduce the 1952 target. The country needed to absorb its immigrants and consolidate its economic position. Holt told the press that Australia was taking a 'breather' from rapid immigration.

The Government's management of the economy was under attack from both sides of the House. Menzies was not giving a clear lead which led some to wonder whether Cabinet thought that either time would suggest a solution or the problems would simply go away. Holt could see that the electorate were losing faith in the Coalition. He produced a document headed 'Suggested lines of Government policy'. Holt believed an election held at the end of 1952 would lead to 'a land slide to Labor' and that there was little time to 'stage a recovery' before the May 1953 half-Senate election. Menzies was about to go overseas and the Christmas recess meant there were 'few suitable occasions for pro-Government prop-aganda'. Holt argued that the Government's problems were obvious. The first and most severe was inflation. The electorate blamed the Government and would hold it accountable. The second was the re-emergence of unemployment for the first time in a decade. And the problem was bound to get worse.

> The political effects flowing from this decline in the employment level need no stressing. We will all be aware that for every person unemployed, there are friends, relatives and fellow workers who react to the unemploy-ment of the person out of work. In the months ahead political considerations will be of far more consequence than the economic. Our policy of diverting labour to the basic industries has been realised . . . We no longer have a 'milk bar' economy. Rather we have an economy of 'all dressed up and no place to go'. We must be prepared to make a realistic appraisement of the political consequences of a continuance or aggravation of the current rate of unemployment.[3]

Holt offered no precise solutions or new initiatives. He simply wanted his colleagues to realise the seriousness of the Party's plight. Treasury produced a 'diversion' entitled 'Proposals for specific action to maintain and stimulate employment' which included some modest proposals for placing defence supply orders with local industry. It was clear that the Treasury intended to maintain existing policy in the hope that the threat of recession would recede. The electorate still expected the Government to deliver an economic boom even as it was fearful of another depression. As political scientist John Murphy has shown, electoral support for the Coalition between late 1951 and mid-1953 was fragile, a series of opinion polls showing solid and growing support for Labor.[4] But the Opposition did not do as well as expected in the half-Senate election, gaining only one extra Senate seat. By the end of 1953, consumer confidence had lifted and the Government's fortunes improved. There was an appreciable rise in standards of living with many more Australians believing they were better off than they were twelve months before. Talk of recession was now criticised as 'irresponsible'. But there had been another element to the Coalition's counter-attack—Holt was integral to making fear of Communism work against the Labor Party at the ballot box.

Holt had been making strong anti-Communist speeches since first entering Parliament. On 19 April 1940 he claimed that the Labor Party was riddled with 'Reds', quoting from the October 1934 edition of the *Workers' Voice* and an exhortation to its readers to 'seize the opportunity of an imperialistic war [in Europe] to cause civil war'. Holt said 'these views are still held by Australian communists . . . today we have a fifth column in Australia and while it consists of only a small minority of Communists its smallness does not reflect the damage it can do if allowed to go unchecked'. Holt demanded that Curtin take action to rid his Party of their malign influence. Holt later called for dissolution of the Communist Party, closure of its offices and prohibition of its newspaper from fomenting industrial unrest. He believed the Government should use its powers to break up strikes and deregister unions.

When the Liberal Party came to power in 1949, it was committed to taking strong action against the Communist Party. In 1947 Menzies said that he was against legal measures because he had 'complete confidence in the sanity of our own people', but by the 1949 election he said he would ban the Communist Party if the Coalition were elected. Several senior party leaders, including Holt and Casey, were against imposing an outright ban. B.A. Santamaria, an influential Roman Catholic layman and Director of the Australian National Secretariat of Catholic Action, says that Richard Casey asked him to meet Holt who then suggested that Santamaria should formulate his views on suppressing Communism in a memorandum that could be brought to Cabinet.[5] Holt also received a letter from the Roman

Catholic Archbishop of Melbourne, Dr Daniel Mannix, concerning possible strategies the Government could adopt. [6]

In April 1950, Menzies introduced the Communist Party Dissolution Bill. Within 48 hours, the report of a Royal Commission into Communist activity in Victoria was presented to the Victorian Parliament. Justice Sir Charles Lowe concluded that the Communist Party was plotting to overthrow Australian State governments and to seize control by armed insurrection. This State inquiry was used as additional justification for the proposed Commonwealth legislation. Menzies' bill not only outlawed the Party and any organisation controlled by it; allowed Party property and assets to be seized; imposed imprisonment on any members who continued to be active; but empowered the Government to 'declare' that an individual was or had been a Communist and thereby was barred from holding any position in the government or in the trade unions. Holt admitted it was:

> an unusual Bill with unusual provisions, but it must be considered against the full background of Communist aims and activities . . . The Government believes the Australian Communist Party (ACP) is an integral part of the world Communist revolutionary movement which is engaged in Australia and other parts of the British Empire in treasonable or subversive activities designed to accelerate the coming of a revolutionary situation. The ACP, as a revolutionary minority, would then be able to seize power and establish a Communist dictatorship.[7]

Holt explained that the onus of proof rested with the Commonwealth and that 'non-Communists have nothing to fear'. This had not been the view of Opposition Leader Ben Chifley who claimed the Bill 'opens the door for the liar, the pimp and the perjurer to make charges and damn men's reputations, and to do so in secret without having either to substantiate or prove any charges they might make'.[8] But in October 1950, after Communist North Korea invaded South Korea and trade union strikes had been staged against the Bill, the Labor Federal Executive directed the Parliamentary Party to drop its opposition to the legislation. The Right wing of the Party had prevailed and the Bill became law on 20 October 1950.

The Communist Party and ten trade unions immediately challenged the constitutionality of the new law. On 21 October they applied for a restraining order in the High Court and gained an interim injunction preventing action being taken against individuals and organisations. The appeal for a restraining order was referred to the High Court which scheduled the case for 14 November. In the House of Representatives, Holt attacked the decision of Labor's Deputy Leader, Dr Herbert Vere Evatt, to appear for the Communist-led Waterside Workers Federation in the High Court of which he had been a member for ten years before election to the House in 1940. In turn, Holt was accused of trying to influence the High Court. He replied:

> I make it clear that I neither challenge nor criticise the right of a member of this Parliament who is a member of the legal profession to appear before the courts of this country . . . [But] this is no ordinary case, and the Honourable Member is no ordinary barrister. The Deputy Leader of the Opposition is now apparently seeking to challenge legislation passed on both sides of this Parliament with the full concurrence of both Houses of Parliament and without a dissentient vote from any member.[9]

It was a blatant political attack designed to exploit Evatt's inability to recognise the electorate's disgust at any assistance rendered to the Communists. If a party was not against the Communists, it was for them. To direct maximum attention to Evatt's decision, Holt claimed the Deputy Labor Leader was 'giving aid and comfort' to a subversive movement.[10] Chifley defended Evatt's conduct in accepting the brief and his right to appear in the High Court, saying that Holt's remarks were 'a disgrace to both himself and the Government'.[11] Evatt said Holt had raised 'the matter for no bona-fide purpose but to embarrass proceedings in the High Court and to try to injure me'.[12] The Victorian Bar Council also issued a statement in response to Holt's speech:

> It is a barrister's duty to accept a brief in the courts in which he professes to practise at a proper professional fee, unless there are special circumstances justifying his refusal to accept a particular brief . . . A barrister is not entitled to refuse a brief merely because of the character of the cause or of the client, or because he does not share the ideals involved in the former or dislikes the latter.[13]

Evatt loathed Holt. He would claim more than once that Holt always waited until he was absent from Parliament before launching a personal attack. While Holt dismissed this as a sign of Evatt's paranoia, there were indeed several occasions on which this appeared to happen. But these personal sentiments had no bearing on the electorate's mood or on the course of subsequent events. On 9 March 1951, the High Court ruled by a margin of 6–1 that the Act was invalid. Chifley applauded the decision. Menzies said 'this is not the end of the fight against Communism; it is merely the beginning'. On 19 March he moved to hold a double-dissolution of Parliament. The immediate reason was given as banking legislation but another aim was a strengthened mandate for action against Communists while gaining the majority in the Senate denied him in 1949 by the change in voting systems.

In a short election campaign, Holt pointed to his achievements in Industrial Relations and said he had forged strong relationships with all bar the Communists. He attacked the Labor Party for obstructing the Government's legislative program and claimed that only the Liberal Party could deal with Communism because Labor was too reliant on Communist union support. Holt said that 'the menace of Communism dwarfs all other international questions' and that Australian Communists 'were willing partners ready to betray and sabotage their own country in time of war and soften it for the day of revolutionary overthrow or Communist invasion'.[14] Holt appealed to the electorate for its vote in the Senate to let the Government implement its mandate. On 28 April 1951 the Liberal and Labor parties each won 52 seats, the Country Party 17 seats. This gave the Government a reduced majority in the House. The Coalition gained a majority in the Senate. On 6 July, Menzies introduced a Bill providing for a referendum on the Communist Party issue. The Government wanted to change the Constitution so as to deal with the High Court judgment and allow the *Communist Party Dissolution Act* to come into operation without further legal challenge. Before the referendum was held, Holt warned that:

> [The] problem is more serious in Australia than any other English-speaking country for in no other part of the free world has the Communist Party been able to obtain the same control of key unions and vital industries. This makes special action necessary against those Communists who hold office in the essential industries. In other countries the Communists have been rooted out by the unions themselves.[15]

Chifley died suddenly on 14 June, the day on which the new Parliament opened. He was replaced by Dr Evatt who claimed that the Government already had sufficient power to deal with Communists under the *Crimes Act*. Arthur Calwell was elected Deputy Leader of the Opposition.

At the referendum on 22 September 1951, 68 electorates returned a 'Yes' vote with 53 returning a 'No' vote. But the 'No' votes had a slim majority of 52 082, or 50.48 per cent of the vote. Holt accused Evatt of turning the referendum into a party political exercise. He claimed this was evidenced by the number of electorates returning a 'Yes' vote equalling the number of electorates with Government members. Despite the setback, Holt said 'the Government will certainly not abandon its fight against Communists. The trade union movement—where Communism gained its most potent influence—now has thrust upon it the responsibility for putting its own house in order'.[16] He also expected 'from the Labor Party and the ACTU firm support in such action as may be taken against Communists under existing powers'.[17] Holt commended unions that had precluded Communists from standing for office—such as the Australian Workers' Union—and unions registering secret ballots with the Arbitration Court. Early in 1951 Holt had claimed that there were 18 000 Communist Party members in Australia. By June 1952 he could say that, as a result of Government pressure, the membership of the Communist Party had been cut in half since 1949. The Government had 'succeeded in bringing home to most Australians the alien, treacherous significance of Communist propaganda and tactics. There has been a well-planned government counter-penetration, of which, obviously little detail can be given, into the ranks of the Communist Party'.[18]

The Government's campaign against Communism was boosted by Evatt's shift towards the political Right following the referendum. He became vehemently anti-Chinese and stridently anti-Communist, but maintained a commitment to civil liberties. Evatt led Calwell, Stan Keon and a number of anti-Communist Labor members in attacking the Government—and Holt, as Immigration Minister, in particular—for allowing a delegation of five Australians led by Evatt's former protégé John Burton (Secretary of the Department of External Affairs, 1947–50) to participate in a 'peace meeting' at Peking in May 1952 while the Korean War was in progress. The strength of political feeling generated by Labor's attack caused the Government to reverse its position and refuse passports to a larger group who wanted to attend a subsequent conference in Peking.[19] In a letter to fellow Communist Stephen Murray-Smith, prominent intellectual Brian Fitzpatrick wrote that Holt confided that he 'had misgivings about the policy but felt that he could do nothing in the prevailing atmosphere . . . he said to kick the Left in such a fashion is bad practice, as the boot may one day be on the other foot'.[20] However, Holt told the press he was 'amazed' by the strength of protests directed against him for refusing passports to individuals wanting to travel abroad for potentially subversive activities and pointed out that requests for passports from individuals who might constitute a security risk were assessed by the Security Services. 'The right to travel is a very important one and should be jealously guarded and not be subject to arbitrary determination by any government. It would require a strong security recommendation to me against the issue of a passport before I would refuse one.'[21]

On 12 February 1954 Cabinet decided to hold an election for the House of Representatives on 29 May. Menzies made an announcement to this effect on 24 February and explained that its timing was to ensure that the election campaign would not clash with the visit to Australia of Queen Elizabeth, scheduled to conclude by 30 March. On 3 April 1954, shortly after the royal entourage had departed, a Canberra-based Soviet diplomat and spy, Vladimir Petrov, sought and was granted political asylum. Menzies announced the defection ten days later. On 3 May, the Government appointed a Royal Commission into Soviet espionage in Australia. The Commission commenced hearings on 17 May in Canberra. Holt then announced that six prominent Communists would not be allowed to leave Australia until the Royal Commissioner had decided they were not persons of interest. Although this was a drastic action, Holt believed it was demanded by national security needs. The Petrov defection and the Royal Commission had a considerable effect on the election campaign. The central issue became the alleged Communist influence on Australian public life. Just before the poll, Holt again defended his decision to refuse passports to Australian Communists wishing to travel abroad. The ban on overseas travel 'would be applied until such time as the implications behind recent Communist developments became clear . . . the Federal Government had reluctantly decided on its ban against a background of Communist activity in Asia and the Petrov disclosures'.[22] The Government also pointed to the dire situation in Indochina where the French garrison at Dien Bien Phu had been overrun by the Communist Viet Minh after a 57-day siege that would bring colonial rule in Vietnam to an end.

In the 1954 election campaign Holt identified the strengths of the Coalition as leadership, philosophy and stability. He pointed to the Government's record on wages and employment, the reduction in strike activity and stable prices. The Coalition had delivered on housing and hospitals, and made progress on improving pensions and services for the aged. He accused Labor of disunity and factionalism, of lacking a national strategy and proposing bank nationalisation by stealth. While the Government had strengthened Australia's relationship with the United States and encouraged a resurgent Japan, Labor had alienated Australia from potential allies while being unnecessarily suspicious of its former enemy. Holt also claimed that the Government was serious about exposing and suppressing Communist influence in so-called 'national uprisings', bogus 'peace campaigns' and major industrial strikes.[23] The central thrust of his campaign was fear of what Evatt and the Labor Party might do once in office. 'With your continued support, we can go steadily ahead developing Australia and expanding an already prospering economy. As a nation, we have never fared better. You know where you stand today under Mr Menzies. Why risk a fall with Dr Evatt.'[24] At the polls, the Government was returned. The Coalition won 64 seats to Labor's 57.

But the passport controversy refused to go away. Australians were yet to be persuaded by the Government's case for restricting their right to travel and free association. By March 1955, and notwithstanding the Petrov defection, the public had become less sympathetic to the Government's refusal to grant passports to alleged 'Reds' to attend what it referred to as 'so-called Peace Conferences'. The turning point proved to be Holt's refusal to grant a passport to the Reverend Neil Glover, vicar of St Matthias' Church in Richmond, Victoria and an executive member of the Australian Peace Council, to attend a conference of the World Peace Movement in Helsinki in May 1955. When Holt was lobbied by a number of senior Anglican churchmen and still refused, Glover threatened to take the matter to the High Court. On 6 April Holt backed down, announcing that the Government would now apply a policy of practically unrestricted issue of passports. He gave as his reasons the end of the Korean War, the fact that unrest in Indochina had not yet escalated into a regional conflict and that the special restrictions following Petrov's defection now could be eased. Glover was granted a passport and another damaging controversy was averted.

Dramas within the Opposition were also drawing attention away from the Government's heavy-handedness. After internal factional brawling and accusations of sectarian meddling by the 'Industrial Groups' established by the ALP after the war to combat Communist influence, the Australian Labor Party (Anti-Communist) was formed in the House of Representatives on 30 April 1955.[25] The Industrial Groups, assisted by the Roman Catholic Social Studies Movement, had selected and supported their own candidates, discredited Communist candidates and opposed 'unity tickets'.

By 1953, the 'Groupers' had achieved considerable success in the union movement and had set their sights on the ALP. An anti-Grouper mood within the ALP was brought into the open in October 1954 when Dr Evatt publicly attacked them as part of an alleged Roman Catholic conspiracy to secure control of the ALP. The ensuing struggle led to a split within the party with the Groupers (not all of whom were Roman Catholics) forming their own party. The parliamentary members of what became known as the Democratic Labor Party (DLP) sat on the cross-benches. Holt said little about the Labor 'split' other than to predict that Evatt would be replaced as Labor Leader by the Member for Bendigo and former ACTU President, Percy Clarey, and that the Party would 'become increasingly dependent on the Communist-led unions for support'.[26] He also accused Evatt of bringing religious sectarianism into a political debate.[27] But he did pay tribute to the Industrial Groups and what they 'were doing inside industry to check Communism'. He said they 'contain men of all religious faiths and political creeds'.

In any event, Holt believed the Government had shown itself to be a good economic manager that deserved the support of working people. During the Higinbotham by-election in January 1955, Holt claimed that, after five years of Liberal Government:

> Australia is more prosperous today than ever before . . . 350 000 new homes have been built, 600 000 Australians have become home owners, 400 000 housewives have bought washing machines, and one million have new refrigerators. According to international polls, more people in Australia are prepared to say they are happy than in any other country in the world.[28]

Ostensibly to synchronise House and Senate elections but seeking to exploit internal rifts within the Labor Party, Menzies called a snap poll for 10 December 1955. Knowing his own seat was safe, Holt travelled across the country supporting the Liberal campaigns in marginal electorates.

On the way back to Sydney after addressing an election rally at Newcastle in the evening of 22 November 1955, Holt was involved in a motor vehicle accident in North Sydney. He was asleep in the back seat of his ministerial car when it failed to negotiate a bend in the Pacific Highway, hit a post and ploughed through the brick fence of the North Sydney Masonic Hall at 1.20 a.m. Holt's driver, Gustave ('Gus') Heister, a 35-year-old ex-serviceman with a wife and two small children, died as a result of his injuries an hour after the accident. Holt was knocked unconscious and was admitted to the nearby Mater Hospital. He had a deep gash on the back of his head that required stitching, abrasions to his back and left arm, and severe concussion. X-rays revealed that no bones were broken. He remained in hospital for more than a week and did not fully resume his official duties until the end of January 1956. Clearly shaken by the accident, he cancelled most of his campaign commitments other than a policy speech in his own electorate. In a statement issued from hospital, he said: 'My doctors [have] said I had severe concussion and that I have to rest for two months. That means I can't return to the election campaign as I hoped to do. But I will be well enough to attend to important Government business'.[29] This happened sooner than he imagined. While in hospital, another patient, Cypriot immigrant Kemal Asilturk, approached him and asked for assistance in having his wife and daughters brought to Australia. He had already written to the Immigration Department in the hope of eliciting his help as the Minister but now Holt offered to intervene personally in the man's case. He spent a few more days in Sydney before returning to Melbourne, but returned to Sydney to attend the Coroner's Inquest into Gus Heister's death on 16 December. He had wanted to attend Heister's funeral but it was delayed by a gravediggers' strike. Ironically, not even the Federal Minister responsible for industrial relations was able to intervene.

Before the accident, Holt had prepared several newspaper articles for the upcoming election, in which he kept to familiar themes. He identified leadership as the key issue. Prime Minister Menzies was 'at his vigorous best and at the highest point of his international influence'. In contrast, 'many within the Labor Party quietly hoped that Evatt was defeated to avoid them moving against him'. Although the outcome in the House of Representatives was almost a foregone conclusion, Holt said 'the Senate is the big question in the election'.[30] Holt implored the electorate to choose stability by casting a vote for the Coalition in the half-Senate election. Holt said the Constitution needed redrafting after the introduction of proportional representation in 1949, especially in relation to the Senate and its power. The Government would 'deal with the matter in a practical way, we will constitute an all-party committee of both Houses to review the working of the Constitution and to make recommendations for its amendment'.[31] The Coalition was returned with an increased majority in the House. The Liberal Party won 57 seats, the Country Party 18 and Labor 47. In the Senate, the Coalition won 16 seats, Labor 12, Anti-Communist Labor 1 and Country-Western

Australia 1. The Government had lost its Senate majority because the numbers were now even. In the seat of Higgins, Labor selected as its candidate the former Victorian State parliamentarian Andrew Hughes. At its first electoral test, the ALP (Anti-Communist) candidate, John Fitzgerald, gained 13.5 per cent of the primary vote almost entirely at the expense of Labor. Holt again secured more than 64 per cent of first preferences with Higgins continuing to be the kind of safe seat that a senior Liberal figure needed if he were to become prime minister.

CHAPTER 5

Heir apparent

MENZIES HAD NOT LONG been Prime Minister before the press were openly declaring Holt to be his obvious successor. After Chifley's death in 1951, Sydney's *Eastern Suburbs Advertiser* ran the headline 'Mr Holt to be Prime Minister'.[1] The article claimed that Menzies would retire before the end of the year to become Chief Justice of the High Court. This was the first of many inaccurate predictions. On 1 December 1954, Menzies became Australia's longest serving prime minister. Including his first term as Prime Minister (1939–41), he had been in office for 7 years and 106 days when he surpassed the record set by Billy Hughes. Talk was of a succession sooner rather than later. In 1954 journalist Rohan Rivett claimed that Menzies wanted Holt because:

> they represent the liberal, middle of the road section of the party and in most major matters of policy are more broadminded and progressive than the majority of the benches behind them. As the whole electoral tendency since the war has been towards a mild, genuinely liberal policy, the Menzies–Holt outlook tends to gain ground at the expense of a more diehard and illiberal philosophy.[2]

But Holt was still ranked fourth in Cabinet. When Sir Eric Harrison, Deputy Party Leader since the Party's formation in 1944, accepted the post of Australian High Commissioner in London in 1956, the outcome of the ballot for his successor was eagerly awaited.

On 26 September, Menzies addressed a meeting of Liberal members and Senators on the Suez Crisis before turning to the matter of electing

Harrison's successor. The discussion on Suez was designed to highlight Menzies' disapproval of Richard Casey's approach to the crisis and to weaken his chances of winning the ballot. There were four candidates: Sir Philip McBride, Bill Spooner, Casey and Holt. The press speculated that McBride and Spooner would be quickly eliminated. Political commentator Ron Watson thought that Holt was 'closest to the man in the street. Younger than the others, he represented a departure from the crusted Toryism that was characteristic of the non-Labor parties pre-war. He could see the other fellow's point of view'.[3] John Bennetts of the *Age* thought Holt's performance 'in the industrial field—in which the Government's greatest blunders have occurred when his advice was ignored—and his administration of the Immigration portfolio show him to be Casey's superior as a politician and administrator'.[4] Many were tipping Casey to win, although most thought that Casey would succeed Menzies only briefly before Holt assumed the prime ministership. This would give Casey the opportunity for national leadership and Holt time to gain more experience. As Casey's biographer, W.J. Hudson, observes, this was the scenario that appealed to Casey.

> As Casey had explained earlier in the year to [his mentor Viscount Bruce], the deputy leadership ballot would be important 'by reason of the current belief that R.G.M. will not continue as P.M. at least beyond the life of the present Parliament'. Casey was convinced that Menzies could not for much longer cope with the physical strain of the prime ministership. Thus, although there was no tradition of deputy leaders becoming leaders, Casey thought that in this instance the man elected to the deputy leadership would soon succeed in leadership, that the ballot really would be for an imminently vacant prime ministership.[5]

According to senior Labor figure Clyde Cameron, Menzies' preference was far from clear, while Billy McMahon had also decided to make a bid for future leadership.

> McMahon claims that Menzies didn't want Holt to take over from him because of the way Holt had let him down during the 1941 crisis when Menzies was thrown out of leadership. He said that Holt had supported Earle Page. I don't believe that. Menzies once told me that Harold's greatest attribute was loyalty. He went on to say that Menzies had approached him [McMahon] to stand for the position of Deputy Leader telling him he had

the party's support. He said Eric Harrison would have been able to swing the New South Wales members who had always supported him on various issues and, in addition, he had good support from the other states as well. He claims to have told Menzies he couldn't take the job of Deputy Leader at that time because he was almost deaf.[6]

The vote did not proceed as expected. Casey was devastated to be eliminated in the first round. The next candidate to go was McBride, the Defence Minister. This left Holt to face Spooner, the Minister for National Development. Born in the Sydney slum district of Redfern in 1897, Bill Spooner served in the First AIF during the Great War. He was promoted to sergeant and decorated with the Military Medal for bravery. After qualifying as an accountant, Spooner did not take an interest in politics until his elder brother Eric lost his Federal seat in 1943. By 1949, Bill Spooner was the Number 1 candidate on the Liberal Party Senate ticket for New South Wales. He was elected and became the most powerful figure in the Liberal State organisation. As a Party heavyweight he was given the Social Services portfolio in Menzies' 1949 ministry. In 1951, he became Minister for National Development. Menzies disliked the Spooners because Eric had played a leading role in his downfall in 1941. Spooner's vote had been increased by members from New South Wales anxious to avoid a situation where both their Leader and Deputy Leader were Victorians. We do not know if Menzies lobbied for Holt, despite Casey's inference that he did. None of those who voted in the ballot later mentioned any contact from Menzies regarding Casey or Holt although the *Adelaide News* would claim that Menzies had managed to divert seven votes from Casey to Holt.

According to the *Sydney Morning Herald*, Holt's victory over Spooner was by only two votes—40 to 38.

> The feeling of Liberal members on the Suez crisis was largely responsible for the weakening of Mr Casey's position in the last two weeks. Members were annoyed at Mr Casey's eagerness to regard the United Nations as the solution to the Suez problem. They said that there was resentment at the emphatic way in which Mr Casey rejected any firm measures to deal with the crisis. The members said these feelings had been stirred up again at a meeting of the Government parties, which Mr Menzies addressed, before the ballot . . . Mr Menzies did not refer to Mr Casey but members said the mere raising of the topic reminded some of their irritation with him. Members said after the election that Senator Spooner was unlucky not to have defeated Mr Holt.[7]

In its analysis of the close result, the *Canberra Times* claimed 'a set against Mr Holt by some elements within his party on the very opposite grounds to those which commend him in national affairs. He has been attacked because he has sought to maintain the immigration programme, and he has been criticised by those on his side of politics who believe he is too close to labour'.[8] An editorial in the *Sydney Morning Herald* described Holt as the 'Heir-Presumptive'. 'It does not follow that he will step into the Prime Minister's shoes when Mr Menzies decides to ring down the final curtain on this part of his career. Much will doubtless depend on what happens from now on, and the Liberal Party will certainly reserve freedom of action on the choice of its future leader.'[9] Political scientist Katherine West would later remark: 'From the time of his elevation, the new Deputy Leader was formally acknowledged as heir apparent, which was the way many of his colleagues had already thought of him for some time'.[10] But Don Whitington identified

> three factors that could block Holt [from succeeding Menzies]. He has antagonised some of those who could have supported him; he lacks the stature that political parties, particularly non-Labor parties, like in their leaders. Bruce, Latham, Lyons and Menzies were all big, handsome men. Hughes was not, but the non-Labor forces rid themselves of him at the first opportunity. Finally, Holt has been the promising protégé for so many years, that like Anthony Eden, he is coming to be regarded in some quarters as the eternal bridesmaid.[11]

On being elected Deputy Leader, Holt became Leader of the House. This position had been established formally in 1951, the incumbent being a Minister appointed by the Prime Minister to organise the business of the House—formerly a prime ministerial task. Although established by Menzies rather than the House and requiring no parliamentary resolution for its creation, it was widely recognised as a positive innovation by both sides of politics. With time, the position was recognised and eventually incorporated into *House of Representatives Practice* which gave the Leader of the House, rather than the Speaker, 'ultimate authority and responsibility for the management of the House'.[12] Harrison had been the first incumbent. Hasluck considered Harrison

> more rigid than his successor and probably less successful than Holt in handling the occasional crises that arise in the routine of parliamentary

business . . . [Holt] got on better terms with the Opposition, managed the business more tactfully and with less fuss, and himself showed more adroitness and skill on the floor of the House than Harrison had done.[13]

Holt's responsibilities as Leader were to supervise the conduct of debates, liaise with departments to ensure draft legislation was ready for introduction into the Parliament and coordinate with the Government and Opposition whips in programming speakers during debates and allocating time for Government business. He was the right man for the job, as he believed that Parliament was 'the greatest monument man has so far devised for the organisation of a free society'.[14] His colleague, Jim Killen, observed:

> Holt was a Parliament man. He would remain courteous to members no matter what the provocation. He would, however, crack back in debate with great effectiveness. He was one of the best off-the-cuff debaters I have seen and heard. He was also one of the few Ministers utterly familiar with the procedures of the House and he knew how to use them. For a senior Minister he spent a lot of time in the House, far more than the majority of private members . . . Parliament to Holt was not a place to be treated with bucolic indifference.[15]

Because he was much more approachable and gregarious than Menzies, Holt developed good relationships with most Ministers and backbenchers. They enjoyed his company and he joined them regularly for a social drink. Menzies announced that given his new duties Holt could 'no longer continue to administer both Labour and National Service and Immigration, each of which is indeed a busy and extremely important portfolio. I regret very much that by sheer necessity Mr Holt should have to terminate his own administration of Immigration'.[16] For his part, Holt was relishing a fresh challenge.

As Leader of the House, in February 1957 Holt proposed measures to 'streamline' parliamentary proceedings. They included annual proroguing of Parliament to provide for the official opening of a new session each autumn; clearly defining sessional periods as autumn and spring sittings; dividing legislation so that the autumn sitting was devoted to general matters or amending or consolidating legislation and the spring sitting to financial measures normally associated with the Budget; and arranging Cabinet and committee meetings to allow Ministers to spend more time in the parliamentary chamber during debates. Holt was supported by the Government Parties. His reforms were, according to Melbourne's *Age*:

> carried out with such thoroughness and thought that he assumed a far more effective control over the House than ever was exercised by his predecessor . . . as a result of these and other measures there is little doubt that Mr Holt has increased his grip on the claim to leadership of the Liberal Party when Mr Menzies retires. He is in a much stronger position with the rank and file now than when by the narrowest of margins he defeated Senator Spooner for the deputy leadership last year.[17]

But not everything he did met with approval. On 29 May, two days after he departed for Singapore bound for Geneva, Holt's office announced that there would be a review of parliamentary salaries and daily allowances. Every politician was delighted with the proposed increases but politically each blamed Holt when press and public protested loud and long. Holt could, however, console himself with the Federated Clothing Industry Council of Australia's decision to name him as one of the six best-dressed men in Australia—along with golfer Peter Thomson and TV personality Bob Dyer.[18]

While the Coalition had won the political confidence of the people, the economy continued to pose problems. The management of labour remained the biggest issue. In August 1956 Holt told the House that in the previous month 9164 people were receiving unemployment benefits, an increase of 2161 on the previous month with Commonwealth Employment Services (CES) vacancies falling from 32 473 at 29 June to 28 784 by 27 July. This variation was due to seasonal factors. Corrections in the labour market reflected imbalances in the economy that the Government was attempting to rectify. There was another rise the following month to 10 333 receiving unemployment benefits although Holt continued to argue that employment was stable. By August 1957, he was conceding that unemployment was continuing to rise but indicated that the Government would announce a package of measures in the August 1957 Budget. He resisted Labor's contention that unemployment was being fuelled by immigration. The Government's short-term solution was to create more jobs in the building and construction industries. Some of the projects that commenced during 1957 were construction of a standard gauge rail track between Melbourne and Wodonga; increased naval ship construction at Williamstown and Cockatoo Island Dockyards; and a program of road construction as part of Commonwealth Public Works. The States received grants for public programs. The economy showed signs of recovery by October when the unemployment figure dropped.

Wage stability was improving. The Basic Wage Decision of April 1957 delivered a weekly increase of 10 shillings to the minimum wage. Holt stated: 'Now that the principal industrial tribunal of the Commonwealth has come down firmly in favour of an annual wage review, those State Governments who still persist with quarterly adjustments will make their own contribution to stability by following the lead of the Commonwealth Commission'.[19] When the Coalition was accused by unions and the Federal Opposition of not disclosing its real attitude to periodic wage adjustments, Holt said the Government had never opposed the adjustment of wages or an annual wage adjustment. What the Government *had* argued against was the continuation of a system of quarterly wage adjustments that had been introduced under a completely different set of circumstances. The Government favoured the annual review arguing that it gave more wage justice. Holt claimed there had been 'fantastic allegations' about the end of quarterly adjustments causing workers in various States to be out of pocket. But details of average weekly earnings in Australia showed that not only had wages kept pace with increases in the cost of living— they had gone well beyond them.

─ ─

As the economy grew stronger, the Government could return to exploiting continuing tensions in the Opposition. Holt led the attacks. In a press release headed 'Socialist objective of ALP' issued after the 1957 Labor Party National Conference, Holt claimed 'the Left-wing element now in control of the Party have brought the question of its socialist objective prominently forward at this time . . . and that the hard core of its socialist program as printed in the constitution and platform of the party remains unchanged'.[20] He also castigated the Conference for its 'contemptible and completely unwarranted attacks upon intelligent and public spirited New Australians', saying that migrants were hostile to Labor because 'they had come to Australia to flee the policies that Evatt and the ALP stood for'. Holt continued to stir the Opposition over its internal split. On 27 March 1957 he claimed in the House that the Labor Party had 'purged itself of Right-wing moderate elements and declared itself clearly, frankly and unequivocally as a Socialist party' and was 'shattered beyond recovery'.

He referred to the Opposition as a rabble 'not only split into three definite groups inside the party, but split elsewhere'.[21] A week later he was accusing Evatt of having a foreign policy consistent with that advocated by the Australian Communist Party, and of naïvety in relying completely on the United Nations (UN) to promote global stability.

> This Government supports the UN and will continue to do what it can to make it effective. But we are not blinded by its weaknesses and imperfections. We can discharge our obligations not as one small voice among 80 in the UN, but through our association with Great Britain, the United States, and the other parliamentary democracies.[22]

In a private letter to Harrison, Holt commented that:

> The Opposition has been showing a little more fight this session, but nothing comparable with the old days of Jack Beasley's team, or our own gallant band in the mid-forties. Most of the infighting is left to left-wingers like Ward and Clyde Cameron . . . We still occasionally get tougher opposition than Labor provides from some of our own backbench boys—Bill Wentworth being, as you might expect, the worst offender . . . [Menzies'] bitterness towards Wentworth is out of all proportion to Wentworth's consequence in the scheme of things, and he has become more sensitive than I have ever known him before to hostile Press comment.[23]

The Liberal Party was also displaying the first signs of complacency and some hints at weariness.

After becoming Deputy Leader and accepting a greater responsibility for the Liberal Party's overall direction and electoral performance, Holt identified two problems in a paper entitled 'The political situation' dated 4 February 1957. First, the Government was not getting the 'degree and warmth of public support' it deserved for its achievements. This had become a familiar lament. Although the Government had weathered the political storms required by 'measures not calculated to enhance our popularity', Holt thought the Government could do better at selling its policies to the electorate or making them aware of the practical fruits of sound public policy. It also needed to improve the relationship between the various elements of the Party organisation. With Menzies as leader the qualities of the organisation seemed scarcely relevant, although some Liberal officials still worried if the Party would be strong enough to survive his departure.[24] Second, the Government plainly needed a new agenda as 'most of the things we set out to do when we were returned in 1949 have been accomplished'.

As the Federal Opposition was divided and dispirited after the 1955 split, Holt believed the Government should demonstrate its unity and vision. With its immediate electoral future assured, 'it would be stupid of us to lapse into complacency'. Holt noted the tendency of the Australian electorate to turn against the Government without being convinced that the alternative was better while Labor polled well despite internal upheavals. He wanted a new appeal to be made to the Australian people. The Liberal Party had successfully secured much of the middle class. It now needed to broaden its appeal and bolster elector loyalty.

> We still lack a sufficiently large following of devoted people who are whole-heartedly for our principles, and enthusiastic about the way we apply them. We have been 'delivering the goods' in terms of sustained prosperity, develop-ment and full employment. We are generally regarded as being 'sounder' on national finance, foreign relations and defence. We have managed to attract enough 'marginal voters' of the artisan, farmer, small shopkeeper type, etc., to ensure our parliamentary majority. But we have never experienced the fervour and unquestioning loyalty which Labour [sic] could confidently expect for so many of its better years from a great mass of people. We have yet to face the challenge of bad seasons, growing unemployment, or a unified Labour Movement under a more popular leadership.[25]

Holt suggested that the only two major national initiatives of the post-war period, the Snowy Mountains Scheme and large-scale immigration, actually originated with Labor. The Government lacked 'imagination' and the public's support was fickle. The Government needed 'a story likely to arouse some enthusiasm towards us from the public'. Holt wanted to tran-scend electoral popularity in reaching for philosophical commitment. The central elements of the story would be industrial expansion and mineral exploration, tied together 'as examples of what is going on in this country, during a period when it is being soundly governed in accordance with Liberal principles'. But Holt also recognised that Australian liberalism had 'so individualised political allegiance, framing citizens as responsible to themselves, their families and their workplaces, that this allowed little vision of a national story'.[26]

Holt's paper angered some of his Cabinet colleagues. They did not believe the Government's program was exhausted. In fact, they did not see what all the fuss was about. The Government's management of the economy had been good and it was not necessary 'to seek all the time after dramatic projects'. Liberal philosophy encouraged the creation of conditions that would 'encourage development through private enterprise'. Furthermore, new projects and increased government spending might lead to inflation. Whereas Holt proposed public meetings and 'mass contacts' that would allow the Government to sell its message to the electorate, Cabinet thought that parliamentarians 'should be their own and the government's best public relations men'. Holt wanted the Government to exude energy and promote excitement, but most of his colleagues seemed to him to be dull and drab. As Murphy points out, 'with his simple, buoyant faith in progress, [Holt] was concentrating, fleetingly, on a public relations exercise to win allegiance, rather than a vision of policy'.[27] But Holt's efforts were designed to renew energy and enthusiasm in a party nearing a decade in office.

By the time of the Federal Election on 22 November 1958, the Government could still attack disunity within Labor ranks while promoting itself as the party of stability. It campaigned with the slogan 'Australia Unlimited'—based on its economic record—and claimed that the 'Battle for production' had been won. Together with McMahon, Holt participated in the first televised political debates in Australian history during November. Their respective opponents were Evatt and Calwell.[28] Menzies, who did not like the new medium, had been unwilling to participate. The polls delivered the biggest Federal electoral victory since 1901. In the House of Representatives the Liberal Party won 58 seats, the Country Party 19 and Labor 45. Of the 32 Senate seats contested, however, the Coalition and Labor both won 15. The Democratic Labor Party (DLP) and Country-Western Australia Party won the remaining two seats. The Government had succeeded in regaining a majority. There was never any doubt about the outcome in Higgins. Given the national trend, however, it is perhaps surprising that there was a 1.3 per cent swing to the Labor candidate, Alfred Shiff, drawn almost equally from Holt and the DLP's Celia Laird. But Holt still commanded more than 60 per cent of the primary vote.

The member for Higgins felt more optimistic about his own position than he did about the standing of the Government.

63

CHAPTER 6

Immigration

1950–56

BY THE END OF World War II, the Chifley Labor Government had recognised the importance of large-scale immigration for Australia's national development and defence. Maintaining a high intake while absorbing the new arrivals successfully would continue to be the challenge it had been for the previous four decades. From Federation to the outbreak of war, Australia's net gain from immigration was just under 60 000, with an annual average increase of 15 000. Most of these immigrants arrived in the three years before World War I or in the 1920s. During the two periods of 1901–05 and 1931–35, the Australian population actually dropped. Immediately after World War II, the initial immigrant arrival rate was hampered by a shortage of ships. By 1947 the number of new arrivals exceeded departures by 12 000; in 1948 the figure was 48 000; by 1949 it was 149 000. In the five years between 1945 and 1950, the number of new arrivals exceeded the entire population of Tasmania at that time. Such an influx required concerted Government effort across a number of departments.

Labor's first Immigration Minister, Arthur Calwell, established the Immigration Advisory Council in 1947. The Council was reconstituted by Holt in 1950, with sixteen members including leading trade unionists such as Reg Broadby, Percy Clarey, H.O. Davis and Albert Monk. Organisational affiliates included the Air Force Association, the Associated Chambers of Commerce, the Associated Chambers of Manufacturers, the Australian Council of Employers Federations, the ACTU, the Australian Legion of Ex-service Men and Women, the Australian Workers' Union, the National Council of Women, the National Farmers' Union, and the Returned Sailors', Soldiers' and Airmen's Association. The Council's

Chairman was Colonel Rupert Ryan, the Liberal Member for Flinders in Victoria. The Council was responsible for settlement issues and the assimilation of migrants. Its counterpart was the Immigration Planning Council, which focused on economic, industrial and developmental issues. In effect, the two Councils gave Holt separate social and economic advice.[1]

Cabinet set the broad policy parameters, but the Minister was given discretion to interpret and implement them in relation to specific cases. Holt took this discretion to its limits and displayed a genuine liberal spirit. His long-term aim was to increase the initial target of 70 000 immigrants per year to 200 000 each year, primarily from Britain, Holland, Malta and Ireland. The initial goal was to increase Australia's population to 9 million by 1953, then maintain an annual population growth of 3 per cent throughout the coming decade.[2] Although there was a preference for British immigrants and their families, Holt would extend the policy of accepting non-British immigrants to accommodate those displaced by the war and the post-war Soviet occupation of Eastern Europe. There was also a need for single male workers for major public works such as the Snowy Mountains Hydro-Electric Scheme. The main hurdle to overcome was lack of housing. Government hostels were overcrowded and the standard of accommodation was basic, although far superior to what most had left in war-torn Europe.

On 27 April 1950 Holt told the House that: 'This Government decided at the beginning of 1950 that it wanted to bring to Australia a larger proportion of British immigrants than had been contemplated by the previous Government'.[3] He appeared to believe that the British Commonwealth had a form of sacred destiny:

> The next century could see our British Commonwealth and our English speaking ally the United States advance to a situation of strength unparalleled in world history. Together we could guarantee democratic freedom and produce a more widely shared prosperity. Together we could assure the peace of the world. War, in our time, would smash these hopes. It is one war which must not be allowed to happen.[4]

Holt explained that 'We Australians are proud of our British origins and of the British way of life, which are the bases of our own. It is natural and commendable that we should seek to preserve the predominantly British character of our population'.[5] Although Australia was taking immigrants from across Europe, it 'can still build a truly British nation on this side of the world. I feel that if the central tradition of a nation is strong this tradition will impose itself on groups of immigrants'.[6] 'New Australians' were expected to make a break with their country of origin—unless they were British. Holt restored the words 'British Passport', deleted by the Chifley Government in 1949, to Australian passports, but this was the extent of his preferences. He would prove to be more liberal and progressive than most in his Party.

The Party's 1946 policy platform had committed the Liberals to preserving the 'ideals of the White Australia Policy'. Two years later, the Victorian State Council claimed that its maintenance was 'vital to the existence of a free Australia'. Although Holt's approach was outwardly consistent with the Party platform, on taking office he officially banned the term 'White Australia Policy' as offensive to Australia's nearest neighbours. He preferred the term coined by Calwell: 'restricted immigration policy'. Holt explained that Australia's Asian migration policy 'rested on a frank recognition that important differences of race, culture and economic standards would make successful assimilation of Asians unlikely. There was no racial superiority in this approach'.[7] When asked in 1952 by a reporter from the Singapore *Straits Times* about the 'White Australia Policy', Holt replied: 'We don't call it that. I have tried to administer Australia's immigration policy with commonsense and humanity during my term of office'.[8] Holt stressed that the policy employed neither a colour nor an economic bar. Holt was widely criticised for his decision to take German immigrants, but replied:

> By accepting as migrants to Australia some of the selected Germans of Western Europe, Australia would be helping ease the strains on the seething occupied zones of Europe. It would be making a humanitarian gesture and a real contribution to the spread of justice and goodwill in the world.[9]

Holt did give a number of assurances over the following months that no former Nazi Party officials or soldiers would be permitted to enter Australia and that accusations of Nazi affiliations would be thoroughly investigated. He also made it clear that he would not make exceptions in dealing with 'prohibited migrants' such as those who were 'stowaways' or came to Australia illegally.

Holt's initial policy statement was praised as 'wise and statesmanlike' by Professor MacMahon Ball (at one time the British representative on the

Allied Council in Japan) and commended for its 'flexible attitude' by Sir Frederic Eggleston, a former Australian Minister to China.[10] A cartoon in the Melbourne *Herald* captioned 'New Hand Out' depicted Holt's extended hand in the shape of the Australian continent. The four fingers were labelled 'Friendship, Tolerance, Discretion, Humanity'. Holt also had to counter the fears of industrial unions and the National Farmers' Union that immigrants would take Australian jobs. He explained that immigrants were already being absorbed into the workforce without difficulty in those areas where additional manpower was required, at a time when unemployment was negligible. He also pledged to prevent any deportation of Asians who had fled to Australia during the war until their cases had been thoroughly investigated. He agreed to extensions to their residential permits although the High Court had upheld the validity of the *Wartime Refugees Removal Act 1949* and the *Immigration Act 1949*. Holt decided that Mrs Annie O'Keefe (see Chapter 3) and 800 other wartime refugees who wanted to stay were 'a special case'. The press detected a clear shift in the management of immigration.

> The difference now is that instead of the merciless rigidity with which Mr Calwell administered the immigration laws there will be under Mr Holt a prudent exercise of a Ministerial discretion that was always permissible . . . The deportation campaign pursued against a handful of wartime refugees and others was rapidly convincing [the new Asian nations] that the White Australia Policy was not a justifiable national measure of self-protection but an expression of racial superiority. The new Minister's humane and balanced approach . . . should repair much of the harm done.

Not everyone approved. The Secretary of the Queensland Branch of the Australian Natives Association, a Mr McGoll, asserted that 'Australians fought and died . . . to keep their country free from dictators, coolie labour, cheap goods and low standards'.[11]

—— ——

In a spirit of bipartisan generosity, Holt had invited Calwell to attend the inaugural Migrant Citizenship Convention in 1950. After all, Holt said, his predecessor had helped to organise the event. More than 150 delegates from around the country gathered in Canberra to consider problems associated with the 'assimilation of new settlers'. The following year,

Holt convened a Commonwealth Jubilee Citizens' Convention at Canberra to discuss ways in which 'New Australians' might become more fully part of Australian society. There was a general confidence that assimilation could and would be achieved, although there were divisive forces to deal with.

In July 1951, Holt warned that Communists were using the poor conditions under which immigrants lived in hostels and camps for political gain, but said the Commonwealth was doing its best. Holt decided to establish a Government-owned corporation administered by his Department to manage the 64 immigrant resettlement hostels (26 000 beds). He also had to act on allegations of an Italian 'Black Hand' crime syndicate establishing itself in Australia; high rates of violent crime among immigrants; the presence of former Nazis among German immigrants; and concerns over whether Japanese women who had married Australian servicemen should be allowed residence in Australia. On 19 July 1952, 200 armed troops and five armoured cars from Bandiana together with officers from the Victoria Police were called into the Bonegilla Migrant Camp when 2000 Italians were threatening to riot if they were not given work. Holt met a delegation in Albury Town Hall, heard their demands and promised to meet with Prime Minister Menzies the following week. The Government then decided on 'special measures' to give 2300 unemployed Italians jobs. He was then forced to defend the Government's immigration policy from the charge that it was creating unemployment.

> The critics cannot have it both ways; they cannot claim that migration added to inflationary pressure and at the same time say that it deprived Australians of jobs. The records of the Department of Labour and National Service showed that the number of empty jobs grew steadily as migration increased. No impartial examination could lead to any conclusion but that migration created jobs, and could be stepped up in a period of economic decline as a valuable restorative of demand and activity.[12]

Holt explained that the absorption of immigrant labour into the workforce had to be directed by use of landing permits and financial assistance and that the Government was sending 'directable' immigrants—mainly from Holland, Italy and West Germany—to rural activity, particularly dairy farming and potato growing, rather than jobs in the cities. Holt was also concerned that manufacturing industries were growing too fast over far too wide a field, causing distortions in the national economy. He attacked Labor's claim that Australia was slipping towards a depression and that the Government wanted to create an 'unemployment pool'.

In a press statement issued in April 1952, Holt noted that 'there had been a further decline during April in the unsatisfied demand for labour . . . the most urgent demand was for skilled tradesmen who were needed to provide great opportunities for unskilled workers in essential industries'.[13] He pledged the Commonwealth Government to finding a job for every person who wanted to work to fulfil its policy of full employment. After a period of over-employment in which industries were competing for workers, Holt forecast a return to a balance between labour supply and demand by May 1952.

By 25 July 1952, however, Holt reluctantly announced that the intake rate would be reduced by half in 1953 to 80 000, to give the country and the economy a 'breather'. The 1952 intake would itself be restricted to 110 000. In an article published in the *Age* on 14 August 1953, Holt argued that Australia could cope with an annual migrant intake of 100 000 'without any serious disturbance to our living standards'. He told a convention of the Australian Association of Advertising Agencies that Australia's population would reach 40 million by 1994.[14] Holt continued to promote the benefits of immigration. The growth in the workforce and in national productivity could be attributed directly to the new arrivals. In a message to the Australian Institute of Political Science Summer School held in January 1953, Holt argued that:

> We are in a period which has brought migration under close review by many of our fellow Australians. Some of these have become more conscious of the discomforts and difficulties of migration, and less appreciative of the benefits in terms of added strength and richer development increase of population has brought with it. Prejudices can build quickly around religious and national differences and become sharpened by personal inconvenience or fears of economic hardship. But those whose vision remains clear will never lose their conviction that Australia must be populated and developed rapidly.[15]

At the fifth Citizenship Convention in January 1954, the Minister reported that the intake for 1953 had been 73 000 (the target was 80 000), but the target for 1954 remained 100 000. Immigration was now increasing at a sustainable rate although Holt was attacked by the Opposition for allowing too many 'Chinese and other Asiatics' into the country. The secretary of the New South Wales Branch of the Labor Party claimed that Chinese were 'breaking down labour standards'.[16] Holt's response to the restrictions on immigration was masterly inactivity: he was prepared to administer the policy but was much less vigorous in defending its restrictions. Although he believed that Government policy ought to reflect rather than direct prevailing community attitudes, he thought that the electorate was still too fearful of immigrant cultures. He was largely indifferent to the idea of accepting token quotas of 50–100 people from several Asian nations when it was raised by General K.M. Cariappa, the Indian High Commissioner, although the proposal met with anger and strident backbench opposition in the Liberal Party room. Shortly after meeting with his colleagues on 8 July 1954 he told the House that 'this Government stands four-square behind the maintenance' of the policy which was 'designed to preserve the homogeneity of the Australian nation'.[17] He also asked Asian nations not to ask for an immigration quota as they would certainly be rebuffed. But the mix of immigrants was set to change.

The initial emphasis of the immigration program was single men and women. By the mid-1950s this had shifted towards single women eligible for marriage and married women. At the 1953 Citizenship Convention, Holt explained the economic rationale behind this shift. In periods of high inflation most immigrants 'should be breadwinners, few or no dependants accompanying them' as this boosted production without increasing consumption. When inflation fell, migrants with dependants created a demand for goods and services that stimulated employment. There was also a genuine desire to do something about the loneliness faced by migrant men unable to speak English and unable to find a female companion. On 6 June 1955, Holt announced that Australia's immigration intake for 1955–56 would be 125 000, comprising 70 000 assisted-passage immigrants and 55 000 paying full fares. He told the House: 'If our expansion is not to be halted we must maintain from migration a supply of labour to all sections of industry . . . The community as a whole shares the confidence of the Government, that Australia can successfully absorb continued population growth on the scale proposed'.[18]

Not surprisingly, the one-millionth post-war migrant was not a middle-aged single male from Europe. She was a young, photogenic, married British woman, Barbara Porritt, who arrived in Australia on board the liner *Oronsay* during the middle of 'Immigration Week'—8 November

1955. The Chief Migration Officer in London had chosen her on advice from the Immigration Advisory Council because she presented an attractive face to the immigration program and because her husband, Dennis, was an electrician contracted to work for the State Electricity Commission of Victoria. At a press conference held in the ship after it docked in Melbourne, Holt said, 'Mrs Porritt, Australia salutes you as the representative of our million post-war migrants. Now we are looking forward to our second million'.[19]

At what would be his last Citizenship Convention in 1956 as Minister for Immigration, Holt argued that the Menzies Government rightly 'came to the conclusion that Australia could sustain a continuing rate of population growth from immigration of the order of 1 per cent [of population] per annum, and [deciding] that for planning purposes, this figure should be adopted as the basis'.[20] This conclusion was a pillar of Menzies' statement on economic policy delivered on 14 March 1956.

By now, the numbers from Europe were slowing as the prospect of another world war diminished and employment prospects in Europe improved although Australia agreed to take up to 10 000 refugees after the Hungarian Uprising. Part of the solution was another long overseas trip in which the Minister would promote Australia and the Government's willingness to assist in immigrants' passage. By this time, Holt had become a seasoned traveller, although he did not travel abroad until after World War II. During the first half of the 1950s, his ministerial duties and leadership of the Commonwealth Parliament Association (CPA) led to him being absent from the country almost as much as the Minister for External Affairs. He enjoyed international travel and proved to be an effective advocate of Australia's interests abroad, especially in attracting immigrants. His first major ministerial trip had been to Colombo and Singapore for a meeting of the Council of the Empire Parliamentary Association on 30 December 1951. While in Malaya, Holt was given an explanation of how the administration was dealing with Communist terrorism. On 22 January 1952 he boarded a RAAF 'Lincoln' bomber for a four-hour mission over northern Perak. Six 1000-pound bombs and eight 500-pound bombs were released as part of an airstrike on suspected Communist positions. He was probably the last Australian Minister to participate in a combat mission.

In July 1952, Holt went abroad for ten weeks accompanied by Zara and his private secretary, Noel Flanagan. They travelled to Singapore (with re-fuelling stops in Darwin and Jakarta), and then to Karachi (with a fuel stop in Calcutta) where he met the Prime Minister of Pakistan. It was then on to Rome (via Beirut) and a private audience with Pope Pius XII at Castelgandolfo. From there, Holt made a short visit to Malta. With Zara and Flanagan he travelled by car into Austria where he visited two refugee camps and noted the unwelcome presence of Soviet troops. It was then to London for discussions with British shipping authorities concerning the lack of available vessels to transport immigrants to Australia before returning to Europe and a whirlwind round of meetings in Geneva, Stockholm, Berlin, Amsterdam, The Hague, Brussels, Paris, Cologne and Bonn. In Berlin, Holt visited the Russian sector, which he found thoroughly dispiriting. He also toured the Berlin Documentation Centre and examined captured Nazi Party documents. As he met European immigration officials, Flanagan noted that Holt explained that 'although Australia is anxious to receive migrants an annual increase of population of some 3 per cent would, after a period of years, place considerable strain on the community. We have to build additional schools, hospitals and houses, and it is necessary to expand our engineering services and this public investment is naturally beyond the present resources of Australia'.[21] Holt then returned to London for several days, for discussions with the British Government and the Anglo-Iranian Company (later British Petroleum) on the proposed construction of an oil refinery in Kwinana, Western Australia. He also made a short visit to Northern Ireland before departing for the biennial CPA Conference in Ottawa via Scotland and Newfoundland.[22] At the opening session of the conference, Holt said the Commonwealth was not unravelling although some countries were moving towards independence or self-government and had demonstrated that the 'brotherhood of man' was no idle dream. The United States was the next stop, where Holt met with Adlai Stevenson, the Democratic candidate in the November 1952 Presidential Election. He was heartened by the American Federation of Labor's encouragement of migration—in contrast, Holt said, to the attitude of the Labor Party in Australia—and Stevenson's insistence on unions remaining clear of politics so as to preserve their independence and individuality. In an article published in the Melbourne *Herald*, Holt said that Australia could learn much from the 'American miracle'. Greater cooperation between employers and employees would lead to both sharing the benefits of increased productivity.[23]

On returning to Canberra on 5 October 1952, Holt stressed that Australia was the most preferred destination for European migrants and that the country was in a position to take the best rather than the poorest.

Holt assured Australians that the screening tests applied by his Department were the best, that Australia had the lowest unemployment level of any developed economy and that immigrants would not long be jobless after they arrived.

In May 1953, Holt was back in London as the Chief Host of the Commonwealth Parliamentary Association's luncheon for Queen Elizabeth six days before her coronation. Holt sat on the Queen's right. The *Buckingham Palace Court Circular* dated 27 May 1953 recorded that Holt proposed the formal toast to 'The Queen'. Before doing so, Holt said: 'The world has had a weary surfeit of bitterness and strife. As your Majesty stands on the threshold of your reign, so rich in promise, you embody the hopes of mankind for another great era of peaceful development'.[24] He presented her with a book containing pictures of the Houses of Parliament of the 50 member countries of the Commonwealth. On 1 June, the London *Times* announced that Holt had been appointed a Privy Councillor. The 'Honourable Harold Holt' was now the 'Right Honourable Harold Holt'. He was sworn in at Windsor Castle on 19 June 1953. There was press speculation about whether Holt would receive a knighthood 'so early in his career'. On the way home, Holt visited Holland to appeal for 20 000 Dutch migrants before heading to Greece with a similar objective. Then it was on to New York to promote American investment in Australia.

In August 1954 Holt travelled to Kenya for the next CPA meeting, where he again chaired the General Council. Holt praised the progress Kenyans were making, regretted that India was not present but stressed that Commonwealth ties were as strong as ever. He declared: 'Let no stranger be misled by the constitutional evolution through these post-war years. The Commonwealth is not breaking up, it is growing up'.[25] In August 1957 he returned from another ten-week trip in which he visited Germany, Austria, Italy, Spain, Holland, England and the United States. He had accompanied Menzies to the Prime Ministers' Conference in London and went on to New York for the opening of the new Qantas office. He also met the UN Secretary-General, Dag Hammarskjöld, and had a conference with the Australian Government's bankers in America, Morgan Stanley. In a ministerial statement, he noted that 'the prosperous condition of Europe generally, strong competition from Canada and a slight easing of demand for labour in Australia has, over recent months, made it rather more difficult to secure suitable migrants in the desired numbers from some countries'.[26] He did not seem to be weary of travel.

He was criticised for the length of his absences from Australia, however, and very occasionally for the nature of his activities while overseas. Typical was Eddie Ward's attack on Holt for visiting 'the Isle of Capri with ex-King Farouk of Egypt'. As the taxpayer was funding Holt's travel, Ward wanted to know 'why he went there'.[27]

In his seven years at the Immigration Department, Holt maintained Calwell's better initiatives with more than Calwell's tact and diplomacy.[28] In fact, the immigration policies of Labor and the Coalition were remarkably similar. The difference was that while Holt publicly upheld the policy, he had already begun to dilute it by the generous application of ministerial discretion. He did this through changing the eligibility requirements for citizenship: extending eligibility for citizenship to non-European spouses of European immigrants; allowing the non-European wives of Australian servicemen to become Australian citizens; admitting immediate relatives as Australian citizens; granting indefinite work permits to allow qualified people to remain in the country; and allowing non-European immigrants resident in Australia for fifteen or more years to become citizens.[29] During Holt's tenure:

> with the exception of a few minor cases, the 1950s were almost entirely free of incidents related to the White Australia policy. Most Australians, due very largely to Holt's more flexible attitude to the subject and new immigration legislation enacted in 1956 and 1957, believed that the general tenor of the policy was changing.[30]

Holt presented a caring and humane public face, and won for himself and the Liberal Party personal and electoral popularity with non-British immigrants.

After nearly seven years as Minister for Immigration, Holt was asked to nominate his greatest success. He replied that it was preventing the winding back of the immigration program despite pressure from within his own party. In his final contribution to the magazine *The Good Neighbour*, Holt spoke strongly of:

> The necessity to avoid destroying carefully cultivated good relations with emigration countries and the need to maintain the confidence of governments, investors and others both within Australia and overseas to emphasise the desirability of avoiding both any permanent reduction in what is deemed the manageable rate of immigration and a major cut in the programme . . . a

continuation of a high level of immigration can ensure the continuation of this progress which will bring in its train improved productivity and other benefits arising from larger scale activity. The simple fact is that immigration is one major influence that leaves the country with a long-term asset on both political and economic grounds.[31]

He relinquished the Immigration portfolio on 24 October 1956, shortly after he became Deputy Leader of the Liberal Party and Leader of the House of Representatives.

CHAPTER 7

Labour and National Service

1950–58

IN THE AUSTRALIAN SYSTEM of industrial relations, government intervention in the labour market has been a constant although contested feature since Federation. It is based in the belief that governments have a role in regulating the terms of employment when there is an inequality in the bargaining strengths of employers and workers, and that strikes and lockouts disrupt the economy and cause social hardship. Government intervention has taken two forms: conciliation and arbitration. *Conciliation* is the process of bringing disputing parties into a voluntary agreement. *Arbitration* is the settlement of a dispute by the decision of an independent third party. As many unions have members across the country and operate as federal entities, many disputes relate to federal awards and, consequently, involve the Commonwealth. Section 51 (xxxv) of the Constitution gives the Commonwealth power to make laws with respect to 'conciliation and arbitration for the prevention and settlement of industrial disputes extending beyond the limits of any one state'. The Commonwealth cannot legislate directly on industrial conditions but it can set up tribunals that are authorised both to conciliate and arbitrate.

In 1904 the Federal Parliament passed the *Conciliation and Arbitration Act*, which aimed to prevent or settle industrial disputes through the creation of the Court of Conciliation and Arbitration. The Court was empowered to make determinations relating to wages, hours and working conditions. Both employer organisations and trade unions were required to be registered before they could appear before the Court. Withdrawal of a union's registration—the foremost source of the Government's coercive power—meant it could not approach the Court for a hearing nor would a deregistered union or its members become a party to awards made by the Court. The members of a deregistered union suffered individually while the union became vulnerable to its members being poached by a registered union covering the same or similar trades and occupations.

Some disputes could not be resolved before the unions felt they had no choice but to bring their members out on strike, although this was always deemed to be a last resort. In the period 1946–50 a large number of working days were lost to strikes. Although the wage limitations imposed during World War II had come to an end and there was excess demand for labour as economic prosperity returned, some employers refused to accept union demands. When the 1949 national coal strike culminated in the defeat of the mining unions at the hands of a Labor Government, it was apparent that neither employers nor employees would be the inevitable victors in any industrial conflict. In the two areas of greatest industrial unrest, mining and stevedoring, an initial under-supply of labour in the first half of the 1950s was replaced by an over-supply when mechanisation reduced manpower needs. In both instances special tribunals were required to deal with the turmoil. The Government's involvement in the management of industrial relations therefore required wise leadership and careful administration.

Harold Holt was given the portfolio largely because he was the Minister most acceptable to moderate elements in the labour movement. He understood their concerns, had sound negotiation skills, believed in government regulation of the labour market and thought an unfettered labour market was both inefficient and contrary to the specific needs of the post-war Australian economy. As Holt's parliamentary colleague Jo Gullett remarked:

> Harold's greatest quality was the ability to see and sympathise with other points of view. This is very laudable in a politician. It meant that for a start he was generally liked and respected in the Parliament, regardless of party. It also meant that he had developed very good relations with the trade union leaders.[1]

Holt saw the industrial relations challenges facing the Menzies–Fadden Government as 'Communist control of key industrial unions; a weakened arbitration system lacking effective disciplinary powers; a hostile Senate, making substantial legislative amendment difficult, if not impracticable; a suspicious and uncooperative attitude on the part of the Trade Union movement'.[2] Holt believed the last challenge not only to be the greatest but also the key to improved industrial relations. He worked hard at establishing and maintaining a close relationship with Albert Monk, the President of the Australian Council of Trade Unions (ACTU).[3] What became known as the 'Holt–Monk Axis' was vital to the conduct of industrial relations. Holt struck an agreement with Monk and the ACTU that all trade union representations to the Government were to come through the national body. Federal ministers were not to receive deputations from federal unions until the ACTU President had been notified.

Holt's main concern was the poor performance of the building industry as lack of housing was restraining immigration. In July 1950, Holt stated that there were 140 000 building workers—compared with 95 000 in 1939—yet fewer houses had been built in the preceding twelve months than in 1939. He considered several possible strategies. He floated the idea of incentive payments to boost productivity and addressed the subject in detail at a forum convened by the Australian Institute of Political Science in July 1950. Holt also appealed to employers: 'There is no substitute for the skill, energy and ingenuity of good management, either in its capacity for solving technical problems, for organising productive processes, or for handling the human problems of production'.[4]

But one union continued to be Holt's nemesis, the Waterside Workers Federation (WWF) led by the towering Communist figure of Jim Healy. The WWF had been founded in 1902 to remedy the appalling working conditions on the waterfront. It had fought many battles with employers and was characterised by a thoroughly militant spirit. On 16 August 1950, Holt convened a meeting of 22 waterfront employers and employee groups to plead for better industrial relations and improved turn-round of ships. He said the Government would not tolerate 'defiant' union acts but insisted that employers were responsible, too, for industrial harmony. A Steering Committee on Waterfront Reform was established as a buffer between irreconcilable employer and employee organisations. It consisted of ten members nominated by B. Foggon, Chairman of the Overseas Shipping Representatives' Association, J.M. Hewitt, Chairman of the Australian Stevedoring Industry Board (ASIB), and Albert Monk, representing the trade unions.

Holt believed that there was a Communist conspiracy to disrupt the coal, shipping and waterfront industries simultaneously. By early 1950, he was predicting 'one of the blackest periods in Australia's industrial history'.[5] In February 1951, he tried to take firm action against the leaders of the Miners' Federation for contempt of the Arbitration Court. He also discussed with senior Army officers the possibility of the military taking control of the nation's coal fields. The Chifley Government had set the precedent for such action in 1949. Holt announced that the Government would consider using the *Crimes Act* against waterfront union leaders if they continued their ban on overtime[6] and to amend the Act so that it could also be used against coal miners for their weekly one-day strikes. When Holt did invoke the *Crimes Act*, the Communist Assistant Secretary of the WWF was sentenced to a year's gaol for contempt of the Arbitration Court. The Acting Prime Minister, Arthur Fadden, and Holt sought Chifley's counsel, as did the ACTU. He told the unionists to take their dispute back to court. The waterfront dispute was resolved on 5 March and the miners' case on 12 March. Holt then introduced the Conciliation and Arbitration Bill to give the Arbitration Court power of injunction to deal with contraventions of orders and awards, and to punish contempt of its powers and authority. The changes were opposed in the Senate and could, in time, have given the Government another trigger for a 'double dissolution'. But before there was time for further action, the Parliament was dissolved for the 1951 election.

Political correspondent Alan Reid praised Holt for his 'successful resistance of pressure from his own Party' to attack trade unions and noted the personal support he had from Menzies and Fadden.[7] Holt had earlier told the Liberal Federal Executive that there was a tendency within the Party to 'over-dramatise the effect and incidence of strikes' and to side too readily and hastily with the employer.[8] But some within the Liberal Party saw Holt as an 'appeaser', while Monk's close relationship with Holt provoked some unionists to side with Left-wing elements in the labour movement rather than moderates such as Monk.

Holt threatened to use Australia's armed forces again in June 1951 when the WWF placed a ban on handling ships from New Zealand which had been worked by new unionists or troops there as part of a campaign of solidarity with New Zealand wharfies. Holt had warned that 'the Commonwealth Government will certainly not tolerate indefinitely a situation which creates cessation of trade between this country and our sister Dominion'.[9] Holt decided to have union officials charged under the *Crimes Act* for inciting an illegal dispute; General Secretary Jim Healy was charged with interfering with overseas trade. Holt also asked the Attorney-General, Senator John Spicer, to seek the deregistration of the WWF. Holt said the action would not be necessary if the union cooperated with the Government. When Healy went to court on 19 July, wharfies around Australia walked off the job in support. On the basis of documents seized during police raids of the WWF's offices in Sydney and Melbourne, Healy was found guilty and sentenced to six months' imprisonment. On appeal, the penalty was reduced to a fine of £100.[10] The union called off their ban and Monk asked Holt to discontinue the court action. By the end of October 1951, Holt was praising waterfront workers, particularly in Melbourne, for the improved turn-round rates reported by the Stevedoring Industry Board. Holt said 'so much unbalanced criticism is directed from time to time against the Australian working man and his rate of work, that it is pleasing to be able to give details of this improvement'.[11] The strike rate for 1951 was the lowest since 1945 with less than one million working days lost through strikes—1.2 days lost for every 1000 days worked. Holt attributed this improvement to closer relationships between management and labour.

In May 1952, Holt was again at loggerheads with the WWF over its right to declare overtime bans. The Arbitration Court had previously refused to hear the WWF's log of claims while overtime bans were in force. On 8 May, the Full Bench of the Arbitration Court directed the WWF to lift its ban, a direction unsuccessfully appealed in the High Court. When the Attorney-General issued a summons against the WWF for contempt of court, it was found guilty and fined £500. When the bans continued into June 1952, Holt threatened to amend Arbitration legislation to allow the creation of a new union if the WWF was deregistered. Holt told the WWF that if it believed:

> there is not enough work to justify overtime it should apply to the Arbitration Court in the proper manner for a variation of its award. We are not judging the merits or demerits of the overtime issue. We are taking our action against the union's defiance of the arbitration system and refusal to obey the court's lawful directions.[12]

Growing financial hardship forced the wharfies to end the bans on 9 July 1952. But the Minister realised some reforms to the machinery for handling industrial disputes were needed. When he introduced a bill for changes to the Act that were designed to reduce delays in resolving disputes, Holt conceded that the Court needed additional judges and an appeals mechanism 'because no commissioner should carry the responsibility of making a decision that could have far-reaching effects on the national economy'.[13] This meant decisions on a large number of industrial principles would be made by the Full Arbitration Court with Conciliation Commissioners allowed to fulfil their original function. Countering the ACTU's accusation that he was taking the side of employers, Holt contended that: 'If the ACTU Executive claims an inherent right of the trade union movement to rectify industrial grievances, the Government certainly has a duty to safeguard the public against a misuse of industrial strength'.[14]

In August 1953 Holt returned from an extended overseas trip to renewed industrial unrest on the waterfront. The WWF was threatening to strike if the Government introduced non-union labour in a number of ports in New South Wales and Queensland, in order to fulfil port labour quotas the WWF had failed to meet. Holt had public support for strong action. The editor of the *West Australian* remarked:

> Mr Holt has a reputation for tolerance and restraint in industrial matters, so that it is improbable that he would have acted without good cause. Morally, but not legally, the Federation is required to obey the [Stevedoring Industry Board]. If it persists in its present attitude it will endanger the whole system of organised waterfront employment.[15]

But Holt took a very different line the following month. A record sugar crop was expected in North Queensland during the second half of 1953 and cane growers wanted an increase in the workforce at the ports. At Bowen, the local WWF branch resisted any such change, claiming that the 'huge seasonal fluctuations in demand for labour in the port . . . meant an increase in the permanently registered watersiders at the port, and since all were entitled to an equal share of available work, this would mean a drop in income for the original Bowen watersiders when work thinned during the off-season'.[16] In July, a dispute over rest periods and meal breaks meant that more sugar cane was piling up on the wharves. The Bowen branch agreed to an increase in the workforce from 130 to 152 but not until the additional workers were registered with the union on 14 September. Holt visited the northern sugar ports and issued an ultimatum that non-union labour would be used if the quotas were not immediately increased. The threat was ignored.

Cabinet agreed to Holt's proposal that troops from Brisbane be sent to Bowen to take over the waterfront. On 2 September, 220 soldiers took control of cargo handling facilities. The next day, when railway workers refused to shunt trains to the wharves, they commandeered the railway yards and locomotives. This had a ripple effect throughout the district where the WWF enjoyed community support. The soldiers were shunned and there were threats of violence. Holt defended his action, explaining that the soldiers had been deployed not to break a strike but to 'supplement quickly the full waterfront workforce to avoid an immediate emergency'.[17] There were threats to extend the strike into a national stoppage. Albert Monk then intervened and insisted that Holt convene a conference between the interested parties. Within three days the union had agreed to increase the workforce at Bowen from 136 to 180 men, with most of the increase achieved by relocating waterside workers from Brisbane. Holt and Monk made a joint announcement of a settlement on 4 September. The troops were withdrawn on 5 September and work resumed at 8 a.m. on 7 September. The Government had won, although Holt was accused of totalitarianism and of unnecessarily departing from his usual policy of moderation.

A cartoon in the Communist *Tribune* depicted Holt as Adolf Hitler. Indeed, he had not acted wisely or entirely in character. His action was secretive, pre-emptive and could easily have led to civil disobedience and violence. It also damaged his standing with some elements of the union movement. But he had felt the need to act decisively to demonstrate to his own party colleagues (especially those from New South Wales) that he was not 'an appeaser'. By bringing the weight of the ACTU to his side, Monk had saved Holt from a potential industrial and political disaster. Despite these difficulties, at the end of 1953 Holt was nonetheless optimistic. He felt he was gaining the upper hand over Communist domination of trade unions and employment figures were good—CES unfilled vacancies rose from 20 858 to 37 453, while those receiving unemployment benefits fell from 42 033 to 12 914. But problems with the WWF would simply not go away. In April 1954, the Australian Government offered to send supplies to the French in Vietnam who were then engaged in combat operations with the Communist-led Viet Minh. The WWF refused to load weapons in the *Radnor* claiming that toilet facilities were unacceptable while the wharfies wanted danger money for loading explosive ordnance. Holt said the dispute was motivated by thinly disguised political motives which 'bore the imprint of Communist policy'.[18] Troops completed the loading.

In August 1954, the Australian and Overseas Transport Association released a report recommending changes to the *Stevedoring Industry Act*. The proposed amendments included giving shipowners the right to recruit their own labour force, the power to sack workers and the prerogative to withhold attendance money. On his return from Kenya in October, Holt was advised that both the ACTU and the Australian Workers' Union would support the Government in any future show of strength against the WWF, but in agreeing to amend the Act, Holt knew he was provoking what would be a bitter fight with the union whose strength derived from its right to control the waterside labour supply.[19] When Holt foreshadowed the amendments, stop-work meetings were held across the country on 14 October.

When he introduced the Stevedoring Industry Amendment Bill into the House early in November, Holt said the Government would 'establish a fact-finding committee of inquiry to examine the organisation and operation of the waterfront industry' and would 'alter the present method of recruiting labour for the waterfront workforce'.[20] The committee would consist of a lawyer together with representatives from labour and management. Holt nominated J.B. Tait QC, Vice-President of the Law Council of Australia, F.J.R. Gibson, National Secretary of the Australian Council of Employers' Federations, and James Shortell, President of the New South Wales Trades and Labour Council, and asked them to report to Parliament by March 1955. The Government's aim clearly was to break the Communist control of the WWF. As the *Herald*'s Canberra correspondent, E.H. Cox, noted: 'If the stevedoring companies are given the right to select men, they will be registered for wharf work because they are competent workers and because the ports need more labour, not because they are dependable supporters of entrenched union officials'.[21]

By 2 November, strike action had commenced in several ports with the waterfront almost completely idle two days later. This prompted Holt to describe the WWF as 'a strike happy union' and the strike as 'a truculent, arrogant attempt to intimidate the Federal Government from proceeding with its policy'.[22] At this point, despite its earlier assurances, the ACTU declared its support for the WWF and issued a joint declaration criticising the Government's action as 'retrograde and provocative'. Allowing shipowners the right to recruit labour was 'deliberately designed to break down past practice and weaken union organisation on the waterfront as a whole'.[23] Monk was publicly critical of Holt for deciding to remove the recruitment concession before the Committee of

Inquiry had met. The Labor Party also joined forces with the WWF. Holt began to feel isolated as the Federation was obviously well prepared for a long, hard fight. But firm action of this kind was nonetheless a clear answer to some in his own Party who had hinted that his ability to avoid controversy stemmed from his capacity to side-step conflict. This was now impossible and Holt told his ministerial colleagues that this dispute 'could blow up into the biggest brawl we have ever had'. The *Sydney Morning Herald* said that after years of relative industrial harmony, the confrontation was Holt's first big fight and an 'opportunity to show whether he can make trouble pay'.[24]

The Bill was rushed through Parliament and passed on 11 November. But the Government's apparent victory presented a problem for the shipowners who did not have any experience in recruiting labour. In fact, they were surprised when Holt decided to embrace as law what they had seen only as a threat. After a ten-day strike, the wharfies ended their strike on 16 November. The WWF had backed down under pressure from the ACTU in the face of Holt's threats to invoke the *Crimes Act*, freeze union assets and deregister the union. Monk had another tactic in mind: to make the new legislation unworkable. The unions would refuse to work with any labour recruited by the shipowners. The men who accepted such employment would be deemed 'industrial renegades'. In the end, such steps were unnecessary. Three days after the strike ended, Healy gave the Stevedoring Industry Board the names of 1000 men to be registered. The shipowners did not provide any names. By February 1955, the situation had become desperate. Shipowners wanted to increase the workforce in Sydney by 500 men (or 8 per cent) to 6900. While the 1928 waterfront strike had been broken by the use of volunteer labour, both Holt and Healy recognised that no such pool of labour existed in 1955. The union would have to provide the workers.

Holt called a conference of the key players to draw up a new agreement on recruiting. In a surprise compromise ahead of the conference, Holt proposed that:

> where extra labour up to the quota was required, the employers would ask the Waterside Workers Federation to supply names of prospective employees. The employers for their part agreed that they would not reject persons so presented except for bona fide reasons. If any rejection were made and was objected to by the Federation, the regional director of the Department of Labour and National Service would be the final arbiter.[25]

Under Holt's plan, if the WWF did not supply the requisite number of names or failed to recruit the workers within ten days, the ASIB could employ additional labour without recourse to the unions. In return, the ACTU would advise the WWF that there were no grounds for holding stop-work meetings for the admission of new members.

Holt was widely condemned for his weakness in compromising with the WWF and accused of mishandling the dispute. The *Sydney Morning Herald*'s banner read 'Costly Defeat on the Waterfront'. 'The Government has no option but to retreat, but nothing can conceal the humiliating terms of its surrender. The handling of this matter must count as one of the worst blunders of the Menzies Government'.[26] The *Newcastle Morning Herald* carried the headline 'Watersiders Win on Port Labour'. An editorial claimed that 'the wharfies are in control—at least until the next showdown'. It implored Healy and the WWF to 'show their good faith by getting the ships moving and keeping the cargoes flowing'.[27] A statement issued by the shipowners said: 'There is no doubt that the full provisions of the Act are not being implemented. But that is the Government's wish'.[28] The *Argus* alone congratulated Holt for his 'lone hand' intervention.[29]

The Sydney *Sun*'s Keith Woodward claimed that the architect of the failed amended Bill was Holt's Departmental Secretary, Harry Bland, whose strategy was to strike at the source of the WWF's power—recruitment—and then work towards the union's deregistration. Like Holt, Bland believed fervently in government intervention when union power threatened the public interest, and they were a good team. Bland later described their 'flexible working arrangement with no rigid demarcation between minister and departmental head'.[30] Bland considered his years with Holt to be his happiest and most productive, but this particular plan went off the rails when Holt returned from overseas to learn that Monk would not support the legislation. Bland thought the core of the Bill—what became known as the 'Tait Inquiry'—would be universally welcomed. He was wrong. Holt told Monk he would reconsider the penal clauses in section 29 of the *Arbitration Act*—which provided for fines of up to £500 on parties to awards who refuse to obey the Industrial Court—on the strength of the ACTU's claim that they were not being applied as a 'last resort' as Holt had indicated they would be when the Act was passed.[31] To demonstrate even-handedness, Holt then criticised shipowners' inefficient management when they requested an increase in international freight charges of 10 per cent. Holt said he could not see the justification for such an increase and told the companies to examine the prospects for internal reform. The Government commissioned an accounting firm, Wolfenden & Company, to consider the shipowners' claims.

Industrial unrest continued, amid growing concern about the validity of the Arbitration Court's coercive powers. Early in July 1955, Holt refused to see a deputation from the ACTU and its metal trades union representatives regarding the Arbitration Court's power to fine unions because the delegation included representatives who were striking at Garden Island and Williamstown Naval Dockyards. Holt said the strikes were evidence that some unionists were 'bent on exploiting the full employment situation with a reckless disregard of the effects of their action on the nation's employment'.[32] Shortly afterwards he told the Melbourne University Liberal Club that:

> undoubtedly full employment strengthens the bargaining power of the employee. Until recently, most reasonably minded trade union officials have realised that this power must be exercised with restraint. They have favoured conciliation. But with the bitter faction fight in the trade union movement, some formerly moderate officials have taken advantage of full employment to attract rank and file support for themselves.[33]

Holt claimed that full employment stimulated more efficient management and led to incentive payment schemes, profit-sharing and attendance bonuses. In 1955 the labour market was stable. Employment was keeping pace with the rise in the labour force produced by immigration and the increased birth rate.[34] Notwithstanding, there was an upsurge in strike action in mid-1955.

Holt blamed the split in the Labor Party for a spate of strikes in New South Wales. More than 70 per cent of the total time lost to strikes nationally was in New South Wales and was caused by two unnamed unions that Holt claimed were under Communist leadership. But Alan Reid claimed that Holt was 'cutting the political throat of every devotedly anti-Communist trade union in Australia' by heaping praise on the 'Industrial Groups' as this would allow the Communists to portray the groups as 'bosses' stooges'. Holt said that Communists and both Labor groups were trying to bribe workers to their respective causes. Monk countered with the explanation that the strikes were in response to the Federal Cabinet's decision to increase public service salaries by up to £900 a year. The Sydney Trades and Labour Council claimed the strikes were the outcome of award anomalies, suspension of basic wage adjustments and the penal provisions in the *Arbitration Act*.

E.H. Cox told his readers that 'Australia's record of industrial stability since 1949 has been partly due to the personal relationships between [Holt and Monk] . . . But there are signs that the [Holt–Monk Axis] is straining towards breaking point'.[35] Monk announced that the ACTU would ask Holt to separate the functions of arbitration and conciliation by abolishing the Arbitration Court. On 5 August 1955, Holt called a conference of unions and employees to discuss the principal source of unrest—the *Arbitration Act*'s penal provisions. The conference did not satisfy the unions and a High Court challenge on the validity of the Act was foreshadowed. Following the wisdom that attack was the best form of defence, Holt argued that any changes to the conciliation and arbitration machinery had to be accompanied by a 'fresh examination of restrictive practices adopted by trade unions—strikes, absenteeism and turnover of labour'.

[The] trade union movement wanted brimful employment (a principle the Government accepted), stabilised prices and free collective bargaining on wages. It does not take much thought to realise that these three things are not compatible unless free collective bargaining is related to an improvement in production and profitability on the part of the enterprise in respect of which higher wages are sought. There has been no evidence on the part of trade unions that they recognise any such limitation.[36]

Fadden argued that the balancing force in a time of inflation and full employment was the willingness of the trade union movement to keep wage demands within the limits of national production. To increase costs would put some industries out of business and create a small pool of unemployment. The Government's position was that the trade union movement had to choose between higher wages and the present level of prosperity. The ACTU responded with a demand for an increase in the basic wage and restoration of quarterly adjustments. Holt claimed that the ACTU's position was based on 'superficial reasoning'. He argued that wage increases would prompt a rapid rise in production costs at the very time the economy was running into difficulties; average take-home pay had risen and there was a higher level of personal consumption.

The unions were not convinced. Twelve months after the 'recruitment dispute' initiated by the Government, in January 1956 the WWF initiated a 'margins dispute'. The union had sought on several occasions to gain a pay rise through the Arbitration Court to restore the purchasing power of wages it had claimed had been eroded by inflation since 1948. When the hearings failed to deliver an acceptable outcome, the WWF decided to negotiate directly with the employers. On 17 January, Holt reported to Cabinet that negotiations between shipowners and waterfront unions had collapsed and that a 'pay and hours' dispute was brewing. On 23 January, 24 000 men walked off the job. Holt said:

> When the parties failed to reach an agreement, the situation clearly called for arbitration. The Federation has rejected the speedy, impartial decision on all matters in issue which the judge offered and shipowners stated their willingness to accept. This stubborn refusal by the Federation to abide by a prompt and just determination throws the obligation on the ACTU or trade unions to withdraw their support for strike action. No mistaken sense of loyalty to a union which has knocked the arbitration process must be allowed to blind the ACTU leaders to the responsibility they have towards hundreds of thousands of unionists whose jobs and living standards are now threatened. Above all, the ACTU leaders have a responsibility to the nation to avoid the halting of essential services and industries.[37]

In reply, Monk told Holt not to 'blindly support the shipowners in their adamant attitude not to attempt to overcome the impasse, at present existing, by increasing the 6d an hour they have already offered'.[38] Monk was emphatic that the waterside workers had not received a pay rise of any kind since 1952 and the ACTU was insisting on an increase of 9 pence per hour while offering a dilution of other claims on condition that the shipowners dilute their demands. Privately, Holt blamed the Arbitration Court for precipitating rather than averting the strike but he nonetheless won Cabinet backing to adopt emergency measures if the parties refused to resume negotiations. 'Before adopting such drastic measures, the Government has felt that it should make another attempt to explore the possibility of a negotiated settlement.'[39]

Holt called a conference of the shipowners, the ACTU and the Federation in Canberra on 2 February 1956. An editorial in the *Sydney Morning Herald* warned the Minister not to sacrifice principles for expediency.

> In calling the conference, Mr Holt said he is not trying to usurp the functions of the Arbitration Court. But do the union leaders or many other people appreciate that? The Arbitration Court is the Commonwealth Government's

sole wage-fixing agency. In taking up the mediator's role where the Court left off, Mr Holt is no doubt aware that this is what some union extremists have wanted all along. They want to destroy the court.[40]

Holt presented a four-point plan to get the parties back to the negotiating table: agreement on a return to work, arbitration of the respective demands with certain agreed minimum gains and an increase in attendance money. Both parties agreed to consider the plan. At the ensuing press conference, Holt made no effort to hide his opinion that the shipowners' attitude was the stumbling block to a resolution, criticising their unwillingness to negotiate. But he also said that the Government would deploy troops to the waterfront if ships did not move within seven days. On 4 February, the ACTU and the WWF rejected Holt's plan and left Cabinet to consider strike-breaking proposals at its next meeting.

Holt then held separate private discussions with Monk and the ACTU Secretary, Reg Broadby, at his Toorak home ahead of a meeting of the ACTU interstate executive. Holt once again threatened to use the Army and by impressing upon Monk and Broadby that the WWF's action was hurting the economy and increasing the possibility of unemployment he also managed to achieve his main objective—isolating the WWF. On 7 February, after considering the matter further, the ACTU directed wharfies to return to work on the basis of Holt's plan and apply to the Arbitration Court for a decision. This was a course of action the WWF had already rejected. The strike collapsed. The margins dispute was a victory for Holt and the Government. By the end of the month, the shipowners and the WWF were back in the Arbitration Court with each side making concessions. The *Sydney Morning Herald* commended the Minister for his 'highly intelligent contribution to a settlement with honour to both sides'[41] that had also preserved the Arbitration Court's prestige and authority. The *Age* believed 'no man could have striven harder to bring the shipowners and the watersiders to some form of agreement acceptable to both bodies'.[42] A week later, the *Sydney Morning Herald* said that 'Holt saw what the hotheads didn't see—that a tough line, calling in troops—would get nowhere while the ACTU was backing the wharfies. He had to detach the ACTU by putting up a reasonable formula, and that was what happened'.[43] Recognising the magnitude of their defeat, the wharfies marched on the ACTU headquarters in Melbourne claiming to have been betrayed by Monk.

But there was an unexpected setback in store for the Government. On 2 March 1956, the High Court decided in the now famous 'Boilermakers' Case' that arbitral and judicial functions could not be combined in one tribunal.[44] In other words, the Arbitration Court could not impose penalties for non-compliance with its own rulings. The Government appealed to the Privy Council but needed to amend the legislation in the interim. Holt welcomed this as the perfect opportunity for an urgent overhaul of the whole arbitration system. His preference was for legislation that made defiance of the Arbitration Court punishable in another court. Accordingly, on 10 May 1956, Holt introduced a bill to amend the *Conciliation and Arbitration Act* to create two separate bodies—the Conciliation and Arbitration Commission, responsible for award-making matters, and the Commonwealth Industrial Court, to deal with judicial matters. Holt argued for a more informal approach to proceedings by abolishing wigs and gowns, giving legal counsel limited access to hearings and relying on industrial advocates who were 'able to get to know each other in a more friendly and intimate way than counsel. There is more probability of conciliation in this kind of atmosphere than in the more formal environment produced when counsel are in attendance'.[45] The response to Holt's reforms was generally favourable, although the ACTU wanted more time to study and assess its implications. Cabinet refused. When the legislation was passed the Attorney-General, Senator John Spicer, was appointed Chief Judge of the Commonwealth Industrial Court and Sir Richard Kirby, formerly of the Conciliation and Arbitration Court, became President of the Conciliation and Arbitration Commission.

By this time, the Tait Inquiry had issued an interim report on Australian stevedoring. It claimed that wharfies had engaged in political stoppages that were unrelated to conditions of employment or the protection of trade union principles. The Committee believed that the WWF had placed very few limits on the issues that were regarded as legitimate reasons for strike action. It proposed establishment of a new statutory authority consisting of representatives from industry and the unions. When the Committee tabled its final report on 7 March 1956, the Government was already working on a new Stevedoring Industry Bill for introduction into Parliament on 30 June. The most controversial element of the new bill was empowering the new stevedoring authority to recruit and register labour. It was a bold move and Holt was criticised by his own colleagues for failing to give the Party room sufficient advance detail of his proposals. Senators Reg Wright and Harrie Seward were among those who claimed that Holt's 'attitude was indicative of the ministerial attitude in legislation of great public moment'.[46] Both were opponents of a statutory body.

The essence of the bill was a triumph for Holt who managed to persuade his colleagues that a statutory authority was the only way of dealing with waterfront unrest. He also believed that stiffer non-compliance penalties could 'usher in a brighter era in industry'. Under the new bill, the Minister would have power to 'control' stevedoring operations only in the event of an emergency. The bill 'will not attempt to define where control begins or ends, or what constitutes an emergency. This will continue to be a matter for the Minister of the day'. As for the use of troops, 'there have been doubts about the power residing with the Government under legislation that now exists to carry out this sort of operation. By this provision we remove, we believe, doubts which might otherwise exist'.[47] In his 'Canberra Comment', Keith Woodward remarked:

> Holt's bill was designed to please neither the watersiders nor their natural enemies, the shipowners and stevedoring operators . . . Apart from a clumsy abortive piece of legislation in November 1954, this bill is the first positive product of the long-range stevedoring plan which Holt's departmental advisers began two years ago.[48]

Holt met with the ACTU Interstate Executive and Jim Healy to discuss the many controversial aspects of the bill, but an ACTU Special Congress held in June condemned the draft legislation. Although the Opposition objected to the bill clause by clause and repeatedly called for divisions in Parliament, it became law. It provided for creation of the Australian Stevedoring Industry Authority (ASIA) which was given a very broad range of responsibilities from paying attendance money to ensuring workplace safety. Joe Hewitt was appointed to chair the new Authority with F.J.R. Gibson and James Shortell as its members. The Act also excluded the WWF from existing bulk-loading sugar facilities in north Queensland and from new bulk-loading terminals elsewhere. Holt had finally struck a major blow against the WWF stranglehold on recruitment of labour although he had done little to curtail Communist influence within the union. Undeterred, on 3 July 1956 the WWF went out on strike over new ship-loading rules. Holt described the strike as 'an act of national sabotage' and told the striking watersiders that if they were 'to enjoy the substantial additional benefits recently awarded them, they had an obligation to accept the conditions which accompanied the benefits'.[49]

In tabling ASIA's first report on 9 April 1957, Holt noted that more working days were lost to strikes in the period 30 June 1955–30 June 1956 than in any year since the war. But there was a marked improvement in the last quarter of 1956 and first quarter of 1957. On 17 May 1957 Holt proclaimed, during a debate on raising the levy paid by wharfies to ASIA, that 'the Australian waterfront is operating more efficiently at present than I can recall in my period in this Parliament'. The improved waterfront performance 'should enable shipowners to pay all or most of the increased charge [1/7d to 2/- per man hour]'.[50]

But Holt's battle with the WWF was not over. In July 1958, Frank Hursey and his son Denis brought their case to the Tasmanian Supreme Court. They had refused to pay their membership dues to the Hobart branch of the WWF on the grounds that these dues included a political levy of 10 shillings to assist the ALP in the Tasmanian State election campaign in March 1957. The Court found in their favour, awarded them both damages and ruled that the levy was invalid. In September 1959, the High Court ruled on appeal that the imposition of the levies by registered trade unions was valid under Commonwealth law but that the Hurseys had been the victims of 'actionable conspiracy'. The original damages claim was reduced. Holt, encouraged by the DLP, had twice in the previous four years attempted to persuade the Cabinet to prohibit political levies. Menzies was steadfastly opposed, believing such a ban would have 'crippled the ALP and prompted a strong reaction from the unions'.[51] By way of compromise, the application of compulsory levies was abandoned and replaced by donations to the ALP from the general funds of trade unions.

Holt attempted a number of other reforms. The Secret Ballots Bill was drafted to prevent further Communist infiltration of unions and to preclude Communist intimidation of workers. In October 1953 Communists active in the Amalgamated Engineering Union challenged the legislation. Holt said the Liberal Party 'always believed that if a faithful expression could be given by democratic means to the wishes of rank-and-file unionists, they would speedily put an end to Communist influence in their midst'.[52] While Holt believed the relationship between unions and the Labor Party was too close and damaged potentially harmonious negotiations with employers, he nevertheless welcomed ALP control of the AEU as a 'stinging rebuff to the Communists'. Holt also resisted the imposition of compulsory unionism in New South Wales. He told the Federal Council of the Liberal Party that it was 'detestable', that it 'indicated the fascist turn of mind' in the Labor Party and was contrary to United Nations and International Labour Organisation (ILO) declarations.

He urged unions to remain with the Commonwealth Arbitration Court rather than moving to State tribunals or other processes of collective bargaining (such as direct negotiation with employers) following the Court's decision on 28 October 1953 to suspend automatic quarterly basic wage adjustments and replace them with annual adjustments based on economic performance and demonstrated productivity. The Court argued that the economy was stable and could not increase wages without affecting costs and prices. Employer organisations had wanted to increase hours and decrease pay in order to maintain economic stability. Holt defended the Court's decision by pointing out that it had previously shortened the working week and increased the basic wage.

Holt's success in managing Australian industrial relations was recognised internationally. At the end of May 1957, he left for the 40th session of the International Labour Conference. The ILO was formed as a result of the Treaty of Versailles. Holt had hosted the first ever ILO event to be held in Australia—a conference on pneumoconiosis (fibrosis and scarring of the lungs arising from chronic inhalation of dust) held at Sydney University from 28 February–11 March 1950. In his welcome speech, Holt had said:

> Labour problems—problems of industry have always in Australia occupied a position of very great importance ... the work of the ILO enjoys the support of the responsible political bodies in Australia, irrespective of the change of governments from time to time ... the Government which I have the honour to represent has already given thought to the question of increasing Australia's representation at future meetings of the ILO.[53]

The focus of the 1957 gathering was the effects of automation and adopting two conventions on forced labour and providing for a 24-hour rest period every week. Holt was elected to the Presidency of the Conference after being proposed by the Government delegations of Thailand, Chile and France, the workers' delegation of Canada, and the employers' delegation of France. There were no other nominations. Claude Jodoin, the Canadian workers' delegate, said in support of Holt's nomination:

> We of the workers group know of the Right Honourable Harold Holt by reputation, and we know that he has always looked upon the requests of the workers of this country with much sympathy. We are sure that through the experience he has acquired, and his loyalty to the ILO, he will certainly be an excellent President.[54]

Holt's presidential address looked to the future:

> Few nations can insulate themselves against what is happening in other countries. The work of this Organisation, therefore, can not only benefit those countries whose living standards are comparatively low . . . but can also help other advanced countries . . . It has become fashionable to gaze into the crystal ball of the future. According to their political outlook some see a world of capitalism, some a world of communism. I believe that if all governments were to direct themselves to the objectives [of social justice and national security], they will find themselves increasingly drawn into a partnership with management and labour in which these differences tend to diminish. I would describe this process as a dynamic and progressive liberalism . . . based on this conception of a harmonious cooperative partnership between these three essential elements in the modern State.[55]

This left no room for class warfare but plenty of scope for incentive. According to Holt, 'no country attaches more importance to matters which are of concern to the ILO, such as the cultivation of good industrial relations and the establishment of international cooperation for these purposes' than Australia.[56] 'Those of us in this conference who have laboured over the years for better relations in industry know that when we find a clash of extremes, we must usually evolve a middle way to produce the desired agreement.'[57] In his closing remarks Holt told the delegates that:

> I shall go back to my own public duties not merely enriched with a great deal of knowledge but understanding, I believe, rather better the point of view of peoples from so many diverse parts of the earth and holding so many diverse points of view, not all of which would necessarily coincide with my own.[58]

The Conference passed a number of important conventions, such as the Convention Concerning the Abolition of Forced Labour that came into force on 17 January 1959, but Holt was criticised for the ILO's decision to grant participation to a delegation from Hungary representing the Soviet-backed Kadar Government. Although the majority of delegates had voted to reject the Hungarian Government delegates, their numbers fell short of the two-thirds majority required under conference standing orders. Holt said the recognition of Hungary and the credentials of its delegates had been a matter that had been left to the United Nations. Australia had abstained from an ILO vote on the matter although Australia shared international opposition to Russian occupation of Hungary in October 1956.

Holt's portfolio also included National Service, although it did not take up a great deal of his time nor did it require creative policy development. From the late 1940s, Menzies had been promising to reintroduce compulsory military training. Repeated Gallup polls showed that it was a policy popular within the electorate, including a majority of Labor voters.[59] In July 1950, Cabinet approved a Three Year Defence Plan costing more than £A2.72 million—nearly double the amount budgeted annually by the Chifley Government. It also approved a National Service Scheme under which 18 year olds would complete 176 days of military training: 98 days in training camp during the first year and 26 days of 'spare time training' with a Citizen Military Forces unit in each of the following three years. The first intake would be about 13 500 men. When fully implemented, the Government expected there to be an annual intake of 21 000 National Servicemen. The aim was to increase the citizen forces to more than 49 000.[60] Not only would Australia's defence readiness be increased, a new generation of young men would be subject to the 'steadying influence' of military discipline. It would also 'improve the physical fitness—using that phrase in the widest sense—of our young manhood'.[61] As explicitly stated in the *Defence Act*, no National Serviceman would be required to serve outside of Australia unless he volunteered to do so.[62]

In a ministerial statement on National Service delivered in March 1951, Holt announced that '95 per cent of the young men believed to be liable to register have registered and registrations are still being received'. There was little community resistance. 'All reports I have received so far indicate that all sections of the community are showing themselves co-operative to the Government's National Service Scheme and this attitude of cooperation is particularly evident among the prospective trainees themselves'.[63] During the second reading of the National Service Bill, Holt warned of the lack of 'breathing space' before the next world war and the magnitude of the challenge of increasing defence spending while expanding the economy and enhancing productivity. Cabinet decided in September 1951 that the citizen forces should be expanded to a total of 68 220 as soon as possible.

On 1 May 1957, National Service intakes were reduced from 33 000 to 12 000, restricted to the Army and training reduced to 140 days over four years. At this point, Holt introduced a system of birthday ballots.[64] Many in the Labor Party believed that compulsory military service in peacetime should be abolished while most in Holt's party believed more in its 'social value' than the modest military capacity it provided. The scheme was finally wound down in late 1957, just after Holt relinquished the Immigration portfolio. This allowed him to spend more time on industrial relations, managing the Government's business in Parliament and his duties as Deputy Leader of the Liberal Party.

Of all his achievements, Holt's administration of industrial relations during the 1950s won him the most generous accolades.

In the Government's first year in office more than two million working days were lost through industrial disputes. Eight years later, the figure had declined to 439 000. During those years, the number had never reached 1.5 million in a calendar year and had not exceeded one million in four of the previous eight years. While Holt's leadership had been a factor, general economic conditions, the growth of hire–purchase commitments among low-income groups acting as a disincentive to taking strike action and the gradual trend in many unions away from political militancy towards legal remedies also contributed to his success. Key unionists had also been directly involved in formulating government policy. As Holt explained:

> For many years I have tried to set up a body which would be representative of the Government and of top management, and the Trade Unions so that we could sit around the table together and discuss . . . national economic problems where we can combine together for the national good. [The Ministry of Labour Advisory Council was the result.] We have already examined such questions as the employment of the older aged, the physically

disabled, safety in industry, the provision of a work force in the seasonal industries; and . . . the problems which a full employment situation creates for us.[65]

Whitington judges Holt's years in Labour and National Service as his most productive:

He brought to the task a humanity, a tolerance, a moderation and a willing-ness to compromise that contributed greatly to the comparative harmony that prevailed for most of his term of office. The country was never as free of industrial trouble as while Holt held the portfolio—in what normally could have been stormy post-war years. The Communists were at the zenith of their peace time strength in the unions; there was an extreme Right wing faction in the Cabinet that wanted a showdown with the unions at any cost, and there was a considerable body of opinion in the rank and file of the coalition parties that would have supported such tactics.[66]

Holt argued that workers ought to 'put pressure on inefficient and slipshod employers' in order to improve production output and raise standards of living.[67] At the official opening of the new ACTU building in Carlton, on 30 June 1954, Holt said that 'no Australian Government, whatever its policy, could deal with great national problems without closely collabor-ating with the trade union movement'.[68] Holt publicly acknowledged the role of the trade unions in accepting immigrants and even commended the more militant unions at the Port Kembla and Newcastle steelworks where nearly ten per cent of the workers were displaced persons. He also recognised that immigrants fleeing from Communism in Europe would be disinclined to vote for a party that had been labelled pro-Communist.

Holt believed that the ACTU did not need to ally itself formally with the Labor Party because an enlightened government could—and should—ensure that capital and labour existed harmoniously. With the prospect of full employment and increasing wages, it was possible that theory could become practice. The *Age*'s editor and later Holt's speechwriter, Keith Sinclair, noted Holt's 'great success was to accommodate conflicting spirits and people in the industrial movement'.[69] He formed close and continu-ing friendships with ACTU officials, especially Albert Monk. His relations with Jim Healy remained cordial and constructive even when they were locked in a bitter dispute. He also worked well with the courts. Sir Richard Kirby, President of the Arbitration Commission, said of the years after Holt left the Labour portfolio: 'It was as useful as having Bill the cat as Minister. The Government put coves in the job who didn't have a clue. I'd see their eyes glazing as I tried to explain things—they literally could not understand what industrial relations was about'.[70] Looking back, Holt said: 'I believe for the first time since Federation we did produce some thawing of the frozen attitudes between management and labour'.[71]

Holt relinquished the Labour and National Service portfolio on 10 December 1958, after nearly nine years in office.

CHAPTER 8

Patience and persistence

1958–65

AFTER HIS ELECTION AS the Deputy Party Leader, Holt expected a major change in his ministerial responsibilities. He had relinquished the Immigration portfolio more than two years previously and had been in charge of Labour and National Service for nearly nine years. In terms of ministerial workload his busiest year had been 1956, when he concurrently held two portfolios and was also designated 'Minister for the Melbourne Olympics'. As Menzies waited to determine the composition of his new Cabinet until after the 1958 election result was finalised, he asked the retiring Fadden to remain Treasurer under a section of the Constitution that allowed a non-elected Minister to hold office for three months. John ('Jack') McEwen, the new Country Party Leader, then made a conscious and surprising decision not to claim the Treasury (which the Country Party had frequently held in Coalition governments since 1923) and remain in the Trade portfolio (later expanded to become Trade and Industry). This gave him scope to oppose those Treasury policies and pronouncements with which he disagreed. McEwen was a vigorous advocate of economic growth and government intervention. The Treasury preferred economic stability and reliance on market forces. The Coalition partners also disagreed on foreign investment and ownership of key industrial assets, particularly food production and processing. As Trade Minister, McEwen would be openly critical of Liberal economic policy and would issue frequent warnings about Australia's growing dependence on foreign investment. For his part, Menzies was pleased that the Liberals had gained the pre-eminent Treasury portfolio—an advantage the Liberal Party still holds more than four decades later. However, the Country Party had a short-term advantage: the hard-working and wily McEwen had a firm grasp of economics and would try to out-think and out-manoeuvre whoever was the Liberal Treasurer over the coming years.

Although keen for a fresh challenge, the Treasury was not a portfolio which intrinsically interested Holt. As the Liberals' second ranking parliamentarian the problem he faced, however, was the limited range of senior portfolios from which to choose. McMahon, who usually had breakfast with Holt before they walked from the Hotel Canberra to their Parliament House offices, desperately wanted the Treasury but Menzies was not considering him for the post. Holt also recognised that if he allowed another of his colleagues to take the portfolio, they might develop a profile that threatened his status as favourite to succeed Menzies. Holt's experience in economic matters was limited and he had never shown a close interest in Treasury questions. He preferred what he called 'human problems' rather than the impersonal character of economics with its emphasis on statistics and factual information. But he was known, however, for emphasising the importance of job creation and industrial expansion. Despite his later uncharitable assessments of Holt, Paul Hasluck was probably correct in noting that Sir Roland Wilson, the Permanent Head of the Treasury, was concerned about Holt's appointment. But Holt had always taken advice and Wilson and others knew 'they could work with him'.[1]

Holt was sworn-in as Treasurer on 10 December 1958. His principal personal assistance came from a succession of private secretaries who later became senior and distinguished public servants, including Austin Selleck, Terry Larkin, Peter Brown (former Liberal member for Kalgoorlie), Keith Pearson (from the Prime Minister's Department) and Jim Short (later a Liberal Member of the House of Representatives, Senator and Federal Assistant Treasurer). Holt had gained a reputation for being one of the best ministers to work for in Canberra. He was invariably kind to those in his office and never overlooked an opportunity to praise his staff. He was repaid with loyalty and hard work. Sensibly, Holt relied consistently on technical advice from Wilson, with whom he had first worked in Labour and National Service nearly twenty years earlier, and the two Deputy Secretaries at the Treasury: Richard Randall (appointed in 1957), who had responsibility for economic policy, and Lenox Hewitt (First Assistant Secretary from 1955 to 1962 and Deputy Secretary (Supply and General) after 1962), who was in charge of budgeting and accounts. Hewitt was widely known as 'Dr No' because of his resolute and sometimes abrasive opposition to any new or additional requests for government funding.

This was, of course, his job and precisely what Wilson expected him to do. Although Holt found it difficult to decline or refuse expenditure proposals he personally favoured, Hewitt insisted that he remain firm. Not surprisingly, Holt was much closer to Randall.

Wilson had by now earned a reputation as one of the country's most formidable and intellectual public servants. But while Fadden sought Wilson's advice when coming to his own mind on a particular issue, he also consulted Dr H.C. 'Nugget' Coombs, the Governor of the Commonwealth Bank, during his frequent visits to the Commonwealth Bank en route to his Queensland home. As Holt was from Victoria, he tended to see less of Coombs and took advice almost exclusively from Wilson.

> The change suited Wilson's Treasury. For years the Secretary had been attempting to restrict the Bank's influence and render it an obedient arm of Treasury. This was not merely a case of bureaucratic power politics. It was also driven by the intense personal rivalry between Wilson and Coombs. The Secretary was by nature unable to refrain from drawing his scalpel whenever Coombs took the initiative. For his part the Governor, a dogged and skilful advocate, refused to surrender meekly which only sharpened Wilson's resolve.[2]

The Commonwealth Bank's central goal was to achieve the highest rate of employment consistent with low inflation maintained through economic fine-tuning, while the Treasury's development strategy was based on tight control over public expenditure, high immigration and capital investment (including foreign capital inflow) and low interest rates with decisive and sometime brutal 'stop-go' adjustments when over-heating and balance of payments crises occurred in an era of fixed exchange rates. Making the most of his skills with people, Holt kept out of the rivalry between Wilson and Coombs while embracing firmly the Treasury line on economic policy.

In addition to his duties with the Loan Council and the annual Premiers' Conferences which increasingly brought him into closer contact with State premiers and treasurers, Holt also enjoyed the higher international profile and recognition accorded to the Treasury portfolio. He attended the annual meetings of the Board of Governors of the International Monetary Fund, the International Bank for Reconstruction and Development, and the International Finance Corporation. In 1960 he would chair the annual meetings of both organisations after suggesting to

Menzies that he 'would be glad of the chance to establish a little prestige for myself in the sphere of Finance Ministers'.[3] Although Holt's critics would regularly claim he was 'fleeing' the country to avoid 'the heat of the budget debate', the annual meetings of the Commonwealth Finance Ministers and the other organisations of which he was Australia's nominee were always held in September.[4]

During his travels Holt spent a great deal of time in the United States and built an impressive network of contacts in the worlds of finance, politics and entertainment, the latter reflecting the theatrical interests he had inherited from his father. He developed close friendships with, among others, the CEO of the Chase Manhattan Bank, David Rockefeller III, the bullion dealer Charles Engelhard (said to be the inspiration for Ian Fleming's *Goldfinger*), and the West Coast entrepreneur, Allan Chase. He was also acquainted with the founder of the Hilton Hotel chain, Conrad Hilton (great-grandfather of celebrity model Paris), and the American television personalities Art Linklater and Bob Cummings. He enjoyed their company and the possibility these friendships provided of attracting foreign investment to Australia. But he did not enjoy airline food. Holt complained, to no less a person that Sir Hudson Fysh, the Chairman of Qantas, that during a flight to Britain he was served 'shishkebab' and there was no alternative. Things got worse. He was offered ice cream when he wanted cheese. Holt suggested that Qantas might consider having 'a couple of tins of Camembert tucked away to meet the requirements of difficult characters like myself'.[5]

When Holt took over the Treasury portfolio, a key Government objective was reform of the banking sector. During the 1950s, debate over the Commonwealth Bank's dual functions as a central bank on the one hand, and a trading–savings bank on the other, favoured legislative reform.[6] In 1957, the Liberal Party's Federal Council had asked the Prime Minister 'to introduce legislation to separate the Commonwealth Trading Bank from the central bank'.[7] Fadden shared his Party's innate suspicion of private banks but acknowledged there was a conflict of purpose within the Commonwealth Bank's structure. In October 1957 he introduced new banking legislation that was depicted by the press as a personal defeat and a setback for the Country Party. On closer examination, however, his proposals strengthened the central bank while the creation of a Development Bank would substantially assist farmers. Labor saw the moves as promoting the private banks and was joined by the DLP in its opposition to the changes. After a month of debate, the bills were defeated in the

Senate, then again in March 1958 when the Senate was tied. Holt said that Labor was still committed to abolishing the Senate (it remained a pillar of Labor's party platform) but had, in the meantime, made it a 'House of Obstruction'. Almost ten years previously, Holt had warned that the Senate might become 'a powerful opposition . . . with a very much stronger voice' that would set it against the Government and the 'people's house'.[8]

Holt reintroduced Fadden's banking reforms on 26 February 1959.[9] Fadden remembered that, 'in his characteristically thoughtful way, Harold sent me a telegram from Canberra: "Proud to be presenting banking Bill tonight in substantially identical terms with your own pioneering work. Affectionate regards, Harold"'.[10] The legislation would establish the Reserve Bank of Australia and empower it to conduct central banking functions, control the issue of currency and administer the Rural Credits Department established by the former Country Party Leader, Sir Earle Page. The Commonwealth Bank's functions would be administered by the 'Commonwealth Banking Corporation' acting in concert with the Reserve Bank. These included the management of trading and savings banks and a new Development Bank to absorb the extant Industrial Finance and Mortgage Bank Departments. The Government believed these structures would make it far more difficult for a future Labor government to nationalise banking in Australia. There were, however, some rumblings from a group of New South Wales Liberals concerned that a future Labor government might use the Development Bank to compete in the area of general banking.[11] Holt was unmoved but tried to placate their fears. As the Government had regained a Senate majority in the 1958 election, the Commonwealth Bank Bill and the Reserve Bank Bill were passed by both houses of Parliament and received the royal assent on 23 April 1959. These changes brought Dr H.C. 'Nugget' Coombs much more into the public eye and displayed something of Holt's political pragmatism.

Prime Minister Ben Chifley had initially appointed Coombs to the Governorship of the Commonwealth Bank. He was respected for his frank and fearless advice and for his solid performance in the role. Despite the mutual antipathy between Wilson and Coombs, Holt never considered having Coombs replaced. Indeed, Holt was adamant that Coombs' independence had to be preserved even as he defended him from criticism. One such example was the 1959 controversy over negotiations between Chinese import agencies and the Australian Wheat Board for the purchase of large quantities of grain on terms. Coombs decided to make his own assessment of Chinese intentions as exports of primary products were financed through the Rural Credits Department of the Reserve Bank. He also thought it an opportune moment to make contact with the People's Bank of China. Holt feared adverse publicity but recommended to Menzies that a low-key visit be permitted. After some administrative delays, Coombs eventually travelled to China in October 1961. On his return, Coombs announced that the head of the Reserve Bank of China would pay Australia a reciprocal visit. Coombs believed that central banks were a link in an 'international chain which spreads throughout the world and most central bankers feel they belong to a family of central banks which accepts a moral tradition'.[12] Kent Hughes led the ensuing back-bench protests. He feared that such a visit would signal de facto recognition of Communist China and frighten some of Australia's South-east Asian neighbours. He complained to Holt:

> surely Nugget Coombs' latest effort is not good publicity for the Government either at home or abroad? In view of the fact that Nugget was recently in Peking, there does not seem to be any necessity for Communist bankers to come here to do what he should have done if it was necessary for him to go to Peking.[13]

Holt advised Kent Hughes that in line with other Reserve Bank return visits arranged in recent years, the visit would be kept at a 'banker' level and would not be considered a political contact. But Kent Hughes was not to be placated, arguing that every contact with the Peoples' Republic was of a political nature.

> As it is freely rumoured that the recognition of Red China is involved in the deal, and we are again going to act as the hire purchase company for Red China to finance her overseas propaganda machines, surely it is time the Government made a statement on what is actually the position and not allow these rumours to circulate around the world.[14]

He then issued a threat that could not be taken lightly as the Government, in the recent Federal elections, had had its majority reduced to the slenderest of margins—one seat:

> I will not stand for the secrecy of the dealings with Red China. If this is

the way the Government wants it, you can count out my vote on the first possible occasion in order to force the Government to an election and let the Australian people decide whether they want to play with the Communists in this fashion.[15]

Holt brought the matter to Menzies' attention, backed Coombs and his judgment, and an embarrassment for the Government was averted for the time being. Holt remained a dedicated opponent of Communism and never shied away from engaging in public debates with leading Communists. He believed—almost naïvely—that their words 'would condemn them' and erode their electoral appeal.

An example was Holt's continuing dialogue with Communist Brian Fitzpartick in the 'Letters' column of Melbourne's *Age*, over the issue of foreign investment policy. During a National Export Convention held in May 1960, Holt said he 'would not like to see capital investment from overseas continue on the present scale indefinitely'. Fitzpatrick declared that 'the growth of foreign investment was inhibiting and undermining small scale Australian private investment, and that this was causing concern to the Manufacturing Industries Advisory Council'.[16] Holt disagreed. He did not believe the increase in overseas investment was 'uncomfortably strong' and took the opportunity to attack Fitzpatrick's partisanship. 'Mr Fitzpatrick is a staunch Labor supporter and an able polemicist for socialist causes. It is not surprising to find him in disagreement with the policies of the Menzies Government'.[17] Holt was content with the rate of Australia's economic growth, but he did commission the Treasury to produce a White Paper on *Overseas Investment in Australia* in September 1962. He claimed the reaction against overseas capital was 'based on emotional and political considerations—as well as on an understandable sense of nationalism—rather than on a realistic appraisal of Australia's needs'.[18] Holt was being lobbied by a number of overseas banks keen to start operations in Australia but Treasury was resolute in its opposition. When Holt's friend Allen Chase sought advice on shaping a proposal for a banking licence, Wilson told Holt that the American banking chains 'would be able to do nothing more than is already done with great efficiency by the Commonwealth Savings Bank . . . my own suggestion would be that you should discourage your friend Allen Chase as soon as possible'.[19] Holt did not press the matter further and told Chase 'there would be formidable difficulties against overseas interests breaking into this particular field'.[20] The Australian banking sector would not have to face foreign competition for another two decades.

In his first Budget, delivered on 11 August 1959, Holt stressed the importance of population growth, infrastructure development and expanding the economy. The immigration target for 1959–60 was increased to 125 000 to reflect the Government's commitment to an annual intake of 1 per cent of population. Holt's statement was dubbed the 'give and take budget' as income tax cuts accompanied increased charges. A 5 per cent income tax rebate and increases in other benefits were offset by an increase in postal charges that would net £20 million. It was a controversial move that angered the Country Party in particular. As Treasurer, Fadden had opposed seeking higher revenues from the Post Office because he believed it would disadvantage rural consumers. The Country Party's Charlie Davidson threatened to resign as Postmaster-General over the proposed increases and McEwen's lack of support for him in Cabinet. Many of Holt's Coalition colleagues threatened to vote against the Government. Menzies pacified Davidson while Cabinet agreed to reduce the planned increases in postal charges, but public feeling ran high. Holt received a Christmas card in which the seasonal greeting had been replaced by:

> Had you left the 3½d mail or even 4d the poor people would not hate you as they do. But your worst sin is that you have done more than anyone else to put that bastard Evatt into power at the next elections. For that decent Aussies will never forgive you. I hope you have an unhappy Christmas.[21]

Holt might have secured a notable victory but he was unhappy with the projected Budget deficit of £122 million.

In 1960, the Reserve Bank warned the Government that, partly as a consequence of abandoning import licensing, the trade deficit was heading out of control. Interest rates would have to be increased to curb domestic expenditure and Australia's international reserves had also declined sharply. The Reserve Bank and the Treasury proposed possible measures to Cabinet and a small group of economists in the Prime Minister's Department, headed by Peter Lawler, provided comment on and analysis of the Treasury recommendations.[22] Dr Wilf Salter, the most influential of those economists, was the strongest proponent of what would later be referred to as the 'unorthodox measures' used to deal with the problems. In his 16 August 1960 Budget speech, Holt identified 'boom' conditions during which 'prices and costs rose sharply over the last year' and the 'rate of increase does not seem to be slackening'. The boom had led to 'shortages of key materials and of some classes of labour . . .

though local supplies have increased, they are failing to match the rise in demand and this . . . is spilling over into a demand for imports'. What was to be done? The Treasurer explained that 'the pace of expansion has become rather too fast and we have to ease off a little. But what the Government proposes to do should in no way be taken to mean that we believe some major interruption of growth to be necessary'. The rise in domestic demand and the inflation rate was draining on the nation's overseas financial reserves, a situation that could not be allowed to continue. Mindful of the enduring political damage caused by Fadden's 'horror budget' a decade earlier, Holt preferred to err on the side of caution.[23] This proved to be a mistake. The October trade figures alarmed the Cabinet. Additional intervention was required but the lack of firm and decisive Government action was a gift for the newly elected Labor Leader, Arthur Calwell.[24]

Calwell, formerly an officer of the Victorian State Treasury, had a much better grasp of economics than Evatt. He expected the Government to act decisively: 'I was upset because the [August] Budget contained nothing to help reduce unemployment, increase production, stimulate consumer spending or restore the flow of immigration. I described it as a "stay-put" budget brought down by a "stand-still" government'.[25] Calwell said Labor would introduce a supplementary Budget with provision for a £100 million deficit to restore full employment. (Holt had budgeted for a deficit of only £16 million.) On 15 November Holt announced a series of 'supplementary measures' designed to flatten domestic demand and eliminate inflationary pressures. Holt warned a Joint Party Meeting that these measures would be unpopular with the electorate, but it was imperative to reduce demand for imports and dampen growth. When the economy responded and prosperity returned, the electorate would forget the pain and commend the Government.

Holt's emergency measures included increased sales tax on motor vehicles, reduced tax deductions on borrowings by industry, a compulsory cutback in bank advances, a requirement for life insurance companies to hold not less than 30 per cent of their holdings in government and semi-government securities, and higher interest rates. Certain forms of interest payments were declared non-deductible against tax, including interest on convertible notes—a very popular security at the time. There was also widespread concern that the plan to limit tax deductibility on borrowings would be difficult to implement through legislation. The All Ordinaries Index at the Sydney Stock Exchange, which had already seen share prices drop in anticipation of the Government measures, dropped a further five points after Holt's speech.

The Government had panicked. Holt's remedial measures were not only excessive, they came four to five months too late to achieve a steady reduction in growth. In fact, they would drive the economy into recession and prompt the worst credit squeeze since 1945. Several major companies would collapse, including Reid Murray, Cox Brothers, Korman and H.G. Palmer, an electrical retail business that based its business on low interest or no deposit sales. As its customers tended to be the worst credit risks, H.G. Palmer suffered a substantial increase in bad debt write-offs before collapsing with enormous losses and bad debts. Sir Frank Richardson, the Managing Director of Cox Brothers which operated 112 retail stores across the country, told Holt in a personal letter that he was 'in disagreement with almost every move made since 15 November 1960. The Government was at least two years too late in imposing restraints' and had ignored his earlier warnings 'to check the unhealthy growth of [the] hire purchase business[es] and the diversion to them of funds which should have gone into Government loans'. Richardson prophesied that the forthcoming election result would be unnecessarily close because 'the restraints were delayed too long, then too harshly imposed and, I fear, will be too slow in removal to restore confidence before the end of the year'.[26]

There was worse to come. Overdraft rates rose from 6 to 7 per cent. By May 1961 unemployment had jumped to 3 per cent—easily the highest rate since 1945. Holt became the focus of community outrage when he claimed (wrongly) that the decline in employment activity was merely 'sectional' and that unemployment was only a problem in those industries that had 'expanded too fast in the boom period'.[27] Holt was infuriated by a newspaper advertisement organised by the Queensland Trades and Labour President Jack (later Sir John) Egerton. It claimed that the Treasurer was planning a 'pool' of the unemployed and that he regarded 5 per cent unemployment as acceptable.[28] The advertisement carried the line: 'You'll be pretty cool in Harold's pool'. The usually calm Holt was incensed by what he regarded as a blatant lie. Queensland Liberal backbencher Jim Killen, who knew Egerton and thought the matter part of the usual misinformation associated with electioneering, offered to speak with Egerton about a withdrawal or retraction of the advertisement. Egerton replied: 'Tell him he can do what he likes. If need be he can send me to Boggo Road gaol and I'll write my memoirs from there'.[29] Holt issued what would be the only writ for defamation of his political career. He was victorious and the Queensland Branch of the Labor Party paid his legal costs. Egerton, who said he had based the advertisement on information received from 'a source which I had until now considered to be reliable', was required to issue a retraction. 'I unreservedly accept his assurances and regret any annoyance caused . . . or any injury that his reputation may have suffered.'[30]

As the economy was beginning to respond to his supplementary measures, in February 1961 Holt decided—against the advice of Coombs— to abandon the increase in sales tax on motor vehicles. The mandatory investment of life insurance monies was substantially altered. Holt's remaining measures, coupled with the removal of import restrictions, prompted the manufacturing industry to seek additional tariff protection. On Treasury's advice, Holt argued against early remedial action. The nation had to endure some pain for its own good and in April 1961 Holt was advised that the Budget and other financial measures were now working as they were intended.[31]

The Government would not initiate any further economic measures, a decision questioned by C.B. Schedvin:

> Why the Government accepted the strategy less than four months before [the 1961] general election with unemployment so recently at a post-war record, remains a puzzle. Holt's intellectual dependence on Wilson is likely to be part of the explanation. What is certain is that on this occasion there was no congruence between the political and budgetary cycles.[32]

The economy may have been responding but the *Australian Financial Review* saw this as being down to luck rather than good management: 'The bitter reaction of the business community to the hodge-podge of economic measures beginning in November 1960 was unquestionably aggravated by the strong suspicion that the Treasurer had only the vaguest idea of what they were supposed to achieve'.[33]

A fairer assessment might be that the measures had been 'overcooked' by an abundance of experts all claiming to have identified the key measure. Despite the subsequent myth that the Department of Trade had opposed the removal of import controls, McEwen had actually proposed their removal in February 1960. He would later complain that the November 1960 'mini-budget' was unbalanced, stressing that the 'survival of the government was inextricably linked with its ability to halt the haemorrhage in employment. This in turn was linked with the need to keep the manufacturing sector alive and well. In that period, therefore, the question of whether or not industry should be protected was never an issue in [McEwen's] mind'.[34] There was also the possibility that Australian access to British markets might be endangered by Britain's entry into the European Common Market and McEwen asked Holt to include in his 1961 Budget speech a pledge that Australian agriculture and industry would be subsidised 'if, as a result of the United Kingdom's policies, our large established market should be materially disrupted'.[35] Holt refused to commit the Government to such action.

Holt continued to experience the full force of public anger in a wave of telegrams received by his office. The crew of SS *Koorine* said 'the people of Australia will remember for all time your complete disregard for their welfare'. The owner of a small business hoped that Holt had 'made allowances in the budget for the £100 000 you owe me for confiscating my property to liquidate communists' and a Sydney accountant issued a one-line demand, 'Resign'.[36] One of few to rally to his defence was Frank Chamberlain, Chief of the *Sun-News Pictorial* Canberra Bureau, who pointed out that Holt 'attracts all the abuse for the frustrations inherent in Government action to curb us from using credit recklessly . . . [but there] is not the slightest sign of any Cabinet differences about the policy now being pursued—but the bad light falls on Mr Holt'.[37] And yet, the Treasurer remained in good spirits. He told his colleague Allen Fairhall:

> There has undoubtedly been some discomfort, even hardship, but it is pretty remarkable that a boom of the dimension we were experiencing, with a threatened liquidity crisis, should have been brought under control with so little disturbance to the great mass of people . . . One can absorb almost an unlimited amount of press and public punishment if one's colleagues have an understanding of what is being done and show a willingness to back it.[38]

He was content that no long-term harm was done to the economy, and by the 1961 election campaign was explaining that:

> The boom had been conquered before it could do much damage to the economy . . . [but] no boom can be checked without disturbances to those sectors of the economy that had expanded most. Since the end of 1960, some industries have suffered a considerable contraction of demand . . . There are signs that the economy has now passed through the phase of readjustment and is beginning a steady advance.[39]

To draw attention away from the 'credit squeeze' and the pain that he had willingly inflicted on the country, Holt used the 1961 election campaign to challenge Labor's claim that it could fund its policies without increasing the total amount of taxes collected. Holt claimed that if Labor didn't increase taxes, it would 'have to tap central bank credit on a vast and increasing scale . . . It would launch the economy on a torrent of newly created money and lead it on again to a state of roaring boom, depreciating values and eventual collapse and disillusionment'.[40] Despite the economy's recent difficulties, Holt emphasised that unemployment had fallen, job vacancies had risen and production figures were improving. The Liberal Party's campaign theme—'Building for Tomorrow'—was 'designed to move attention from the past to the future'. A draft Federal Council Strategy Document asserted that 'the most appealing line to the electorate is the deterioration in the morale of the Parliamentary Labor Party, the ineptness of its leadership, and its incapacity to govern'.[41] But many within the Liberal Party were deeply angry with Holt.

Believing that Holt was personally responsible for the current economic hardship, some in the Liberal Party demanded a preselection conference for his seat of Higgins. According to Party rules, sitting members in Victoria were protected unless at least one-fifth of their local branches asked for a conference to be convened. From a total of ten party branches, three (Stonnington, Manning and East Malvern) resolved that Holt should not receive automatic endorsement for Higgins. His most vocal critics were women. Earlier in the year, one of Holt's strongest supporters in the electorate, Alex Rosenblum, had urged him to cancel a gala dinner being held in honour of his 25 years of parliamentary service. He stressed the need for austerity after the credit squeeze and believed 'such an ostentatious display with its accompanying extravagance would have been a gift to your opponents inside as well as outside the party'. Rosenblum told Holt that many of his 'keenest supporters and hardest workers are middle class "new poor" with limited fixed incomes and many would be unable to attend such a function'.[42] As it turned out, none of the leading party figures from Higgins was invited and the dinner went ahead in the Bamboo Room at the Chevron Hotel in Melbourne, with Robert Menzies proposing the toast. The Prime Minister noted that only he and Holt remained from the wartime UAP parliamentary party.

But things were not well in Higgins. George Knox had decided to run as an 'Independent' Liberal. Holt heard that 'his backers include some Sydney business types and, unless my recollection is astray, he was one of the prime movers behind a Brigadier Cremor who stood as an Independent against me in 1943'.[43] This was a veiled allusion to the Murdoch family. Holt expressed a private hope 'that George Knox's medical adviser urges him to keep out of the campaign. It would be a strain at that time of life for any man not accustomed to electioneering, and success could bring even greater stresses'.[44] The Acting Federal President of the Party, Bob Cotton, consoled Holt: 'a Federal Treasurer appears by reason of his position to be a natural target for hostility and criticism from time to time. But to find some fellow like Knox who is so completely lacking in appreciation of almost a lifetime of generous service to the people makes me, literally, sick!'.[45] For reasons that were not disclosed publicly, Knox did not contest the election and by October Holt had managed to defuse local Party hostility, boasting 'my branches have indicated they are solidly behind me, and I detect no signs of defection on their part. The improved economic and political climate should reduce the number of disgruntled Liberals disposed to vote away from the Party ticket'.[46]

Holt shared the Liberal Party's confidence that it would perform well in the 1961 election although he acknowledged that a few seats might be lost. He told his parliamentary colleague Keith Wilson that he would be 'disappointed if we don't come back in at the same strength as when we took to the polls'.[47] In a letter to Menzies outlining the Coalition achievements to be cited in the election campaign, Holt emphasised the new financial arrangements that had been concluded between the Commonwealth and the States, the return of economic stability and the Government's support for new development projects.[48] The Treasury reported likely 'disturbances' in a number of local industries but these would be resolved as unemployment steadily improved. Rather than offering the electorate a detailed legislative program and a comprehensive set of financial measures, Holt thought that attention ought to be focused on regional concerns—the growing instability in South-east Asia and the future of West Papua (also known as Irian Jaya)—and international affairs—the spread of Communist hegemony and the possible consequences of the European Common Market for Australian trade. These were issues that would highlight the Government's experience and the 'divided, inexperienced, debilitated Opposition'.[49] In sum, the Coalition should promote a 'steady as she goes' message. The campaign was subdued and largely uneventful. Holt would describe it as 'the quietest and most apathetic I can recall. I'm sure that most people had their minds firmly made up before the campaign began'.[50] It was the first campaign in which television played a significant role. Holt was the Government's best exponent of the new medium. On 3 December he appeared in his first live television interview—with Gough Whitlam—on the Brisbane station BTQ's 'Meet the Press'.

The Government was still confident of victory when the people went to the polls on 9 December 1961. It was in for a rude shock. The Coalition won 45 Liberal and 17 Country Party seats to Labor's 60 and would govern with a majority of one, after a Speaker was elected in the House of Representatives. Of the 31 Senate seats contested, the Coalition won 15 and Labor 14, with one Country-Western Australia Party senator and one 'other'—Holt's school contemporary at Wesley College, Reg Turnbull. It was the Liberals' worst electoral result for the House of Representatives since 1946, and the swing away from the Liberals in Higgins was the greatest Holt would ever suffer. For the first time, Holt polled less than 60 per cent of the primary vote (56.7 per cent) with a 4.6 per cent swing to Labor's Roger Kirby and 1.9 per cent to the DLP's Celia Laird. He was re-elected but the public's anger at his Budget had been made plain. The Country Party's vote also fell. Under Arthur Calwell, whom many commentators regarded as an unattractive option as prime minister, the Labor Party had come within a seat of achieving Government. The Coalition had lost 15 seats and only the Liberal Party's strong showing in Victoria and the allocation of DLP preferences had saved it from losing office. The post mortems were not long in coming. In addition to accusations of over-confidence and conceit, there was a general consensus that the disastrous mini-budget had almost cost the Government office.

For all of that, the 'credit squeeze' of November 1960 did manage to halt inflation. In the first half of 1962 prices remained steady although unemployment figures for January rose to approximately 132 000—a post-war record. A 'Committee of Economic Enquiry', tasked with making recommendations to the Government for restructuring the economy, was established. However, despite the manifest need, Menzies did not appoint its members for another twelve months. It was chaired by Sir James Vernon, the Managing Director of CSR, with Sir John Crawford, former Head of McEwen's Trade Department and now Director of the Research School of Pacific Studies at the Australian National University, as Deputy Chair. Drafts of the Committee's report were provided confidentially to the Treasury as each section was prepared.[51] When finally delivered on 17 May 1965, the Vernon Report recommended a number of significant changes in economic policy as well as new machinery for economic consultation between business, unions, professions and governments. It also made recommendations on foreign investment and economic growth that accorded with those known to be held by McEwen. By the time it was published the Australian economy had recovered and the Government rejected most of its recommendations. Menzies and Holt were particularly critical of the report's caution over foreign investment. Holt insisted 'the Government was not prepared to make a given percentage increase in a statistical estimate the "target" or over-riding aim of policy. It prefers more practical and concrete objectives than that'.[52] There was some support from financial journalists, one of whom, Peter Samuel, questioned what he referred to as the Vernon Report's 'statistical fetishism'.[53] This was rightly seen by political commentators as a major victory for the Treasury over the Department of Trade.

There can be no doubt Holt's public standing had been damaged by the credit squeeze. He described 1960–61 as 'my most difficult year in public life' in which he had to endure 'a period of very hostile criticism from some quarters in New South Wales' where there would be a State election early the following year.[54] After Christmas, Holt spent two weeks recuperating at the new sea-side holiday home he and Zara had purchased at Portsea. This property was the fruit of Zara's successful business interests. Her shop on Toorak Road had expanded steadily and had a branch within the Myer Store after 1953. The *Sun* newspaper's 'People in the News' column ran a feature on Zara on 12 April 1959. After explaining that she now employed 35 people in three 'fashion' shops (two in Melbourne and one in Adelaide), Zara readily volunteered that she had become wealthy. She said: 'I must be good because of the way people buy my dresses and the prices they pay . . . None of the things I sell are cheap. After all they're individually designed and made and I think they're every bit as nice as the imported models which are very expensive'. Zara would design several 'Gowns of the Year' in the 1960s, including that worn by Tania Verstak when she won the Miss International beauty pageant, and in 1966 would be described by the press as 'dressmaker to the establishment'. However, she had earlier (1959) decried her husband's meagre salary of £6450 and thought the gradual increase in his parliamentary salary to £8850 was insufficient. 'How are you going to get ambitious, intelligent young men into Parliament if they know they can look forward to only a few thousand pounds a year?'[55] Zara's son Andrew had married and left home, and both Nick and Sam would soon follow suit. As the boys were now providing for themselves, Harold and Zara had also decided to buy a property in North Queensland.

The Holts first went to Bedarra Island in the Great Barrier Reef in the mid-1950s, to visit their friends John and Alison Büsst. John Büsst was at Wesley College with Harold. He had been a newspaper reporter before moving to North Queensland, where he became widely known as an artist and conservationist. Alison Büsst (the sister of leading Canberra Parliamentary Press Gallery member Ian Fitchett) had been close to Zara since they were young. When the Büssts moved from Bedarra Island to the mainland in 1956, the Holts purchased 300 acres of rainforest at nearby Bingil Bay, 30 miles from Innisfail and four hours by car from Townsville. Around 300 people then lived at Garners Beach and Bingil Bay. Two years later the Holts bought a one-acre block with a small two-storey wood and fibro home set on rising ground at the southern end of Garners Beach, about 200 yards from the waterfront.[56] There was no electricity or town water. Gas was used for lighting and cooking and there was an outside toilet. There was, however, a 'silent telephone' connected. After the usual round of Cabinet and departmental meetings in June and July preparing the details of the annual Budget, Holt routinely spent the first half of August at Bingil Bay finalising his Budget speech and celebrating his birthday (5 August), with some snorkelling and skindiving thrown in. It also gave him time to ponder some of the more substantial policy initiatives the Government was committed to implementing before delivering his Budget and then spending most of September overseas attending to his international responsibilities.

When everyone returned from holidays early in 1962, Menzies and Holt were the subject of a 'censure' from the Victorian Party Executive when it asserted that the Government was indifferent and arrogant. One member of the Executive, John Buchan, described the Treasurer as 'not terribly receptive', while F.R. Wright suggested to Menzies that Holt be given an overseas posting. This was Holt's first real experience of strident criticism from within his own Party but it reflected a wider malaise.

Holt lacked Fadden's instinctive shrewdness, his aptitude for financial dealings, his insistence on his own point of view when he believed in something firmly enough. Holt was in constant trouble because Ministers and Government backbenchers found it convenient to blame him as Treasurer for the Government's inconsistent financial policies—as they had Fadden—rather than share the responsibility as members of the Government. It was impossible for Holt to translate the essentially conservative policies of the Treasury into the expansionist, even adventurous, actions the public demanded. Holt's public standing was damaged considerably as a result.[57]

Menzies stood by 'Young Harold', reminding his critics that the credit squeeze had been the result of a Cabinet decision and that Holt should not be singled out for blame. Holt, however, had to improve his standing with the Party organisation.

On 15 November 1962 he wrote to Menzies proposing a review of the Party's Federal Council to give the Party a clearer approach to policy development and to achieve a more productive relationship between the Party's organisation and its parliamentary members. Holt suggested that when the Council met, it should not discuss matters without the relevant Minister present. Holt believed that during recent meetings 'certain resolutions were adopted which conflict with current policies of the Government . . . after Cabinet and Party Room decision. Were the present Government to give immediate effect to these resolutions in the terms carried by the Council, some freakish consequences would result'. By way of example, the Council had resolved that the Government should prohibit unions from collecting political levies although this was contrary to the views of the Parliamentary Party. Lest the Council be seen as controlling the Liberal Parliamentary Party in the same way the ALP Federal Executive dominated the Labor Caucus, the Council, according to Holt, must not seek to direct the Parliamentary Party into accepting its resolutions. But Holt also recognised that unless Party members felt they had a voice in policy development, 'we promote a sense of frustration amongst Council members and plant seeds of mischief within the organisation and Parliamentary wings'.[58]

Holt wanted the State Divisions to work closer together to promote 'a national outlook'; a better appreciation of the Party's fortunes and prevailing opinion in each State; a review of the composition and structure of Party committees; and a forum to be created in which parliamentary leaders could make statements for broad dissemination among the electorate. The establishment of a Joint Standing Committee on Federal Policy with representatives from the State Divisions, the Parliamentary Party and the Cabinet would ensure that Party policy reflected ordinary members' opinions while being consistent with the Government's legislative program. The Federal Council would also review the Party's constitution and policy platform and survey the prevailing political mood. This, Holt argued, would prevent the Party from being caught unaware by shifts in public sentiment such as the one that nearly ousted it from office in 1961. Menzies, who tended to see the Party organisation as his servant rather than his master, was not convinced there was a serious problem requiring action. Nothing came of Holt's proposals and the Party organisation continued to feel that its advice on policy matters counted for little. But Holt had nevertheless personally heeded the Party's message after the 1960–61 Budget disaster.

In his February 1962 'mini-budget', Holt outlined a 5 per cent cut in personal income tax for more than four million Australians, increased unemployment benefits, an additional £25 for capital works, reduced sales tax on a range of household goods including furnishings and electrical appliances, and import controls on goods affecting local manufacturing industries. These measures not only dealt with unemployment but restored fluidity to the economy. By the time of his August 1962 Budget speech, one widely described as being as dull in tone as the Coalition's economic measures, Holt could claim that the underlying strengths of the economy would ensure its long-term health while the Government would not allow any repeat of the inflationary boom of 1960 nor stall the current recovery. Indeed, the Government would stimulate the economy by expanding export income and generating employment opportunities in primary and secondary industries. Menzies and Holt had now changed their mind on deficit financing, something Labor had advocated in 1961, and the cash deficit was estimated at £118 million, a substantial increase on the previous year. The theme of Holt's speech was stability. It had almost become a mantra. Holt told the House of Representatives: 'When I am told, as I am from time to time, that we are preoccupied with stability, I readily admit that charge . . . To me, stability means three things, all related to and dependent upon one another—steady growth, a balance between current supply and demand and stable costs and prices'.[59] What had happened to the economy in 1959–60 was, apparently, an aberration and nothing like it would be allowed to happen again. But its legacy remained for Holt.

Despite Menzies' clear anointing of Holt as his successor, McEwen still believed that he had a chance of leading the Coalition and becoming

Prime Minister. Political scientist H.G. Gelber pointed out that the tension between Holt and McEwen over the succession was reflected in the continuing struggles between the Treasury and the Department of Trade.

> During the discussions on the 1962 budget . . . Holt blocked McEwen's attempt to secure more concessions to taxpayers. The Treasurer not only stressed balance of payments and cost stability considerations, but added that rural spokesmen had been particularly worried about this. It was a clear hint that if McEwen, in his attempts to broaden the basis of Country Party support, went too far in wooing secondary industry, he would lay himself open to having his primary political support, among his own farmers, undermined by the Liberals. Yet if he ceased to woo industry, his claim to the Prime Ministership would be weakened. All this was apt to reinforce the long-standing Country Party suspicion about Liberal intentions, a sense of weakness also reflected in the discussions on electoral boundary reform at about this time.[60]

McEwen also had a public fight with Liberal Minister Les Bury over the effect of Britain's entry into the European Economic Community (EEC) which McEwen had hoped to exploit as a 'wedge' issue in the forthcoming election. The Cambridge-educated Bury had been a leading Treasury official before being elected to the safe Liberal seat of Wentworth in 1956. Bury had considerable experience with the World Bank and the IMF, and was made Minister Assisting the Treasurer because of his understanding of economics and knowledge of the Treasury's inner workings. Bury was also a close personal associate of Richard Randall. Bury argued in a speech delivered in July 1962, correctly as it turned out, that Britain's participation in the EEC would have a negligible effect on Australian trade. This effectively prevented the Coalition from exploiting the issue for domestic political gain. An angry McEwen took issue publicly with Bury. After reading the speech, Menzies requested and then accepted Bury's resignation on 27 July 1962. Holt publicly denied that he had prompted, been party to, or even known of Bury's remarks before they were uttered although most observers assumed that they would have discussed the matter. At the meeting of Commonwealth Finance Ministers held in Accra in September 1961, when he emphasised the benefits of providing global trading opportunities rather than foreign aid for developing countries, Holt had spoken for many when he expressed a general fear for the Commonwealth's future as a consequence of Britain's evolving relationship with Europe.

When Parliament resumed for the Budget a few weeks later in August, Clyde Cameron asked Holt whether he shared Bury's views. Holt's only reply was that his views were in accord with those of Cabinet. Allan Fraser, a long-standing member of the ALP Caucus Executive, asked Holt whether Menzies had been advised of the Treasury's attitude towards Britain's entry into the EEC. Holt replied that the Prime Minister knew his views. While Holt was privately sympathetic to Bury, he could not support him publicly. Despite the tension within Cabinet, the Coalition was projecting an image of unity and purpose. But the *Sydney Morning Herald* thought Bury's speech had exposed 'the rather shabby war of the Canberra succession'. The *Australian Financial Review* noted: 'Holt had more to gain probably than anybody else in the Cabinet from Mr Bury's gaffe'. Although some collusion is possible, there is nothing in Holt's papers to suggest it. This incident damaged the Coalition and embittered many Liberals against McEwen, whose chances of becoming Prime Minister ended abruptly and permanently as far as most Liberals were concerned.[61]

In June 1963, Holt advised Menzies that the economy was recovering too quickly and that the Government might not be able to grant tax and other concessions in the 1964 Budget. It was also possible that wage margin increases would pump so much additional money into the monetary system that inflation might rise, requiring remedial action that would not be popular with the electorate. To avoid a repetition of 1960–61, Menzies and Holt discussed the desirability of an election in late 1963 or early 1964. Menzies also spoke with Sir Garfield Barwick whom some (most notably McMahon and Spooner) suggested was in danger of losing his seat of Parramatta. Barwick assured Menzies that he would not lose. The economy was doing so well that Menzies decided to call an early election to exploit the favourable conditions. The 1963 Budget had met with a very positive response from the business community and Holt was praised by the press for keeping the economy on 'an even keel'. By August 1963, the unemployment figure had dropped to 1.5 per cent and there were 67 229 job seekers—the lowest since the boom of 1960. Two months later, unemployment had fallen below the December 1960 figure. It was time to act. On 15 October 1963, Menzies told a Joint Party Meeting that he had settled on 30 November 1963 as the election date and that he would accept complete responsibility for its timing. This was the first time in Australian history that the House was dissolved early for reasons other than defeat of the government (1929), a double dissolution (1914 and 1915) or to realign House and half-Senate elections (1955). The Government pledged to introduce a Home Savings Grant Scheme for young married couples, raise medical benefits, provide funding for non-Government schools, purchase TFX fighter aircraft (later known as the F-111) for the RAAF and establish a joint naval communications facility with the United States at North West Cape.

The Coalition continued to target the Labor Party's Federal Executive's '36 faceless men'. Although most were not parliamentarians, they nonetheless controlled Labor policy in Parliament without being directly accountable to either Parliament or the people. Sydney's *Daily Telegraph* led the press in undermining public confidence in the leadership of Calwell and his deputy, the youthful member for Werriwa, E.G. Whitlam.

Menzies' decision and the Party's optimism about the result were justified. The Liberal vote increased by 3.5 per cent and the Coalition's parliamentary majority was increased.[62] Holt was greatly relieved. The economy had become an electoral asset rather than a liability. Criticism had been replaced with applause. The new Cabinet was sworn in on 18 December 1963 (the remainder of an enlarged Ministry had to wait until 4 March 1964, after enabling legislation had been passed). Holt remained Treasurer, a position he had held now for more than five years. He was finding that the greatest challenge was managing the many demands upon his time but as a devotee of parliamentary processes he especially enjoyed his powerful role as Leader of the House.

Ministers and backbenchers approached Holt constantly about the conduct of parliamentary business, offering their views on how it could be improved. For example, in late 1959 six backbenchers reported that 'most, if not all of the government private members feel there is too wide a gap at present between the Ministry and the private members'.[63] The letter acknowledged that the private members were partly to blame and suggested that a better Party Committee system might involve the backbench. Holt attempted to implement their proposal but encountered ministerial resistance. Throughout the early 1960s he received a steady flow of letters on parliamentary procedures as well. Recognising the need for a thorough overhaul, Holt drafted changes to parliamentary standing orders that took effect in 1963. They would be lauded by all subsequent parliamentarians but criticised by political philosophers as giving the Executive Government a great advantage over the House.[64]

Notwithstanding his high view of Parliament, Holt was unconcerned by the accusations that further parliamentary powers and prerogatives were being ceded to the Executive.

The main example affected the House's financial procedures, which were reformed to prohibit any member other than a minister from even introducing proposals relating to taxes or duties. A second example was the reversal of priority for committee-stage examination of bills before the House, henceforth no longer required unless so ordered by the House. Since this change, over three-quarters of all legislation have been exempted from committee-stage consideration in the House. A third and final example was the consolidation of the rules for question time in their current form so as to guarantee that this whole accountability exercise remains a non–onerous ministerial game of enduring 'questions without answers'.[65]

Holt was prepared to delegate the compilation of the list of speakers during the parliamentary debates to the Whips, Fred Chaney from Western Australia and, later, Peter Howson from Victoria. But there were moments when he intervened personally. Although noted for his mild manners and even temperament, two incidents recorded by Howson and confirmed by others suggested that Holt was capable of aggression and even rage. Before 1963, with a House majority of one, it was important that all Government members attend divisions unless a 'pair' was arranged. On one occasion, Harry Turner, member for the safe Liberal seat of Bradfield in New South Wales and often a dissenting backbencher,

> put his head into the office of the Leader of the House and said off-handedly to Holt that he would not be in Canberra next week because of other arrangements. Holt, absorbed in reading, said 'OK, Harry'. A minute later, recollecting that the government had a majority of only one, and that Turner was it, Holt leaped to his feet and pursued Turner into the corridor. He pinned Turner to the wall, and waved a fist under his chin. 'You *will* be here next week, won't you Harry? . . .'. Turner nodded, and fled. Holt was slow to arouse but when finally aroused would act without caring about the consequences.[66]

The second incident occurred during a debate in the next Parliament. Howson had listed the Reverend Dr Malcolm Mackay considerably down the list of Government speakers. Without consulting either Holt or Howson, Bill McMahon went to Menzies and sought his approval for the order of speakers to be changed to increase the likelihood of Mackay, a fellow New South Wales Liberal, having a chance to speak.

Menzies, not knowing the background said, 'Oh yes, change Mackay'. [Howson] stormed into Harold and told him: 'How much longer do I have to put up with this?' Harold was just as wild, leaped out of his chair to see Menzies, and as he walked into the corridor there was McMahon. Harold picked him up by the shoulders, whisked him round the corner and said, 'McMahon, if you interfere in my side [of the House] any more I'll have you right out of Parliament'.[67]

Holt and Howson were a close team, with Holt rapidly gaining confidence in Howson's ability to organise the Government as a team. In the Senate, Shane Paltridge became Government Leader on 10 June 1964, succeeding Sir William Spooner who had resigned for health reasons. On 22 June 1964, after a conversation with Menzies, Paltridge told Holt that Denham Henty would become Deputy Leader in the Senate and that he would also replace Paltridge as the Treasurer's representative in the Senate. Paltridge said, 'I am certain that Denham is the most suitable Senate Minister for this important and heavy representation'.[68] Events would prove otherwise.

While Menzies led from the front by force of personality, Holt's colleagues appreciated his consensus style and personal warmth. Although most had only known Menzies as their parliamentary leader, they seemed prepared to embrace Holt as a steady and consistent performer. He was still considered the most likely candidate as Menzies' successor, and he was also Deputy Liberal Leader. Possible rivals would either have to gain by Holt's mistakes or grab the attention and affection of the electorate. Back in 1958, the leading Sydney barrister, Sir Garfield Barwick QC, had decided to seek Liberal Party preselection for the seat of Parramatta. In his gossip newsletter *Things I Hear*, widely referred to as 'Things I Smear', Frank Browne confidently asserted:

For Harold Holt, it means no leadership. For the New South Wales Cabinet aspirants it means no Cabinet. All in all, to the Liberal Federal politicians, the entry of Sir Garfield Barwick means exactly what the acquisition of a Derby winner means to the other stallions in the stud. Prosperity for the stud, but the first step towards the boiling down of the other stallions.[69]

But Sir Frank Packer's *Sunday Telegraph* asked whether Sir Garfield's 'hide was tough enough'.[70] It reported that Barwick's swearing-in 'was a good humoured occasion'. Barwick's biographer, David Marr, notes that 'among members of Parliament that morning there was a sense of being honoured by Barwick's arrival. Congratulations were warmly offered. "Bad luck Harold", the Labor wit Jim Cope called across to Holt. As the new member was led forward Arthur Calwell called, "Now the fun starts"'.[71]

Barwick is adamant, however, that Menzies did not offer him the leadership as a means of enticing him into Parliament nor did the Prime Minister subsequently offer to help him gather parliamentary support in the leadership succession. In fact, Barwick seems to have believed that Holt's experience and competence made him the likely successor. He also maintained a personal affection for Holt, who recognised and sympathised with Barwick who suffered from diabetes. During an acrimonious debate in 1959 over changes to the *Crimes Act* Barwick wanted to make as a consequence of the Petrov Royal Commission, Barwick had returned from the Despatch Box and slumped into his seat, placing his head in his hands. As Leader of the House Holt was called upon to retrieve the situation. Barwick later recalled: 'Holt, always a kind man, came to the table and suggested that I leave the Chamber and rest awhile. I went out with him. The media said I was in tears. I certainly was very upset and had tears in my eyes'.[72] It was plain that Barwick did not have the inner strength and resilience for effective parliamentary leadership. Although the press and the Opposition continued to paint Barwick as a threat to Holt, Barwick was adamant that he 'would not have contested the leadership if Menzies were to resign . . . my own nature would have prevented me from being so political as to put aside friendship and personal loyalties . . . I felt Holt had earned the opportunity to succeed Menzies'.[73] And when Holt did become Party Leader and Prime Minister, Barwick believed that Whitlam, whom he prophesied correctly would replace Calwell, would not be able to 'defeat Holt for at least two terms'. By then, Barwick would be far too old to contest the Party leadership.

Notwithstanding Barwick's generous attitude towards Holt, the Treasurer had a lot of ground to regain after the disastrous 1960 Budget. There was even a rumour that Menzies' position was far from secure and if Menzies fell, Holt would probably fall with him. *The Times*' Australian correspondent, citing Billy Wentworth as his source, reported on 2 March 1962 that:

Menzies had never been more unpopular among Liberals and Country Party members. He [Wentworth] thought the Prime Minister would have retired by the end of the year, having been (if necessary) edged out by his colleagues . . . Barwick could succeed Menzies as PM (Wentworth told me that Harold would never get the succession now), although McEwen is now favourite to succeed, despite the fact that he is only Leader of the minority party in the Coalition.[74]

But Menzies' electoral appeal quickly recovered.

Just before his sixty-ninth birthday (in December 1963), the Prime Minister was shown to have a dominating 79 per cent support in the Coalition parties, compared with 2 per cent for John McEwen and 1 per cent for Harold Holt. His lieutenants were still hidden in his shadow, as they had been in 1960 when more than half of the Government supporters polled had no idea who they would want as Menzies' successor—21 per cent wanted Holt, 19 per cent were for McEwen with Barwick trailing as an 'also-ran' with 3 per cent.[75]

There were sections of the media, especially those controlled by the Murdoch family, that were always ready to champion McEwen's cause. On 18 December 1961 the *Sun* newspaper had claimed that: 'Pressure is mounting within the Federal Liberal Party for a merger with the Country Party so that Mr McEwen could succeed Mr Menzies as leader . . . Mr Holt's stocks have slumped so dramatically most observers believe he can be irrevocably ruled out of leadership calculations' and that 'Mr McEwen was the only minister to raise any doubts about Mr Holt's economic measures last November'.[76] In his *Management Newsletter* dated 9 March 1962, Maxwell Newton, who had drafted speeches for Calwell after the Fairfax newspaper management abandoned Menzies in the lead-up to the 1961 election, claimed that:

Mr McEwen is being freely mentioned as a successor . . . at this stage there is strong opposition to that happening among the majority of members of the Liberal Party executives. Mr Holt is temporarily suffering a political eclipse because unjustifiably he is being blamed by too many for the recession, when after all the economic decisions were corporate Cabinet decisions. But that is the way of politics.[77]

Although Menzies held McEwen in high esteem, he had made his preference for Holt clear. The Liberal Party's Federal Executive told

Menzies the thought of him being replaced by McEwen was unthinkable.[78] Holt had a capacity for calmness in situations where others may have been disposed to panic. He was composed and collected even in a crisis and many of his colleagues took refuge in his company and counsel. His even temper and constancy when other Ministers seemed rattled prompted a renewed sense of confidence among backbenchers.

Few thought that Menzies would fight another election after 1963. The Liberal Party would be looking for a new Leader and attention returned to Barwick. In his hostile biography, David Marr claims that:

> It was clear to Barwick, looking around the party, that he had not managed to cultivate a body of followers to match the strong Victorian caucus backing Holt. Barwick calculated he would need forty to fifty members willing to 'stick behind him through thick and thin' to become Prime Minister. He put his failure to muster this support down to arriving in parliament too late . . . There was little affection for Barwick among backbenchers. The warmth they felt was directed to Holt, a more charming man who masked his ambition with urbane ease, a man who wanted to be generally liked. Barwick did not see himself in Holt's Cabinet: 'There is no way I'm going to be Harold Holt's foreign minister'.

It is noteworthy that Marr does not provide a reference for Barwick's alleged remark. Indeed, in an interview I conducted with Barwick in 1993, he denied ever making such a comment. Menzies provided an alternate and more accurate assessment. He told journalist David McNicoll: '[Barwick] didn't understand parliament. He didn't understand the art of getting along with that fellow over in the corner, and making him think about something . . . he was a disappointing politician'.[79] The out for Barwick was the retirement of Sir Owen Dixon as Chief Justice of the High Court. Barwick and Menzies spoke about the appointment and Holt encouraged Barwick to consider the job, promising to support his nomination in Cabinet. Barwick detected no sign of personal interest in Holt's encouragement: 'Holt genuinely thought that judicial life would be less strenuous for me'.[80] Barwick accepted the post and served with distinction, and a measure of controversy, as Australia's most senior judicial officer for the next seventeen years. As Prime Minister, Holt would accede to Barwick's request to put up a building for the High Court in the Parliamentary 'triangle' in Canberra.

Holt's standing within the Party and with the public had also been rejuvenated. London's *Financial Times* awarded the Australian economy an

'Oscar' for its overall performance in early 1964, and the August 1964 Budget was praised by commentators for its balance and responsibility. Maxwell Newton said the Treasurer's decision to raise personal income tax for the higher income groups 'earned him considerable respect both within the Government and among the Government's supporters'.[81] Holt's stature was also raised by his performance during trade talks in the United States in April 1965 after the British and American governments proposed 'arbitrary and unilateral' restrictions on overseas capital. It was apparent to many in the Liberal Party that Holt had maintained a useful network of contacts, particularly in the United States, and that he was widely respected internationally for his judgment and negotiation skills. He was also able to work effectively with the Democratic Party in the United States and the Labour Party in Britain which had both formed governments.

When Menzies celebrated his seventieth birthday in 1964, there were suggestions that he would retire after the 1966 election and that he might even succeed Viscount De L'Isle at Yarralumla. Howson's diary records a discussion on 21 October 1964 with lobbyist Frank Davis on the 'problem of succession':

> There is a general impression that the PM is visibly tiring and that he will retire early next year . . . I favour, of course, Harold Holt with Paul Hasluck as his deputy. Frank suggested Harold and John Gorton. I told him that in my opinion John Gorton is losing ground in the Cabinet arena.[82]

Holt told Sir Eric Harrison in London that he would be 'glad to learn that Bob has been in excellent form physically and politically since his return. The discomfiture and division of our opponents seem to increase day by day. The budget has had a very good reception from our backbenchers'.[83]

But the Murdoch press continued to promote McEwen. In an article published in the *Australian* on 15 January 1965, Brian Johns remarked that:

> Mr Holt's years in Treasury have not been happy and he has lost the public standing . . . [while Mr Hasluck] has been steadily making ground as a potential leader. Time is not on Mr Holt's side and as the months go by there could be greater evidence of the fact that he is not able to match the abilities of Mr McEwen.[84]

Johns thought that the political trust shared by McEwen and Menzies that had made the Coalition so strong was not evident in relation to Holt.

Johns also alleged that Holt 'has told friends that he will resign unless the Prime Minister retires in a year' so as to allow him 'to assume the leadership in time to lead the Government to the 1966 Federal poll'. This was far from true.

━ ━

Holt drew a great deal of personal satisfaction from the August 1965 Budget which, he said, 'has had the best reception yet of any in the series I have presented. There was a good reaction beforehand in the Party Room and this has also been the case in the subsequent comment from the press and industry'. Although he received only nine hostile telegrams—all from trade unions—the experience of 1960–61 remained in the back of his mind and militated against unrestrained optimism. He told former private secretary Terry Larkin: 'I will be keeping an anxious eye on imports over the months ahead'.[85] He had also conducted successful economic and trade negotiations with the Johnson Administration in the United States, despite the President announcing 'arbitrary and unilateral restrictions' on overseas capital in April 1965. Holt found that new doors were opened to Australian interests after Menzies announced on 29 April that Australia would commit combat forces to the war in South Vietnam.

In October 1965, the loyal deputy commented that 'Bob is in great form and shows no sign of flagging' although Menzies had shown Cabinet 'the flag of the Warden of the Cinque Ports . . . and has been giving us some detail about his uniform, accoutrements of establishment, etc.'.[86] It was clear, however, that the Menzies era was drawing to a close, as he would have to retire in early 1966 in order to give his successor a chance to consolidate before the November election. Holt's time as Treasurer would, finally, be over. Although he recognised his own limitations as Treasurer, Holt had influenced a number of important decisions—principally the notably successful transition to decimal currency.

After decades of political lobbying, Holt established the Decimal Currency Committee and directed that it report by August 1960, giving broad guidelines on achieving an efficient conversion. After exhaustive consideration, Holt announced on 7 April 1963 that Australia would convert to decimal currency in two years. He outlined the advantages of conversion, pointing out that decimal currency would drastically simplify arithmetic for primary school children. In all, it was a complicated undertaking involving a public education campaign, the withdrawal of the old currency, the manufacture and introduction of new coins and banknotes, the need to avoid conversion problems—especially inflation—and the construction of a new 'Royal Australian Mint' in Canberra to produce the currency. Given the high level of demand, during the initial conversion phase the Perth and Melbourne branches of London's Royal Mint would share in the task of making the new coins with some of the cupro-nickel coins being minted in London and shipped to Australia.

From the outset, Holt recognised that as every Australian handled currency, everyone would have an opinion. He was bombarded with ideas about possible names for the new currency and suggestions for its appearance. A few things were made clear very early in the discussion. The basis of the conversion would see the 10 shilling note replaced by the new unit of currency which would represent 100 cents. The issue of new banknotes was a statutory responsibility of the Reserve Bank. Nugget Coombs wanted Australia to be more adventurous than South Africa, which had introduced decimal currency in February 1961 but made minimal changes to the existing banknotes. Convinced the Reserve Bank Note Issue Department could produce banknotes with an entirely new design, Coombs asked Holt to support a creative approach. Holt readily agreed. On 24 March 1964, Menzies, Holt and Wilson approved a set of designs for the new banknotes submitted by artist Gordon Andrews.

The name of the new unit of currency, however, was causing a row. There is some confusion over Holt's preference. On the basis of former Country Party Minister Peter Nixon's recollection, Peter Golding claims that Holt wanted the 'Royal': 'McEwen and the Country Party hated it and there was quite a ruckus in the Country Party room. But McEwen said, "If Harold wants Royal, he can have Royal". It wasn't important enough to kick up a fuss about'.[87] This is unlikely as Holt had always proposed a distinctively Australian name and instituted a public competition on 9 April 1963. Downer remembers Holt liking the 'Austral' but feared it might be called the 'nostril'.[88] Cabinet had considered calling it the 'Royal', the 'Pound' and the 'Dollar' but had settled on the 'Royal'. Menzies was against any change in name because sharing pounds, shillings and pence was one of Australia's abiding links with Britain, but if there had to be change he wanted the 'Royal'. On 5 June 1963 Holt announced that the new unit of currency would be called the 'Royal'; the 50-cent coin would be called a 'crown'; 20 cents would be known as a 'florin' and the 10-cent piece a 'shilling'. It was an unpopular announcement, which suited Holt because he thoroughly disliked the 'Royal'. The next day he released a five-page document listing all of the public suggestions with everything from the 'Barton' to the 'Booma' and the 'Kelpie' to the 'Kangaroo'. Holt told the press that 'it soon became evident that there was wide and deeply felt opposition to the name'. In the ensuing public resistance to the Royal, he said there emerged a clear preference for the 'Dollar' as using the 'Pound' for a new currency might cause confusion with the old currency. In September 1963, in a forthright, personally prepared submission, Holt persuaded Cabinet to revise its decision and select the 'Dollar'.[89] Well-managed public opinion had given Holt a triumph over Menzies.

In announcing the change, Holt explained that a Decimal Currency Board would be created to manage the introduction of the new currency.[90] One particularly sensitive aspect was the extraction of precious metal from the existing silver coins after decimalisation. Holt explained to his friend (and Charles Engelhard's son-in-law) Rupert Gerard that pre-1947 silver coins contained 92.5 per cent silver while those minted after that date were 50 per cent silver. Holt received many letters from companies offering to provide an extraction service for what was expected to yield 69 million ounces of silver.[91] The Royal Australian Mint began producing the new range of coins and banknotes in February 1965. A previously unknown Melbourne designer, Stuart Devlin (later Royal Silversmith in London), prepared a range of wonderful drawings of Australian native wildlife for the new coins. Arnold Machin RA, a London artist, produced a profile of the Queen for the coins' reverse. The Latin inscriptions on the obverse of the old coins would be dropped in favour of 'Dignity with Simplicity', Holt's personal decision which followed the lead of New Zealanders who had simply put 'Queen Elizabeth II' on their coins since 1953. During the parliamentary consideration of the Currency Bill in February 1965, Holt said 'we are debating a currency which [will] endure, I am convinced, for many years—perhaps centuries—to come'.[92] He managed to secure bipartisan political support and the Bill was passed unopposed. Although Holt was no longer the Treasurer when 'C-Day' came around—14 February 1966—the conversion was achieved efficiently, without fuss and without affecting inflation. The initial cost of conversion had been estimated at $60 million and later revised to $75 million. Actual expenditure was $45 million. It was an administrative and educational triumph and, for Holt, a conspicuous feat of political management from which he rightly drew great personal satisfaction.

As Christmas 1965 approached, Holt felt justified in telling the Australian people that they could look forward to 1966 in 'good heart and with full confidence'.[93] The economy was buoyant and there were strong upward forces that would lead the country into the greatest ten years of advance in its history. He was confident there would be no repeat of 1960–61 as the economy was more diverse and continuing to grow at a sustainable level. There were a few 'soft spots', such as the fall in housing construction and the need for consortia to finance national development projects that the Government could not undertake alone. The drought in Queensland and New South Wales was causing hardship but the Commonwealth was assisting the States in providing adequate relief. Speculation about Menzies' retirement plans escalated after a house was purchased for him and Dame Pattie by Liberal Party members and friends at Malvern (within Holt's electorate) in November 1965. *Sun* reporter Herschel Hurst wrote on 7 December 1965 that Menzies would retire in February or March 1966. A national Gallup poll conducted a week later had 27 per cent of respondents saying that McEwen should succeed Menzies with 22 per cent nominating Holt. Four per cent mentioned Hasluck. For his part, Holt had enjoyed an extremely productive year and was entitled to believe that he was both ready and likely to become Prime Minister of Australia. After 30 years in Parliament, his long period of political formation for national leadership appeared to be coming to an end.

CHAPTER 9

The bloodless succession

January–February 1966

MOST AUSTRALIANS THOUGHT THEY had witnessed the political demise of Robert Gordon Menzies in 1941. As he walked out of Parliament House after being rejected by his own party, few could have imagined that Menzies would become the longest-serving Prime Minister in Australian history. There had, of course, been persistent rumours that Menzies would retire after every election since 1951. Over a meal at Kirribilli House on Boxing Day 1965, Menzies disclosed to his Press Secretary, Tony Eggleton, that he intended to retire. No one else was present at the lunch. As Cameron Hazlehurst notes: 'Exactly when [Menzies] decided to go was a secret, well-kept from even his chosen successor'.[1] By mid-January 1966 Holt had certainly been tipped off that Menzies would probably make an announcement soon but he had been disappointed more than once before. At the conclusion of a scheduled Cabinet meeting on 19 January during which Menzies made no mention of his future, there was a sense of disappointment and even despondency in the air. It seemed that again reality had confounded rumour. It was nearly lunchtime and Holt 'had his head slumped almost on his chest in despair, and Billy McMahon was also looking very glum indeed. Just before Cabinet rose the Prime Minister said to them: "Well, gentlemen, this is the last time I shall be with you", and he ended his long rule with a few simple sentences'.[2] Menzies' decision was conveyed to a meeting of the joint Government parties at 11 a.m. on 20 January. At his final press conference, Menzies was asked to nominate his most lasting political achievement. Putting to one side his founding of the Liberal Party, he nominated 'the fruitful and constant alliance with the Country Party in the Federal Parliament'.

The obvious candidate as his successor continued to be Harold Holt. The combination of his roles as Deputy Party Leader, Treasurer and Leader of the House meant that he commanded considerable power and prestige. He supervised access to the Prime Minister, influenced whether a politician's parliamentary profile was enhanced or diminished, facilitated liaison between the Party organisation and the Parliamentary Party, and exercised the ministerial supremacy that flowed from controlling the public purse strings. There was no shortage of people who owed a debt to Harold Holt or who relied on his goodwill in some way. He had survived the 1960 credit squeeze and shown himself to be resolute in the face of political hostility. He had not cracked or even wavered under intense pressure, nor had he tried to evade responsibility by blaming his department, damning a hapless public servant or offering feeble excuses for the pain he believed the country needed to endure at the time. In the years that followed he had been persistent but patient in pursuing his personal and political goals. He had proved himself to be steady under fire and a reliable colleague who valued solidarity. No one else in the Liberal Party had such depth or breadth of experience. None had proved themselves so thoroughly for so long. Many Liberals simply believed that Holt was entitled to the office.

No surprise contender emerged in the days that followed. Sir Alexander Downer asserted that Menzies had, in fact, groomed a single successor in order to avoid internal party conflict:

> Menzies manifested a paternal disposition, not approving of every aspect of Holt's character, more than once criticising his parliamentary speeches as 'lacking in edge', but regarding him as his successor. In numerous aspects Holt exercised great influence with him—for example, over ministerial appointments, the Government's program, party management.[3]

Hasluck was characteristically begrudging: 'As far as I could tell, [Menzies'] judgement was much the same as mine, namely that Holt was the best available—no higher than that'.[4] Several years earlier Menzies had apparently confided to Richard Woolcott, then a junior official in the External Affairs Department, that he 'expected Harold Holt would lead the Liberal Party after he retired' but that Hasluck was 'highly intelligent and a good Foreign Minister and was also a possible successor'.[5] Hasluck may have had the capacity, but he did not appeal to either his colleagues or the electorate. Tony Eggleton remembers Menzies expressing great confidence in 'Young Harold' as he still referred to him, and the belief that he would be a worthy successor. While the two men had been friends for more than 30 years, theirs could not be described as a close or intimate relationship. They had not sought each other's company beyond their formal duties or shared family holidays. There is nothing to suggest that Menzies ever visited Bingil Bay or Portsea, although he did dine from time to time at St Georges Road. Menzies was not, of course, intimate with anyone much beyond his immediate family. However, he knew Holt would never challenge him for the Party's leadership, that Holt was loyal and trustworthy, and would never presume upon Menzies' goodwill. There is no evidence that the two men ever discussed the leadership succession. There was probably no need. Holt seemed quietly confident that if the Liberal Party retained power the prime ministership would one day be his.

Holt was characteristically candid about comparisons between Menzies and himself. A few years earlier he had told Dame Enid Lyons, widow of Prime Minister Joe Lyons: 'You and I know that without Bob there are half a dozen of us that could do a workmanlike job, but not while he is with us. His stature overshadows the rest of us'.[6] Newspaper editorials noted the need for a 'conscious effort to grasp the fact that Sir Robert Menzies is leaving the political scene'.[7] But Holt was far from being an unknown quantity. He had been a member of the House of Representatives for 30 years, 5 months and 9 days—it was the longest wait for the post in Australian history.[8] Of his successors, William McMahon, Paul Keating and John Howard were parliamentarians for 22 years before becoming Prime Minister, and Gough Whitlam and Malcolm Fraser 20 years. Since Federation, the average age for incoming Australian Prime Ministers is 53 years. When Menzies retired, Holt was 58 years old. Only Ben Chifley (60) and William McMahon (63) were older on taking office. Not surprisingly, some felt that Holt would essentially be an interim prime minister. His age meant that he would not lead the Government for an extended period. Certainly he would not rival Menzies' recently established record.

Holt was unique in that he had not been associated with any particular group or faction in the Party organisation. There had always been tension between the Liberal Party's upper middle-class 'old money' members and the middle-class business and professional people. S.M. Bruce, Richard Casey and Malcolm Fraser were representative of the former; Harold Holt, John Gorton and Billy Snedden the latter. Accordingly, Holt's inclinations and sympathies were those of the political centre.

Not surprisingly, he was a pragmatist rather than a philosopher, but he nonetheless claimed a philosophical lineage connecting him with Alfred Deakin and approvingly quoted his statement that 'we are liberal always, radical often and reactionary never'. In noting the conditions of change and continuity that prevailed in his prime ministership compared with the situation facing Deakin, Holt claimed that:

> [there has] inevitably to be change in emphasis according to the needs of the times. There are today issues of great importance to the nation which occupy the attention of politicians but they are not of a nature that attracts radicals nor do they call for radical thinking in the terms of these early years of federation . . . New systems and methods of communication between the politician and the public have changed our habits and the tasks which fall on Ministers and backbenchers alike. But the old values remain. It is because of the very fact of our pledge to political liberty and individual freedom that we can absorb change and maintain our identity.[9]

Holt preferred to maximise his political scope for policy and action. Like most other political leaders of his day, Holt would not come to the nation's highest elected office with a comprehensive vision for Australia or an agenda for wholesale political, economic, social or diplomatic reform or restructure other than a program of 'taking Australia into Asia'—as he described it. Rather, he was committed to preserving a certain approach to public policy and a specific mood in public discourse.

> The principles which attracted me to the Liberal Party in the first instance are a truly Australian outlook, a determination to preserve for the Australian people freedom for the individual, opportunities and incentives for the individual, with emphasis on freedom of the individual. These things have endured throughout the life of the party, and I believe these principles are the reason why we are attracting at this time so many young people either to our ranks or to our political support.[10]

Holt believed that public demands shaped public policy. This meant that every politician needs 'in-built radar systems which will sense when something he proposes is likely to have serious electoral repercussions'.[11] Thus, Holt was not an innovator but a searcher after consensus. 'In this country the margins for movement are not very great and the politician must judge as accurately as he can the likely impact of his policies upon public opinion if he wishes to retain office'.[12] Holt did not intend to embark on an ambitious legislative program or attempt major constitutional change (although he would be one of the few prime ministers to sponsor a successful referendum).

In fact, his only detailed statement on the status and standing of the Constitution while Prime Minister would be a Foreword to Justice Percy Joske's *Australian Federal Government*.

> The existence of a written constitution has affected the political, economic and social life of the Australian people less than is generally supposed. While in Australia neither the national nor any one of the state governments is individually in the position of exercising full legal sovereignty over the whole field of government, this very fact has encouraged a spirit of active cooperation and partnership. This process has become increasingly evident in recent years. There is less disposition in the present than in the past on the part of Commonwealth governments to look for new heads of power which might be employed without being unduly troubled by the attitudes of the state governments. The reluctance of the electorate to make changes in the Constitution is well recognised and, in modern times, resort is made to consultation and conference discussion between heads of governments or the ministers appropriate to particular subject matters . . . One of the traditional objections in British thinking to the existence of a written constitution that might prove difficult to amend is the fear that it will prevent governments from meeting the known wishes of the people as changing circumstances occur. Australian experience has been otherwise . . . successive administrations have been responsive to the needs of the time, and that, with rare exceptions, the Constitution has not proved an insurmountable barrier. [13]

This led some to be critical of Holt's capacity for compromise and possibly for opportunism. In a savage attack mounted before he assumed the Liberal leadership and possibly designed to influence the Party vote, an editorial in the *Australian Financial Review* criticised Holt for his lack of philosophical convictions and political commitments: 'The most outstanding characteristic of Holt's politics is their elusiveness. Unkindly one could say that he was a plasticine man—imprinted with the philosophy, beliefs, arguments of the last person with whom he came in contact'.[14] This was unfair but it highlighted the need for the likely new Prime Minister to declare firmly the things for which he and his Government would stand. As someone who maintained the discipline of confining himself to matters within his own portfolio, he would have some deep and creative thinking to do in terms of a domestic agenda. Holt had a very different approach, however, to defence and foreign policy where he believed the Government had to show leadership consistent with its particular ability to survey regional trends and the Commonwealth's responsibility to act internationally on behalf of all Australians.

Holt enjoyed the goodwill of parliamentary colleagues on both sides of politics (with the possible exception of the Liberal Member for Bradfield, Harry Turner, and the late Opposition Leader, Dr H.V. Evatt), senior party officials, public servants and electorate office staff. He was polite, courteous and considerate of others. He neither shouted at nor abused departmental staff. He never resorted to bad language and avoided alcohol during his public duties. Indeed, his alcohol consumption was usually limited to an occasional sherry before lunch and a G&T or whisky and dry ginger ale late in the afternoon. He did not usually drink beer or table wines. Not considering himself superior to others, no one ever accused him fairly of snobbishness. He was a genuinely thoughtful and compassionate man. He rose early and worked late. In Zara's words, Harold 'had an alarming habit of waking up, sitting up, getting up and then usually going off singing'.[15] When asked whether he suffered from stress, she replied, 'I can't say that Harry has ever worried me by overworking. He isn't the nervy type. He works methodically not sporadically.'[16] Holt tended to work 15–16-hour days and looked forward to relaxing at weekends by skindiving, playing tennis or attending horse races (something Zara loathed).[17] If he had any vices, they were probably gambling and politics. Before it became customary for Parliament to be adjourned for the running of the Melbourne Cup, Holt could be observed sitting on the front bench listening to the big race through the earpiece of a hidden pocket radio.[18] Some thought that there was something wrong with his hearing before they realised his devotion to the Cup.

This was a rare distraction from his work as Holt was committed to his parliamentary duties to the point of slavishness. Some thought he was obsessive. He did not take long holidays and was an irregular sleeper who needed only about four hours a night to survive. He often read Cabinet submissions until 4 or 5 a.m. Cabinet Secretary, Sir John Bunting, noted that whereas Menzies would not arrive in his office until 9.45 a.m., Holt's day usually 'began at 7am, or even 6am with the first newspapers, and continued from his office as from 8am. But his was a day that mainly wound down'.[19] Holt may have lacked Menzies' flair but he was more diligent and hard-working than his predecessor. Holt 'recognised there were areas in which the most he could acquire was a broad knowledge, and sought and welcomed advice in the fields in which he felt insecure'.[20]

— ◄

As expected, Holt was elected to the Party leadership unopposed a few hours after Menzies announced his resignation. He considered this a great personal achievement but was humbled at the same time. He proudly told Zara that he would become Prime Minister without 'stepping over anyone's body'. After the débâcle of Menzies' deposition in 1941, this was the way he always wanted it to be. He was also relieved to be free of the Treasury and its complexity, remarking, 'I'm back on familiar ground, that of general politics, and away from the heavy specialisation of Treasury. This is my field'.[21]

The differences between Menzies and Holt were apparent from the outset—indeed Holt made no effort to conceal them. Party official Edgar Holt (a former parliamentary press officer and no relation to Harold) remembered that 'Menzies and Holt were dissimilar in appearance, in temperament, in outlook. The methods of the one were not those of the other. From the day Holt took over the very atmosphere of Parliament House was different'.[22] Towards his own party, Holt was 'open and approachable by nature, he always seemed willing to discuss [younger MPs'] personal problems and proffer advice'.[23] Towards the public he was courteous and affable, stopping to speak with tourists visiting the building on the way to his office in Parliament House.

Billy McMahon was elected Deputy Leader, although Menzies had done little to hide his preference for Hasluck. He had deliberately made him a Privy Councillor, he later told Senator Reg Withers, as a form of 'blessing' on his leadership aspirations.[24] The change of Liberal Party leadership was, however, achieved with remarkable ease and without any destabilising lobbying. There were no discontented rivals to provoke either ministerial resistance or backbench revolt. Over ten years, Holt had simply 'emerged' as Menzies' successor. Yet Allen Fairhall thought that 'one would have supposed that having elected a new Prime Minister there might have been some spontaneous celebration in the Party Room if only as an opportunity to express the Party's support and goodwill to the incoming leader. In fact, there was none'.[25] Perhaps this was because although no one was surprised everyone was quietly relieved that a change in the Liberal leadership had been achieved without conflict or controversy?

Although the Liberals had elected a new Leader and the Coalition had a large majority in the House of Representatives, the Governor-General, Lord Casey, was a stickler for protocol and custom.

> Harold Holt called on me and assured me of his ability to form a Government. I said I would like to ask John McEwen to come to see me to give his personal assurance of support, with which he agreed . . . John McEwen called . . . and showed me his letter to Harold Holt which appeared to be supportive. He assured me personally of his complete support without reservations, assuming, he said, that Harold Holt did not seek to destroy the Country party. He made no conditions as to any Country Party portfolios.[26]

McEwen provided a 'record of certain fundamental points' to guarantee the Coalition. It preserved most of the arrangements agreed with Menzies and emphasised that:

> policies to be pursued would be those designed to maintain stability in Government, to ensure the security of Australia in association with our traditional Allies and the UN Charter, to foster fast balanced growth of the nation consistent with economic stability, and the objective of raising living standards for all sectors of the community.[27]

A working draft of this document marked 'Destroy' and 'Not for Record' at the top included three statements: 'PM not to be a "Treasury" man'; Fix up "Industry" division of Trade and Industry; Interior with CP over next redistribution'. Holt filed his copy and was able to recognise some of McEwen's unwritten expectations of his leadership. He told McEwen in reply that he was 'confident that, on the basis of these understandings and the spirit in which they were reached, we shall work happily and successfully together'.[28] On the eve of assuming the Liberal leadership, Holt wrote to Fadden:

> I wanted to tell you tonight how grateful I shall always be for your encouragement and guidance, your self-effacing generosity in giving prominence to me—as with the Child Endowment and Housing Bills—when it would have been entirely appropriate for you to have occupied the centre of the stage, and my appreciation for all the years of warm friendship between us.[29]

Holt had enjoyed a sound working relationship with McEwen over more than twenty years, although without the close friendship that had accompanied his dealings with Fadden. There was not the rapport or the mutual respect that had existed between McEwen and Menzies while Holt's relationship with McEwen was also coloured by Holt's seven years as Treasurer during which 'there was increasing antipathy between Trade and Treasury'.[30] By this time, the Country Party had tried to combine its rural base with the manufacturing sector, a move that resulted in the kind of protectionism opposed by McMahon and the Treasury. But tension within the Coalition was almost entirely organisational: the Liberal Party wanted to contest rural seats. There was also the continuing Coalition Agreement which stipulated that 6 out of the 25 Ministerial positions and 3 of the 12-member Cabinet be Country Party members. (In 1956 Menzies had adopted a system of a Cabinet of senior Ministers and an outer ministry whose members were called into Cabinet only when matters affecting their portfolios were under discussion, a practice Holt would continue.) There were some within the Liberal Party who felt the Coalition Agreement was too generous to the Country Party but Holt decided to allow the Agreement to continue.

Having been assured that the Coalition was sound, Casey felt he was entitled to give advice to the new Prime Minister as well as to receive it.

Casey urged [Holt] to increase the country's defence capacity by means of deferred payment for purchases from the United States, to appoint assistant ministers, to lend a senior adviser to the Indonesian Government, to let the CSIRO station a liaison officer in Japan and further to liberalise immigration policy. In March 1966 he asked Holt to consider setting up a Royal Commission to report on how the impact of droughts might be lessened. In April he suggested tax concessions to encourage investment in research and development . . . Just before a Commonwealth Prime Ministers' conference, he urged Holt to do all he could to encourage and support the British Labour Prime Minister, Harold Wilson, whom he saw as struggling valiantly to cope with Britain's economic woes . . . After a visit to Western Australia, Casey warned Holt of 'intense feeling' and 'quite an unhealthy attitude' there towards the Commonwealth.[31]

Having secured the Party leadership, guaranteed the Coalition and received a commission from the Governor-General, Holt could now turn to the composition of his Cabinet and ministry. The Party had become accustomed to the Prime Minister playing a dominant role in determining the shape and composition of the Cabinet, and in the conduct of Cabinet's affairs.[32] But given the ease with which he ascended to the leadership and the absence of any genuine rival, Holt could have embarked on a major restructure. He did not take the opportunity.

— · —

Although Holt had been part of every Menzies' Cabinet since 1949, there was nonetheless a feeling that the mood had changed. One of Menzies' founding philosophical principles he carried over into his political life was constant emphasis on mutual obligations arising from implicit contract. This created a necessary tension between obligations and responsibilities that built on loyalty and trust. It was soon apparent that Holt saw things differently. One commentator noted:

> Loyalty and trust are notions also basic to the philosophy and attitudes of Menzies' successor, Harold Holt. Both have had legal training and experience, but the new Prime Minister's conception of loyalty and trust reflects not the relatively sophisticated and abstract notion of contract, but rather a perhaps naively optimistic belief that voters and colleagues behave as if they were part of a public school football team. Herein lies a crucial difference between Menzies and his successor, both of them dedicated to public service, but on the basis of vastly different assumptions.[33]

Holt disliked the idea of an elected ministry because it would not allow him to have representation from every State and both Houses. After becoming leader, Holt asked his colleagues at a Party Room Meeting whether they wanted an elected ministry. They did not and also declined to have a Committee of the Party established to develop a proposal for such a practice.[34] The Prime Minister would continue to select both the Cabinet and the ministry. Later in the year, Alexander Buchanan (the Member for McMillan in Victoria) proposed that the Prime Minister select the Cabinet while the backbench chose the ministry.[35] This was, in part, a reflection of backbench frustration that there were so few new opportunities for ministerial advancement. Holt put the matter to the Parliamentary Party Room and Buchanan's motion was defeated by 42 to 20 votes.

While Holt wanted a *selected* rather than *elected* ministry, he made few changes to the Cabinet and ministry he inherited. The Menzies years had been characterised by stability. There had been few Cabinet reshuffles as Menzies believed that ministers needed time to understand the issues facing their portfolio and to shape their policy accordingly. Some ministers had been in the same department for a decade. Knowing that McMahon desperately wanted the Treasury job, that he was the best qualified Liberal minister for it, and recognising how destabilising his presence in Cabinet would be were he overlooked, Holt had little alternative but to appoint him. McMahon was also the Deputy Party Leader and it had been assumed (unjustifiably in the view of some) that the Treasury accompanied his party seniority. The only other name put forward was Alan Hulme, although no one was convinced he was suited for the job or understood its complexities. When Sir Roland Wilson was appointed Chairman of the Qantas Board in July 1966 (he was replaced at the Treasury by Sir Richard Randall later in the year), the press started to talk about the end of the Holt–Wilson era and the start of the McMahon–Randall era. McMahon's appointment to the Treasury was also deemed a 'win' for the New South Wales Division of the Liberal Party which had felt itself to be less influential than the Victorian Division.[36]

Menzies' retirement and the death of Senator Sir Shane Paltridge on 19 January created the need for two new Cabinet Ministers—Les Bury and John Gorton. Allen Fairhall succeeded Paltridge as Defence Minister and Henty took Paltridge's place as Leader of the Government in the Senate. Bury and Gorton were described by the press as the big 'winners' in the reshuffle. Bury shifted from Housing to Labour and National Service. David Fairbairn succeeded Holt as Leader of the House. Dame Annabelle Rankin, who succeeded Bury in the Housing portfolio, became the first woman to hold ministerial rank since Dame Enid Lyons. Holt also needed to consider the ministerial aspirations of Malcolm Fraser. His relationship with Fraser was cordial but not close. After being elected to the House of Representatives in 1955, Fraser had delivered speeches and published articles on immigration that were critical of Holt. Other 1955 entrants to Parliament—Snedden and Howson—already had portfolios. Fraser attributed his 'failure to be selected for the ministry before Snedden and Howson to Holt's hostility'.[37] Following Menzies' retirement, Fraser asked Holt: 'What are my prospects? Do you want me in your Ministry or not, because if not, I'm perfectly happy to get out and make room for someone else'.[38] Fraser recalls that Holt did not answer directly. But when the Minister for the Army, Dr Jim Forbes, who entered the House in 1956 after winning a by-election, told Holt that he wanted a change of portfolio (he preferred Health), Holt asked him about possible replacements.

> I said, 'Well, what about Malcolm Fraser?', and he said, 'But Malcolm Fraser isn't an ex-serviceman, he was too young to go to the war'. I said, 'Look Harold, the world's moved on, you know. There must be a point at which you have non-ex-servicemen from the Second World War to take over the service portfolios [65 of the 93 Government MPs had served in the world wars]. Malcolm Fraser is one of the few non ex-servicemen who's taken an active interest in defence'. Harold pricked up his ears and said: 'Oh, has he?' I said, 'Yes, didn't you know he was Chairman of the Government Members Defence Committee?' He said, 'No'. He didn't even know! Harold didn't say anything more, but in due course he announced his Ministry. I was Minister for Health and Malcolm Fraser was Minister for the Army.[39]

The trouble for Holt was the lack of new faces and growing ambition—and frustration—among younger backbenchers. The average age of Holt's Cabinet Ministers was 59 years in comparison with 61 years for Menzies' last ministry, but the best days of several ministers were behind them. They had run out of ideas, vision and energy. Others had become too comfortable in their portfolios, preferring continuity to change in a society that was being rapidly transformed by the 'Swinging Sixties'. It was perhaps for these reasons that Holt said publicly that his entire ministry was 'on trial' until after the 1966 election. No one, he said, had a monopoly on any portfolio while he had no personal right to the leadership and intended to earn his entitlement to the job of Prime Minister.

In addition to those who felt frustrated at not being given the chance to experience ministerial work, Holt inherited a number of backbench mavericks including Bill Wentworth, Billy Kent Hughes, Jim Killen, John Jess and Senators Ian Wood and Reg Wright. All were inclined to criticise the Party's leadership and to vote against the Government. Firm action was needed to keep them in line—at least, this had been Menzies' approach. Menzies had concluded that 'his position as Leader of the Government would be intolerable if I had to exist at the whim of one or two or five persons, and I don't propose to live so precariously as that'.[40] Holt should have found an alternative to Senator Denham Henty as Leader of the Government in the Senate. He was neither cunning nor ruthless and had not performed well while he had deputised for Senator Shane Paltridge, a gruff ex-publican from Western Australia. A strong man was needed to keep the Coalition senators in line and force the Government's legislation through a Senate in which the Government did not have a majority. Not appointing such a leader would prove a costly mistake for the Coalition.

Holt's leadership style was to guide Cabinet towards a consensus consistent with the Party's philosophy and the practical needs of the nation. Shortly after becoming Prime Minister, he explained his 'activist' approach:

> Leadership can take various forms. There is the type of leadership which is so far out in front of the team that there is danger of lack of cooperation, lack of warmth and some loss of effectiveness. There is the leadership which can lead but, at the same time, be close enough to the team to be part of it and be on the basis of friendly cooperation. I will make that my technique of leadership.[41]

Holt also wanted to distinguish between his role within Cabinet and his office as national leader, and public perceptions of both.

> I don't think we get from the public, as yet anyhow, the veneration which apparently develops around a President of the United States. The Prime Minister here is very much in the firing line of political action. The events of recent years are tending to accentuate this because the publicity media— [television] particularly, the press and radio—all tend to concentrate attention these days on the head of government, and whereas sitting around the Cabinet table he should be regarded as the first among equals, in the eyes of the public he tends to be regarded as, not only the leading figure, but virtually a dominant figure in the administration.[42]

Holt's consensual approach saw him taking Cabinet through each submission page by page or even line by line if necessary. Each member was given a chance to comment and to be part of the decision-making process although this could make meetings long and tortuous. Holt's problem was trying to satisfy everyone or, at least, attempting to accommodate their viewpoint. As political scientists Clem Lloyd and Gordon Reid note:

> [Holt] observed the conventions of the Cabinet system of government as developed in Australia. He viewed himself as chairman of a committee, the first among equals, vested with the responsibility of giving leadership but where the consensus of Cabinet opinion was clearly against him, the instrument and executor of the majority decision.[43]

Because Holt had been 'an equal' for so long, it was not surprising that parliamentary colleagues such as Iain Sinclair said he thought of the new Prime Minister as a 'colleague and a partner'.[44]

Cabinet members soon realised that Holt could be quite determined, occasionally to the point of obstinacy, and he could rarely be deflected from the agreed course of action. He did not, however, feel the need to speak on every issue as Menzies had done, nor did he have an ambitious legislative program. It was perhaps for this reason that Holt did not direct his ministers to be more disciplined in their Cabinet submissions. Sir John Bunting, Secretary to the Prime Minister's Department under Menzies and Holt, and later McMahon and Whitlam, remembered that:

> Menzies received the commentary of his department, observed it, savoured it and, if he liked it sufficiently, digested it. Later, starting with his successor and running on, the practice of receiving Prime Minister's Department's briefs continued, but the art that previously went into their use did not altogether survive. The briefs were another document in the Prime Minister's file—unprivileged, undistinguished from others. It had been the practice of Treasurers to use Treasury briefs as part of their ammunition or armoury by getting the attention of Cabinet at a suitable time and quoting in confident terms what was there written. There was nothing wrong with that; it was, on the contrary, a wise and proper course and all the more so because Treasury was in the habit, again wisely, of writing its brief so that it included a section expertly designed, even sometimes with a little cunning, to be read to the Cabinet. The Prime Minister's Department briefs, for Menzies, had no such paragraphs . . . We found that Mr Holt was very much, and to some extent his successors were also, apt to say: 'I shall read you the Prime Minister's Department notes'. We learnt soon enough to write in a quotable fashion.[45]

On Australia Day 1966, the Government was sworn in at 11 a.m. at Government House after which Holt chaired his first Cabinet meeting. Some were a little weary after returning from Perth for the funeral of Sir Shane Paltridge, the Defence Minister.

The public warmed quickly to Holt's elevation. One commentator remarked that:

> On the eve of Menzies' retirement most of the electorate could think of no one to fill his shoes and similarly with Evatt. Yet so completely may any leader

overshadow his colleagues in the political coverage of the media that when Holt succeeded Menzies three-in-four Liberals and one-in-two Labor voters declared him the person best suited to head the party.[46]

Whereas many journalists had taken an active dislike to Menzies, the press looked for reasons to praise Holt. The following contemporary observation was typical:

> Holt presents a personality more in keeping with contemporary Australia. The new Liberal leader has always enjoyed extremely good relations with his parliamentary colleagues and in carrying out his ministerial duties. Menzies, in contrast, was the most friendless politician in Canberra, projecting there a patronising private image in direct contrast with his protective public one. Holt genuinely likes people and wants to be liked in return. Holt talks smoothly but is without Menzies' oratory. His physical appearance is that of an active rather than a spectator sportsman. Privately a hard, methodical, cautious worker, Holt takes care to project a gay, debonair, vaguely reckless public image.[47]

During his first major address to the Liberal Party in February 1966, Holt was keen to emphasise that the Party was not synonymous with Sir Robert Menzies; that it had an organisation which had accounted for its electoral success as much as his predecessor's leadership. It was a young party, developing its own customs and the traditions to give it stability and vitality. Furthermore,

> Australia has need of the Liberal Party. We had reached [in 1944] a point in our affairs when we needed a party which would stand for all sections of the Australian community, which would cast aside, once and for all, the old bitter concept of class warfare, the struggle between employer and employee; that would see in the needs of Australia a need for a party of unity, a party which could develop a co-operating democracy with the Parliaments of the States; not trying to make Federation work by imposing authority from the centre or by so construing the Federal powers that the States were reduced to nothingness, but a true Federation based upon a spirit of cooperation rather than on a strict definition of powers.[48]

In seeking to differentiate itself from Labor and the '36 faceless men' of the ALP Federal Conference, the Liberal Party stressed that:

145

> Our Council is not a council of Party bosses. If we reach conclusions about Federal policy, we send them to the Government as recommendations. We don't give orders to the Government. We don't make policy for the Government and don't compel the Government to carry it out. It is our belief that the final responsibility for policy rests with the Government elected by, and responsible to, voters.[49]

Menzies' legacy to Holt was a healthy majority in the House, a harmonious party, a united Coalition, a vibrant economy and a war that had driven a wedge into the Opposition. There was virtually no inflation, essentially no unemployment, mineral exports were supporting a trade boom, and living conditions were steadily improving. But the Opposition thought its prospects would improve. Calwell believed that there was a great chance of success in the 1966 election as Holt would not be as formidable an adversary as Menzies.[50] Indeed, he told Lee Kuan Yew that as 'Menzies has gone our chances have improved considerably. Harold Holt is a nice fellow, but he has little of the ability and astuteness of his former leader'.[51] Although Holt was naturally critical of Labor policies and party procedures, he nonetheless maintained a good rapport with the Opposition, and with Calwell in particular.

The first test of strength of Holt's leadership would be parliamentary debate. As an impromptu speaker he had no superior. He was lucid and confident, able to identify the flaw or weakness in an opposing argument while avoiding personal abuse. But,

> he was not so successful when making set speeches. One suspected outside assistance in their preparation. He possessed neither Menzies' language, cadences, dramatic pauses, nor depth of thought. Not being widely read, he lacked the cultivation of mind of some of his contemporaries. Though fluent, his greatest admirers could not claim that he was an orator. Words came easily but they did not make him an inventor of epigrams. Yet his ready sense of humour, quick repartee, and amiability in most situations reaped a harvest of popularity greater than any member in my time in the House.[52]

Holt's popularity would, of course, be influenced by the manner in which he was depicted by the media.

Journalists were given easy access to Holt. He was always willing to explain the Government's policies and decisions. Journalist Keith Dunstan recalled seeing journalists approaching Holt in King's Hall at 1am after a long session of Parliament when he was almost out on his feet with exhaustion. Yet, there was still this fantastic courtesy in the man. He answered all questions with that famous smile . . . Press conferences before were rare, to be remembered . . . but Mr Holt gave them whenever they were wanted.[53]

All of this was in stark contrast to Menzies, who had coped with the prying press and the curiosity of the public by 'reducing the area of his private life to a minimum, and rigidly segregating even that reduced private area from the public arena'.[54] But in the grey area where public and private lives struggle to co-exist, 'Holt always saw that he emerged as Holt, the "with it" Prime Minister, rather than as Holt, private citizen possessed of slightly bohemian tastes and outlook'.[55] 'In one sense', Peter Bailey recalled:

> he was our first modern prime minister. He was the first prime minister to hold regular press conferences, under Tony's [Eggleton] influence, and he rarely slipped up in them. He went on TV frequently; he would go out and meet people. My problem was to balance all that with the job of getting the Government business done.[56]

Eggleton would be the Prime Minister's almost constant travelling companion. His role as Press Secretary was evolving and was yet to be completely formalised. The Secretary of the Department, Sir John Bunting, supported Holt's interest in public relations and media liaison and believed the Prime Minister ought to take the Press Secretary with him on all public occasions attended by the media. Eggleton was encouraged to make contributions on methods of communicating Government policy and to obtain departmental briefing notes, to allow him to respond promptly to questions from the media. Eggleton succeeded in helping Holt get his message to a press corps delighted that the new Prime Minister not only understood their needs but recognised that press conferences represented an opportunity rather than an obligation.

Holt was 48 years old when television first went to air in Australia. Unlike Menzies, who did everything he could to avoid appearing on television, Holt was prepared to learn how to exploit this new and powerful communication medium. As programs were live and editing technology in its infancy, there was considerable pressure on participants and Holt occasionally lacked composure and confidence. Clem Lloyd remarked that Holt:

was shrewd enough to realise that the Prime Ministership had to be brought into closer touch with the electorate. In his early days as Prime Minister Holt adopted a populist approach, generating interviews and picture opportunities in the tabloid press which Menzies had largely spurned. Holt also acknowledged the importance of the political media and strove to build better links with it.[57]

That being said, Holt did try to ensure his contact with the media was on his own terms.

Holt encouraged more regular access by the media, but there was also a discriminatory element in his approach. He was wary about full-scale press conferences with a general right to question, preferring to brief a small group of press gallery journalists known personally to him and representing the principal media organisations. Effectively, this meant that two representatives of each office attended Holt's briefings on an invitation basis. Holt also recognised that by the mid–1960s electronic media was well established in the press gallery and their special needs had to be met. If he made an important statement for attribution at a briefing, he summoned TV and radio reporters to his office and repeated the remarks for the cameras and tape recorders.[58]

These briefings were conducted in accordance with protocols devised by Eggleton and the Parliamentary Press Gallery Committee. John Bennetts recalls that:

At these sessions, Holt encouraged a lively exchange of questions, answers and views which were tape recorded and transcribed by his staff. At the end of the session he quickly reviewed what he said, and circulated to the Gallery a memorandum which indicated which statements were for attribution, which were for publication without attribution, and which were 'off the record'. This procedure allowed Holt second thoughts and an opportunity to avoid publication of ill-considered replies to unexpected questions.[59]

Holt also embraced the innovative television current affairs programs. Shortly after the launch of the ABC's *This Day Tonight*, Holt agreed to an extended interview. This, according to former ABC staff member Robert Moore, was 'a big deal' and 'rules of behaviour were invented overnight'.[60] No one had ever engaged the Prime Minister in this manner before but, within a decade, such interviews would be commonplace.

Not everyone approved of Holt's accommodating attitude to the media because of its impact upon the business of government. Hasluck claimed that the principles of the Public Service eroded by Labor during and after World War II had been re-established by Menzies, but under Holt:

> the deterioration was slow and slight and resulted mainly from the increased attention he gave to public relations and creating 'a good image' so that occasionally the argument in Cabinet gave less weight to the expertness, experience and objectivity of the senior public service than to the rather preposterous notions of some urchin on the fringes of politics about what story would get the best run in the Press Gallery.[61]

Making himself so available to the press and the public also carried with it certain risks for Holt, especially after the assassination of President John F. Kennedy in November 1963. This was an area of exploration and uncertainty for both sides of politics and the press.

Menzies had declined the offer of a bodyguard and Holt initially followed his example, until a disturbed teenager, Peter Kocan, attempted to kill the Leader of the Opposition, Arthur Calwell, during a political rally in June 1966. Even this did not convince Holt of the need for greater security. But one night:

> a lone sniper fired a single rifle shot at [Holt] from a tree near Parliament House, as he worked in his corner office at night, lights ablaze and curtains open. The bullet cracked a window, Holt was not hurt, and according to police the sniper was caught and charged with a different offence, and there was virtually no publicity.[62]

Holt then agreed to be protected in Canberra and at Parliament House. He was accompanied by security officers during the 1966 election campaign and when travelling overseas. Although there had been a number of threats to Holt's life by telephone and mail, he refused to be 'watched' when at his holiday retreats at Portsea and Bingil Bay when he desperately wanted to be left alone.

Increased concerns about security affected Holt's travelling arrangements. For most of his prime ministership, Menzies had travelled on commercial aircraft. He later decided to order two British TSR-2 Viscount aircraft as the genesis of an RAAF VIP Fleet. By the time the aircraft arrived (one had been used by the Shah of Iran and the other

by the Union Carbide Company) Holt had assumed office.[63] The second
of the two aircraft was more luxuriously appointed and would be first used
for a prime ministerial trip to South Vietnam in April 1966. The second
was chartered by the Press Gallery with Holt agreeing that there would be
no prime ministerial selection or veto of the journalists permitted to
report his visit.

— —

Departmental and personal staff mediated Holt's contact with the Executive arm of government, the press and the people. Sir John Bunting, born
in 1918, had been Secretary of the Prime Minister's Department and
Cabinet Secretary since 1959.

> In the period between Chifley's innovative use of his 'official family', and the
> election of the Whitlam Labor Government in 1972, [Coalition] govern-
> ments largely relied on traditional patterns of staffing ministerial offices.
> Elements of an 'official family' remained, for instance, in Menzies' friendly
> relations with key PM's officials such as Bunting, ready interaction with
> Wilson and Randall in Treasury and resort to Liberal Party figures such as
> J.R. Willoughby and Edgar Holt; in Harold Holt's appointment of journalist
> Keith Sinclair (to PMs rather than his office) as speech writer and extra
> intellect.[64]

Keith Sinclair, editor of Melbourne's *Age* newspaper for the previous seven
years, would undertake detailed research and produce a final draft of Holt's
speeches before passing them to Eggleton, who further massaged them
before they were handed to Holt for final review and delivery. Mary
Newport served as Eggleton's assistant. Acknowledging his lack of confidence about public speaking without notes and his tendency to ramble,
Holt was the first Prime Minister to employ a speechwriter. Sinclair
enjoyed a close rapport with Bunting and Bailey, and the arrangement
worked well. This was the first time Holt had enjoyed the services of a
press secretary and a dedicated speechwriter. Previously he had largely
managed his own contact with the media and had his department prepare
first drafts of most of his speeches. As in most things, Hasluck was critical
of Eggleton's influence on Holt and thought he ought to have 'paid much
more attention to the counsel of John Bunting and faced up to such re-
alities as might have been presented to him by his senior ministers, rather

than being lured into Eggleton's strange and glamorous but quite fanciful world of "public relations"'.[65] Holt had many other staff on whom he relied as heavily as Eggleton.

For a very brief period his personal secretary was Hazel Craig, Menzies' long-standing secretary. Frank Jennings had been Menzies' Private Secretary and remained with Holt for much of 1966 although Holt had initially wanted Jim Short to come with him from the Treasury. Bunting advised against the appointment on the grounds that it might look as though there was a 'Treasury takeover' of the Prime Minister's office. When the transition from Menzies to Holt was complete, Craig returned to Sir Robert Menzies' service and was replaced by Pat de Lacy, a member of Holt's personal staff at the Treasury. Bernadette 'Bernie' Long continued to serve as the Assistant Private Secretary although her duties were mainly associated with electorate matters. She was especially valued for her ability to read Holt's scrawling handwriting. Betty Greenwood and Jan Moore were Secretarial Assistants. These were essentially minor changes although political scientist Tony Griffiths would later accuse Holt of attempting to 'set up an American presidential style of leadership in Australia' by surrounding himself with 'a battery of aides' when the appointment of the 39-year-old Peter Bailey as Liaison Officer was announced in February 1967.[66] Whereas Jennings (who left the public service in late 1966 to grow bananas in Queensland) fulfilled the traditional duties of a private secretary, Bailey, whose formal title was First Assistant Secretary (Prime Minister's Office), was essentially an 'on-the-spot' departmental adviser. He was also in charge of Holt's private office. Holt had the official Prime Ministerial vehicle, a black Bentley limousine with the registration plate C★1, and an official driver, Ray Coppin, who had also served Sir Robert Menzies. There was also the official residence, The Lodge, and its staff to manage.

When he became Prime Minister, Holt was the longest-standing permanent resident at the Hotel Canberra. For her part, Zara was not attracted to Canberra as a place to live. She did not visit the city other than for 'gala' occasions and was bored by parliamentary proceedings. The arrival of the Holts prompted a frenzy of activity at The Lodge, a two-storey, 35-room Georgian-style house that was built in 1927 as a temporary residence for the Prime Minister. Although it was the Holts' home for less than two years, this would be the most intense period of building and renovation seen since the building's completion. Not surprisingly, the impetus came from Zara who 'found The Lodge bare, dingy, and depressing, with discoloured walls and carpets, and scanty furniture in rooms too numerous and too small'.[67] This was all about to change. Most of the work directed by Zara was carried out while the Prime Minister was away from Canberra as security requirements necessitated him living elsewhere while tradesmen were employed in and around the building. She had a great deal of the dark wood panelling painted white to make the rooms seem brighter and had the billiard table removed. The Melbourne *Sun* newspaper said 'the look is neo-Zara' while the *Mirror* reported on 'a new "wild" look for The Lodge'.

In addition to re-ordering the internal layout, Zara also recruited a domestic staff of five members. Ray Coppin was the only one who had served the Menzies family. As Sir Robert and Dame Pattie did not vacate The Lodge until 28 February 1966, Harold and Zara lived at the Hotel Canberra during March so that work Zara had proposed for the dining room, entrance hall and sitting room could be completed before the arrival of the Queen Mother in Canberra on 3 April 1966. So proud was Zara of her initial renovation that she allowed the *Australian Women's Weekly* to produce a colour feature on the changes she had made.[68] While overseas with Harold during 1966, Zara spent most of her free time purchasing furniture and fittings for The Lodge. These acquisitions were complemented by a few personal items, principally artworks, Zara had transported from St Georges Road. But neither the building's exterior nor the landscaping were affected by Zara's renovating zeal.

> Although she had such a major impact on The Lodge, Zara Holt appears to have taken little interest in the garden, and changes to the exterior seem to have been minor, such as installation of striped awnings on all the eastern windows at the front of the house, although in 1967 she proposed that a portico be built at the front entrance.[69]

In addition to The Lodge, the Holts also had access to the Prime Minister's Sydney residence, Kirribilli House, although he rarely spent much time there. Tiny Lawless kept St Georges Road fully functioning as the family's main place of residence, now occupied by the Holts' two Siamese cats, 'Cha' and 'Cha Cha'. Although Holt realised he would not be able to spend much time at Bingil Bay, he planned regular respite visits to the house at Portsea which he referred to as the 'Bathing Box'. The cost of maintaining three private properties and two official residences was not inconsiderable. The principal family income continued to be the substantial profits from Zara's fashion shops although, as Prime Minister, Holt received an annual salary of $17 000 in addition to the $7000 he received as a Member of Parliament; an annual special allowance of $8000 to cover living and entertainment expenses at The Lodge; and a further $2200 as an electorate allowance. He also designated Canberra as his home base for the calculation of travelling allowance.[70] In other words, they were reasonably wealthy people who enjoyed a very comfortable lifestyle. Most of what they earned was spent. Neither Harold nor Zara ever tried to build a personal fortune. Notwithstanding their affluence, neither was ever accused of being proud or conceited. Such characteristics were political poison in a place like Australia where people still believed in egalitarian ideals, even if the Prime Minister had five residences at his disposal.

The long wait for Harold Holt was finally over. It was now for him to demonstrate that his potential could be translated into performance.

PART 2
And Death

CHAPTER 10

From good to better

March–December 1966

HAROLD HOLT BECAME AUSTRALIA'S seventeenth Prime Minister on Australia Day 1966, as the nation and its people were truly coming of age. The formative years of the nation experienced within the British Empire were nearing an end, and he told the Young Australian Foundation at the University of Melbourne that while the country once looked to Britain and the Royal Navy, 'we have now realised that Australia is a national independent entity of its own and that Australia faces problems and has obligations which are quite unlike anything the earlier generations of Australian had to meet'.[1] The unifying symbols of Crown, religion and race were becoming less relevant to an increasingly multicultural society. But what would replace them? Holt recognised the nation was in a period of social, economic, political and moral transition. He was willing to lead but did not seem to be sure about the direction he should be taking. The almost indecipherable handwritten notes handed to speechwriter Keith Sinclair that were the outline of some of his speeches bordered on incoherent. They were a grab-bag of subjects and themes, mixed with second thoughts and adjoining arrows to suggest a logical flow of ideas that plainly did not exist in the Prime Minister's mind. He hoped the people would provide a lead but emphasised the importance of harmony and homogeneity in the meantime. No one should have been surprised when Holt said that 'if we're going anywhere, we're not going American, we're going Australian, and there is, I think, a stronger sense of nationalism, a growing feeling of pride in Australia, its achievements, its potentialities, even its hazards'.[2]

In any event, Holt believed national unity would arise from the common life of the people; they would be drawn together by those things in which they felt a shared future and a common destiny. The Government or the Prime Minister could not impose it on the people. As Prime Minister, he said, 'it is my responsibility to reflect the modern Australia to my fellow countrymen, to our Allies and the outside world at large'.[3] Government, according to Holt, was an institution conferring rights and entitlements. He did not believe in expansionist government and adhered to the Liberal ideal of restraining government intervention in people's lives. But with the economy in good shape and the country on the verge of a mining boom, the Government recognised it needed to focus on social policy although it would reflect rather than determine its direction. Holt was looking to the 'forgotten people', the moral middle class he had inherited from Menzies, whose mood and mind he claimed to understand. He had long believed that 80 per cent of the electorate would invariably vote Liberal or Labor. This left 20 per cent of the voters who could make or break the Government and Holt believed these were the 'forgotten people'. What could he say or do that would attract and retain their votes? Holt was prepared to compromise and seek consensus in order to find the answer.

With such an outlook, Holt emerged very quickly from Menzies' shadow. He was so much more relaxed with the media that within a few weeks, profiles of the new Prime Minister featured in every major newspaper. The differences in style were obvious. At a Party rally in Melbourne, Holt reiterated his understanding of the Party's platform. Its four pillars were a positive philosophy of liberty, enhancing opportunities for freedom, encouraging incentive for effort and ensuring a minimum of government interference with daily life. His Government would maintain a policy of full employment and promote national growth. New, major infrastructure projects would absorb some of the labour from the Snowy Mountains Scheme which would start to wind down in April 1966.[4] And what about immigration? What kinds of new arrivals would Australia accept? Holt naturally turned to a field in which he had already achieved notable success to demonstrate the shift in social policy he wanted to promote. In his first statement as Prime Minister, broadcast on national television on 20 February 1966, Holt foreshadowed a change to Australia's immigration policy to allow for 'more flexibility . . . [and] a spirit of humanity' particularly in relation to non-European migration. The changes being proposed would go further than those of the previous decade because, Holt argued, the White Australia Policy had proved an international embarrassment and a problem for Australia's external relations.[5] But, he assured the electorate, this 'did not mean fundamentals of the restrictive policy would be changed'.[6] In fact, as Holt well knew, this is exactly what would happen.

In late 1964, the Minister for Immigration, Hubert Opperman, had asked Cabinet to consider a five-year residence requirement for non-Europeans and widening of the categories for accepting migrants. Menzies had rejected the proposals outright. Within weeks of becoming Prime Minister, Holt resurrected these initiatives with the aim of securing bi-partisan support in an effort to promote Australia's image abroad. Before any decisions were made, the Secretary of the Immigration Department, Peter Heydon, advised the Immigration Advisory Council of the Prime Minister's request for the proposals to be reconsidered. Menzies learned of the initiative from the parliamentary grapevine and was not impressed. At a dinner held at the Chinese Embassy on 2 April 1966, Menzies told Heydon's wife Naomi that he was contemplating a chapter in his memoirs critical of Heydon, adding 'it may be written but it won't be published'. Heydon noted Menzies' reaction in his diary: 'he is finding this change hard to take, especially as he realises it is symbolic of great changes everywhere'.[7]

Opperman now took the unprecedented step of addressing the Council personally, to outline the key elements of the changes being sought. A significant shift was the proposal to reunite 'well-qualified' Asian migrants who had been resident in Australia and separated from their immediate families for fifteen years. The main legislative reform was reducing the qualifying period a non-European was required to be in Australia before becoming eligible for residency and citizenship, thus giving non-Europeans from fifteen to five years parity with European migrants. The Government also intended to assist in family reunions and to admit certain 'well-qualified' non-Europeans.[8] Opperman secured the Council's support, with only minor objections being raised.

Although a political conservative, Opperman supported Holt's reform agenda. He had been Minister for two years and knew that Holt not only took a continuing interest in his old Department's work but was driving his legislative changes from personal convictions, not political pressure. As Immigration Minister in 1956, Holt had introduced the first legislation to allow non-Europeans to become Australian citizens. A decade later, he told the House of Representatives that 'many of the peoples of Asia can point to cultures dating back centuries before those of Western Europe'.[9] He was effectively supported by the Deputy Leader of the Opposition, Gough Whitlam, who rebuked the Government for continuing racial discrimination in Australia's immigration policy. The case of Aurelio Locsin, a university graduate man from the Philippines denied permanent residence in Australia in 1965, prompted the Filipino delegate at the United Nations (UN) Commission on Human Rights to declare the 'growing resentment in this country to the White Australia Policy' and the need for a resolution to eliminate racial discrimination 'in all its forms, wherever it exists'.[10]

By the time a series of UN resolutions on discrimination were formally tabled, the Australian Government had modified its conditions for naturalisation and expanded entry conditions for non-Europeans. A pamphlet outlining the changes, entitled *Australia's Immigration Policy*, was produced and distributed to all non-European embassies. The Malaysian Prime Minister, Tunku Abdul Rahman, said the reforms were 'a step in the right direction' and showed Australia had a genuine 'desire to be more friendly with Asian countries'.[11] The Madras newspaper, *The Hindu*, told its readers that the White Australia Policy had been 'a major stumbling block' but the 'liberalisation that is now planned would help Australia forge firmer friendships with Asian countries'.[12] The Adelaide *Advertiser* suggested that while Holt and Opperman 'may not have finally buried the White Australia Policy with their announced changes . . . they have at least given it a decent covering'.[13] There were other reforms. In August 1967, the word 'British' was dropped from the front cover of Australian passports (Holt had reintroduced it in 1950 after Labor removed it the previous year) and the Government announced that it planned to amend the *Nationality and Citizenship Act* to change the designation 'British subject' in the text. Australia was no longer an overtly nor purely 'British' nation.

Between March 1966 and March 1968, approximately 3000 Asians were granted Australian citizenship. This was almost as many as those requesting Australian citizenship in the decade before the policy changes were announced. Within three years (1965–68), the percentage of Asians in the total number granted permanent residency more than doubled from 3.7 per cent to 7.7 per cent. But the extension of citizenship to Asian migrants was slightly less than 1 per cent of the number of Europeans granted citizenship in the same period.[14] Not everyone applauded the changes. Vestiges of the old Australian racism persisted. Holt was told by one angry correspondent that:

I have been a life time Liberal supporter and a strong believer in our part in the Vietnam War but I strongly object to our soldiers fighting and being killed to protect our country while the government gives it away to the Maltese grubs, Italian, Arabs and other coloured people so readily seen in Australian streets.[15]

It is noteworthy that the Labor Opposition indicated that it would oppose any further relaxation of the White Australia Policy. But Holt regarded these reforms as 'of fundamental importance in the development of Australian foreign policy and the search for friendly relations with non-European countries'.[16] Although these policy changes were cautious and constrained by qualifications, Holt should nonetheless be credited with beginning the formal deconstruction of the White Australia Policy. The Whitlam Government would complete the task by removing race, colour or creed as a basis for immigration control. No change in legislation was needed as, thanks to Holt, the old policy had gone. 'The policy that had been a necessary precondition for Australia's status as a homogenous nation and a founding principle of national life was no longer at the heart of national self-determination.'[17]

For the greatest part, Holt found that the job of Prime Minister was more reactive than proactive. He was confronted not only by the continuing routine business of government but a succession of real and purported national crises. Although the economy was buoyant, business and trade union leaders were disappointed that Holt's first statement on economic matters was neither adventurous nor creative. There was evidence of a slight increase in unemployment, real wages were declining, housing approvals were down and the growth in Gross Domestic Product was minimal. Sections of the media noted that Australia's 'stop-go' economy had 'come to a Holt'. While business wanted the Government to stimulate economic growth, the ACTU asked the Government to consider the needs of pensioners and social security recipients. Although McMahon showed very early that he was willing to dispute and reject formal Treasury advice, Holt was disinclined to initiate a major government spending program for fear of increasing inflation. When rising costs caused problems for major projects such as the Ord River Scheme and the Mount Newman Mine, Commonwealth investment was at the lower end of expectations. The same was true of drought relief. The persistence of a severe drought that had begun in 1965 occupied Holt's first weeks in office and provided a chance to accumulate some goodwill with his Coalition partner. Holt said that Commonwealth financial assistance 'would cover whatever deficit [the States] might have in their budget as a result of drought relief measures their Governments might take'.[18] A month later he announced the establishment of a new system of farm loans. The scheme would cost $50 million and 'provide primary producers with greater access to medium and long term finance through the banking system for farm development purposes, including measures for drought recovery and mitigation of future droughts'.[19] He was criticised by various lobby groups for giving too little too late as he prepared for his first major overseas visit (described in detail in Chapter 11).

After being absent in South-east Asia for a month, Holt hosted the Premiers' Conference on 16–17 June 1966.[20] Later in the month he departed for his second overseas trip, this time to Washington and London. On his return in mid-July, he was occupied with economic consultations and the Budget session of Parliament. McMahon gave the tag 'stimulative' to his first Budget, delivered on 16 August 1966. The critics thought it was more a case of 'half speed ahead' as increases in government spending were less than expected. The exception was in Defence spending which increased by 34 per cent to 1 billion dollars. There were small increases in age and war pensions, education and foreign aid. This meant the Government did not need to increase taxation, something it wanted to avoid before the election the Liberal Party organisation sought in early November. In late August Holt departed for the Commonwealth Prime Ministers' Conference in London. He returned on 17 September, suffering from a mild bout of viral pleurisy that confined him to bed for a few days. When he returned to work, Holt began to prepare for US President Lyndon Johnson's historic visit to Australia.

Johnson was three weeks younger than Holt and entered the United States House of Representatives in 1937. He served in the South Pacific with the United States Navy during World War II and met Holt for the first time at Melbourne in 1942. After assuming the Presidency on John F. Kennedy's death, Johnson managed to secure 61 per cent of the vote and the biggest margin of victory in any American presidential election. There were, then, many parallels between the two men's political careers. Johnson and Holt hit it off from the start and developed a deep and mutual affection. Holt had invited Johnson to visit Australia as a prelude to the Manila

Conference on Vietnam to be held on 24 October 1966. The visit, the first by an incumbent President, was also timed to allow its residual effects to be felt at the ballot box at the House of Representatives election set for 26 November 1966. Johnson wanted to visit Australia for personal reasons— he had spent some time in various parts of Australia during June 1942—but the visit suited the Johnson Administration politically as well. Given that Calwell had pledged a Labor Government to the immediate withdrawal of Australian forces from South Vietnam, the United States hoped that the Coalition would be returned to office although Johnson told Holt on 15 October that he hoped there would 'not be any partisan implication' in his visit.[21] Johnson knew, of course, that his trip would assist the Coalition at the ballot box. Although Presidential adviser Walt Rostow told Johnson on 28 September 1966 that Holt was 'likely to be returned',[22] such a visit would further increase his chances of winning. A United States President had never visited Australia, but opinion was divided on the visit's merit and timing. Calwell thought and said the visit was a political propaganda stunt and referred to the major American political parties as 'two empty bottles'. But the Liberals were concerned that the visit would elicit electorally unhelpful anti-American sentiment. Holt was obliged to state that there were 'no political motives behind the visit'.[23] He told Johnson on 7 October that there had been some adverse comment from Labor but it reminded him of a comment by a former colleague about one of his critics: 'he would find politics in the Lord's Prayer'.[24] In developing the President's itinerary, Holt said his aim was to give him a 'wide exposure' to Australia and its people.

Johnson arrived at RAAF Base Fairbairn in Canberra on the afternoon of 20 October and was accommodated with his entourage at the Canberra Rex Hotel.[25] David Moore's famous photograph of Holt standing behind Johnson and appearing to bow in submission (he was actually looking down at a microphone cable) was taken during the press conference held at Fairbairn. After dining at The Lodge, Johnson returned to the Rex Hotel via a back door, thus avoiding the 1000 anti-war protesters who maintained a vigil outside the hotel for the duration of his visit. The President visited the Australian War Memorial the following day and then made a short visit to Melbourne, returning to the Rex Hotel in the evening. On 22 October Johnson went to Sydney.

The Askin Liberal Government organised the distribution of 100 000 Australian flags and the same number of lapel badges to children lining the route of the motorcade. The official theme was 'Make Sydney Gay for LBJ'.

Sydney's Anzac Parade was temporarily renamed 'President Johnson's Way'. Holt was in the car with Johnson, along with Premier Robin Askin and the American Ambassador, Ed Clark. When anti-war demonstrators threw themselves on the road in Liverpool Street ahead of the Presidential motorcade, Askin is supposed to have told a police superintendent to 'ride over the bastards'. According to another version of the event, when the President's vehicle came to a halt, a police superintendent put his head through the car window and was asked by Askin, 'What's the trouble?' The police officer replied, 'Oh, some commos are lying on the road, we'll pull them off.' At a subsequent luncheon hosted by the American Chamber of Commerce, Askin quipped that it was 'a pity we couldn't run over them'. Although a private function, Askin's remark was overheard by journalists and duly reported. As his audience had laughed at Askin's remark and seemed to concur with his description of the demonstrators as 'the great unwashed', he evidently concluded that this bravado would help rather than hinder him politically so did not protest about its reporting. In 1981, Askin gave another, sanitised version. He claimed that after he told the police superintendent to ride over the demonstrators, the policeman asked, 'What do you really want me to do?' Askin replied, 'Grab them by the heels and drag them away.'[26] In her own inimitable style, Zara said she could:

> respect the feelings of people who demonstrate against things in Australia if they're dedicated. Possibly it is the only way they can get a public hearing. They can't get on TV. They can't get into the papers. They can write letters but they'd probably never be printed. Perhaps demonstrations are the only way they can get a hearing, but I don't understand their logic when they are demonstrating against violence, to be violent themselves.[27]

Johnson returned to Canberra for a reception at Lanyon Homestead (an historic farmhouse in the south of the Australian Capital Territory) to which 750 official guests were invited. After another night at the Rex Hotel, he left for Brisbane, Townsville (where he had also served with the US Navy during World War II) and then the Manila Conference. On leaving Australia Johnson wrote to Holt: 'My visit to Australia has indeed been all for which I might have hoped. In addition to evoking many wartime memories, it has shown me the amazing progress made by Australia in the post-war period'.[28]

After the Manila Conference, Holt began campaigning for the 26 November election. This would be his first electoral challenge as Prime

Minister and he needed an emphatic victory after two disappointing by-elections earlier in the year. The Dawson by-election had been held on 26 February 1966 following the death of the sitting Country Party member, George Shaw, on 9 January 1966.[29] Although depicted in the press as a popularity poll for the new Prime Minister, local infrastructure development emerged as the key issue. Holt was expected to take a low-key part in the campaign but made several appearances in support of the Country Party candidate, John Fordyce, to demonstrate his personal commitment to the Coalition. In the belief that the Government would win comfortably, Holt nonetheless set himself up for a fall by claiming that a 'Government victory was important to the nation and as an indicator to people overseas of the state of the electorate'.[30] Holt was unnecessarily tying the Coalition's fortunes to a minor by-election, whose result could not influence the government of Australia.

Despite personal appearances by the two most senior members of the Government (Holt and McEwen), the Labor candidate, Dr Rex Patterson, won the seat with a swing of 13.7 per cent (in the absence of a DLP candidate). Although both the *Courier Mail* and the *Australian* believed that Holt had helped Fordyce's campaign, Patterson was a very good candidate and well known through his previous work as the Director of Northern Development in the Department of National Development.[31] This was the first Coalition by-election loss since 1952 and it led Holt to concede that by-elections are 'notoriously unreliable guides to the state of public thinking on national issues, and the special local features of this campaign put the result very much in that category'.[32] The media did not remind Holt of his previously fulsome remarks. In any event, no blame for the disappointing result could reasonably be laid on the new Prime Minister, but there were those who mistakenly claimed that Menzies had never lost a Government seat in a by-election (the seat of Flinders was lost in 1952). Holt had lost one within his first month as leader.

The second by-election of Holt's tenure as Prime Minister was prompted by his predecessor's resignation from the House of Representatives.[33] The Liberal candidate in the Kooyong by-election was the youthful Andrew Peacock, the Victorian State President of the Liberal Party. Menzies had supported a move to persuade Victorian State Minister Rupert Hamer to run for preselection. Hamer declined the offer, believing (correctly) that he would be Henry Bolte's successor as Premier of Victoria. Peacock was well known to Holt, not only through the Party's State organisation but also because the legal firm in which Holt remained a partner had merged with the firm in which Peacock had a practice. The Labor candidate, William Cooper, tried to make the by-election a poll on the Vietnam War, while Peacock's campaign launch was disrupted by violent anti-Vietnam demonstrations. Unsurprisingly, Peacock's strategy was to highlight Liberal Party unity in contrast to ALP disunity. Speaking in support of Peacock, Holt tried to outline the 'Domino Theory' and the need to halt Communism in South Vietnam before it 'spread unchecked through South-east Asia'. When the protests became so loud he could not be heard, and a woman threw marbles at him to symbolise 'the [conscription] lottery of death', he wisely abandoned his speech.[34] The campaign launch had turned into a fiasco and Holt had become the focus for hostility and anger. No one believed the Government would lose Kooyong but there was a marked swing of 7.1 per cent away from the Liberal Party, evenly split between Labor and the DLP. While Calwell claimed it was the start of a 'downward slide for the Government', Holt replied that it would be 'unrealistic and misleading to attach too much significance to the Government's reduced majority'. Holt also pointed out that this was the first time the Labor Party and the DLP had run serious campaigns in Kooyong.[35]

The Federal election campaign had effectively started from the middle of the year. On 28 June Calwell said that if he did not win he would resign and serve under someone else's leadership until his term expired. This was an attempt to placate Whitlam, who could now be clear about Calwell's intentions and how long he would have to wait for the leadership. Aware that Whitlam was more attractive to the electorate than Calwell, Liberal Party tacticians said 'the attack should not be directed to Mr Calwell but to what we might call the Calwell–Whitlam axis. It is demonstrable that Mr Whitlam has consented to repudiate his so-called Right-Wing beliefs and identify himself with the Left-Wing policies sponsored by Mr Calwell. It should be our aim to show the electorate that the Parliamentary Labor Party has elected to follow the Left-Wing master of the ALP'.[36]

It was an election campaign marred by violence. Not only did Peter Kocan shoot Calwell outside Mosman Town Hall but Holt faced the rowdiest meeting of his political career in Rockdale where he was heckled and jostled.[37] The election campaign also revealed simmering organisational tensions within the Liberal Party. In June the Queensland Division of the Liberal Party called for nominations for all eighteen House of Representative seats, including those held by two Country Party ministers—Charles Adermann (Fisher) and Charles 'Ceb' Barnes (McPherson). The Country Party was outraged by the Liberals' decision to make these elections three-cornered contests. Within 24 hours, Holt intervened to express his disapproval of the Division's action. He said 'he could not join in opposing loyal Cabinet colleagues'.[38] Holt met with the Queensland State President, Dr Hartwig, and the decision was reversed.

On 8 November Holt delivered a pre-recorded policy speech for television and radio. It was a tightly controlled event and confined to the issue of 'external security coupled with a forward-looking domestic program'. The Liberal Party organisation had earlier told the Prime Minister that 'Great Debates' between the main party leaders had 'no positive vote-winning value and should be avoided if possible'.[39] It had been decided not to deliver the main policy speech at a public meeting because it 'would involve serious risk of demonstration and interruption'. Described by a *Sydney Morning Herald* media commentator as a 'recitation', Holt had clearly 'been over and over his lines so that he used the teleprompter rarely. His voice was expressionless and utterly without force. The script was so crammed that the most ardent Liberal could not digest a fraction of it'.[40] Holt could, however, draw consolation from the fact that Calwell's performance was described as far worse.

The 'core' of the Government's election policies revolved around national security and defence with its campaign slogan taking the form of a question: 'It's your choice: where do you draw the line against Communist aggression?'. Holt pledged to increase the size of the Australian Army from 22 750 to 40 000 with the assistance of National Service intakes. He contrasted the stability of the Coalition Government with the 'disunity and disarray' evident in the Labor Party after Whitlam's unsuccessful challenge of Calwell in May 1966.

> All that we plan and hope for Australia must not be put at risk—so far as we Australians can order events—by what occurs outside Australia; and we have much to hold fast to and build upon inside our country . . . [The ALP] refuses to acknowledge, or it runs away from, the great central fact of modern history—the tremendous power conflict between the communist world and the free world. The foreign policy of every country is affected incessantly by this conflict . . . Yet the Labor Party dismisses all this as a bogey. What a delusion! . . . [The] support we and others are giving in South Vietnam is not only helping the people of South Vietnam resist aggression. It is providing a shield behind which the new Asia can emerge and grow stronger. The presence of ourselves and other friendly forces is not a commitment to war; it is a commitment to peace and freedom.[41]

Holt's speech was long on the familiar anti-Communist rhetoric but short on details of how and when the war would be won. On the domestic front, Holt said the Government would create a new Ministry of Education and Science; allocate funds for new teacher training colleges; double grants to independent schools for the building of science blocks; ease the means testing of pensions; increase investment in water conservation projects; expand research in the wool industry; and establish an Australian Tourist Commission.

At Labor's campaign launch on 10 November, Calwell pledged his party to increased social service benefits; $20 million in new funding to the states for schools; additional investment in northern development projects; introduction of stricter controls on foreign investment; creation of a national fuel policy; and the conduct of a referendum to give the Commonwealth control over prices and interest rates. Calwell reiterated his promise to end conscription, discharge all National Servicemen and withdraw Australian troops from South Vietnam. The *Australian Financial Review* thought that Calwell's speech was 'not so much a policy as pop-art pastiche; something for everyone, so long as it has been rejected elsewhere'.[42] There was little new and nothing much to excite. Calwell had recently turned 70 and was depicted as a tired, old man. In sum, the media lamented, his speech was a restatement of past policies with which the electorate had already expressed its disapproval. Labor's position was weakened further when Calwell's pledge to withdraw all Australian troops from South Vietnam was contradicted by Whitlam, who was quoted as saying that a Labor Government would consider withdrawing the conscripts while leaving Regular Army personnel in place. Holt had earlier told President Johnson that Whitlam believed the Vietnam War was winnable within two years.[43] Calwell spiced up the debate with uncharacteristic personal abuse. He accused Holt of 'checking out' of World War II and alleged that his three stepsons were doing the same over South Vietnam.[44] These rather cheap shots did nothing for Calwell's electoral standing.

The *Bulletin* spoke for many when it said that Calwell would lose the election for Labor more than Holt would win it for the Coalition.

Mr Holt has been far too generous in his assessment of the Labor Party . . . Mr Calwell would like to see Australia a cosy little isolated British community, without people from continental Europe, let alone any other fearful regions. This is the dream of a very old man, living in the Australia he knew

168

before his days as Minister for Immigration a quarter of a century ago. A harmless enough dreamer perhaps, but to dream of an Asia from which we can disengage and isolate ourselves is in fact very dangerous in a person with aspirations of power.[45]

Most commentators predicted a Government victory, with public support for the Coalition hovering around 50 per cent for most of the year while that for Labor rarely topped 40 per cent. The Morgan Gallup polls had Holt's personal approval rating at 60 per cent, Calwell's at 24 per cent. For most of 1966, it appeared that the Federal Labor vote would fall below the 1963 figure of 46 per cent.

The only unknown factors were the Liberal Reform Group which ran candidates to express Liberal 'dissent' over Holt's policy on Vietnam and the activities of the Basic Industries Group (BIG). This was a lobby group allegedly bankrolled by the wealthy Queensland grazier Charles Wilfred Russell. Russell had fallen out with Sir Arthur Fadden in the 1950s and BIG was funding Liberal candidates to campaign against incumbent Country Party members. But in a much larger sense, BIG symbolised the hostility between McEwen and McMahon and reflected deep ideological differences within the Coalition parties. BIG opposed protection and believed that high tariffs had actually increased costs for primary producers. As BIG claimed it did not wish to harm the Coalition, its campaign was limited to five rural seats where Country Party voters would be urged to vote for Liberal candidates—Corangamite, Indi and Wimmera in Victoria, and Canning and Moore in Western Australia. But dissent within the Coalition was not restricted to BIG. Liberal Minister Gordon Freeth openly attacked the Country Party generally and McEwen personally while campaigning in rural Western Australia. McEwen responded in kind, alleging that the Liberal Party was behind BIG. This was untrue and McEwen probably knew it but, for the sake of unity, Holt publicly assured the Country Party that no endorsed Liberal candidate was supporting BIG's activities. He also insisted that all Cabinet members accepted the Government's tariff policies. Despite the controversy, BIG would fail electorally; all Country Party members it targeted would retain their seats. As the campaign drew to a close, Menzies sent Holt a telegram from the United States: 'Good wishes for a great Government victory on Saturday. It will be well received here'.[46]

When counting was complete, Labor had lost 12 seats and was reduced to 41 Members in the 123-seat House of Representatives. The Liberals captured 50 per cent of the vote which translated into 61 seats—just two short of an absolute majority. Holt enjoyed a sizeable swing of 3.2 per cent in his own electorate of Higgins, almost entirely at the expense of Labor's Bruce Phayer who polled only 25.2 per cent of the primary vote. (First preferences for the DLP's Frederick Skinner remained virtually unchanged at 11.6 per cent.) Holt's only worry had been the possibility of facing a candidate who had changed his name to Holt, presumably in order to confuse the electorate. The man did not become a candidate although the Electoral Commission said he was free to use the name Holt. In securing a primary vote of 63.3 per cent, Holt returned to the level of support he had experienced during the 1950s. He had also recovered all of the first preferences lost in the disastrous 1961 election. For its part, the Country Party gained only 1 new seat to bring its total to 21. The Government had increased its overall majority by 20 seats.

This was the ALP's biggest electoral defeat in any poll since 1931. Graham Freudenberg thought the 1966 election 'was a decisive rejection of the leadership—not just Calwell for the people had decided that in 1963—but for the whole way the Party had developed in the previous decade . . . whether they knew it or not, the Australians in confirming Harold Holt as their continuing Prime Minister had also vested Gough Whitlam with the leadership of the Australian Labor Party'.[47] But Calwell refused to be the scapegoat or to give Holt any credit for the Government's victory. He claimed that Labor's defeat could be attributed to 'the long sustained attacks on my leadership by a vicious press campaign and other means. The party was defeated because of whipped up fear of communism that was quickly forgotten once the elections were over. I was not responsible for our defeat'.[48] Well, yes and no. Calwell was vulnerable because it was evident to the press and a large section of his Party that he could not defeat Holt. He also failed to present any practical solution to widely held fears that Communism would destroy most of the democracies in the region. Holt deserved to win as much as Calwell deserved to lose. But the Government could not count on the continuing prospect of an unpalatable Opposition being rejected by the electorate. Holt had to attract votes, not merely assume them. This first election victory had been so easy that it led to complacency and a confidence that would prove misplaced.

There were two other down-sides to Holt's tremendous success. The first was the composition of the Senate. During the previous Parliament, five Senators had died. Four were from the Coalition (Seddon Vincent,

Harrie Wade, Sir Shane Paltridge and Robert Sherrington) and one from Labor (Charles Sandford). Sir William Spooner, a Liberal Senator from New South Wales, had also resigned. It was customary for 'casual vacancies' to be filled by nominees from the same party.[49] Section 15, paragraph 2 of the Constitution required those filling casual vacancies to face the people at the next scheduled Federal ballot, irrespective of whether it was for the Senate or the House of Representatives. In the case of the six Senate vacancies created between 1964 and 1966, this was the November 1966 House of Representatives election. There were single vacancies to be filled in New South Wales and Queensland, and two in both Western Australia and Victoria. New South Wales and Queensland would have a single ballot paper for each 'special' election and the Coalition was expected to retain both positions through the system of proportional representation.

In relation to Victoria and Western Australia, the Coalition received internal legal advice that there could be three ballot papers in each State: one for the scheduled House of Representatives election, and one for *each* of the two Senate vacancies. In other words, the Coalition could have separate ballots for each vacancy and would be able to retain its seats by achieving a 'quota' in each of the two separate Senate elections. The issue of a single ballot paper did not matter in Victoria—one Senate seat had been held by the Coalition, the other by Labor. In Western Australia, where the Coalition held both seats, it was crucial.

But Holt had also received advice from the Attorney-General's Department. It was concerned that the conduct of two separate elections would be challenged in the High Court.[50] This presented Holt with a dilemma that would in all probability affect Government control of the Senate. If he conducted two separate elections to fill the vacancies, he would possibly win both seats but probably have the outcome contested by the Labor Party in the High Court. Indeed, Whitlam said in the House that Labor would have challenged the result in the High Court if the Government had conducted two separate elections.[51] Melbourne *Herald* journalist Harold Cox had mentioned as early as 21 January 1966 that the two vacancies would have to be filled by a single election and that the Government would probably lose control of the Senate.[52] Holt was not inclined to risk legal action to preserve his majority.

Cabinet decided to act on the advice it had been given and Parliament passed the *Senate Elections Act 1966* ahead of the scheduled election. In instances where there were two or more causal vacancies in one state, 'the election to fill those vacancies shall be conducted as one election'.[53] This meant there had to be one ballot paper for both vacancies in Western Australia and virtually assured Labor of one Senate place. Reg Withers, who had replaced Sir Shane Paltridge earlier in the year, was placed after Peter Sim (who had replaced Seddon Vincent) on the Liberal ticket. As expected, Withers lost his place in the Senate. (He would regain his place at the November 1967 half-Senate election and resume his place in mid-1968.) The Coalition no longer had a majority in the Senate. After the election, the Federal Director of the Liberal Party, J.R. Willoughby, reminded Holt of a proposal made by the 'All Party Joint Committee on Constitutional Review' to change the Constitution to allow a Senator to 'hold his place until a) the expiry or dissolution of the second House of Representatives to expire or be dissolved after he was chosen b) the dissolution of the Senate, whichever happens first'.[54] It was all too late to help the Government in 1967.

The second down-side was the sheer magnitude of the Coalition's victory. The Government's enormous majority had some unexpected and unwanted consequences. One observer at the time later remarked:

> the size of his victory carried its penalty. The new Liberal members knew little of the old days of defeat and struggle before 1949. They knew little about Holt and he knew little about them. The disarray of the Opposition was so great, the causes of its defeat so obvious that the new Liberals held little personal gratitude towards Holt. No member of the Government believed that Holt was the architect of its victory. Certainly there was great goodwill towards him, but that was because he was such a decent, likeable fellow. No one regarded him as the indispensable man.[55]

Despite having a mandate to choose whomever he wanted after such a stunning success, Holt's Cabinet remained largely unchanged. Nigel Bowen QC, an eminent Sydney barrister, entered the Ministry as Attorney-General. Hubert Opperman became High Commissioner in Malta; Fred Chaney became Chairman of the Joint Public Works Committee after failing in a bid for the speakership and was replaced as Navy Minister by the Victorian Liberal, Don Chipp. Holt explained the exclusion of Chaney by pointing out that there were too many West Australians in the Ministry although some suspected it was a judgment on his handling of the tragic loss of HMAS *Voyager*. Chaney's departure concerned Hasluck who doubted the Liberal Party would win three of the five seats it needed to secure in the 1967 half-Senate election to hold its present position. 'The good results you have had in other parts of Australia in establishing a favourable impression of yourself as Prime Minister have not yet been felt in Western Australia.' He spoke of an anti-Federal mood and resentment towards New South Wales in particular. 'While I would not go so far as to say there is any anti-Holt feeling there is "non-Holt" feeling to contrast with the "pro-Whitlam" feeling'. He urged Holt to make an extended tour of Western Australia in 1967.[56]

By Christmas 1966, Holt appeared to be at the pinnacle of his political career. His brother wrote: 'What a win! You have now won the office the way you've always wanted to win it and have proved that you can win votes with the best of them'.[57] He had achieved what was then a record majority. He had proved himself a popular leader at home and abroad. The Parliamentary Party was in good shape and appeared to be standing in unity behind him. He was also enjoying his work. And he had every reason to believe the fresh mandate the people had given him would sustain the Liberals in office well beyond the next election. Holt could realistically expect to remain in power at least until the 1972 election. By that time, he would be considering retirement. But there was still much to be done.

CHAPTER 11

'All the Way': External Affairs

1966–67

ON ASSUMING OFFICE IN January 1966, the new Prime Minister felt that his Government's main concerns would arise from Australia's dealings with the wider world. Although he had been in Parliament for more than 30 years, Holt could not claim any special expertise in security or diplomacy. But as a senior Minister he had become a foundation member of Cabinet's Foreign Affairs and Defence Committee when it was formed on 22 January 1963. He had also had extensive dealings over the previous fifteen years with foreign governments in relation to immigration and financial institutions. The Committee's records reveal that Holt's opinions did not vary substantially from those of Menzies on foreign policy although he advocated shifting the diplomatic focus from Britain and Europe to the United States and Asia. While Menzies believed Asia was 'a land mass to be crossed over, preferably on the way to London', Holt saw it as a place 'where millions of people live, representing half the world's population'.[1] He was also in favour of expanding Australia's commitment to the war in South Vietnam, although Hasluck and McMahon both believed that Australian involvement should not be extended beyond the Australian Army Training Team Vietnam (AATTV), first deployed in 1962. Holt argued in favour of Cabinet's decision to deploy a combat battalion to South Vietnam in April 1965.

Holt's personal approach to the conduct of foreign affairs was, however, substantially different from that of his predecessor. Whereas Menzies was given to acting unilaterally and consulting Cabinet only in relation to major decisions, Holt thought of himself as a 'roving ambassador' whose role extended well beyond theory to its practice. Holt saw his overseas visits as 'primarily of an educational kind, with the added objective of establishing personal relations with heads of governments in other countries'.[2] Most observers recognised that Holt excelled in diplomacy of this sort where his personal charm and outgoing character built bridges of friendship and enhanced bonds of trust. This was in striking contrast to the Minister for External Affairs, Paul Hasluck, who shunned publicity and did not approve of Holt's strategy of building diplomatic ties on the strength of relationships between national leaders. Indeed, Hasluck remarked:

> When he went to some Asian country for the first time and was received with honour and goodwill he imagined that his own 'instant diplomacy' had immediately created the goodwill and that the honour was due to a personal diplomatic triumph, while of course we knew that the goodwill had resulted from years of conscious, careful and calculated effort by the Australian Government, and its officers in a succession of situations.[3]

This is quite unfair on two grounds. First, Holt's personal style added to each overseas visit and its value to Australia. He was liked and respected. He was not a diplomatic liability and tended to gain the confidence of foreign leaders more than most. Second, Holt recognised that his role was to lubricate the wheels of government and diplomacy and, other than in a few isolated instances, did not seek to supplant Hasluck nor claim credit for achievements that belonged properly to the Department of External Affairs. Holt also managed to maintain very close and productive relationships with Democratic President Lyndon Johnson and Labour Prime Minister Harold Wilson although they both led parties of a rival political persuasion.

The day after Holt became Prime Minister, the UK Secretary of State for Defence, Denis Healey, met the Australian Cabinet to discuss Britain's contribution to defence and security 'east of Suez'.[4] Although a 1965 Gallup poll had found that 43 per cent of respondents named the United States as 'Australia's best friend', followed by Britain with 39 per cent (New Zealand was third with just 6 per cent), Holt believed emphatically in the Commonwealth and stressed the unifying link of the monarchy. Although personally more attracted to Americans than Britons, Holt recognised the continuing importance of Britain in Australia's affairs. In 1965, he privately told the High Commissioner in London (former Cabinet colleague Sir Alexander Downer) that he was concerned for the political plight of Harold Wilson's Labour Government after it had won the 1964 election with a majority of just five seats, a margin judged insufficient for a full term in office.

> The well-being of the United Kingdom whether it be in the economic field or its status in international affairs means so much to Australia. There is no satisfaction to be felt in the discomfiture of a Government drawn as it is from a rival political camp. I should add that nothing which has so far emerged from the Conservative camp has given us much cause for enthusiasm. I think they would be foolish to dislodge the Socialists so early in the Government's life when so much must be done inside their own ranks before they can make convincing claims to govern again.[5]

In one of his regular missives, Lord Casey told Holt that 'Harold Wilson deserves all the support he can get and I believe he'd appreciate your support and that such support will rebound to our benefit in other directions'.[6] Holt was aware, however, of Wilson's reputation for deviousness and his propensity to change his policies without warning. Sensibly, in seeking Britain's engagement with South-east Asia he did not appeal to any residual Imperial sentiment but to the need for regional stability and British self-interest. (Wilson's Government would be re-elected in March 1966 with an increased majority of 99 seats, the second-largest in Labour's history.)

Healey informed Holt that the British Labour Party believed that defence spending was absorbing too much of the national Budget although Britain had 'no intention of ratting on any of our commitments'.[7] The Wilson Government was determined to reduce expenditure even as it hoped that Australia would be prepared to play a greater part in regional affairs. In effect, he sought an annual Australian financial commitment of around $120 million to maintain British naval and air power in the Indian Ocean and South-east Asia. As Treasurer, Holt had used the occasion of the Sixteenth Annual Citizenship Convention to announce that Australia could not afford to assist financially with regional security because 'any increase in defence expenditure would be at the expense of the present growth rate' and that 'Australia had a balance of activities, including development and defence, which could not be readily altered without creating new problems'.[8] To complicate things further, the Chancellor of the Exchequer, James Callaghan, placed restrictions on British overseas investment in the sterling area. As a rapidly developing nation dependent on an uninterrupted flow of international capital, Australia would be directly affected by the Chancellor's policy as British investment in Australia was greater than that of any other nation. The Chancellor later eased his policy by abandoning the compulsory element in controlling capital exports to the sterling area, but Holt remained concerned about the future shape and substance of the relationship. He was adamant that Britain should not 'turn its back' on South-east Asia. When a British Defence Review was released in late February 1966, Holt welcomed 'its recognition of the retention of the Singapore and Malaysian military bases'.[9]

Holt's other principal concern was South Vietnam. He was told by Australian Defence intelligence that the military situation in Vietnam was favourable but victory was not imminent. By this time, the conflict was already a decade old and Australians had been in Vietnam since 1962, when 30 Australian military advisers had been sent to South Vietnam as the Australian Army Training Team Vietnam (AATTV).[10]

On 29 April 1965, Menzies had announced that Australia had received an additional request from the Government of South Vietnam for combat troops. The AATTV was joined by the First Battalion, Royal Australian Regiment (1RAR), a logistic support group and six RAAF Caribou transport aircraft in January 1966. The United States had also substantially increased its military presence and was bombing selected strategic targets within North Vietnam, yet government and allied forces were still barely holding ground in the face of enemy troop increases. More forces were needed. The United States decided to increase its military commitment while making clear its desire to see Australia do likewise. The Australian Army preferred a two-battalion taskforce rather than the deployment of a separate battalion to South Vietnam although it was severely stretched with units concurrently stationed in New Guinea, Thailand and Malaysia. For its part, the Australian Government continued to be concerned about the internal stability of Indonesia where an unsuccessful Communist coup in 1965 had led to possibly as many as one million deaths.

Within a week of becoming Prime Minister, Holt received President Johnson's advice that he intended resuming the bombing of North Vietnam and hoped for continuing Australian support.[11] On his own initiative, Holt publicly supported Johnson's decision despite Britain's opposition to the strategy.[12] He received another personal note from Johnson thanking him 'most warmly . . . your own personal message of understanding and friendship gave me great encouragement'.[13] Holt then announced that Johnson's running mate in the 1964 election, Vice-President Hubert

Humphrey, would visit Australia on 18–19 February 1966 with roving ambassador Averell Harriman and Special Presidential Assistant Jack Valenti.[14] Although Humphrey said after his arrival in Australia: 'I have not made any request to the Government of Australia for additional forces in Vietnam',[15] the Americans explained privately that they were not satisfied with the proposed Australian increase. The Administration noted that the American Defence budget was 9.7 per cent of its GNP whereas in Australia it was only 4.6 per cent. But first Holt had to convince the Australian people that the war had to be fought and why Australian forces were needed in such numbers.

Holt explained the importance of Australia's presence in South Vietnam in his first 'Report to the Nation', which was delivered on his first day in the House of Representatives as Prime Minister—8 March 1966. (He had already agreed to consider the extent of Australia's continuing commitment to South Vietnam following the Vice-President's visit and after consulting the White House on 5 March.)

> Measuring the availability of Australian troops in the light of our other commitments and in consultation with our allies, and at the request of the Government of South Vietnam, the Government has decided that the battalion will be replaced by a self-contained Australian task force under Australian command . . . and enlarging our contribution to a total of some 4500 men—in effect a trebling of the current strength of our military forces there.[16]

Johnson told him this was 'the most welcome news I have had for a long time'.[17]

Holt explained that the taskforce would comprise a headquarters, two infantry battalions, a SAS squadron, combat support and logistic units, and a team of 100 military advisers, together with a flight of eight RAAF Iroquois helicopters and a flight of Caribou aircraft. Holt also stated that the two battalions to leave for South Vietnam in mid-1967—5RAR and 6RAR—would 'contain a proportion of fully trained and integrated National Servicemen as will all future substantial Australian Army units deployed overseas in that theatre'. The need for such a substantial contribution, Holt said, was plain.

> Australia cannot stand aside from the struggle to resist the aggressive thrust of Communism in Asia and to ensure conditions in which stability can be achieved. Our own national security demands this course. We cannot

be isolationist or neutralist, placed as we are geographically and occupying, as we do, with limited national strength, this vast continent. We cannot leave it solely to our allies—and their national servicemen—to defend in the region the rights of countries to their own independence and the peaceful pursuit of their national way of life.[18]

Holt identified three key elements in the Government's Vietnam policy. The first was assisting South Vietnam in its efforts to resist Communist aggression; the second was to create the conditions in which 15 million South Vietnamese could choose their own form of government; and third, Australia needed to honour treaty commitments and obligations to its allies. In reply, Calwell stated: 'As the Opposition sees it, the Holt Government is just the same old firm the Australian people have had to suffer under for the past sixteen years'.[19] Holt retaliated by questioning the Labor Party's patriotism and its loyalty to the United States alliance. Holt told Johnson that their critics 'will have to admit that we made the right and necessary decisions'.[20] He did not hint at when this admission would be forthcoming.

As part of his emphasis on the growing importance of Asia, Holt commenced a tour of South Vietnam, Thailand, Singapore and Malaysia on 21 April 1966. He was accompanied by the Chief of the General Staff, Lieutenant-General Sir John Wilton, Peter Lawler from the Prime Minister's Department, Private Secretary Frank Jennings and Press Secretary Tony Eggleton.[21] On arriving at Saigon's Ton Son Nhut airport, Holt was met by the Prime Minister of South Vietnam, Air Vice-Marshal Nguyen Cao Ky. Holt's visit was planned to coincide with Anzac Day and included a tour of Australian units. He visited 1RAR at Bien Hoa and met the newly appointed Commander of the Australian Task Force, Brigadier David Jackson.[22] Political commentator Wallace Brown remarked:

Nobody in attendance doubted his sincerity, his political savvy, his showmanship and his bravery, when deliberately conspicuous as a potential sniper target in sparkling white safari suit, he stood on a dais at Bien Hoa airport and addressed 1RAR while in the background Viet Cong mortar bombs were exploding along the heavily guarded perimeter.[23]

As Holt's prepared remarks had been left behind, he was forced to speak 'off-the-cuff' at Bien Hoa and delivered, many believed, one of his best speeches as Prime Minister. Menzies sent Holt a telegram on 2 May: 'Welcome home after a most successful and valuable journey. You have consolidated your position at home and enhanced our reputation abroad. In short, I am proud of you'.[24]

On returning to Australia, Holt angrily denied the claim that National Servicemen were being kept out of the most dangerous operations until after the Federal elections. He said, this 'is a typical piece of Calwell fiction, utterly without foundation, recklessly made, mischievous in its effects and offensive in its implications'.[25] His denial was tragically upheld only two days later, when Holt offered his 'personal sympathy to the parents and relatives of Private Noack . . . Australia has, in its short history, paid a heavy price in human life in the cause of liberty and national survival. no one can foretell what the price will be in South-east Asia'.[26] Errol Noack was the first National Serviceman to be killed in South Vietnam. Although there had been only 51 operational deaths involving Australian servicemen from 1950 to 1 June 1966,[27] and many more men would be killed before Australian forces were withdrawn from South Vietnam, Holt felt Noack's death personally. Bill McMahon's press secretary Peter Kelly recalled being told that Holt was in tears when informed of Noack's death.

Holt was quickly proving himself to be an effective diplomat, able to communicate his Government's desire for closer relationships between Australia and the region. This sincerity did not go unnoticed.

> Observers even in Asian countries not visited by Mr Holt noted the new Prime Minister's excellent style in personal contacts, his concern to maintain effective relations with the press, and above all the fact that he chose to regard Asia as deserving a trip . . . all of which could be described as constituting nothing less than dramatic change in the diplomatic style of Australian prime ministers.[28]

Holt stressed Australia's commitment to regional economic development through the Colombo Plan, the Economic Commission for Asia and the Far East, the Asian Development Bank, the Development Assistance Committee and the United Nation's Conference on Trade and Development. It was obvious to Holt that Australia needed to play a more active part in Asian life to preempt the possible British withdrawal and the identification of South-east Asia as a 'critical battleground for free peoples'.[29] Britain's role continued to be the unknown factor but Holt was grateful for its continuing diplomatic support for the war in South Vietnam despite objecting to facets of its conduct. He explained to Harold Wilson that:

> We and the Americans share the belief that if we can reduce Communist activity to nuisance point or less, the country can be built up economically to form one of the strong links in the chain of friendly countries running around the arc from South Korea to Thailand. Korea and Taiwan are two more case histories of successful resistance to Chinese communism. If South Vietnam can be held, and we believe it can, the whole region will be strengthened.[30]

In announcing that he would visit Britain and the United States in June and July 1966, Holt said 'there were no specific issues which require settling on this occasion, and the purpose of the visit is to make personal contact with the leaders of Government'.[31]

Holt set off for the United States on 27 June with five accredited newspaper reporters on his flight: Alan Reid, Harold Cox, Douglas Wilkie, Frank Chamberlain and Max Walsh. Holt arrived in Washington on 28 June to find that President Johnson had personally upgraded the status of his visit.[32] The main event, originally a small luncheon at the White House, had become a formal reception and was preceded by a ceremonial welcome on the South Lawn with an honour guard and a 19-gun salute.

In reply to the President, Holt delivered what should have been an unremarkable formal address. He began by explaining that Australia was in South Vietnam not because the Americans were there but because his Government wanted to 'hold the line' against Communism.[33] In a rather rambling speech, albeit one read directly from notes, Holt thanked the President 'for the warmth of your hospitality to me today' and assured him that Australian forces would remain in Vietnam 'as long as seems necessary to achieve the purposes of the South Vietnamese government and the purposes that we join in formulating and progressing together'. Holt then departed from his text and concluded with some extemporary remarks he had been thinking about in the car en route to the White House:

> And so, sir, in the lonelier and perhaps even more disheartening moments which come to any national leader, I hope there will be a corner of your mind and heart which takes cheer from the fact that you have an admiring friend, a staunch ally that will be 'All the Way with LBJ'.[34]

The speech had ended on a rousing note and the audience applauded enthusiastically. This was the kind of friend the President needed. Holt's use of the Democratic Party's slogan during the 1964 Presidential election campaign was much appreciated given Holt was on the other side of the political spectrum. It was meant to be a light-hearted gesture of goodwill towards a generous host, but it was a serious mistake. Holt did not understand the sensitivity of Australians to any hint of sycophancy at a time when their nation was emerging from Britain's shadow and asserting its independence.

While the main body of Holt's address was completely ignored and is no longer remembered,[35] those who heard the speech could not have imagined the furore created by its ending or its enduring notoriety in Australian history. Immediate attention was elsewhere. The journalists accompanying the Prime Minister noted with surprise the phenomenal reception Holt received in Washington. One even described it as 'royal'. The Australian Ambassador, Sir Keith Waller, later told Holt that the warmth of Johnson's welcome 'has not gone unnoticed among the diplomatic missions in Washington'.[36] He also remarked that local commentators made much of the contrast between Holt's support for the President and that grudgingly offered by Harold Wilson.

Holt spoke at Washington's National Press Club the following day. After having two days to recover from a packed official and social program, he addressed the Australian–American Association in New York on 5 July before departing for London the next day. Holt said his visit to Britain was an opportunity to become acquainted with the challenges facing the Labour Government and the consequences for Australia of a future British decision to join the European Economic Community (EEC). As most of his engagements would be held in the capital the Prime Minister's party was accommodated at the prestigious Savoy Hotel.[37] He had a 20-minute audience with the Queen on 7 July and was somewhat disappointed that this was not expanded to include lunch. Instead, he received and accepted an invitation to dine with the Governor of the Bank of England. The following day was devoted to meetings with the Commonwealth Secretary and his leading officials. The Australian High Commissioner, Sir Alexander Downer, told Holt before his meeting with Wilson that relations between the United States and Britain 'have seriously deteriorated' and that Holt might use Australia's 'special position' to help both nations resolve their differences.[38] When Holt met with Prime Minister Wilson, he explained that Australia understood Britain's difficulties but merely wanted a British presence in the region and not a massive force.[39]

At a press conference held in Australia House before his departure on 13 July, Holt attacked France's attitude towards the war in Vietnam and seemed to be genuinely mystified by its refusal to offer diplomatic support to the American campaign to preserve the integrity of South Vietnam.[40] He spoke of a number of other European nations but did not mention any by name. He certainly did not mean Britain which had remained generally supportive of the combined efforts to contain Communism in South-east Asia and also maintained a military force to support Malaysia in the face of Indonesia's continuing threats of aggression. Holt spent the weekend with Wilson at Chequers and came away believing that Britain and Australia would continue to share close and cooperative defence and security arrangements in the region. But Johnson had a sense the British were going to change their position and asked Holt on 10 July to make an unscheduled stop on the way home. Holt was told that 'the President would like your views on the atmosphere in London and would like to have a further word with you about the situation in our part of the world'.[41]

By the time he arrived back in Australia on 17 July, Holt had begun to grasp the depth of feeling prompted at home by his now infamous 'All the Way' remark. Max Walsh, who travelled with the Prime Minister, wrote an article for the *Australian Financial Review* headed: 'All the Way with LBJ—But how far with Haiphong?' Gough Whitlam commented that 'Menzies would not have abased himself as much as "All the way with LBJ". He'd reserve that sort of thing for the Queen, "I did but see her passing by . . .". But he wasn't as trivial or as crass as Harold'.[42] Hasluck thought that Holt's remark was 'one of the most harmful slogans we had to counteract in our Asian diplomacy'. Ambassador Waller is alleged to have said that Johnson was 'horrified by Holt's speech, which he saw as politically dangerous for Holt'.[43] (This was completely untrue. Johnson actually thought it quite amusing. During a meeting with President Thieu and Air Vice-Marshal Ky of South Vietnam later in the year, Johnson mentioned the public reaction to Holt's White House speech. One of the Vietnamese leaders said in reply: 'Better all the way with LBJ than half a win with Ho Chi Minh'.) Bruce Grant considered it 'grotesque' and 'the most humiliating statement of single-minded Australian dependence . . . if this was the price of loyalty to the alliance, it had become very high for a self-respecting nation to pay'.[44] Bill Hayden, later Australian Foreign Minister but then a Labor backbencher, said the remark 'shocked and insulted many Australians. Its seeming servility was an embarrassment and a worry'.[45]

Holt was genuinely surprised by the emotion he had aroused and insisted that his statement 'doesn't mean, certainly, that Australia has any lack of independence of mind and anyone who knows the President would be paying him no compliment if they felt that he was looking for the kind of friend who was never prepared to have an argument with him'.[46] In a rather indifferent Press Club speech, Holt attempted to defend his remark by claiming that 'when it comes to American participation, American resolution to see the issue through in South Vietnam, Australia undoubtedly is "all the way"'.[47] On being made aware of the criticism Holt was facing for his show of gushing support, Johnson sent him a personal letter.

> It gave me much pleasure to have you visit Washington last month, and to learn at first hand that you and I see the problems in Vietnam and in the Pacific in the same way . . . I wish others would stand up and speak out in public with the same forthrightness. Too many leaders are saying in private that they support us, but they will not say so in public. Perhaps you can prevail on some of the Prime Ministers attending the Commonwealth Conference—especially those from Asia—that they have a duty and an interest to speak out as you have done. I want very much to stay in touch on these important matters. Do write whenever you feel there is something I should know, and I shall do the same.[48]

While his visit had done much for Australian–American relations despite the local resentments, press reporting of his National Press Club speech had also created problems. The *New York Times* had reported that Holt was critical of British and European apathy and indifference towards Southeast Asia and the Pacific, without including Holt's subsequent statement that the British Government was determined to 'support the American presence in Vietnam' and that the two great democracies would 'maintain a close comradeship in the affairs of the world'. Wilson was angered by Holt's use or misuse of the press coming so soon after what the British Prime Minister thought had been positive meetings. On his return to Australia, Holt's embarrassment was obvious. He told reporters at Sydney Airport that the American press:

> read more into what I said than I intended . . . having regard to his own political difficulties and to the problems he faces at home, Mr Wilson has shown great courage and firmness in the line he has taken in relation to

South Vietnam. It is true that he did not see North Vietnam in the same way that the United States and we did, but he made it clear he was still supporting the American purposes and presence in South Vietnam.[49]

The Australian Prime Minister had learned a hard lesson about international diplomacy and the media. He should have been much more circumspect in his remarks at the White House and avoided any allusion to the British position on Vietnam. He had, however, an opportunity to explain his remarks to Wilson face to face, when he returned to London the following month for the Commonwealth Prime Ministers' Conference.

Nearly half of the 23 Commonwealth countries sent ministerial delegations in lieu of their head of government while President Nyerere of Tanzania refused to attend or be represented. Although Vietnam was on the agenda, the most controversial subject to be discussed during the nine-day conference was Rhodesia and the collective action that ought to be threatened or taken against Ian Smith's rogue government which had issued a 'unilateral declaration of independence' (UDI) from Britain. Most of the African nations were unconvinced by Wilson's apparent hostility to Smith and wanted firm and forceful action to be taken. Holt was emphatically opposed to a military solution, an opposition shared by Malaysia, Canada, New Zealand and Britain. Jamaica and Cyprus preferred UN-endorsed mandatory sanctions. During the discussions, Holt chided the other leaders for being unfairly critical of Britain, and impractical in their prescriptions for the way ahead. He regretted that 'race' had been raised as an issue and noted that Britain, Canada, New Zealand and Australia had all refused to recognise the Smith regime. Holt claimed that the British Parliament would not endorse the use of force while he preferred that the Commonwealth try to resolve the situation, before involving the UN. He would later remark to his friend Rupert Gerard:

> The Africans succeeded in narrowing Harold Wilson's room to manoeuvre, but this did not seem to displease him too much. I rather gathered the impression that this pressure was not too unwelcome as it strengthened his hand in meeting Opposition criticisms in his own Parliament. Whatever his motive, the UK is now under obligation to support the application of sanctions by the UN.[50]

Although reluctant to involve the UN, Holt argued that selective and targeted sanctions were preferable to complete and mandatory embargoes which he felt would ruin the Rhodesian economy and harm its people. Holt said Australia would only agree to mandatory sanctions if Britain were also persuaded of their efficacy.

It was with some relief to the Australian delegation that the Conference finally turned to wider issues of peace and development. Holt believed that the greatest threat to world peace existed in Asia and that recognition of 'mainland' China must include living with other Chinese diplomatic aspirations and admitting China to the United Nations while not overlooking the existence of Taiwan and its fourteen million people. (Two months after the conference, Australia signed a record contract to sell 65 million bushels of wheat to China although accusing the Communist regime of being behind much of the unrest in Asia and the instability in South Vietnam.) Holt told his Commonwealth colleagues that as a member of the South East Asia Treaty Organisation (SEATO), Australia had a duty to assist in the self-defence of South Vietnam. He rejected any suggestion that this was an expansionary policy by reminding the conference that Saigon was closer to northern Australia than Sierra Leone was to Salisbury (the then capital of Rhodesia). In his view, the war in Vietnam was more integrally related to Australia's security than to that of the United States.[51]

A month after Holt returned from London, President Johnson visited Australia. Speaking in the House of Representatives Holt described Johnson's visit as 'one of the most distinguished and notable in the whole history of the Australian Parliament'.[52] Johnson said in reply:

> There is a widening community of people who feel responsible for what is happening in South Vietnam . . . The unilateral use of power is out of date in an age where there can be no losers in peace and no victors in war. And the unilateral reach of compassion is limited. What is required—and what we are seeing emerging in Vietnam and throughout all of Asia—is a concert of effort on the part of diverse nations that know they must work together.[53]

He also attempted to reverse the effect of Holt's White House speech when he said 'Every American and LBJ is with Australia all the way'.

Holt and Johnson departed separately on 23 October for the 'Seven Nation Summit Conference' on the situation in South Vietnam, convened by President Ferdinand Marcos of the Philippines. Holt and Johnson were joined by the leaders of New Zealand, the Philippines, South Korea, Thailand and South Vietnam. Before he left for Manila, Holt was told by Australian Defence intelligence that 'the military situation has improved over the last twelve months despite the efforts of the North Vietnamese and the Viet Cong, but with Allied forces at present available defeat of the military aggression from North Vietnam is unlikely to be achieved for some considerable time'. Holt was also warned by the Australian Ambassador in Manila, Francis Stuart, to expect public criticism of Australia's immigration policy from Filipino officials as 'they do not accept (as many of our other neighbours do) that they cannot gain by criticising the principle of an exclusion policy'.[54] The two-day 'Manila Conference' was widely agreed to have been a success. On his return to Australia on 26 October, Holt told the waiting media, 'I have not attended a conference where there has been readier disposition to find agreement together on matters that counted'.[55] He highlighted the importance of the charter signed by all seven leaders, known as 'Goals of Freedom'. These goals were 'to be freed from aggression; to conquer hunger, illiteracy and disease; to build a region of security, order and progress; and to seek reconciliation and peace throughout Asia and the Pacific'.[56] The tenor of the charter reflected Holt's broader objective on leaving Australia, to respond to Communism on a number of fronts. When asked whether Australia would increase the size of its military contribution to South Vietnam ahead of the forthcoming election, Holt replied, 'I don't make a decision in the absence of my Cabinet . . . I wouldn't accept firm commitments on behalf of Australia in relation to matters of this sort without my Cabinet colleagues being fully informed and having an opportunity to engage in any discussion'.[57] In reality, he had already decided to increase the size and the scope of Australia's involvement in a war of indeterminate length.

Holt made the Vietnam War the principal campaign issue of the November 1966 Federal election although senior Ministers, including Hubert Opperman, had advised him months before that electorate polling had shown that prices and inflation were the key issues. In Opperman's seat of Corio, conscription had ranked seventh and withdrawing Australian troops from South Vietnam thirteenth.[58] Holt nonetheless believed that Vietnam was the defining issue. The Government issued a new Vietnam Policy Statement on 8 November 1966.

Unless there is security for all small nations there cannot be security for any small nation. Unless principles of international conduct are preserved in all international situations they are not likely to be preserved in any. That is the essence of our foreign policy . . . That is why we played our part in the making of the SEATO and ANZUS Treaties which carry with them responsibilities as well as benefits. Because of those responsibilities, Australian soldiers are fighting in South Vietnam. We know and share the genuine concern of responsible Australians about what has been happening there. But we believe our decisions have been right. We seek a peaceful settlement of the conflict through negotiation, but think of the consequences of abandoning our objectives—and the people of South Vietnam. The impact of our complete withdrawal, as proposed by the Labor Party, would be felt through South-east Asia. We, too, would come under threat.[59]

The war gave the electorate a clear choice between the two major parties as well as provoking violent protest and civil unrest. During the campaign, Holt arrived in Brisbane to a warm welcome but during a public address was chastised about his war service by a veteran from his old unit who had lost both his hands in combat.[60] The man said that Holt had 'squibbed out' before the unit went overseas. A similar charge had been levelled at Menzies regarding World War I. At least Holt had joined the Army and had fully intended to serve overseas. Killen recalls that 'his reaction was most unlike him. Harold leapt at his interrogator with the ferocity of a wolf'.[61] With this depth of feeling the November 1966 poll would undoubtedly be a 'khaki' election. Calwell claimed the war in South Vietnam was 'a cruel, unwinnable, civil war, aided and abetted, of course, by the North Vietnamese Government, but neither created nor principally maintained by it'.[62] Labor was committed to the complete and unconditional withdrawal of Australian troops and 'would be completely happy to fight the election on the issue of conscription . . . Our view is that conscription for service in Vietnam is immoral, unjust and a violation of human rights'.[63] Calwell asked 'the Australian people not to cast a blood vote for the Holt Government and conscription. A vote for Labor will be a vote against conscription. Conscription is the issue that faces the nation'.[64] Within the Labor Party itself there was a range of views towards Australian involvement in Vietnam. Those of the anti-Communist Right felt the war was necessary and Australian participation justified. Those on the Left were calling for immediate withdrawal of Australian troops and an end to the fighting. Jim Cairns, surprised that other Asian countries were not perturbed about the presence of Australian forces in Vietnam, believed that 'immediate withdrawal would be not only impractical but inhumane'.[65] The Left wing of the Party believed Cairns had betrayed them and Labor principles. The Government quietened the DLP by listing defence as the Government's top priority. Between 1962–63 and 1967–68 defence spending increased from $420 million to $1.118 billion. The best that the DLP could do was criticise the Government for not countering anti-war sentiment more effectively or pushing for greater defence self-reliance.[66]

— —

Holt's electoral success could be attributed, in part, to his defence and security policies. The *Courier Mail* concluded: 'By voting as they did on Saturday Australians have approved participation in the Vietnam War alongside America, our alliance with America, and the maintenance of a growing army, if necessary by compulsory call-ups or national service'.[67] In a congratulatory telegram, Johnson said:

> The world has taken note of the great vote of confidence given you by your countrymen yesterday . . . With steadfast devotion we will stand by your side as long as freedom is being challenged and peace is being threatened. We know we stand with a man of conviction, integrity and wisdom. We know we stand with a friend.[68]

Calwell protested that Johnson was interfering in Australian politics. This was true but no one was listening.

Buoyed by the electoral landslide and his continuing conviction that US-led forces would be victorious in South Vietnam, Holt proposed increasing the Australian commitment with the deployment of a third infantry battalion.[69] Not all of Holt's Ministers supported the increase. Some thought it unwise given Britain's projected withdrawal east of Suez and could see no pressing need for such a move. Others suspected that Holt had already given a personal undertaking to President Johnson. Senator John Gorton was strongly opposed to any increase:

> if decisions on our force levels are <u>not</u> going to affect the United States' decision one way or the other, I believe that instead of spending the money envisaged on Defence we should spend it on developing and strengthening Australia itself and that that will be of far greater benefit to the progress, safety, and stability of our country [original emphasis].[70]

Rather than providing another infantry battalion or redeploying the battalion then stationed in Malaysia, Holt was persuaded to accept the Defence Committee's advice that an increase in Australia's participation could be achieved by deploying a RAAF Canberra bomber squadron, a RAN guided missile destroyer and another 900 troops. Holt then announced that Australian strength in South Vietnam would increase from 4500 to 6300 personnel.[71]

The Holt Government supported the American military in other ways. On 9 December 1966, the Commonwealth negotiated an agreement for an American satellite base at Pine Gap, near Alice Springs. The joint defence space research facility was an integral part of the US missile early warning defence system. In an interview published in December 1966, Holt said the United States is 'following the path of wisdom and good sense—this is the practical way to prevent areas of Asia from being brought under the domination of an aggressive Communist power ... Without the American shield most of us who live in Asia and the South Pacific would have a continuing sense of insecurity'.[72] Holt also approved the establishment of four new Australian Security Intelligence Service (ASIS) stations in Saigon, Bangkok, Rangoon and Manila. The latter two were opened the week after Johnson visited Australia and partly in response to Britain signalling it was closing its SIS station in Manila in addition to making staff cuts in Rangoon.[73] By this time, Australia was now the most substantial centre for American missile and space operations outside continental United States. As civilian Defence commentator Robert Cooksey observed: 'with its technological and logistic facilities, its political stability and external security, [Australia] is the most suitable piece of real estate for such operations in the southern hemisphere'.[74] In September 1967 Holt opened the North West Cape Naval Communications Station at Exmouth Gulf. Deep space tracking stations were established near Canberra at Tidbinbilla and Honeysuckle Creek. In all of this, Holt never questioned the validity of the domino theory or the American policy of containment.

In his first year as Prime Minister, Holt travelled 125 000 miles. After he increased Australia's commitment to South Vietnam, the Prime Minister of South Vietnam, Air Vice-Marshal Nguyen Cao Ky, expressed a desire to visit Australia. Without consulting his Cabinet colleagues, Holt agreed despite the visit's potential as a diplomatic disaster.[75] In an attempt to counter political and press hostility, Holt despatched Richard Woolcott from the Department of External Affairs to South Vietnam, where he was to brief President Ky on the reception he might receive in Australia but Holt had made a risky decision without adequately weighing all the possible consequences. Ky's arrival on 19 January 1967 drew protest crowds of 6000 people in Sydney and Melbourne. For many, he embodied all that was wrong with South Vietnam. Calwell referred to him as a 'quisling gangster', a 'butcher' and a 'social and moral leper'.[76] But Ky proved to be a humble man and a most capable diplomat. Richard Casey told Holt that Ky 'was able to stress so effectively the progress towards democratic institutions' that his government was making.[77] Although the *Bulletin* described the visit as 'a personal triumph' for President Ky and commended Holt for agreeing, public opposition to the war and Australian involvement in particular was growing.

On 22 February 1967, Federal Cabinet convened to meet with the British Commonwealth Secretary, Herbert Bowden (later Lord Ayle-stone).[78] Bowden assured Holt and the Cabinet that Britain was standing by its decision of the previous year to maintain its military presence East of Suez—for the time being—and discounted backbench pressure for a complete and immediate withdrawal. He claimed that less than 50 Labour parliamentarians supported such action but explained that Britain's annual defence spending was running at 6 per cent of GNP and needed to be cut. The Wilson Government's objective was to maintain the 1964 figure but this was proving difficult. The British presence in Malta would be reduced and, possibly, its NATO contingent. With the end of Indonesia's 'confront-ation' with Malaysia, between a quarter and a third of Britain's 52 000 troops in Malaysia would also be withdrawn and redeployed. But Bowden was adamant that Britain would maintain its commitment to Singapore. Speaking more broadly, Bowden told Cabinet that the Commonwealth could hold together despite its many trouble spots and, in response to a question from Holt, lamented that some on the Labour front bench and even within the Conservative Party doubted whether the Commonwealth remained a worthwhile entity. On economic matters, Bowden explained that Britain was interested in joining the EEC but the reaction of Presi-dent de Gaulle of France was not encouraging. If Britain did negotiate with Europe, there would be full discussions within the Commonwealth about any possible consequences. He also assured the Cabinet that Britain would not depart from the present position of sterling (in which Australia had large reserves) while the Chancellor wanted to end the voluntary restraints he had imposed on investment in the sterling area. No one doubted Bowden's integrity or the right of the British Cabinet to keep possible changes in the value of sterling confidential. Subsequent events, however, showed that the Wilson Government had intentionally misled the Australian Government on the exchange rate of sterling.

From 28 March to 10 April Holt visited Cambodia, Laos, Taiwan and South Korea, flying some 16 000 miles. He was the first Australian Prime Minister to visit these countries and had now covered ten Asian countries in fourteen months. During a stopover press conference in Singapore, Holt talked of the 'special relationship' that existed between Australia and Cambodia, claiming that Australia represented American interests in Phnom Penh and Cambodian interests in Saigon.[79] Holt explained that the purpose of his visit was 'to make contact with four countries of the region, which I've not previously visited, and I hope in this way to make Australia and its policies better known . . . Geography brings us together and, at the same time, there are mutual interests to be served'.[80] He was still optimistic about the role Britain would play in the region but this changed after a regular meeting of the SEATO partners, held in Washington in April. The abrasive British Foreign Secretary, George Brown, told Hasluck that Britain would announce new defence plans in July 1967. In order to reduce military spending further and preserve foreign exchange, Britain would close its Singapore naval base in 1971 and vacate all its facilities on mainland Asia by the mid-1970s. Thereafter, Britain could not provide a forward defence capability and would in all probability be limited to a small civil and support contingent in its colony of Hong Kong. Hasluck sent a cable to Holt. The United States and New Zealand governments were informed at the same time. In addition to alarm among South-east Asian nations, the Americans were furious that the British should even be contemplating a withdrawal at what they considered the worst possible moment in the region's affairs.

On 21 April, Holt urged Wilson to reconsider his proposed reduction in defence outlays in the light of the damage such a policy would have on the United Kingdom's world standing.[81] Appealing to British self-interest, Holt asked Wilson to imagine Asia's future and the economic prospects it offered for British investment. He also suggested to Wilson that he weigh the consequences of America's inevitably hostile reaction. In a tone that bordered on entreaty, Holt reminded Wilson of the abiding importance—military, moral and material—of a British presence in Asia and those parts of the world that aspired to prosperity and stability. Holt told Wilson that developing Asian nations would welcome greater British participation, but a withdrawal would lead many of the newer nations to conclude that

Britain had abandoned them to an uncertain fate when it had the capacity to help them achieve greater independence and responsibility for their own affairs. Wilson replied immediately: 'Our defence expenditure in the Far East represents at the present time a disproportionate amount of our total defence expenditures'. He then outlined Britain's withdrawal options before mentioning that 'None of this as you will understand affects our firm intentions to stand by Australia as Australia stood by us in two world wars'.[82] Holt told the Malaysian Prime Minister, Tunku Abdul Rahman, that:

> My own military people are not happy with technical aspects of British thinking. They cannot see that the British would be able to honour their obligation simply by moving forces into the region from outside . . . I myself very much doubt whether, if the British once withdraw their forces from the Malaysian region, we can confidently expect them to send them back again however sincerely they may intend it now.[83]

Holt did not know that Wilson was already committed to the proposals which, according to some, had been deliberately leaked by Whitehall to the London press.

High Commissioner Downer told Wilson's two Principal Private Secretaries that Holt felt he had been deliberately misled. He was advised that Britain simply could not afford to retain a physical presence 'East of Suez'. The preferred British solution was a highly mobile response force rather than expensive overseas bases. Holt had already decided that a British withdrawal would 'require the recasting of Australian external policy in fundamental terms'.[84] Holt was realistic, telling the British High Commissioner in Canberra that he knew from experience that 'it was impossible to persuade another government to do what they believed to be against their national interest'.[85] The line he adopted was unchanged: maintaining a British presence in Asia was in the United Kingdom's own interest. Holt did not want a British base in Australia nor would the country support its establishment.

In his prompt reply, communicated through the British High Commissioner in Canberra, Wilson assured Holt that he would confer with the Australian Government before any final decisions were made. Holt thanked Wilson for this undertaking, which he believed was sincere, and suggested that Wilson should visit Asia to assess the region's needs and the consequences of a British withdrawal for himself. Holt told Wilson he looked forward to speaking with him further in person when they met in London for official discussions in June. By this time, Britain had decided again to seek membership of the EEC but would again struggle to meet the financial conditions. In private discussions between Callaghan and Downer, it was becoming clear that the price of EEC membership would have to be drawn from substantially reduced defence expenditure. The British people would no longer be denied improved services at home and were prepared to sacrifice Britain's position as a world power. Downer advised Holt to extend his visit to London while suggesting that he ask the Americans and New Zealanders to bring greater diplomatic pressure to bear on the British Government.

Holt told Tunku Abdul Rahman that he would raise Malaysia's concerns when he met Harold Wilson. He explained that Australia accepted Britain's need to reduce expenditure:

> and in this they are entitled to look to understanding from all of us. But withdrawal is another matter altogether, affecting not only defence, but also confidence and development and stability generally . . . without a significant presence the degree of British interest would greatly diminish.[86]

Holt told President Johnson he feared Wilson had made up his mind on withdrawal 'but I nevertheless propose to trade heavily on Wilson's assurance that there are not yet any final decisions'.[87]

The Prime Minister departed on 28 May 1967.[88] He would be absent for four weeks. Holt spent several days on the United States' West Coast, during which he addressed the World Affairs Council in Los Angeles, before travelling to Washington for a White House meeting with President Johnson on 1 June. He then visited Canada for EXPO. He was present at Australia's special day on 6 June. In talks with the Canadian Prime Minister, Lester Pearson, Holt tried to generate new interest in Australia and Canada working together as Pacific powers. The next stop was London for talks with the British Government on the future shape and substance of the British presence east of Suez. Holt met Wilson on 13 June at 10 Downing Street. After a preliminary private conversation, they decided that their discussions should be limited to defence policy as the most pressing issue between the two nations. Wilson gave Holt advance notice of a statement he would make to the House of Commons on 15 June that British intended 'to take speedy action in withdrawing from the Far East every unit whose continued presence there ceases to be necessary'.[89]

Holt told Wilson that this decision had come as a great shock, especially given his previous assurances. Holt again urged him to consider the trade opportunities for Britain in Asia, and highlighted Britain's existing stake in countries like India, Malaysia, Australia and New Zealand. While the Americans were prepared to invest in non-Communist Asia, they considered Malaysia and Singapore to be Commonwealth countries and the responsibility of Britain as the former colonial power. Furthermore, Holt believed the British were morally obliged to consider the effect of such a decision on the Commonwealth as a whole. Although he understood Britain's economic difficulties and accepted the likelihood of some reduction in the British military presence after Indonesia's 'confrontation' with Malaysia:

> We never understood this would precede a complete withdrawal. It is the unanimous wish of the Commonwealth countries, as well as the United States, that in the short term you will retain some flexibility in your thinking regarding the Commonwealth Brigade. It is an example of Commonwealth teamwork—there are not many others. We hope for a sufficient British military component to make it viable. As to your proposed withdrawal from the area by the mid-1970s, we earnestly press you to take no final decisions at this point of time, or announce such decisions.[90]

Healey, who was also present, told Holt that Britain had expected better economic growth than had been achieved during the previous twelve months. Consequently, all areas of government expenditure—not just defence—had to be reduced. As an alternative, the British had in mind an amphibious force based either in Britain or, if the Australian Government agreed, at Cockburn Sound (the site of the present HMAS *Stirling* in Western Australia) that would meet and respond to crises as and when they developed. Wilson emphasised that the proposed force would give the British greater mobility and the opportunity for a wider presence in Asia. As for Malaysia, the internal security of that country was a matter for its government. Healey explained that the British Government had to announce a decision if it was to save the target figure for EEC entrance of £300 million by 1975. He also claimed that most British Ministers wanted the withdrawal to be immediate and it was only through the persistence of Wilson, Brown, Healey and Bowden that such an outcome had been averted.

Although extremely disappointed, at this stage Holt did not feel that the meeting had been a complete failure. His understanding was that Britain would continue its contribution to the Commonwealth Brigade based at Singapore until 1970–71 but that no firm decision had been made for beyond that date to avoid setting off 'a highly damaging chain reaction'. He was also led to believe that Britain had 'decided to maintain a capability for use in the Far East after 1975'.[91] In further talks the next day, Holt urged Healey to find a way of explaining the proposals that would prevent critics from alleging that Britain had abandoned Asia in favour of Europe. Sir Alexander Downer remarked:

> Holt had fought hard not merely for Australia but for all Commonwealth countries affected by Britain's sudden change of course, to which should be added American interests in South-east Asia. His main success lay in a somewhat nebulous promise of a small amphibious British presence in that theatre.[92]

Whether it would be effective was another matter.

But Wilson did not keep his word. A month later, Wilson informed Holt that a Supplementary Statement on defence policy was about to be tabled in the House of Commons. He explained that Cabinet had 'decided to reduce our forces in Singapore and Malaysia to about half the current levels by 1970–71 . . . [and] withdraw our present contributions to the Commonwealth Brigade and complete this process by 1 April 1970 . . . we must plan on giving up our bases in Malaysia and Singapore by the mid-1970s'.[93] To avoid speculation and rumour and to aid forward planning, he would announce as much of the policy as was possible to the British public. In an understatement, he told Holt that 'these have been difficult decisions and we are well aware of the anxieties which you and other partners feel'. It was obvious to Holt that all his arguments had been rejected except for the date of closing the Singapore base. He replied immediately: 'Having had a series of messages from me . . . we regret that they have made so little impact on the collective mind of your Cabinet. We cannot escape the conclusion that involved in your decisions is very much more than economics'.[94] Holt, with some justification, felt betrayed. He believed that Wilson had deliberately deceived him over the previous twelve months. Complete British withdrawal from east of Suez had never been mentioned and Britain's 'Commonwealth partners' were not consulted as promised. Holt felt he had failed completely and was despondent. Wilson could say little in reparation:

> I recognise and fully understand your disappointment that we have not been able to go further to meet your wishes. I am sorry that I have been obliged to convey to you decisions which I knew would be unwelcome to you.[95]

At a hastily convened press conference, Holt expressed Australia's deep disappointment with the decision and referred to Britain's 'lotus land' attitude. His remarks were viewed as controversial and bound to cause offence to the British. Holt did not care:

> we very much regret that the British Government should feel itself impelled to plan now for final withdrawal from Malaysia and Singapore at a date so far ahead, and when it is so difficult to predict how the situation in South East Asia will move.[96]

While he still believed that Britain would continue to be an active player in Asia, Holt had gone to the United States for private talks with Johnson at his Texas ranch. But there was a late change of plan. As the Soviet Prime Minister, Aleksei Kosygin, was travelling to New York for a United Nations' emergency debate on the Middle East, the weekend meeting was relocated to Camp David on 17–18 June. The debate was in response to the Six Day War which had raged during the week of 5 June 1967. When President Gamal Abdel Nasser of Egypt closed the Gulf of Aqaba, Johnson wanted a multinational naval taskforce to break Nasser's blockade. Johnson stated that:

> besides Great Britain and the United States, two other nations had agreed to take part in a naval taskforce. The Dutch had expressed their intention to us in writing. Harold Holt . . . assured me personally in a visit to Washington on 1 June that his country would assign two of its fastest cruisers to the joint task force.[97]

Holt was reported to have described the war as 'only huffing and puffing', not his own words but those of Tony Eggleton, taken from a draft speech prepared within the Prime Minister's Department. Holt was trying to downplay the conflict in order to prevent any diversion of American interest from South-east Asia. The taskforce was not needed. In any event, Australia had no cruisers in its order of battle while the RAN ships that were operational were preparing for deployment to the Far East Strategic Reserve and service off South Vietnam.

Although Johnson and Holt addressed questions of international diplomacy, the main focus of their meeting was on trade and economic questions, particularly the American *Wool Tariff Interest Equalisation Act*. It was a relaxed and largely informal discussion conducted mainly by the poolside. Holt then returned to New York where he addressed the America-Far East Council. He touched on trade and economic relations and said that Australia had received a 'raw deal' from the United States in the recent past. Holt then appeared on NBC's popular 'Meet the Press' television and radio program, which had an estimated audience of 9 million. On his way back to Australia, Holt took part in the inauguration of the American–Australian Association of Honolulu before arriving back in Canberra on 22 June. In a personal letter to Holt, Johnson remarked:

> It was a comfort and a delight as always to have your company, your ideas, and your thoughtful advice these last days at Camp David. They are trying and testing times for us as well. I feel better and stronger, as we face our common trials and the problems of our troubled world, knowing that we understand each other and that we and our peoples are tied together by a friendship and a confidence that will not be severed.[98]

Johnson gave Holt a watch inscribed: 'To HH with the affection of his friend LBJ'. But Holt remained dissatisfied with their discussions on trade and finance, making the point to Johnson that 'the kind of defence contribution we can make, and the pace of national growth, depend upon our trading strength'. The areas of conflict were wool, tobacco and dairy products with Holt claiming that the United States 'takes an unreasonably tough line with us'. He pointed out that Australia's support for the Administration's policy on Vietnam did not seem to influence other areas of the relationship. Holt told Johnson that 'useful gestures' and a 'positive response' were necessary if he were to answer criticisms of trading arrangements.[99] This led some to accuse Holt of exchanging 'diggers' for 'dollars'.

Not long after returning to Australia, Holt hosted the President's special mission in Canberra. General Maxwell Taylor and civilian adviser

Clark Clifford (Secretary for Defense from 19 January 1968) met with Holt and the Cabinet on 29–30 July for 'an exchange of information and views' on Vietnam.[100] The American party was told that Australia was contributing to western security in several places beyond South Vietnam and its forces were, therefore, fully extended. Holt was also in favour of the continued bombing of North Vietnam in an effort to persuade Hanoi that 'the continuation of the war on the present scale is too damaging and costly'.[101] But Clifford was disappointed with the practical elements of Australia's position:

> Surely there was hope here. But Prime Minister Holt, who had been fully briefed, presented a long list of reasons why Australia was already close to its maximum effort. I returned home puzzled, troubled, concerned. Was it possible that our assessment of the danger to the stability of Southeast Asia and the Western Pacific was exaggerated?

And even after Holt subsequently increased the Australian force to three battalions, Clifford remarked that 'Australia, then with a much smaller population, had been able to maintain over 300 000 troops overseas in World War II. They had sent only 7000 to Vietnam'.[102] In a long letter to President Johnson, Holt tried to explain why Australia was constrained economically from doing more in Vietnam, and pointed to the added burdens created by Britain's withdrawal and Australia's increased contributions to Singapore and Malaysia. He concluded: 'I do not mention these things to argue there is nothing more we can do . . . I mention them to demonstrate the complexity of our problem and so that you will have full understanding of our situation'.[103] But Holt faced more than simple logistic problems.

Despite his close personal relationship with President Johnson, the Australian people were rapidly becoming restless about the war in South Vietnam. Australian military personnel had been in South Vietnam for five years, more than 250 Australian servicemen had died and the war appeared no closer to ending in late 1967 than it did in mid-1965 when Australian combat troops were first deployed. When Holt delivered the inaugural Alfred Deakin Lecture on 31 July 1967 he tried to explain the need for perseverance. According to political commentator Gerard Henderson, who was present in the auditorium, 'it had become evident that the Prime Minister could not explain Government foreign policy—and, in particular, Australia's military commitment in Vietnam'.[104] Holt was greatly affected by the steadily growing list of Australian casualties, but sceptical that suspending American bombing raids on Hanoi and Haiphong would bring North Vietnam to the conference table. Holt offered a six-point defence of the bombing campaign[105] which led Whitlam to criticise his enthusiasm for military solutions that would prolong rather than shorten the war.[106] By this time the Johnson Administration had already decided that Whitlam was much more 'realistic' and moderate on Vietnam than Calwell.[107]

President Johnson wrote to Holt indicating the need for even greater Australian support in South Vietnam in the form of an additional 'two-battalion combat team'. With nearly 500 000 American troops already deployed to Vietnam, the foremost effect of the Australian contribution would be political, rather than military. Johnson told Holt: 'I simply cannot exaggerate the favourable effect it would have here if we were able to tell the Congress within the next month that your Government has reached a firm decision along the lines I have suggested'.[108] The Australian Defence and External Affairs departments were concerned that a refusal to send additional troops would have a negative effect on American domestic policy and its continuing bearing on support for the war but they were also anxious to avoid Australia's military forces being over-stretched, given Britain's planned withdrawal from the region. Holt again insisted on the deployment of a third battalion. Howson, the Minister for Air, recorded his concern that Holt had been overly influenced by the American President and 'wanted to send up as much aid as possible, leaving ourselves with absolutely no room to manoeuvre in any other direction should the need arise'.[109] Fairhall, Hasluck and McMahon shared Howson's general reservations, but when the matter was put to Cabinet on 6 September, Holt had his way although there were widely held suspicions that the Prime Minister's foremost intention was to achieve favourable political and commercial concessions from the Americans, including a more favourable trade environment.

This view was reinforced when Holt spoke with the American Ambassador the following day. He stressed the difficulties facing the Australian economy and the impediments to an expanded military commitment without disclosing that the decision to deploy a third battalion had already been made. McMahon was instructed not to mention Cabinet's decision when he visited Washington and met President Johnson on 2 October. McMahon reported the 'extremely strong' pressure being applied by the President and persuaded Holt to inform him that a decision had been made. Holt sent a message to President Johnson on 6 October. A third battalion would be made available for service in South Vietnam. Holt also told the President that Australia and the United States needed to reach an agreement on the handling of security concerns elsewhere within the region and that Australia could not, and would not, contribute any further forces to the war. Its military capacity to assist had reached a definite limit: 'to attempt to go beyond this would involve us in military, economic and political decisions which my colleagues and I would regard as publicly unacceptable in the existing climate of opinion apart from other considerations of national security'.[110]

On 17 October 1967, Holt told the Australian people that a further 1700 troops would be sent to South Vietnam in addition to a tank squadron and more helicopters, bringing the total Australian presence in Vietnam to more than 8000 personnel. This was the fourth and final increase in Australia's commitment to the war. But allocating additional men and equipment did not seem to embody a consistent or coherent Government policy or guarantee an end to fighting. An editorial in the *Age* commented that Holt's announcement was:

> impressive in its honesty, its resolution and its recognition of personal responsibility. But it said very little to clarify the Government's beliefs about the course of the war, it did not satisfy the public nervousness that escalation may have already gone past the point of logic, it did not adequately relate our new commitment to an overall strategy, it did not indicate that the Government has any view of the war's future other than to accept Washington's decisions and accede to reasonable requests for help. All these doubts demand satisfaction during the election campaign debate. It is a pity the Labor Party has not given Mr Whitlam a Vietnam policy which might put Mr Holt under test.

It is noteworthy that the *Age*, a newspaper that had previously supported both the war and the Government's policy, was expressing concern about its conduct and progress. By this time, opinion polls were revealing that more than half of the population were opposed to further increases in Australian participation in the war. There were also widening divisions within the Liberal Party about policy on Vietnam. While Australian soldiers were dying, the British were still engaging in trade with North Vietnam. Killen was outraged and spoke to Holt privately after Hasluck ignored his concerns:

> I cannot understand why we cannot ask the Brits to stop their ships going to Haiphong . . . If I were a digger in the field, being shot at by angry men, I

would not feel like singing 'Land of Hope and Glory' knowing that British flag ships were going into the enemy's ports with impunity.[111]

Holt replied: 'The British Government is desperately seeking a political solution and, as a consequence, if they do what you propose then their actions will be regarded as hostile and their efforts will be useless. That's the position'.[112]

By 2 November 1967, Holt still hoped that Labor's attitude to Vietnam would damage its electoral appeal. In a campaign speech for the half-Senate election, he claimed that:

> despite the facelift and despite the glamorous new leadership, [the ALP stands] where it stood at the last general election. It still stands for a troops-out policy in Vietnam. As long as that is the policy honestly presented by the ALP then the Australian people will have no truck with it.[113]

During the election campaign, Holt is alleged to have said 'off the record' to several members of the Press Gallery: 'You know, I still think I'm right, but these casualties our boys are suffering are terrible, for everybody. I believe I know how John Curtin felt during World War II'.[114]

Holt wrote another long letter to the President on 5 December in which he told Johnson that the half-Senate election showed 'the people still want my government and its basic economic, foreign and defence policies'. He proposed another Manila Conference for mid-March 1968.[115] On the weekend of 16–17 December, Holt and Eggleton discussed the possibility of a major European tour in 1968 to 'sell' the possibilities and potentialities of Asia, and to explain the security dilemmas being faced by its emerging democracies. Holt believed that during his previous visits to Europe 'it became clear that Australia has been accepted as a member of the Asian and Pacific community. We are not on the outside looking in, but we are regarded as one of the countries of the area, involved in its problems'.[116]

— ◼ ◼ —

On a personal level, Holt achieved a great deal in the field of diplomacy and foreign policy. He strove to have Australians think more creatively about trading with Asia and helped them to overcome historic fears and anxieties. He met most of South-east Asia's leaders and tried to convince them that Australia wanted to play a constructive and positive part in regional affairs while he worked to overcome the residual effects of the White Australia Policy. He deserves credit both for his willingness to tackle the problems and for building closer relations with Australia's nearer neighbours. But he was less successful in dealing with the two big issues he faced on taking office.

There was probably nothing any Australian leader could have done to prevent the British withdrawal east of Suez. The sun was setting on the British Empire and, on a strategic level, it was unreasonable to ask Britain to underwrite the security of its former colonies, especially as many of them resented continued British involvement in their affairs. But Holt could have proposed some further alternatives to a complete British departure from the region. With the British Government thinking almost exclusively in terms of reduction in expenditure, Holt might have focused on a range of options linked to the development of local infrastructure; in effect, he should have helped the British find ways to make military involvement in South-east Asia produce some economic dividend. Thankfully for Australia and the region, the British withdrawal did not have serious adverse strategic or military consequences in either the short or long term.

The second big issue Holt faced was the war in South Vietnam. It is easy to be critical of Holt's policy and decision-making with hindsight. In early 1966, the Australian Government believed that without a substantial contribution of friendly forces South Vietnam would have fallen prey to Communist insurgency. The flaw in Holt's approach was to concentrate much too heavily on a military solution while failing to determine the nature of Australian interests in South Vietnam and the extent to which they needed to be preserved. Holt never deviated from his whole-hearted support for American bombing of North Vietnam and the hope that steadily increasing the number of foreign troops deployed to South Vietnam would lead to military victory and a solution to the crisis. By the end of 1967, it was not that these strategies were not working but that Holt could not say how long they would take to succeed or at what price. The Australian people were not prepared for an open-ended conflict and not willing to accept an increasing long casualty list. Holt failed to convince the nation that the human and material cost of the war was justified in terms of Australian interests. Lyndon Johnson was no more successful. In their mutual embrace, the two men pursued a policy that left too many questions unanswered. Both inherited the war from their predecessors, neither handled it well and both suffered politically as a result. The tragedy for Australia was that more than 500 servicemen would die before the nation's leaders realised the futility of the strategy they were pursuing.

CHAPTER 12

From bad to worse

January–October 1967

HOLT MAY HAVE SECURED a huge victory in November 1966 but Australian society and the electorate were changing more rapidly than ever before. The social mores that had underpinned suburban harmony were being freely challenged; and a previously compliant society was displaying widespread civil disobedience. The Battle of Long Tan on 18 August 1966, in which 18 Australian soldiers were killed and another 21 wounded, had demonstrated the human cost of Australian involvement in a conflict to which no end was in sight.

In his 1967 Australia Day Address, Holt noted that Australians 'are finding their thoughts dwelling on the challenges, opportunities and the obligations which derive from our proximity to the teeming countries of Asia and our neighbours in the Pacific'.[1] While Australian society was still being described as 'British', Holt observed that its geopolitical location was starting to influence the national outlook. There was, however, an element of continuity in that Australia's potential adversaries were still located to the north. The trouble for Holt was that many in his own Party doubted both the character of their intent and the wisdom of the Government's response.

The new Parliament sat for the first time on 21 February 1967 with a record majority in the House and a minority in the Senate for the first time since the Parliament of 1950–51. Holt then learned that Clive Hannaford, a Liberal Senator from South Australia, had decided to sit as an Independent as a protest against the Coalition's policy on South Vietnam.[2] There was further change ahead. Gough Whitlam had become the Labor Leader on 8 February 1967 and few doubted his electoral appeal.

The Coalition needed to respond. Billy Wentworth told Holt that the Government was almost entirely dependent upon the Communist issue.

> [Although] our electoral position is excellent and I think that you are a better vote-getter than Menzies . . . the reaction towards Whitlam is quite strong and could be overwhelming if he took a strong anti-Communist line. Under such circumstances many of our marginal seats would go at the next election and we might even lose Government.[3]

Whitlam's Deputy was the dour Tasmanian Lance Barnard, who was content to leave the public stage completely free for his charismatic leader. He remarked: 'The party does not need star quality in its deputy if the price it would have to pay for it is division in its leadership'.[4]

When Holt faced Whitlam as the new Leader of the Opposition, he remarked that Whitlam's first speech would reveal whether he would make a better Opposition Leader than Calwell. Whitlam replied, 'Thank you, Mr Prime Minister . . . Actually I have always thought that you would make a better Opposition Leader than either Mr Calwell or myself.'[5] But at least some of Holt's colleagues, including Andrew Peacock and Iain Sinclair, felt that Dr Jim Cairns was a more potent parliamentary adversary although he could be more readily 'neutralised' by exploiting anti-Communist fears. As for the former Labor Leader, Holt wished him well for the future, to which Calwell replied, 'It is true, as you said, that we have never been personal enemies and we never will be'.[6] Holt then wrote to Prime Minister Harold Wilson at 10 Downing Street in London, recommending Calwell's appointment to the Privy Council. The two men would remain fierce political rivals but close friends.

For Holt, 1967 would be very similar to 1966. As well as a series of overseas trips, he had planned tours of rural areas where the Coalition vote was faltering ahead of the half-Senate election which had to be held by mid-1968. On 2 February Holt went to New Zealand for a six-day visit, the first prime ministerial visit across the Tasman since Menzies was there in 1954. The *Wellington Post* said it was heartening that 'Mr Holt did not come here attempting to toss us a bauble or two and avoid some of the really sore points that do exist'.[7] The main purpose of the visit was to discuss the Limited Free Trade Agreement. On his return, Holt hosted a special financial mid-year review of the Premiers' Conference. The Premiers praised Holt's personal handling of the conference (he dealt with them directly in the Cabinet Room) and were generally happy with the outcome. This was followed by official visits to Australia by Princess Alexandra and the Duke of Edinburgh, Prince Philip.

Then, with little warning, things began to deteriorate both personally and politically for the Prime Minister. Holt was becoming a target of personal attacks by demonstrators. On 1 May 1967 Holt's house in Toorak was the subject of a demonstration and personal harassment while Victoria Police looked on, claiming the protesters were on public land and they were unable to act. Holt wrote an angry letter to Premier Henry Bolte:

> The episode outside my own home is not an isolated incident. There was an earlier demonstration which took the form of a burning of National Registration Cards and a night long vigil. My garage doors have been defaced with offensive posters. I am not only concerned for myself in this matter. I think that unless the harassment of public men going about their duties is dealt with firmly, it will tend to increase.[8]

Holt wanted State and Commonwealth authorities to determine whether the demonstration was legal and, if not, who would take action. ASIO became involved as Holt considered the prospect of new legislation to protect Commonwealth ministers from 'democracy by demonstration'.

There was much worse to come. On 24 March 1967, Holt's much-loved brother Cliff died at the age of 57 after a 15-month battle with pancreatic cancer. He had served in the RAAF during the war and had established a very successful public relations consultancy in Sydney. Cliff, who converted to Roman Catholicism, was survived by his wife Maura and three children, Peter, Carrol and Susan. His funeral was held on Easter Saturday and conducted by Father Coleman at St Mary's Catholic Church in North Sydney.[9] The Prime Minister described his brother's death as 'a terrible blow'. A year earlier he had learned of the death of his aunt, Vera Annie Pierce (Holt's late mother's half-sister), who died of a heart attack in London aged 70. Her more valuable personal effects were shipped to The Lodge.[10] He was keen to collect personal effects, photographs and portraits of family members, especially of his mother as he had very little to remind him of her or their life together. But now there was little time to mourn Cliff's death before he had to depart for a twelve-day trip to South-east Asia on 28 March. After enjoying widespread praise among regional leaders and the Australian press for a successful series of visits, Holt returned to a divided and hostile backbench.

Many believe that the beginning of the Liberal Party's loss of confidence in Holt's leadership can be identified to within a minute. The turning point was a debate in the House of Representatives into the loss of HMAS *Voyager* after she collided with HMAS *Melbourne* on 10 February 1964.[11] In a motion moved by Arthur Calwell censuring the Government for the succession of naval accidents that had culminated in the loss of *Voyager*, Victorian Liberal backbencher John Jess criticised the Government's handling of the tragedy. He was disappointed with both the conduct of the Royal Commission established by Menzies and its *Report*.

Following the resignation of *Melbourne*'s captain, John Robertson, a campaign had gathered momentum within the naval ex-service community to have certain matters related to the loss of *Voyager* re-examined. The officer who had served as *Voyager*'s second-in-command during 1963, Lieutenant Commander Peter Cabban, was dismayed by evidence that *Voyager*'s captain, Duncan Stevens, had apparently been served alcohol immediately prior to the collision and agreed to speak with Robertson about what he had observed of Stevens' behaviour in the year before the collision. Cabban agreed to make a tape recording of his experiences which was later transcribed. Jess handed a copy to Prime Minister Menzies, who was not persuaded that it was relevant to the causes of the collision or that Cabban's allegations, if proved true, would have influenced the Royal Commissioner's findings.

After raising the matter with Menzies three times, Jess confronted Holt with the 'Cabban Statement' shortly after he became Prime Minister. When Holt asked Jess what he expected him to do with the document, Jess replied, 'That, sir, is hardly for me to say.' The Government had everything to lose and nothing to gain by a new Inquiry unless, of course, there was a backbench revolt. Holt decided to play for time in the hope that Jess would lose interest, but in August 1966 Jess told Holt that Cabban was thinking of making his statement public. Holt agreed to look into the matter after the November 1966 election and the '*Voyager* problem' went away again until the new year. In March 1967, Jess and another backbencher, the Reverend Dr Malcolm Mackay, met with Holt and left him in no doubt that they wanted to pursue the matter. Another delegation consisting of Bill Kent Hughes, Bill Wentworth and Max Fox gave Holt the same message. The Prime Minister put the matter to Cabinet on 27 April with a joint submission from the Departments of Defence and Navy. On 2 May, Holt informed Jess that Cabinet had decided against reopening the case and that it could not agree to any compensation being awarded to Robertson. Only days later, the press was aware that a backbench revolt was brewing. The *Australian* told Holt on 5 May that he was 'wrong to think that . . . he can shut off all public uneasiness about the collision off Jervis Bay'.[12] Jess issued Holt with an ultimatum: he was prepared to commit political suicide to have the case reopened. The new Liberal Member for Warringah, Edward St John QC, had also taken a personal interest in the case. The contents of the 'Cabban Statement' became public on 9 May when the Melbourne tabloid *Truth* published its main allegations against Captain Stevens.

Holt was under siege from his own backbench, the press and the Labor Party which had now realised that the Liberal Party was tearing itself apart over *Voyager*. The Prime Minister's relations with the press became particularly strained after the General Secretary of the Australian Journalists Association (AJA) wrote to Holt complaining about comments Holt made in the House on 18 April concerning an item on ABC television's *This Day Tonight*, presented by Mike Willesee. The AJA claimed that Holt had 'cast a serious reflection on Mr Willesee's journalistic integrity and objectivity. In the opinion of the Federal Executive this was for no other apparent reason than that his father is a Labor Parliamentarian'.[13]

The Prime Minister bowed to the pressure and announced that *Voyager* would be debated on 16 May. The debate was opened by the Attorney-General, Nigel Bowen, who was followed by Jess. After outlining the need for a new inquiry, Jess told the House that this 'should not be a party issue. This is an issue of justice'. The Navy Minister, Don Chipp, argued that the 'Cabban Statement' was unreliable, grossly inaccurate and irrelevant. His speech ended any prospect of negotiation or compromise. St John, the next speaker, was still very much an unknown quantity. In fact, this was his maiden speech. By convention, its content should have been non-controversial and its delivery uninterrupted. But Holt had every reason to fear the worst after St John's opening words: 'I rise to make my maiden speech conscious of my loyalty to the party . . . but conscious above all of my sovereign obligation to speak the truth as I see it in the interests of the people of this, my country'. St John expressed his belief that Cabban was a truthful man and that if his statement constituted truthful evidence, how could it possibly be irrelevant? 'Is not this one of the facts and circumstances leading up to the *Voyager* disaster? Or have I lost the meaning of the word "irrelevant"? Are we playing a battle of semantics? What is the meaning of the word "irrelevant"?' Holt could contain himself no longer. He broke convention, interjected, 'What is the meaning of the word "evidence"?' St John cut Holt in two with his reply:

> I did not expect to be interrupted by the Prime Minister. We have all been invited to debate what comes to us second hand. The Prime Minister's interruption demonstrates better than anything else that this kind of matter can be sifted only by a proper judicial committee.[14]

The big winner in this very brief exchange was St John. Everyone was aware that Holt, the great stickler for parliamentary custom and convention, had been embarrassed by his failure to observe protocol. Bowen, who was sitting next to Holt, placed his hand on Holt's arm to calm the outraged Prime Minister. The press claimed St John's address was a triumph for Parliament and restored the public's faith in the national debating chamber. In adjourning the debate, McMahon said: 'the Government has not closed its options. The Prime Minister after considering all points that have been raised will take the matter back to the Party Room and then decide exactly what is to be done'.[15] When debate resumed, Holt addressed the House and said the matter would again return to the Party Room. It appeared that he was buckling. The rebel backbenchers were encouraged further by the news that the major newspapers were joining their cause. On 18 May 1967, Holt announced in the House that 'the Government has concluded that there should be a further inquiry and that it should be a judicial inquiry conducted probably by three judges'. Holt subsequently confirmed that the form of inquiry would be a Royal Commission. Holt had made his decision without consulting Bowen—who would have advised against it—or his Cabinet, where there was a substantial body of opinion opposing another inquiry. Senator John Gorton, whom Holt had appointed to the new Department of Education and Science after the 1966 election, maintained that he would have resisted another Inquiry whatever the political cost. Bowen felt that Holt had been too easily swamped by political posturing and media pressure.

The second *Voyager* Inquiry heard submissions over 85 days. The findings of the three Royal Commissioners departed substantially from those of Sir John Spicer, concluding that Spicer's criticism of Robertson was not justified. They recommended *Melbourne*'s captain receive a government gratuity of $60 000. Those who lobbied for the inquiry felt justified. For Holt, it was the beginning of backbench suspicion that he could not stand up to intense public pressure and was, therefore, inadequate as party leader. Many were heard to comment: 'It would never have been like this under Menzies'. Graham Freudenberg remarked:

> It is seldom that the beginning of a politician's decline can be placed with any precision. In Holt's case, it can be put down to the minute—8.07pm on 16 May 1967—the moment at which Holt interjected on St John's maiden speech.[16]

Holt had been seen as an able leader until a crisis developed.

The Government had other problems in defence. In 1963, the Cabinet authorised the acquisition of 24 F-111 strike aircraft for the RAAF with delivery planned for 1967. Built by General Dynamics in the United States, the first F-111s flew in 1964 but the aircraft were plagued with major technical problems, lengthy production delays and cost overruns. The planned delivery date of the Australian aircraft had to be postponed and F-4E Phantoms leased from the United States as an interim measure. Although the F-111 eventually emerged as the world's finest strike aircraft, those built for the RAAF did not arrive until 1973. In 1967, the Holt Government was being criticised for buying a defective, expensive plane. This was an embarrassment the Government did not need so soon after the *Voyager* controversy.

In the midst of this political turmoil, two constitutional questions were put to the Australian people at referendum. The timing was far from ideal, but the referendums had been scheduled for some time and could not again be delayed.[17] Killen wrote to Holt imploring him not to proceed with the referendums because there was little energy for them in the Party and he discerned a lack of interest in the community.[18] The Western Australian Division of the Liberal Party urged Holt not to delay. It argued that the first referendum, in particular, could be lost if the Government waited until after the 1966 election, because Whitlam would replace Calwell and possibly seek to thwart the Government by opposing the question.[19]

The first question was an amendment to Section 24 of the Constitution to remove the requirement that the House should be, as nearly as practicable, twice the size of the Senate. If this requirement was deleted it would be possible to increase the number of members of the House of Representatives without proportionally increasing the size of the Senate. Not surprisingly the DLP, as a minority party represented in the Senate, opposed breaking the nexus for its own self-interested reasons but portrayed the referendum as an attempt to reduce the power of the Senate. There was official bipartisan support for the proposal although four Liberal Senators—Alexander Lillico, Edward Mattner, Ian Wood and Reg Wright[20]—and two Country Party Senators—Tom Bull and Edgar Prowse—publicly opposed the 'Yes' vote. The Queensland Liberal Executive considered expelling Wood at its meeting on 2 June. Moves were underway elsewhere to expel Wright. McMahon, who was present at the meeting because the Queensland Liberal Division's finances were in crisis with its bankers seeking to call in a $70 000 overdraft, suggested that Holt 'would not think it prudent to take action on both Wright and Wood together'.[21] He was correct. Holt tended to shy away from all talk of expulsion as he portrayed the Liberals as a party committed to free speech and respect for individual conscience.

On 15 February 1966, the Prime Minister announced that the Government would defer the referendums because it was heavily occupied with other matters and a Federal election was already scheduled for later in the year.[22] He also wanted to avoid approaching the electorate so soon after becoming prime minister. Waiting until 1967 would give him time to earn the people's trust and allow the Government sufficient time to 'sell' the propositions to an electorate usually suspicious of referendums.

Despite official bipartisan support and unanimity among Members of the House, the proposal was defeated nationally with 60 per cent opposed and only 40 per cent in favour. Only in New South Wales was the proposal carried. The campaign was a personal blow for Holt for two reasons. First, he failed to achieve a majority despite securing bipartisan support, a humiliating result for any Prime Minister. Second, he had failed to control the mavericks in his own Party and was unable to project an image of solidarity. While not even Menzies would have been able to silence the renegade Senator Reg Wright, Holt failed to isolate Wright politically by threatening or dissuading his would-be supporters. Holt was finding that he could not be what, at times, he needed to be: at most, a strong leader or, at least, a threatening ogre. He seemed unable or unwilling to deal with those who refused to adhere to Party discipline or declined to show loyalty to its Leader. Discipline and solidarity were becoming elusive within Liberal ranks.

The second referendum question was designed to remove discriminatory clauses in the Constitution relating to Aborigines.[23] On becoming Prime Minister, Holt had been advised that this proposal might not receive majority support. The original 'Yes' case proposed by Menzies was limited to removing section 127 of the Constitution, which stated: 'In reckoning the numbers of the people of the Commonwealth, or of a State or other part of the Commonwealth, aboriginal natives shall not be counted'. Menzies said this was 'completely out of harmony with our national attitudes'.[24] The Federal Council for the Advancement of Aborigines and Torres Strait Islanders (FCAATSI) also wanted the phrase 'other than the aboriginal race in any State' deleted from section 51 (xxvi). This would empower the Commonwealth to legislate specifically on their behalf, especially in preventing discrimination against Aborigines in the States. Menzies believed that this was not an exclusion from equal rights but a protection against the Commonwealth making laws that discriminated against Aborigines. He saw no need to amend section 51 (xxvi). Labor's Gordon Bryant argued that the Commonwealth cannot 'possibly take up the challenge in respect of Aborigines unless it takes to itself the power to do so'.[25] Menzies did not, however, favour direct Commonwealth involvement in Aboriginal affairs as he was not convinced that the Commonwealth would be any more effective than the States in delivering social services or addressing community problems. By this time, legislation had already (1962) been enacted to give Aborigines the right to vote in Federal elections,[26] although Queensland only did so in 1965. The Commonwealth had also been involved in Aboriginal affairs in the Northern Territory since 1911 and could, although legal opinion was equivocal on this point, have played a role within the States through the provisions of section 96 of the Constitution, which probably allowed the Commonwealth to make grants to the States on such terms and conditions as it saw fit.

The advice that Holt received in relation to section 51 (xxvi) was that the extant wording was not discriminatory; that adding a new provision invalidating any Commonwealth or State discrimination on the grounds of race would prompt litigation; that the best protection for Aborigines was to treat them for all purposes as though they were Australian citizens; and that inserting a third matter in the referendum might work against a 'Yes' vote. Aboriginal leaders felt, however, that leaving section 51 unchanged could mean that Aborigines were the only racial group mentioned in the Constitution and thus give the impression they were unable to manage their own affairs. Aboriginal advocates firmly believed it was necessary for the Commonwealth to be able to legislate for the benefit of Aborigines on a national basis.[27] Holt was, however, persuaded that both sections of the Constitution should be changed 'because they have been widely misinterpreted' and because there was 'a general impression that they are discriminatory' although the Government nonetheless regarded this opinion as erroneous.[28] On 14 March 1967 Holt announced the successful passage through Parliament of the Constitution Alteration Bills with the changes to both sections of the Constitution to be put in one question to the electorate rather than two. Holt made no firm undertaking to use the additional legislative power the referendum would deliver to the Government, although the press made it clear that the success of the 'Yes' vote would deny the Commonwealth any excuse for not doing more for Aborigines. A 'No' case was never formulated, printed or circulated.

On one level, Holt was deeply distressed by the need for the referendum. As a former Minister for Immigration who had welcomed people of many different nationalities to his country, he was not convinced that Australia had the same kind of serious race problems he had observed elsewhere. But he was unable to see beyond his own attitudes, which he sincerely believed were free from racism. While conceding that there were 'occasional and unrelated acts of discrimination' reported from time to time, he asserted that they were dealt with once publicised. And where there was discrimination, it would end once 'the habits, manners and education of the race more nearly approached general community standards'.[29] In Holt's mind—and many of his contemporaries felt the same—Aborigines could participate in Australia's public life but they had to think and act like Europeans. The historian John Hirst is right, therefore, when he says that Holt was 'more concerned about Australia's image in the world and he wanted to show that he was sympathetic to the Aboriginal cause'.[30] But at the same time he did not want to 'magnify the Aborigine problem out of its true reality'.[31] On the eve of the referendum Holt said, 'anything but a "yes" vote to this question would do injury to our reputation among fair-minded people everywhere'.[32]

As the first referendum had shown so clearly, bipartisan support for the 'Yes' case was no guarantee of success. This time, however, and despite some last-minute anxieties within the Aboriginal community, the 'Yes' vote was carried in every State, with a national majority of 90.77 per cent. More than five million Australians had voted in favour of constitutional change. It was, and remains, the most successful referendum in Australian political history. It was followed by calls for immediate Commonwealth action, including the creation of a new Commonwealth department. En route to Europe, Holt gave a statement about the results.

He was disappointed by the failure of the nexus question and surprised that 'the majority of voters chose to ignore the advice of those to whom they normally look for guidance on political matters'. As for the question on Aborigines, he said the strong result 'will contribute to Australia's international standing by demonstrating to the outside world our over-whelming desire to give full acceptance to the aboriginal people within our community'.[33] Holt could now confidently claim that Australia was not a racist country. But he continued to promote the importance of assimilation despite allegations that it was intended to eliminate Abor-iginality and Aboriginal culture. In his view, 'it may be that this will happen but if it does it is a matter of individual decision and not of policy'.[34]

While Holt had publicly expressed no doubts about the likely result of the second referendum, Barrie Dexter recalls that Holt was privately astonished by the obvious strength of feeling. In fact,

> [Holt] had not really expected the referendum to succeed. When it did, and so overwhelmingly, he realised that there was something about the electorate which he, as a politician who prided himself on interpreting the public mood, had not understood. He was determined to come to grips with this, and to achieve what the people so clearly wanted—strong Commonwealth leadership.[35]

But no specific plans had been made and Holt was under pressure not to develop any. The Aboriginal Welfare Conference of State and Common-wealth Ministers held in Perth in July 1967 voted for a preservation of the status quo with the Victorian Minister for Aboriginal Welfare arguing that 'uniform Commonwealth legislation would be a retrograde step'.[36] Initially, Holt agreed: 'there is a big variation in circumstances and needs of Aborigines in the States. For this reason, administration has to be on a regional or State basis if it is to be effective'.[37] But he soon realised Commonwealth coordination was vital.

Holt consulted Nugget Coombs, in the belief that the challenges posed for the Government by the referendum were similar to those Coombs and his colleagues had dealt with in the Department of Post-war Reconstruction. Coombs recalled:

> When we talked it became clear that Holt had little knowledge of Abor-igines and was puzzled to know how the Government should go about

creating an appropriate administrative agency to deal with the problems associated with them . . . Here was a problem which seemed to call for an agency concerned with all the functions which might need to be performed for a section of the community only. I agreed to think about the problems and to submit some ideas . . . Accordingly, I suggested that the Prime Minister as an interim solution should establish a small Council backed by a small but powerful research staff to identify the major problems, to establish communication with Aboriginal groups, and then to submit some possible bases for the Commonwealth approach to policy and plans for a continuing organisation.[38]

Holt then visited Aboriginal communities, met with leading indigenous spokesmen such as Charles Perkins, and read whatever he could obtain on Aboriginal history and culture. Bill Wentworth had earlier suggested that Perkins might convene an 'Aboriginal Advisory Panel'.[39]

Having firmly committed the Commonwealth to leadership in Aboriginal affairs, on 2 November 1967 Holt established a three-member Council for Aboriginal Affairs to 'advise the Government in the formulation of national policies for the advancement of the Aboriginal citizens of Australia . . . and to provide the machinery necessary for joint consultation as the need arises with the States and with relevant Commonwealth departments'.[40] Its members would be Coombs (soon to retire from governorship of the Reserve Bank), former diplomat Barrie Dexter and Australian National University social anthropologist, Professor W.E.H. 'Bill' Stanner.[41] Coombs, probably recommended by Bunting who had worked with him at the Department of Post-war Reconstruction, was prepared to join the Council and to act as its Chairman only after Holt 'assured me that it was his firm intention to use the new Commonwealth powers genuinely to transform the status and welfare of Aborigines and his actions gave evidence of his sincerity in that undertaking'.[42] Dexter was made Executive Member of the Council and Director of the Office of Aboriginal Affairs which was created to service the Council. Stanner, a senior academic at the Australian National University, only consented to join the Council because Coombs and Dexter had already agreed to do so. Stanner was quickly impressed by Holt's newly found personal interest and commitment to Aboriginal people, and that the Prime Minister intended to take personal responsibility for Aboriginal affairs by locating an Office of Aboriginal Affairs within his Department and using the authority of his position to implement the Council's policy initiatives. Bill Wentworth, a long-time advocate for indigenous peoples, was later appointed Minister-in-Charge of Aboriginal Affairs. On 23 November 1967 he was urging Holt to expedite action as 'our supporters in the Aboriginal field are being whittled away from us and humiliated by reason of delay in practical Commonwealth initiative.'[43]

'Ceb' Barnes was now Minister for Territories, but Paul Hasluck was surprised by Holt's enthusiasm for Aboriginal affairs and openly critical of the arrangements that Holt had put in place.

> When I heard of the decisions it seemed to me that Holt may have purposely excluded me from any discussion about what should be done. Perhaps he worked on the principle that if you are getting a new broom, you do not mess about with the old broom. Because of my ignorance of how and why things were done in the way they were done I am puzzled about Holt's role as innovator in aboriginal affairs. In sixteen years with him in Cabinet I had never known him to show any interest in Aborigines and when he was Treasurer he had certainly been much less responsive than Fadden had been to my bids for funds for Aborigines. While I have no first hand knowledge, my guess is that the moves following the referendum were mainly due to the efficient and methodical practices of . . . Sir John Bunting. The result of the referendum meant that the Commonwealth Government had the constitutional power to do something, hence it had to decide what it should do.[44]

Not only was Hasluck mistaken in his facts, this was another instance in which Hasluck seems reluctant to give credit where credit was due. Dexter thought that Hasluck's antipathy 'reflected hostility to the prospect of anyone, especially amateurs, tampering with the assimilation policy he had laid down as Minister for Territories from 1951 to 1963'.[45]

But why did Holt become so committed to indigenous affairs? Coombs believed that he 'turned to initiatives in the Arts and for Aborigines' because his Government 'lacked major agreed tasks or objectives to unify the energies of its ministers and supporters'. He also believed that these two areas 'better expressed his own generous and human spirit'.[46] Whatever Holt's reasons, and genuine concern and empathy were among them, he had taken the initiative and shown his determination to improve the well-being of Aboriginal people. Coombs reported that with the Prime Minister's own support, the Council's 'morale was high'.

Holt also approached Coombs about other areas of public service he might offer. Given his life-long interest in theatre and ballet, Holt was open to Coombs' argument that the arts in Australia needed a broader government agency than the Australian Elizabethan Theatre Trust. Late in 1967, he established an Australian Council for the Arts under Coombs' direction, commissioning it to coordinate policies on government support.

Holt had initiated other significant reforms. In May 1967, he floated the idea of ending appeals from the High Court to the Privy Council in matters of Federal jurisdiction. It met with widespread support but some disapproval within the Liberal Party Federal Council.[47] Holt would have only two formal contacts with Barwick while he was Chief Justice of the High Court and this was one of them. Barwick told Holt that he supported the move because he felt that Australia needed to make its own legal mistakes.[48] On 6 September the Government formally announced its intentions, although the abolition of Privy Council appeals did not become law until 6 August 1968. Holt had earlier written to Prime Minister Harold Wilson to explain that there was nothing sinister in the timing—so close to his publicly stated disappointment with Britain's decision to withdraw its forces east of Suez. He said: 'we regard the decision as a desirable expression of national maturity, and I am sure that you will so recognise it'.[49] He also wanted to relocate the statue of King George V from King's in Parliament House and remove the memorial to the former monarch situated at the front of the building.[50] Although he wanted to sever some of the strings that tied Australia to the United Kingdom, Holt was nonetheless thrilled to be appointed a Companion of Honour (CH) on 14 June 1967. This was considered a great honour and perhaps superior to a lesser knighthood, as there are only 65 Companions of Honour at any one time.

———

Despite his innovative reforms, Holt's public image at home, already tarnished by the *Voyager* controversy, continued to slip. In June, the Government faced protracted industrial trouble with postal unions over the provision of Saturday services. The unions' members threatened to disrupt postal services if the Government did not accept their demands. Holt said that if the unions were to 'cancel all proposed stoppages for 1 July and withdraw all other threats of direct action' the Acting Postmaster-General would consider their representations.[51] The unions refused. Although most postal employees defied the unions' instructions and turned up for work, the dispute continued with the Government insisting on 19 July that 'the public wanted Saturday services'.[52] But another aspect of the postal service had caused the Government more difficulties and Holt's leadership again to be brought into question.

The Government planned to increase various postal charges through the simple device of changing the figures in certain regulations made under the *Postal Act*. Cabinet had approved an increase in May 1967 but the Labor Party and the DLP delayed consideration and then disallowed the regulations in the Senate on the grounds that as the imposition of a fee was involved the matter should have been included in the Budget and been made the subject of broader debate. This meant that if the Senate wanted to continue its opposition to the increased charges, it had to reject the two Appropriation Bills that formed the legislative basis of the Budget. Holt repeated his well-worn complaint that the 'house of review should not reject financial decisions of the popular house'. The Prime Minister claimed that there would be:

> many staunch Labor supporters disgusted by the cynical abandonment of a long-held principle and this blatant exercise of political opportunism in the teeth of so many firm and clear public declarations of the past. If this is the new look Labor leadership, then it is revealed as having no basis of consistency or principle nor any respect for historical democratic tradition and practice.[53]

Although the DLP was in favour of such action, the Labor Caucus considered postal charges as a 'money bill' and decided not to obstruct its passage despite Lionel Murphy's vigorous opposition to it. Whitlam declared his strong belief that 'the Senate should not cut off money for a Government which has a majority in the House of Representatives'.[54] The Senate also amended the Aged Persons' Homes Bill which the Government subsequently declined to resubmit. Holt had underestimated the power of the Senate and the Government seemed stuck on the back foot. Exhausted, Holt returned to a custom he had observed every August while Treasurer—he fled Canberra and its cold winter weather and travelled north.

Holt's first and only visit to Bingil Bay as Prime Minister was 3–13 August 1967. He did a limited amount of work but largely wanted to be left alone. He was feeling tired and worn out. His friend John Büsst, recently elected President of the Wild Life Preservation Society of Queensland, briefed Holt on his efforts to prevent the Great Barrier Reef from being mined near Ellison Reef, adjacent to the Prime Minister's favourite fishing ground at Beaver Cay. This was also a chance for him to celebrate his 59th birthday with friends. Departmental officers vetted all papers sent to him, with non-urgent material being held over until his return to Canberra. His private secretaries were accommodated in Townsville. His old friend Grant McIntyre was seconded from the Immigration Department to be with the Prime Minister and then to remain at Bingil Bay until 25 August 'so that he could continue telephone and other official duties on behalf of Mrs Holt'.[55] This part of the Queensland coast was starting to become famous, after the Melbourne *Herald* carried a feature on 'Holt's Hideaway'. One of the locals, Bernie Brook, told reporter Ray Saunders:

> We see Mr Holt often. He's just like one of us when he comes up here, no snob—a beaut bloke. We leave him alone and never talk politics. He comes up here to get away from all that, and we don't want to spoil that for him.[56]

Although Bingil Bay seemed remote to most Australians, the Commonwealth Police identified a number of possible security threats to the Prime Minister's safety: 'anti-Vietnam groups, Italians, Yugoslavs, Townsville university students, resident criminals, cranks, new residents, Dunk Island tourists, political factions and the press'. Although Inspector Hamilton of the Commonwealth Police was 'not able to identify any group or individual likely to pose a threat', he strongly recommend that a 'Commonwealth Police Officer accompany the Prime Minister to afford immediate additional protection and ensure more satisfactory and effective security'.[57] Sergeant Walliker had been Holt's usual personal escort in 1967. But Holt told the Commissioner (Ray Whitrod) that he did not want a security officer present at Bingil Bay. Holt thought demonstrations were unlikely to occur in such an isolated place and that he 'did not see that much protection could be provided against a determined assassin'.[58] He was happy for the local Queensland Police to respond to any security alert.

He thoroughly enjoyed his time in North Queensland and returned to Canberra refreshed and ready for the Budget session of Parliament. But Holt knew he needed to demonstrate his ascendancy over Whitlam during debate. Rumours of a double dissolution were circulating around Canberra although the Government did not have any 'triggers' at its disposal.[59] Calling an election might have exploited the growing tension between Whitlam and Dr Jim Cairns, the volatile leader of the Party's Left, but the omens were not favourable. The two by-elections in 1967 had shattered any notion that the Coalition was invincible. As Holt well knew from experience, by-elections frequently produce unexpected results. The voters realise they are not electing a government and shifts in political allegiance are more pronounced. Applications for postal votes must be made early in the absence of facilities for absentee voting.

The resignation of the Immigration Minister, Hubert Opperman, necessitated a by-election in the seat of Corio. This caused 'particular irritation' in parts of the Victorian Division because 'it is believed in some quarters that Mr Opperman's retirement was decided on before the election'.[60] It was rumoured that Opperman fought the November 1966 election merely to ensure the Government retained the seat of Corio before he was apparently sacked and given the High Commissionership to Malta as an inducement to depart without fuss. Holt denied Whitlam's allegation that there had been some kind of deal: 'there was no discussion between me and anybody else . . . until after the results of the general election were known . . . It would have been much more convenient for the Government to win the seat . . . with a new candidate, than subject ourselves to the inconvenience, effort, expense and hazards of a by-election'.[61] Opperman wrote to the *Geelong Advertiser* and denied that any deal was done.[62] The truth is that Holt was disappointed with Opperman's performance as Minister for Immigration but wanted him to leave with dignity. He thought Opperman lacked creativity and had proved a poor public communicator at a time when he needed to persuade the electorate of the need for further reform in immigration policy. Holt chose Billy Snedden as Opperman's successor, believing him to be both innovative and able to explain clearly apparent and actual contradictions in Government policy. Holt also thought Snedden shared his own liberal attitude towards immigration although he was not considered to have been a very 'liberal' Attorney-General.

Opperman had held Corio for the Liberals since 1949 when he had defeated the former Labor minister, John Dedman. In 1963, he had defeated the Labor candidate, R.J.L. Hawke. Although a predominantly Labor area, Opperman had a staunch personal following. He achieved a majority of 8000 votes in an electorate of 52 000 at the November 1966 election. An ex-Olympian, Opperman was much respected and well-liked around Geelong. It is unclear why the Liberals selected a 28-year-old research officer from Melbourne, Ronald Hay, over eight local candidates to stand for the seat. When pressed for an explanation, Holt made it sound as though the Geelong branch was rather inferior and bereft of talent. Opperman was also unhappy with aspects of the Federal Council's handling of the campaign, especially advertising. He told the Federal Director, J.R. Willoughby, that 'if the Corio by-election publicity is conducted in this way, with the Whitlam might of organisation against such efforts, then we can give it away now'.[63] The Labor candidate was Gordon Scholes, a 36-year-old engine driver active in local government. Whitlam had a high profile in the campaign and was able to criticise the Liberal Party for importing a candidate against the wishes of the local branch.

Although the DLP Leader, Senator Vince Gair, thought a Liberal victory was a foregone conclusion,[64] the electorate liked Scholes and gave him their support. He polled more votes than his four rivals combined and was elected to Parliament. Labor's vote increased by 9.5 per cent and there was an 11 per cent swing against the Government. As the first head-to-head electoral contest between Holt and Whitlam the Corio by-election was a deep disappointment for the Government. The Liberal Party defended its poor showing by claiming the convention that by-elections always go heavily against the Government.[65] While Whitlam had campaigned on local issues, particularly health and education, Holt had tried to focus on Vietnam, Australian security and disunity within the Victorian State Branch of the Labor Party.[66] Opperman blamed Holt's 'desire to please everybody' for the Party's serious loss.[67] Holt offered Opperman his own, candid, *post mortem*. After mentioning that attendance at campaign meetings was very low, he remarked that:

> most of the press pundits thought that we would win with a reduced majority . . . I felt it probable that we would hold the seat. I was, therefore, unprepared for the size of the swing. In retrospect, it has been of the same order as we experienced in Higinbotham, Latrobe and Kooyong . . . Perhaps our defeat will have the good effect of alerting the troops to the fact that they may have a tougher fight on their hands than they were anticipating in 1969, and making them pull together better between now and then, including the lead-up to the [1967] Senate election.[68]

The previously impossible now seemed distinctly possible: Labor might win the 1969 election. Whitlam seemed to have the edge on Holt, who had to accept responsibility for the timing of the by-election, the choice of candidate and the tenor of the campaign. After such a poor result, it was widely speculated that Holt might even delay the half-Senate election expected in late 1967 until well into 1968 in the hope that Whitlam's electoral 'honeymoon' would end. Others were not so sure. Bill Wentworth told Holt:

> when you look at Corio and Dawson you have got to reckon on the appeal of Whitlam. Our election in November 1966 went well because Calwell pushed Whitlam into the background and the Communist issue flared up for us against Labor over Vietnam. Vietnam is now going sour.[69]

Given the circumstances, the last thing Holt needed was another by-election.

The death of George Grey, the Labor Member for the Central Queensland seat of Capricornia, greatly grieved the man's family and the Federal Government. It drove Holt to despair. The member for Lilley, Kevin Cairns, told Holt that the Liberals 'would not win' the seat and that delaying the poll until it coincided with the half-Senate election would not help.[70] The Queensland Liberal Treasurer, Gordon Chalk, thought the Liberals might have an outside chance if the endorsed candidate 'is a good one'.[71] The General Secretary of the Queensland Branch suggested to Holt that 'the campaign will probably be fought more on local parochial matters in which development will feature rather than on the big national issues'.[72] Holt was also advised that the 'ALP choice seems to be between mainly Left-wing candidates'.[73] Perhaps there was a glimmer of hope.

The new Labor candidate, Dr Douglas Everingham, was not Whitlam's choice. He was a self-proclaimed atheist and political agitator on the Left of the Labor Party.[74] Grey had been such a popular local member that Holt started to believe the Government did indeed have a chance of regaining the seat it had held from 1949 to 1961. He began to invest heavily in the campaign. In an electorate message headed 'Bring Capricornia Inside the Government', Holt focused on 'education, social services, housing, dairying and wool, and the Bankers' Refinance Corporation, designed to mobilise Australian capital for national development'. Although he recognised the importance of local issues, Holt claimed that since November 1966, nothing had happened 'to change the great central issue of external security, and I would remind you that the ALP still clings to its discredited policies'.[75]

Despite his own opposition to three-cornered contests, Holt invited the Country Party to field a candidate, in the hope of reducing Labor's primary vote. By stating publicly that he wanted to win the seat rather than just maintain the Coalition vote, the Prime Minister imperilled his own political standing once again.[76] Had he been better briefed and ready to employ more subtle tactics, Holt would have learned that Dr Evering-ham was a highly respected Rockhampton medical practitioner who had treated many of the people voting in the by-election. He was also the Liberal candidate's brother-in-law, which enhanced his acceptability to the electorate. While McMahon attacked Everingham's atheism, Whitlam argued that the Government lacked a Department of Northern Develop-ment. The poll was held on 30 September 1967. Everingham managed to achieve a slight increase in the Labor margin but the Coalition vote also increased, at the expense of the DLP. Not surprisingly, the Prime Minister told the press: 'By-elections notoriously run against Governments and there can be few on record when a government has actually gained a better percentage of the vote than it did at the preceding general election'.[77] He tried to mask his disappointment by stating the obvious: 'the Labor Party retained . . . a seat it had held for the past six years'.[78] But Holt had thought the Liberal Party would do much better and the news-papers were not going to let him off the hook so easily. The *Australian* noted: 'Mr Holt cannot have it both ways. Only a fortnight ago he declared he was leading the Liberal Party into the campaign to win'.[79] Holt's personal prestige had suffered unnecessarily. As Graham Freuden-berg astutely observes:

> There never had, in fact, been any chance of Holt securing a Government victory in a by-election in an established Labor seat. The conditions for victory never existed. But he had unwisely committed himself, not just in public to his supporters, but privately to himself. He really believed he could win. The failure to win Capricornia hurt him psychologically and harmed him politically far more than the actual loss of Corio had done. Holt lost something of himself in Capricornia.[80]

According to Laurie Oakes, 'some Labor theorists are convinced that the Capricornia by-election was responsible for the slump in Holt's confidence and the deterioration of his performance which was evident throughout the 1967 Senate election'.[81] There is some truth in this observation.

Holt had certainly become synonymous with electoral defeat. In a con-versation with New South Wales' Premier Robin Askin, McMahon was told that the Federal Government was performing poorly and the swing against the Liberals in the most populous state 'is strong and persistent.

Vietnam has gone sour for almost inexplicable reasons. Businessmen are fed up with the effort that is necessary to keep the battle going'.[82] Holt was also being outperformed by Whitlam, whose public speeches were more lively and incisive. While the public were largely unaware of Whitlam's superior parliamentary skills, 'the performance of the Leader in Parliament is more important to the morale of his party than the electorate'.[83] Holt's colleagues were starting to worry and to grumble. As his Navy Minister, Don Chipp, recalled:

> [he] was a gentle man who rarely showed signs of temper or of adopting the firm authority of a strong leader . . . Holt did not have the personality to control the dissidents: his softness bordered on naivete . . . During 1967 backbenchers were becoming increasingly critical of the prime minister and the Government. The Party Room debates featured growing aggression and new-found bravado, which would never have been contemplated in Menzies' time. Holt allowed this to happen and so it increased. I remember one party meeting where the criticism had reached an abusive level which brought John McEwen to his feet. He was angry not only at backbench stirrings, but that Holt had allowed the situation to deteriorate. I remember his words clearly: he said, 'Okay, if you want leadership, I'll give you bloody leadership. This is what the Government has decided and this is what we are going to do'. It had a remarkable effect on the Party room, which accepted this strong rebuke, but it left a clear feeling with the Liberals that their own Leader had suffered by comparison.[84]

Even his predecessor was concerned about his performance. Menzies remarked that Holt's 'besetting sin' stemmed from the fact that he 'wanted everyone to love him . . . the result was he had made a muck of everything in his second year. He would have lost the next election. It was a dreadful performance. Dreadful'.[85]

CHAPTER 13

Controversy and complaint

November–14 December 1967

HOLT'S NEXT CHALLENGE WAS the 1967 half-Senate election.[1] Although he could have waited until the result of the Capricornia by-election before making a fresh assessment of the Coalition's electoral fortunes over the next few months, Holt decided during the Capricornia campaign to hold the half-Senate election on Saturday 26 November 1967. The poll could have been held as late as May 1968 but Holt was determined to show he was not afraid of facing Whitlam. He also wanted to get the half-Senate election out of the way in order to give himself a full two years without elections before the 1969 general election which he, and most commentators, still expected the Coalition to win given the enormity of the swing required for Labor to be victorious. But the omens were not good. The Capricornia by-election result had shaken the Coalition's confidence while the Government's credibility had been damaged by the HMAS *Voyager* controversy. The military and political situation in South Vietnam had also deteriorated with a growing Australian casualty list and little sign of an end to hostilities.

Luck was also against the Government in the draw for positions on the ballot paper. First place gave the party listed at the top of the ballot paper the 'donkey vote'—the voter simply numbers the ballot paper consecutively from top to bottom. Victoria was the only State in which Coalition candidates headed the list. In New South Wales and South Australia the Labor Party was in first place, with the DLP candidates heading the paper in Queensland, Western Australia and Tasmania. Before the election, there were 29 Government Senators, 28 Labor, 2 DLP and one Independent. The Government needed to win a 3–2 majority in five States in order to regain a majority in the Senate. This was a real challenge, not made any easier by what became known as the 'VIP Airline Scandal' ('the scandal') which would reach its climax as the campaign was about to begin. Although the timing could not have been worse for the Government, it had been some two years in the making.

The scandal began on 20 November 1965 when Menzies approved Arthur Calwell's use of a VIP aircraft from RAAF 34 Squadron to attend a Labor State Conference in Perth. The flight was made available to allow Calwell to travel for an existing commitment after the House of Representatives decided to depart from convention and sit on Friday. Seeking to embarrass Calwell as part of the campaign to replace him as Leader of the Labor Party with Whitlam, Opposition frontbencher Fred Daly asked Holt a Question on Notice about the use and cost of VIP flights over the previous twelve months. Before the answer could be provided (Holt eventually replied on 13 May 1966), Calwell and Daly managed a rapprochement. The Opposition Leader told Holt that Daly would not press the question. Senator Vince Gair, the DLP leader, then tried to embarrass the Labor Party by asking about Calwell's flight with emphasis on the identity of passengers including 'a number of ALP officials' and the political nature of its purpose. Senator Denham Henty, the Leader of the Government in the Senate, told Gair the flight details were not available. For reasons that are still not clear, the answer provided to Holt by the Department of Air was changed within the Prime Minister's Department by the addition of the italicised sentence that appears below. When Holt eventually answered Daly's original question in the House he said: 'Passengers' names are recorded only so that aircraft may be safely and properly loaded. After a flight is completed, the list of names is of no value and is not retained for long. *For similar reasons, no records are kept of the places to which aircraft in the VIP flight have taken VIP passengers.* The answers to these questions are therefore not available'.[2] The Minister for Air, Peter Howson, said he was 'shocked' because the 'amended' answer was completely untrue. He did not, however, inform Holt of the effect of the changes because he believed the Prime Minister wanted to bury the matter. Officers within Howson's department were also unhappy that their Minister's original answer was, in any event, inaccurate.

Both Holt and Howson should have been aware or, at least, been made aware that the Flight Authorisation Books (RAAF Form No. A71) for 34 Squadron were fully maintained. They contained details about the date of the flight, the aircraft type and its side number, the names of the pilot, navigator and crew, a description of 'Duty or Practice Ordered' and a record of take-off and landing times together with the duration of the flight. These books also recorded the name of the VIP who had ordered the flight (one name only appeared) and the sectors flown. The only information not recorded in the Flight Authorisation Book was the names of the passengers who accompanied the designated VIP. These appeared on passenger manifests (RAAF Form No. AAP 873) that were produced before the aircraft's doors closed. The manifests were usually handwritten and contained the names of all passengers, the weight of any luggage (usually shown as an approximate), the date travelled and the sectors completed. As the form was produced in triplicate, two copies were filed, with the top copy being retained by the Squadron.

There is no evidence Holt was aware that his answer was untrue either at the time it was given or in the months that followed. As his only concerns were to preserve the general confidentiality of Government activity of this kind and not to disclose the complete cost of the VIP fleet which the Government had absorbed into Commonwealth outlays on Defence, Holt showed no further interest in either the question or his answer. He believed the matter was dead although the press had by now drawn attention to the allegedly improper deployment of VIP aircraft by the Prime Minister's office which had authorised their use by the Holt family, a small number of Holt's personal friends, and Sir Robert and Dame Pattie Menzies.

One year later, Senators Frank McManus (DLP) and Reg Turnbull (Independent) both asked questions about the VIP flights. Holt was challenged about the matter during a press conference in March 1967. He responded that flights using VIP aircraft were approved by the responsible Minister (Howson) and that they were integral to the efficient conduct of Government.[3] He did not comment upon or correct his earlier statement that passenger and destination records were not kept. But Turnbull, who had known Holt personally since they were at Wesley College together, was not placated. He felt the use of VIP aircraft was both extravagant and unnecessary when commercial air travel was readily available. By now senior RAAF officers were unhappy about Parliament consistently being misinformed about the operations of 34 Squadron. A memorandum drawing attention to the existence of the passenger records reached the offices of Holt and Howson in late August 1967 but was apparently 'filed' before it reached the Prime Minister. A week later Holt realised that use of the VIP fleet was developing into a political controversy that he could not ignore. Holt spoke with Howson about VIP flights on 9 September. There is no record of their conversation, but departmental staff were directed to draft an answer to Turnbull's questions which did not contradict the earlier claim that the information was unavailable. On 26 September, another fourteen Questions Without Notice relating to VIP aircraft were asked in the Senate. On 6 October Holt told the House what he had told the press: VIP aircraft were integral to the efficient conduct of government business, costs were kept to a minimum, their operations fulfilled RAAF training objectives and only once had his family used VIP aircraft in his absence. The latter statement was true only if one accepted Holt's description of a VIP flight. There were actually three occasions on which Holt's family had flown in a VIP aircraft without the Prime Minister but on two of these occasions the aircraft was returning to Canberra before deploying to other destinations. The Holts were passengers on what would have otherwise been an empty plane.

The media were unimpressed. The Senate was not placated. Opposition, DLP, Independent and three Government Senators who crossed the floor combined to pass a resolution ordering the Government to table in the Senate all relevant documents relating to VIP flights dating from 1 July 1966 to 5 October 1967. Holt was initially inclined to reject the demands. At its meeting on 12 October, Cabinet decided to resist making any information available but asked the Attorney-General to determine the extent of the Senate's power to acquire the documents. Howson attended the Cabinet meeting and produced a bundle of documents, including passenger manifests. Bunting immediately took charge of these to prevent their circulation. In his belief that the crucial issue was presenting the cost of VIP flights in a favourable light, Holt overlooked the consequences of his previous inaccurate answers. He had misled the House and the circle of people who knew continued to grow.

On 16 October, Holt had an opportunity to strengthen his hand. Charlie Adermann, the Country Party Minister for Primary Industry, 'felt it necessary to resign to ease his load of work' and was replaced by Doug Anthony. Peter Nixon became Minister for the Interior and Ian Sinclair came into Cabinet as Minister for Social Services. The *Daily Telegraph* cited observers who claimed Holt 'may have been prepared to go further in his reshuffle' but feared giving the appearance 'of panic so close to the Senate election'.[4] Denham Henty allegedly told Holt he too wanted to retire and allow his successor time to consolidate before the election. Holt then announced that 'Senator Gorton, at my request, has agreed to assume responsibility as Government Leader in the Senate'.[5] But immediately on assuming his new responsibilities, Gorton told Holt that refusing the Senate's demand for documents would prompt 'an unholy row'. In any event, Gorton believed the Senate had a right to such information. At a Cabinet meeting held on 17 October it was decided that Holt, Gorton and Howson would confer on a strategy for dealing with questions on VIP flights and that Holt would make a statement on the matter. Gorton's biographer, Ian Hancock, states that Holt knew that Flight Authorisation Books and passenger manifests existed from mid-August 1967 but does not say how Holt came by this information nor can he prove that Holt was party to a cover-up. On 21 October, Geoffrey Yeend, a First Assistant Secretary in the Prime Minister's Department, informed Holt (presumably, but not necessarily, on the advice of Bunting) that parts of his earlier answers were incorrect. This suggests that Holt was still unaware of the truth or that Yeend wanted to avoid being implicated in the developing scandal.

It is quite possible that Holt did not know until mid-October (most likely 18 October) that both Flight Authorisation Books and passenger manifests existed and that his answers were incorrect. It is much more likely, however, that he probably did know. Indeed, he should have taken a much greater interest given that his personal integrity and the Government's honesty were being questioned. All Holt had to do was to ask his personal pilot, Wing Commander Warwick Addison, during one of more than 80 VIP flights he boarded after May 1966, about the records generated by these flights and kept by 34 Squadron. He then would have known the truth.[6] For eighteen months Holt failed to be curious when he should have been, and this was a serious lapse of political judgment. He ought to have practised the lesson he learned as a young man from Jack Beasley, leader of the New South Wales (Lang) Labor group in the 1930s: Beasley had advised Holt to 'answer every question—hostile, humorous, insulting or loaded—as though it is a serious search for knowledge . . . they'll never trap you or score off you if you do that'.[7]

Holt made a statement in the House of Representatives on 24 October that focused on the cost of VIP flights and the importance of their availability. He tabled a set of documents relating to flights between 1 January and 21 August 1967. The following day Senator Colin McKellar, representing the Minister for Air who was attending a Commonwealth Parliamentary Association conference in Uganda, again stated in reply to a question that passenger lists were not retained and the information the Senate wanted was unavailable. The Leader of the Opposition in the Senate, Lionel Murphy, threatened to call the Departmental Secretary, A.B. 'Tich' McFarlane, to the Senate in Howson's absence.[8] A political storm was building. Gorton, as the newly appointed Government Leader in the Senate and a former RAAF fighter pilot, then contacted Jack Bunting in a desperate attempt to prevent McFarlane being dragged before the Senate. Bunting claims to have told Gorton that Howson's advice to Holt in March 1966 was incorrect, although he was unable to say when he knew this to be the case. But neither Bunting nor Gorton could explain why Holt had not been told that the information he had repeatedly supplied was false. Gorton then telephoned McFarlane to be told that the information the Senate sought was indeed available.

Without consulting Holt, McFarlane brought a bundle of 34 Squadron records to Gorton's office. Gorton maintains he then informed Holt that the relevant records had been obtained and that they had always been available. Gorton recalls that Holt was shocked to learn of their existence and horrified that he had persistently misled the Parliament and the press. Howson's account of these events is substantially different. He claims that Holt was furious to learn that not only had Gorton failed to tame the unruly Senate but he was actually intending to table the records. Gorton, however, was definite that Holt made no attempt to prevent or restrain him from tabling any documents in the Senate. At 8.50 p.m. on 25 October, Gorton sought leave of the Senate to table three 'Flight Authorisation Books' and thirteen 'passenger manifests'.[9] Gorton told the Senate that if it 'wished to have the names of the passengers, they could be provided after a little more dissection'.[10] Gorton's statement was rather curious given that the Flight Authorisation Books recorded the name of the VIPs ordering the flights while the passenger manifests showed the names of every passenger on every flight.

Hancock notes: 'It remains unclear precisely when Gorton learnt that the passenger manifests were available, and in what condition'.[11] The last manifest included in the bundle tabled by Gorton is dated 6 October 1967—the end of the period for which the Senate had sought records. There are various others in a file that are undated (from the period August 1966 to October 1967) although several can be dated by the inclusion of foreign dignitaries whose itineraries are on record. There are a number of formal requests and authorisations for VIP flights beginning in April 1967 but these thin out considerably over the ensuing three months. There is nothing to suggest that any flight details for this period are missing (although five monthly bundles are not secured to a file) or that they have been amended or altered in any way. However, the third of the three Flight Authorisation Books was still in use by 14 October (the previous two books had covered the half-year periods from January–June and July–December) when a routine entry was followed by the words 'Book Closed 14 October'. As the book was in daily use, it is clear that 34 Squadron was directed to end its use immediately. But there is no record of who ordered this action or why they chose this particular date, nor anything to indicate the book's whereabouts between 14 October and 25 October when it was handed to Gorton. This leaves plenty of room for conjecture.[12]

The effect of Gorton's brief statement was devastating for the Government. It was now clear that both Holt and Howson had consistently misled the Parliament while the apparent ease with which Gorton had obtained the relevant records made Holt and Howson look either deceitful or incompetent,[13] or both. In a later interview,[14] Gorton said he thought Howson told the Prime Minister what he wanted to hear rather than the truth, and that Holt had sincerely believed that both Howson's initial advice and subsequent explanation were truthful. This was a view shared by some of Holt's colleagues, who were convinced that Holt was 'too experienced a politician to prevent the disclosure of information so readily available'.[15] It was a political disaster for the Government as it prepared to face a sceptical electorate.

In the House of Representatives, Whitlam moved a motion of no-confidence in the Government 'because of the untrue and misleading information' given by Holt and Howson. Whitlam argued that 'if the Parliament cannot rely on the information that is given to it, then the whole fabric of the parliamentary system would be destroyed'.[16] After a turbulent four-hour debate, the motion was lost 65–35 on party lines. Holt remained firm that he did not know passenger information was available when he made his original statement to the House, while Howson would later state that Holt merely relayed what he had been told.[17] In a Foreword to Hancock's recently published study of the affair Howson claims that documents relating to the matter are missing from the Prime Minister's Department files and that Bunting played an active part in withholding the passenger manifests.[18] Bunting's motives in doing this are not clear. Nor is there any evidence of Howson's claim that one set of documents were being 'doctored' while Gorton obtained another set for tabling in the Senate. To avoid the Prime Minister being an advocate in his own cause,

Eggleton issued a press statement on 28 October: 'At all times the answers which the Prime Minister has given have been in good faith. He has set in train inquiries to establish how he came to be provided with certain information and answers'.[19] There seemed to be few courses of action now open to Holt. On becoming Prime Minister he outlined what he called the 'battleship theory' of government: 'the duty of the rest of the fleet is to protect the battleship even at the risk of losing some of the escort vessels. So it is in politics. The Prime Minister is brought into major engagements; it is the duty of the rest of the [Cabinet] team to protect him'.[20] Under such a model, Howson had to go.

Holt decided, however, to extend the sitting of the House until Howson's return from Uganda to allow him to make a personal statement in which he would explain the 'error'. Howson said in the House and to the press that he believed his answer was truthful but that he should have been more diligent in pursuing the information. He subsequently offered Holt his resignation.[21] It was referred to Cabinet and refused for two reasons. First, as Holt had misled the House also, he felt the matter should be referred to Cabinet for consideration rather than him dealing with it personally. Second, Holt believed that resignation was too severe a punishment for what he deemed to be an honest error. Gorton believed that Holt should have ignored Howson's offer of resignation and sacked him immediately. The consensus within Parliament was that Howson should have been sacked. But as Alan Reid has noted, Holt had a 'distaste for providing the electorate with merited scapegoats in the shape of discarded colleagues'.[22] Holt had accepted blows he could have avoided, but his political wounds were now much deeper. Political scientist David Butler noted:

> The bulk of the Australian press professed itself almost as dissatisfied as the ALP with the final explanations of Mr Howson and Mr Holt and the argument was bound to echo onwards, almost necessarily to the detriment of the Liberal–Country government. The acceptance of Mr Howson's resignation would have cleared the air and ended the matter. It might have been unjust—but since when has justice determined the allocation or the continued tenure of portfolios?[23]

In an editorial headed 'VIP—RIP', the *Sydney Morning Herald* concluded: 'The issue of credibility has not been scotched and it would be astonishing if the Labor Party did not try to make the most of it . . . Obviously it is better to be convicted of inefficiency than of dishonesty; but inefficiency is still a serious matter'.[24] The *Australian* thought the issue:

> exemplified an extraordinary measure of ineptitude, carelessness, vacillation, dissimulation and arrogance on the part of an elected government. It had caused patently false information to be presented to the national parliament, and it does call into question the vital issue of ministerial responsibility . . . Mr Holt is a man of integrity and generosity. He is unfortunate in not being the type of ruthless tactician and autocratic leader that seems to be necessary in the type of government he has inherited.[25]

The whole affair was electorally damaging to the Government. But it was a controversy that could have been avoided. When made public, the information sought by the Senate showed the Government *had* observed the rules applying to the use of VIP flights. But it was too late by then. As Louise Overacker observed at the time:

> no one likes paying for other people's privileges, and in this generation there is no more potent symbol of privilege and extravagance than what came to be called the 'Golden Jets'. It was an issue which fascinated the press and the public. Of course the planes were needed, but did they need to cost so much? And shouldn't those who used them be expected to exercise discretion in how they were used, and the passengers they carried?[26]

In the same way that Holt had mishandled the *Voyager* controversy, his handling of the VIP airline scandal was extremely poor. His own Party was deeply disappointed. In a private letter dated 14 November 1967, Howson said: 'I'm only sorry that I helped to get us into this mess over the VIPs: but with your help and encouragement, I was able to assist in extricating the Government'.[27] But this was far from the case.

The Commonwealth's obsession with secrecy meant that government information was routinely withheld unless there was an express reason to disclose it. This made Gorton's tabling of these documents so unexpected. Indeed, Senator Murphy was so surprised by Gorton's action that he needed time to develop a new line of attack. The press also displayed a degree of deference to Ministers. The aggressive investigation that accompanied the VIP scandal heralded a new era of political reporting. Furthermore, the Senate was now the arena in which the Labor Opposition could most effectively confront and compete with the Government.

Gorton's actions were the most surprising, and perhaps more so than those of Holt and Howson. He broke with custom and had no hesitation in acceding to the Senate's demands which led to his leader being embarrassed. Whether or not Holt encouraged or discouraged the tabling of the documents depends on which account is accepted as the more reliable. Gorton's gives credit to Holt; Howson's damns him even further. To my mind there is still too much that is unknown or unclear to explain what happened and who was to blame. Certainly Holt was responsible.

With his integrity badly tarnished, Holt's campaign speech for the half-Senate election was televised nationally on 9 November 1967. He attacked Labor's foreign and defence policies, claiming they were 'suicidal' for the nations of South-east Asia that were being threatened by Communism.[28] On a more positive note, he foreshadowed increased Federal spending on health and education[29] in addition to the $80 million he had already promised for northern development projects.[30] As this was a Senate election, Holt criticised the ALP for using 'its representation in that chamber to thwart the democratically elected majority of the House of Representatives'.[31] The Prime Minister appealed to the Australian people for a Senate majority to carry out the 'mandate' on foreign policy that had been overwhelmingly endorsed by the electorate in 1966.

> The Government has two years of its three-year term to run, but the numbers remain against us in the Senate. Unless this situation is resolved favourably for the Government, Australia faces a period of political uncertainty and confusion. Effective Government is impossible unless we can carry out the policies and program you have endorsed. And this becomes the more necessary in what is clearly a very difficult period when you consider the international scene. The broad question you have to decide is whether you give the Government the means to do its job in the firm, speedy, decisive way you would wish it to perform.[32]

In his campaign opening speech, Whitlam said a Labor-controlled Senate would initiate inquiries into a range of domestic issues and would keep the Government honest. Attacking what the Government thought was its strength, Whitlam pointed to lack of vision in the Coalition's policy on Vietnam, claiming the choice was between 'the continued bombing of

North Vietnam or the eventual desertion of South Vietnam'.[33] Opinion polls consistently predicted a swing to Labor. Whitlam campaigned much more effectively than Holt although most commentators believed Holt performed particularly well in the final week of the campaign. Privately, Holt was satisfied that he had done enough and that stressing the Government's need for a 'majority voice in both houses of parliament' would persuade the electorate to support the Coalition.[34]

On polling day, the Government did poorly, gaining only 43 per cent of the vote compared with Labor's 45 per cent and the DLP's 10 per cent. The Government won three of the five vacancies in Western Australia and South Australia, something Labor could only achieve in New South Wales. In Victoria and Queensland, the DLP took the fifth vacancy while in Tasmania, Independent Senator Turnbull claimed the final place. In the new Senate, the Government had 28 Senators, the ALP 27. The DLP held the balance of power with four Senators (two each from Victoria and Queensland) and there was one Independent. Although Labor did not control the Senate, the Government's vote had fallen by 7 per cent in twelve months while Labor's vote had increased by 5 per cent in the same period. The real victor was the DLP. Its vote rose from 7 to 10 per cent. Although this was the Government's worst electoral performance in six years, Holt could only say that 'the people have taken the opportunity to give the Government a nudge'.[35]

There had been a major shift in electoral fortunes. A July 1967 poll revealed that 56 per cent of Liberal Party respondents approved of Holt's leadership. This was a decline of 4 per cent over twelve months. The same poll showed, however, that Whitlam's approval rating among Labor respondents was 69 per cent compared with 24 per cent for Calwell a year earlier. Labor under Whitlam was becoming a viable alternative. Part of the Government's problem was the extent of Holt's victory in November 1966. He had achieved a level of popularity that the Coalition could not, realistically, maintain. But according to Katharine West, Holt had to keep winning by margins unrealistically determined by 'party optimists rather than electoral realists'.[36]

The Government's problems were not over. The long-running feud between Treasurer Bill McMahon and Trade Minister John McEwen was threatening to fracture the Coalition. Their differences were philosophical, political and personal—McEwen was a protectionist and McMahon a free-trader. They also had different views on foreign investment and equity. In April 1967, McEwen had advocated establishment of an Australian Industry

Development Corporation. It would be a government-owned corporation that would borrow from funds abroad to help finance Australian enterprises seeking to develop natural resources. This initiative became known as the 'McEwen Bank'. For his part, McMahon proposed creating the Bankers' Development Refinance Corporation in an attempt to gather Australia's trading banks under one roof so that larger amounts of Australian money could be invested in development projects. McMahon's Corporation would accept direct investment from the public and the Reserve Bank. Sir Richard Randall, who succeeded Sir Roland Wilson as Secretary to the Treasury in October 1966, was angry that the Department of Trade and Industry had sought to influence Cabinet on this matter when its proposal 'challenges long established financial policies and procedures such as the practice of confining Australian borrowings abroad exclusively to one authority . . . In brief, it is a challenge to the hegemony of the Treasury over one of its most important and difficult fields of responsibility'.[37] McMahon told Holt that 'the Government corporation of the kind Mr McEwen is proposing could hope to do little good of itself and would be bound to do harm to our credit standing abroad'.[38] Holt sided with McMahon and the Treasury. After several months of simmering resentment, the feud was reignited late in November 1967. The spark was the continuing debate over protection for Australian industry in the wake of the British Government's unexpected decision to devalue the pound, an issue that revealed fundamental ideological disagreement between the Coalition partners.

Mention has already been made of BIG's role in the November 1966 election (see p. 169). But it was wrong to accuse McMahon, as many including McEwen did, of cultivating the benefits of BIG's existence for his own political fortunes. Tom Fitzgerald, the financial editor of the *Sydney Morning Herald*, alleged that McEwen was 'turning his anonymous enemies of the Basic Industries Group into a political asset'.[39] Holt had made a conscious decision to avoid commenting directly on BIG's activities or the philosophical underpinnings of its objectives. However, he believed its demands were excessive. On 29 June 1967, Holt commented directly for the first time on the continuing BIG controversy to counter the internal disunity that the organisation was causing. He stated that criticism of McEwen or the Country Party over tariff policy was unfair. Furthermore, McMahon had assured Holt that 'neither he nor so far as he could ascertain any of his Liberal Party colleagues' had any connection with BIG or its interests: 'the activity of any organisation which could be regarded as prejudicial to the harmonious working of the coalition is certainly not in the interests of myself or any of my colleagues in the Coalition'.[40] But, as Golding observes:

> No doubt Holt was hoping that by coming out into the open on the issue the problem would go away. That it did not go away, one suspects, was at least partly due to the probability that McEwen could see a very real and urgent need to 'exploit the secrecies of BIG', as Fitzgerald put it, as a tactic to divert attention from the disadvantages of the Government's protection policies which were coming under increasingly critical scrutiny in the rural sector.[41]

There was also a lingering suspicion that McMahon was aiding and abetting BIG's activities. Holt's biggest problem was that very few members of Cabinet trusted his Treasurer's integrity or believed he would honour his word.

As early as July 1967, Lord Casey thought the feud was getting out of hand. He suggested to Holt that he should talk to McMahon and try to salvage the Treasurer's deteriorating relationship with McEwen. When Holt called them both into his office, however, the meeting degenerated into a bitter exchange of accusations and insults. McEwen accused McMahon of orchestrating a campaign against him and the Department of Trade by leaking potentially harmful material to Maxwell Newton and Alan Reid. McMahon denied any improper relationship with Newton, who operated a tariff information service to overseas embassies and trade organisations. McEwen was far from convinced. Holt concluded that there was no substance to McEwen's allegations but asked McMahon to sever all contact with Newton as an indication of his commitment to Coalition harmony. Holt brought the meeting to a close by insisting that the two men shake hands. There is no record of whether they did but the gesture failed because they remained implacable enemies. McMahon did end his contact with Newton and subsequently refused his requests for interviews, although he did warn him when a warrant was issued to raid his premises. But Casey, who continued to meddle in Party Room politics, thought the poor state of the McEwen–McMahon relationship was affecting the stability of the Coalition and, therefore, the Government. He insisted on 'sending for McMahon'. While it could be argued that both McEwen and McMahon had contributed to the situation, the Governor-General advised Buckingham Palace that 'from my knowledge of the matters at issue between McEwen and McMahon I laid most of the blame for the controversy on McMahon'.[42]

The feud then assumed another dimension. The Japanese External Trade Organisation (JETRO) was an official Japanese organisation based in Sydney. Because Newton was contracted by JETRO as a consultant, he was accused by McEwen of being a 'secret paid agent of the Japanese Government'. A 'top secret' ASIO document headed 'JETRO' and dated 21 August 1967 revealed the extent of McEwen's willingness to destroy McMahon by whatever means.

> On 18 August 1967, the Director General [Spry] discussed a plan of action against [JETRO]. The Secretary, Department of Trade [Sir Alan Westerman] ... had drawn the attention of the Director General to the activities in Australia of [JETRO] and expressed the view that, whilst its ostensible functions were similar to those of the Department of Trade, it appeared it was attempting to campaign against the [Australian] Government and was involving itself in domestic issues which indicated the possibility of subversion.[43]

The document also suggested an investigation into Newton's personal affairs. Holt was given a further memo regarding Newton on 30 October 1967. It was stamped 'Top Secret' and claimed that Newton was now being employed exclusively by the United States Information Service. An undated attachment, marked 'Document B', stated with confidence:

> Bill McMahon is using Newton as a mouthpiece to further his own ambitions to take over the leadership of the Liberal Party and, therefore, ultimately the prime ministership. As I [the author's name is not shown on the document] said earlier, for months Newton has been carrying out a bitter campaign against McEwen through 'invective' but more recently has eased up on McEwen and switched the attack to Holt. Throughout these attacks, the theme has been that while McEwen nor Holt can do anything right, McMahon cannot put a foot wrong.[44]

There was allegedly evidence of this strategy in Newton's *Management Newsletter*. Under the heading 'Mr Holt's low standing', Newton claimed that: 'Mr Holt has led his Government into this week's parliamentary recess with his personal standing among his colleagues probably at its lowest level in the 20 months since he has been Prime Minister. Mr Holt has lost the confidence and authority he showed in the earlier parliamentary session this year'. Newton also said that backbenchers in marginal seats 'are blaming Mr Holt personally for their impending political extinction'.[45]

No evidence of espionage or subversion was ever produced in relation to JETRO but McEwen later obtained information from a report prepared by the Director General that eventually found its way into the *Australian* newspaper. It led with a story headed 'Foreign agent is the man between two leaders' and cited Newton's JETRO contact.[46] McMahon was damned by association.

Relations between the two men were, however, relatively stable during September and October 1967. McEwen played no part in the half-Senate election campaign, as he was attending General Agreement on Tariffs and Trade (GATT) meetings in Geneva and Paris.[47] A week before the election (18 November 1967), Britain devalued the pound by 14.3 per cent. The Australian Government had not anticipated this as the British Prime Minister had publicly rejected devaluation for many years. Wilson alerted Holt to his change of mind: 'I know that the decision will be unwelcome to you . . . indeed the interest of Sterling holders was one of our strongest reasons for trying so hard and so long to avoid taking the step which we have now taken'.[48] Australia had considered similar action since 1964 and Menzies had quietly reduced the proportion of Australia's reserves held in sterling. As Treasurer, McMahon issued a press statement in which he said the Australian economy was sound and that no deval-uation of the Australian dollar would be necessary. This was despite simultaneous increases in consumer spending, public authority outlays and private capital expenditure, a balance of payments deficit and a fall in overseas reserves from $1.672 billion to $1.2 billion.

Recognising the need for political and practical action, both Holt and McMahon withdrew from the election campaign. On 20 November, Cabinet was asked to consider two submissions. Treasury recommended no devaluation whereas the Department of Trade considered that devalu-ation was the sensible option. After speaking with McEwen, both Anthony and Sinclair told Cabinet that export industries would have to be compensated if the dollar did not follow the pound. In an historic moment in which the economic fortunes of Australia diverged sharply from those of the United Kingdom, Cabinet decided in favour of Treasury's submission although Holt gave a public assurance that if exporters suffered as a result of the Government's decision, a review would be ordered.[49] Despite unfair criticism that the Government was being indecisive, Holt announced that:

> The Australian dollar today is a currency in its own right. It has to stand on its own feet and it has shown itself capable of doing so. We have an enviable reputation abroad for political and economic stability . . . It is, of course, one thing for us to take the decision and another thing to live with that decision. But we are in a strong economic position with a comfortable level of external reserves. It was imperative that we do nothing to undermine confidence in the Australian dollar. We believe that by acting as we have we are protecting the dollar.[50]

The *Bulletin* noted the significance of the decision: 'the sterling devaluation is quite certain to mean the end of any remaining special relationship between Australia and Britain'.[51]

Initially McEwen appeared to accept the decision in a press statement issued from Geneva. On his return to Australia, McEwen met with Anthony, Sinclair and Westerman, his Departmental Secretary. By this time, Anthony had delivered a speech critical of the effect high tariffs were having on rural industries. The next day, McEwen issued a long public statement in which he questioned Cabinet's decision, predicted that Australian exporters would suffer and proposed the establishment of an advisory authority on export compensation to monitor the situation: 'it is sad and serious that the decision strikes in a most selective manner at our wealth-producing industries, both primary and secondary'. He concluded: 'there must be a competent unbiased authority to ascertain the facts on damage and make recommendations to the government'. Arguing that a refusal to devalue was effectively to appreciate the value of the currency, 'neither suffering industries nor the government itself can afford haggling later on'.[52]

Holt was outraged that McEwen had broken with the principle of Cabinet solidarity and taken such a contrary public position without having the decency to speak with him first. Holt asked his Departmental Adviser, Peter Bailey, to confirm that the Liberals could govern in their own right if two of the Country Party's members defected to the Liberal side. Some of Holt's colleagues felt he should have withdrawn the Deputy Prime Ministership from McEwen. An editorial in the *Daily Telegraph* before the most recent controversy claimed that 'McEwen is a menace and a trouble maker. And he is disloyal. Mr Holt deserves better from a deputy . . . and Mr Holt could sack him without a ripple of protest'.[53] Holt called McEwen into his office for a meeting that lasted half an hour. Peter Bailey later recalled that McEwen walked out of Holt's office and slammed the door. He looked tense and annoyed. After five minutes Bailey entered

Holt's office and asked the Prime Minister how he was feeling. Holt replied, 'OK, the Government's still going. Now I'm off to Portsea.'

McEwen's public statement had been pure politics. He later told the Country Party's Federal Council that he *had* discussed the matter with Holt and had not sought permission to make the statement because it would not have been granted and:

> my views and the views of the Country Party would not have been known to the rural industries. I said I had a dual responsibility being his partner in government and also being the leader of a great national party dedicated to looking after the rural industries which had been affected by the Government's decision.[54]

Holt issued a statement in which he claimed that because McEwen was abroad 'he did not have the advantage of participating in the wide-ranging Cabinet discussions, nor did he have the detail before him of the latest appreciation of the likely effects of British devaluation on our own economy'.[55] The press reported the meeting between Holt and McEwen as a decisive victory for the Prime Minister. Holt was praised for the tough stand he had taken and, for the first time in 1967, lauded for a display of strong leadership. Freudenberg remarked:

> It was a worthy action of a Prime Minister protecting the currency and asserting the principle of Cabinet responsibility; it was a courageous action of a coalition leader asserting the collective policy against a sectional interest and a party faction. In a year of drift and decline, it was Holt's best day.[56]

With hindsight, however, Holt may have won that particular battle but McEwen would be the victor in a larger war. He later persuaded the Cabinet—against Treasury advice—to introduce 'devaluation compensation' to cover instances in which overseas trade contracts were expressed in sterling which may have had a lower value than the dollar. But for the time being, Holt was in good spirits. He had gained a tactical victory over McEwen and may have thought the poisoned relationship between McEwen and McMahon could be healed or its worst effects ameliorated. Casey thought his private talk with McMahon 'may have done some good' but McMahon resented his interference.[57]

Casey had summoned McMahon to Admiralty House in Sydney. The Treasurer believed that McEwen had actually suggested the meeting to

Casey who, McMahon believed, had no right as Governor-General to call for him in such a manner. Although Casey claimed he was concerned with the state of the Coalition, his actions amounted to unmistakable interference that could have severely compromised his position. The next day, the Governor-General sent Holt a confidential summary of their conversation, including his observation that the 'notorious relationship' between McMahon and McEwen 'reduced the prestige of the government in the public mind and so might well affect the election results'. Casey told McMahon that his relationship with Newton was clearly manifest in the journalist's obvious support for him and disdain for McEwen and Holt. When McMahon claimed that he had tried to repair his relationship with McEwen, Casey instructed him to keep trying. The Governor-General also told McMahon that he had earlier encouraged McEwen to remain in Parliament for as long as possible because there was not a suitable Country Party successor. McEwen had replied that his relationship with McMahon had caused his health to suffer and reduced the likelihood of him staying in politics.

Casey's summation leaves no doubt that he considered McMahon to be the culprit. He also felt McMahon adopted a rather sanctimonious attitude to the dispute. Of course, Casey had no business involving himself in Party Room matters while his coloured opinions of McMahon, freely offered to both McMahon's supporters and adversaries, only added to the layers of intrigue. The Prime Minister did nothing to restrain the politically active Governor-General. Holt and Casey had spoken with Peter Howson, the Minister Assisting the Treasurer, in the hope that he might be able to build bridges between the two belligerents but this, too, was unsuccessful. The initiative was back with Holt. He 'told Casey by phone that he planned to take Casey's letter [summarising his conversation with McMahon] with him to his holiday home at Portsea where he could give it fuller consideration over the Christmas holidays'.[58] As the end of the year approached, there were other party tensions that Holt needed to resolve.

In late 1967, Dudley Erwin, Government Whip in the House of Representatives, approached Gorton as Government Leader in the Senate to convey apparent backbench discontent about Holt's leadership. Erwin wanted a larger stake in Party affairs than he had been given and was described by several of his colleagues as a 'cunning schemer'. Why Erwin spoke to Gorton is not altogether clear but the most likely reason is that he could not get Holt to take these concerns seriously. Erwin also felt at ease in speaking candidly with Gorton, who as Government Senate Leader was a regular visitor to the Whip's office and also socialised with Erwin. Eggleton also noted that Holt's leadership was allegedly being discussed at regular informal meetings of a group of Sydney Liberal Members including St John, Mackay, Wentworth and Bridges Maxwell.[59] He did not 'think this could be described as a meeting to plot a coup. It had not got to anything like that stage. There seems to have been no connection between this and the Erwin-Gorton-Fraser group'.

After the half-Senate election, Erwin again approached Gorton and showed him a draft letter outlining Party criticisms that he proposed showing to the Prime Minister in the hope that Holt would take remedial action. Gorton thought the draft letter containing the Party Room 'soundings' was 'far too abrasive and hurtful'.[60] Gorton suggested that a toned-down description of the matters causing concern should be forwarded to Holt as a more encouraging line would evoke a better response. Erwin's secretary, Ainsley Gotto, also consulted Allen Fairhall. In addition to speaking personally with Holt, Fairhall offered to be part of a delegation that would approach the Prime Minister about the difficulties facing the Government. Fairhall believed that unless the Government learned from recent experiences, the Coalition would be out of office at the next election. Even Holt's close friend Peter Howson was concerned. He wrote in his diary on 22 November 1967:'I had a talk with Jock Pagan [Federal President of the Liberal Party] about the PM's need to rest and relax so that he doesn't get too close to detail and has time to see the wider issues. I think Jock agreed with me; we both must try and find ways of getting the PM to do this in the coming weeks'.[61] A week later he recorded:

> I had a talk with Jack McConnell of the Liberal Party organisation. We both felt that the PM has concentrated too much on administration and not enough on politics this year, and that he needs more political advice, particularly from the Party. He does not appear to have listened to Willoughby or to McConnell or to Carrick this year, and we would need to do more about this in 1968. Dudley Erwin also rang me and expressed similar views.[62]

Hasluck echoed Howson's concerns.

> Fairhall, Hulme and Fairbairn had apparently objected strongly to his tendency to try to do the work of his ministers and all, including Bury,

deplored either that they could never get a chance to speak to him or that, if they did, they could not gain his concentrated attention. He was trying to busy himself with too many aspects of government and missing the big issues.[63]

Erwin also talked to Tony Eggleton, who shared his concern about Holt's recent performance but believed that things could and would get better in the new year. Eggleton wrote to Holt about ways of improving the service his staff were offering to him. He was particularly concerned about Holt's public speeches:

> Gough Whitlam and his team are putting great emphasis on polished speeches to get maximum mileage out of Whitlam's public appearances. Clearly the Leader of the Opposition has much more time to devote to this kind of exercise than the Prime Minister. This is all the more reason for ensuring that the PM has the proper backing . . . [to] justify the preparation and time that the PM has to put into a speech, we should ensure that we are going to obtain a reasonable dividend from it . . . It may not be a bad thing to undertake rather fewer speaking engagements but to make each one a 'winner'.[64]

Eggleton encouraged Holt to visit public works projects in Australia and New Guinea to show 'an active Prime Minister taking a close personal interest in the development and progress being stimulated by his Government'. He thought it important to further 'the "Holt era" image in our relations with Asia' and to anticipate the likely lines of attack when the Opposition tries 'to make as much mischief as possible for us over the VIP business and the *Voyager*'.

It was hard to imagine how 1968 could be worse than 1967. Having started the year with the largest House of Representatives majority in Australian history, the Coalition lost both the Corio and Capricornia by-elections and the 'nexus' referendum. The Government had been forced to hold another Royal Commission into the loss of HMAS *Voyager*, it had suffered throughout the VIP airline scandal, the Senate had overturned increases to postal charges on three occasions, McMahon and McEwen were still feuding and the Coalition did not do well enough in the half-Senate election. The Government's fortunes had to change soon or its next term of office—assuming it was victorious in 1969—would be its last. And given the Liberal Party's tendency to dispose of its leaders after a poor

Wesley College, Melbourne cricket team, 1921, with Holt on the far left in back row. Future Independent Senator for Tasmania R.J. Turnbull is in the back row fourth from left. NAA: M4297, 7 (8852017)

Holt in his early twenties, before entering parliament (and prior to his teeth being capped). NAA: M4294, 3 (4982235)

The eligible bachelor MP, magazine portrait, 1938. NAA: M4297, 7 (8852022)

Holt attends AIF recruiting office, May 1940. NAA: M4294, 6 (8852097)

Holt with a group of children after he introduced the Child Endowment Legislation and was pronounced the 'Godfather of a million children', 30 May 1941. NAA: M4294, 3 (8852030)

Swearing-in of Menzies' ministry, 1950. Holt seated in front row on far right. NAA: M4297, 10 (8852032)

Holt addresses the Third Citizenship Convention as Minister for Immigration, Canberra, 29 January 1952. Zara is on his right. NAA: M4294, 5 (8852025)

Holt receives a presentation doll during the Third Citizenship Convention, Canberra, 29 January 1952. Zara is on his left. NAA: M4294, 5 (8852026)

Holt in Switzerland, 1952.
NAA: M4294, 6 (8852096)

Portrait circa 1953. NAA: M4294, 3
(8852031)

Metal Trades Exhibit, Careers Exhibition, Sydney, 29 August 1955. Henry Bland,
Secretary of the Department of Labour and National Service, is on his right.
NAA: M4294, 6 (8852100)

Holt with Mrs Pat Nixon, wife of US Vice President Richard Nixon, at the Melbourne Olympic Games, 1956. NAA: A7135, 3 (3458048)

Holt with the Federal Minister for Labour and Welfare of the Federation of Nigeria, Chief Festus Sam Okotie-Eboh, ILO Conference, 1957. Mr Alfred John White, Past President of the Hobart Trades Hall Council, is also pictured. NAA: M4294, 6 (8852098)

Holt with US President John F. Kennedy at the White House, 1961. NAA: M4294, 6 (8852099)

Holt at the annual Board of Governors' meeting of the World Bank, September 1962. This is one of the very few occasions Holt was photographed with a cigarette in his hand. NAA: M4294, 7 (8852015)

Holt about to enter the House to deliver his budget speech, 13 August 1963. NAA: M4297, 7 (8852019)

Holt with Governor-General, Lord Casey (left) at Government House after the swearing-in of his ministry, 1966. NAA: A1200, L53617 (11196677)

Holt ministry swearing-in at Government House, 1966. NAA: A1200, L53615 (11198590)

Ladybird Johnson, Harold Holt, Lyndon Johnson and Zara Holt at the White House, June 1966. NAA: A1200, L56295 (11336939)

Zara and Harold having coffee at Portsea, Victoria, 1966. This was their favourite photograph together. NAA: M4294, 4 (8852001)

Zara and Harold at Portsea, 1966.
NAA: A1200, L54295 (11196679)

Holt at Portsea, 1966. NAA: A1200,
L54298 (11196682)

Holt spear fishing at Cheviot Beach, Portsea, 1966. NAA: A1200, L54303 (11145687)

The Queen Mother and Prince Charles at The Lodge in Canberra with Harold and Zara, March 1966. NAA: A2405, RT2/162 (11376109)

Holt inspects the military guard at the opening of Lavarack Barracks, Townsville, 29 July 1966. NAA: M4294, 5 (8852027)

Holt jostled during a November election rally in Rockdale, 1966. NAA: M4294, 7 (8852013)

Holt in spear fishing gear with friend Peter Lynch, 1967. NAA: M4297, 7 (8852020)

Holt with grandson, Christopher, 1967.
NAA: M4297, 1 (8852028)

Holt addresses Moral Rearmament Action
Assembly, Monash University, 6 January
1967. NAA: M4294, 7 (8852016)

Holt and W.C. Wentworth MP with lobbyists from the Federal Council for the
Advancement of Aborigines and Torres Strait Islanders, Parliament House,
February 1967. From left to right: Gordon Bryant MP, Faith Bandler, Harold Holt,
Pastor Doug Nichols, Burnam Burnam, Win Branson and W.C. Wentworth MP.
NAA: A1200, L62232 (11198523)

Harold and Zara arriving at Parliament House for the opening of the 26th Parliament, February 1967. NAA: A1200, L60776 (11198453)

Holt is welcomed to Cambodia at Phnom Penh airport during his trip to South-east Asia, March 1967. NAA: A1200, L63268 (11469279)

An Ansett-ANA helicopter searching for Holt's body off Cheviot Beach, Portsea,
17 December 1967. NAA: A1200, L69832 (11420860)

Police and those who were with Harold Holt when he entered the surf at Cheviot
Beach reconstruct his final movements, 17 December 1967. NAA: A1200, L69850
(11420878)

Phillip Lynch MP speaking at a memorial service for Harold Holt, Cheviot Beach, 1969. As part of the service a plaque was bolted to the sea floor where Holt disappeared. NAA: A1200, L79740 (11458534)

Sailors marching on board USS *Harold E. Holt* after the ship was commissioned, May 1969. The ship's badge featuring the name 'Harold E. Holt' is on the left hand side. NAA: M4297, 10 (8852033)

electoral performance, Holt had reason to be anxious. Only one non-Labor leader, having lost an election, has gone on to fight the next as leader: Menzies lost in 1946 but led again in 1949. But Holt had been in politics most of his adult life, had survived more than 30 years of Parliament by determination and resilience, and knew that political fortunes change rapidly. At any rate, the Liberals had not yet begun to think about Holt's successor. He had been Leader for such a short period, and most expected him to lead for at least another four years. A candidate would have emerged in two years but there appeared no need to encourage succession speculation so early in Holt's reign.

Then Holt received Erwin's much redrafted letter.

During the last six months of the Parliament and to this present time, various members at all levels within the Party have expressed to me feelings of disquiet. This same feeling seems to be permeating the electorate and is being followed up in the Press. Do you personally feel that there could be some reason for this attitude? Do you think it is of sufficient importance for me to probe more deeply into these problems, if you feel that, in fact, there are problems? And to make a further report to you? I am writing to you only in view of what I think is the seriousness of the situation at the moment and leave it to your evaluation and judgement as to whether you would like a summary of the situation.

Holt read the letter but did not respond immediately. These were matters upon which he could and would reflect over the coming Christmas holidays.

CHAPTER 14
Fate and destiny
15 December 1967–12 March 1968

FEDERAL CABINET'S LAST MEETING of 1967 began in the evening of Thursday 14 December and continued into the early hours of Friday morning. After only a few hours' sleep, Holt returned to his Parliament House office at 8.30 a.m. to complete a Statement outlining measures the Government proposed implementing to assist industries affected by the Cabinet decision not to devalue the Australian dollar.[1] He also signed the last of his official Christmas cards which were then bundled up and made ready for posting. At 11 a.m., he walked out of Parliament House and boarded a RAAF Mystere VIP jet at RAAF Base Fairbairn bound for Melbourne. Zara was spending the weekend at The Lodge entertaining Allison Büsst, and finalising preparations for the annual Christmas party to be held the following Tuesday. On arriving in Melbourne Holt, accompanied by his personal secretary, Pat De Lacy, travelled to his city office in a Commonwealth car. He was there for around thirty minutes while he dictated a number of letters before he was driven to St Georges Road. There he announced to 'Tiny' Lawless that he was leaving immediately for the family beach house at Portsea as it was 'such a lovely day'.

The Mornington Peninsula was a favourite place for Harold and Zara. They had spent many summer holidays at nearby Sorrento after they were married. Although land was difficult to acquire, in 1960 Zara had bought what had been the tennis courts and orchard of a property owned by Winton and Marjorie Gillespie. A 'modest' timber beach house had been built shortly thereafter, and the Holts and Gillespies became good friends. There was no dividing fence between the two houses and they shared a garden. While Lawless packed clothes and gathered provisions for the weekend, Holt drove to Sorrento (on Port Phillip Bay) in his deep red Pontiac Parisienne—a demonstrator model—where he happened to meet Marjorie Gillespie at Johnson's Fish Store and accepted her invitation to drinks that evening. Lawless arrived in Portsea at 5 p.m. At 6.45 p.m., Holt called on Winton and Marjorie Gillespie as planned but stayed for less than an hour, explaining that he was playing tennis the next day. The Prime Minister ate dinner with Lawless and retired to bed about 9.30 p.m.

Holt rose at 6.30 a.m. and ate his customary light breakfast of tea and toast. He then telephoned Tony Eggleton, at around 8.30 a.m., to inquire about the media's reaction to his Statement on devaluation and to discuss his proposed approach to a press conference scheduled for the following Tuesday. Eggleton remarked that the media response was generally supportive. During the next half an hour Holt 'reflected on the year and the need to get things in perspective.' There was a danger that the public 'might not be able to see the wood for the trees'. Although a 'few matters' had been exaggerated by the media, Eggleton remarked that the Government had performed solidly during 1967. Holt replied: 'We should not be leaving the impression that this is not a well-governed country. A few pertinent facts and figures will make people realise just how well governed they are'. He returned 'to his theme about lack of world appreciation of the importance of Asia and the Pacific, and the need to make people understand that our Region would be the powerhouse of the future'. As he had visited most of the regional leaders, he told Eggleton that in the coming year he would 'visit European capitals to encourage them to take more interest in our part of the world . . . before Christmas, he would raise with the Department the need to start planning an appropriate travel program for next year'.[2]

The rest of Saturday morning was devoted to a telephone conversation with stepson Nicholas in Melbourne and the impromptu removal of an unwanted and overgrown ti-tree near the house. Holt then worked on some official papers until eating lunch at around 1.30 p.m. He followed his lunch with a short rest before playing tennis with Dr Bruce Edwards at his Sorrento home. On returning home at 5 p.m., the Prime Minister spent some time with his stepson Nicholas, his daughter-in-law and granddaughter who had arrived from Melbourne. After attending a neighbour's cocktail party from 6.30 p.m. to 7.30 p.m., Holt returned home for a dinner party. The fourteen diners rose from the table around 11.15 p.m. While the other guests went to a neighbour's house and listened to music until midnight, Holt went to bed.

Just before 6.30 a.m. on Sunday 17 December, Holt rose and had a light breakfast while attending to more official papers. At around 8 a.m., he telephoned Zara and they spoke about the previous evening, and their plans for the forthcoming Christmas season. The Prime Minister made at least one other call. According to Lawless, Holt spoke with McMahon. During the conversation she heard Holt say: 'All right Billy, if that's the way you want it, that's it'. Holt then turned to Lawless and, rather enigmatically, said: 'That's it, Tiny'. He did not elaborate further on the contents of the conversation or its consequences. Mid-morning, Holt drove to the Portsea General Store and collected the weekend newspapers and the latest edition of *Time*, which had not been delivered as arranged. The front page of the previous day's *Australian* carried two stories of interest to him. The first was under the headline 'Holt hits out at feather-bedding' and reported his statement that the Commonwealth would no longer support uneconomic primary producers, particularly in the dairy, canned fruit and sugar industries, with government subsidies. Holt had announced that the Minister for Primary Industry, Doug Anthony, would conduct an inquiry into several industries ahead of possible government-assisted reconstruction. There was another two-paragraph story of personal interest under the heading 'PM advised to swim less'. It continued: 'The Prime Minister, Mr Holt, is having specialist treatment for a painful shoulder. A spokesman for Mr Holt said yesterday that although the Prime Minister was carrying out a full work schedule, his doctor had advised him to cut down on swimming and tennis'.[3] Dr Marcus Faunce had examined Holt on Friday morning before he left Canberra.

Armed with the newspapers, he also bought four bags of salted peanuts and two cans of insect repellent. On returning home, Holt was invited to share a barbeque lunch with his neighbour, Jonathan Edgar. Holt then telephoned Marjorie Gillespie and said he was going to the old fort near the tip of Point Nepean and asked whether anyone in her family wanted to accompany him. Lawless was then informed that the Prime Minister and some friends were going to watch the around-the-world sailor, Alec Rose, enter Port Phillip Bay in his yacht *Lively Lady*, from a vantage position at Point Nepean. Holt would then be lunching with the Edgars and, after a short spearfishing trip with Jonathan Edgar planned for 4 p.m., he would dine with the Gillespies in the evening. The group that set out for Point Nepean at 11.15 a.m. included the Prime Minister and Marjorie Gillespie, Vyner Gillespie (Marjorie's daughter) and her friend Robert 'Martin' Simpson, and Alan Stewart (a houseguest of the Gillespies). As the sea was rolling and *Lively Lady* was some way off the coast, there was not much to be seen of Rose's arrival. At Holt's instigation the group decided to move on. As the air had become hot and sultry, Holt suggested that they drive to Cheviot Beach for a quick swim before lunch.

This part of the coastline, also known as 'Portsea Backbeach', took its name from the wrecked 1226-tonne passenger steamer SS *Cheviot*. After losing her propellers in heavy seas and with her anchors unable to hold her, the *Cheviot* was driven towards the beach on 19 October 1887. By the next morning, the steamer was wrecked and 35 people had drowned. Only seven bodies were ever recovered. The loss of the *Cheviot* has been described as 'the most tragic wreck ever to occur in the vicinity of the heads', but this was and is a notorious part of the coastline.[4] The records of the Melbourne Harbour Trust reveal that 61 vessels had been sunk within a 2.5-mile radius of the area between 1840 and 1967. Most of the bodies from the wrecked ships, as was the case with the *Cheviot*, were carried into Bass Strait and never seen again. Very few were washed ashore. Holt knew the beach and its waters very well. In January 1960, he salvaged a porthole from the *Cheviot* in 25 feet of water in a place he said was only accessible after 'a strong northerly has flattened out the sea'. He made the relic available to the Museum of Modern Art in Melbourne for an exhibition entitled 'Found, Contrived and Revered Objects Exhibition'.[5] Holt, patron of the Underwater Skindivers and Fishermen's Association of Australia,[6] was always very keen to get into the water. In a letter to his friend Arnold Glass a few weeks earlier, he said he had 'been in the water at Portsea on each of the last two weekends . . . The water is still too cold for an extended hunt [for abalone] and conditions have not been right yet at the back beach [i.e., Cheviot Beach]'.[7]

After clambering down a steep sand dune to the beach, the group led by the Prime Minister noticed a substantial quantity of sawn timber planks that had been washed up on the sand. They had most probably been used as dunnage to secure cargo in passing merchant ships. Holt, who was wearing light blue shorts, a dark blue shirt, a green bush hat and old sand-shoes, ducked behind a rock and changed into a pair of black and green bathers. He kept his lace-less sandshoes on. While the others debated about whether it was safe to go swimming given the size and strength of the waves pounding the beach, Holt walked towards the water and, without hesitation, jumped in and started to swim in the shallow water. He had remarked a few moments before: 'I know this beach like the back of my hand'. It was high tide and the water was swirling with currents and eddies. The youthful Alan Stewart was encouraged by Holt's actions. He told Marjorie Gillespie: 'If Mr Holt can take it, I'd better go in too'. He entered the surf but kept his feet firmly on the bottom.

As Holt swam into deeper water, he appeared to enter the end of a deep Y-shaped pool near a rock ledge which was hidden by the sea. The tail of the Y was the outlet from the rock ledge and was affected by a strong undertow of several knots' strength. Stewart felt the undertow even in the shallow water and moved towards the shore as Holt was enveloped by swirling turbulent water that appeared to drag him further out to sea. Marjorie Gillespie called out, 'Come back! Come back!' Stewart asked, 'Does he usually swim this long?' Mrs Gillespie replied, 'No.' Holt did not call for help or raise his arms. The waves seemed to gather and then envelop the Prime Minister, whose silver hair disappeared from view. She later remarked: 'It was like a leaf being taken out. It was so quick and so final'. A few moments later and still he could not be seen. Gillespie and Stewart continued to scan the water for any sight of the Prime Minister. It was now about 12.15 p.m. Vyner Gillespie and Robert Simpson returned from a brief walk down the beach to find a frantic Marjorie Gillespie saying, 'He is gone. We can't see him.' After ten minutes Holt was clearly in desperate trouble. Stewart got into his car and drove at speed to the front gates of the Army's Officer Cadet School at Portsea. While remaining calm, he explained to the sentry, Private Peter Morgan, that the Prime Minister 'is in difficulties as he went swimming and he has not been sighted owing to the very big surf'. As most of the personnel were on annual military leave, the School was almost deserted. There could be no delay if Holt was to be rescued—wide-ranging assistance was requested.

The Victoria Police were contacted together with lifesavers, spotter aircraft, helicopters and military personnel. Stewart returned to Cheviot Beach at 1.30 p.m. with three amateur skindivers, Corporal Neville Woods and two of Woods' friends, John Haywood and Neville Lynch. They tried to enter the sea but found diving in the turbulent water virtually impossible. At 1.30 p.m. Tony Eggleton received a call from Herschel Hurst, a Canberra representative of the Melbourne *Sun*, who had heard a rumour that a 'VIP' was missing off Cheviot Beach. He apologised for disturbing Eggleton on what he thought was a 'long shot' but asked if there was any possibility of it being the Prime Minister. Eggleton agreed with Hurst that there were plenty of VIPs in the Portsea area but offered to make inquiries. He rang The Lodge and spoke with Ray Coppin who, as general supervisor at The Lodge, usually kept himself informed about anything that was happening. Coppin told Eggleton that there had been no reports of concern and that Mrs Holt was at a Christmas party being given by Grant McIntyre. At 1.50 p.m., Eggleton received another call from Hurst. The Melbourne radio station 3DB was now reporting that the search off Portsea was definitely for the Prime Minister. Eggleton rang Peter Bailey, who was having lunch with his colleague Clarrie Harders, Deputy Secretary of the Attorney-General's Department, and had not heard anything. He then contacted the house at Portsea and spoke to 'Tiny' Lawless, who could not say where Holt was. Eggleton would later write in his diary: 'I hung up with the realisation that there was definitely something wrong. I felt concerned but had no doubt there would be a logical explanation'.[8] A telephone call to the Victoria Police confirmed that the 'missing VIP' was Prime Minister Holt.

By this time, one of the largest search operations in Australian history had begun. Inspector Laurie Newell was placed in temporary command of the police component and made overall coordinator of the search. He was flown in a two-seater Hughes helicopter from his home in the Melbourne bayside suburb of Moorabbin to Cheviot Beach. The helicopter then began to search an area seaward of where Holt entered the water. It was soon joined by two commercial J47 Bell Ranger helicopters from the domestic airlines TAA and Ansett. Four police divers attempted to enter the water but were forced back by the heavy seas. Various other craft had also started to gather off Cheviot Beach and assist in the search.

The Port Melbourne Naval Diving Team based at HMAS *Lonsdale* had been hastily assembled. The team was led by Lieutenant Commander Phil Hawke RANR, the first RAN College graduate to qualify as a clearance diver. After hearing about the Prime Minister's disappearance on the 2 p.m. news bulletin, Hawke went immediately to *Lonsdale*. By 2.30 p.m., most of the team was ready and Hawke contacted the Victoria Police offering their assistance. They would remain at *Lonsdale* for another 90 minutes until instructed to proceed directly to Cheviot Beach. At 4 p.m., a Navy Search and Rescue (SAR) craft left HMAS *Cerberus* at Westernport with two Navy ships' divers embarked. 'Ships' Divers', as distinct from 'Clearance Divers', were not specialists and were limited to shallow water operations. Given the conditions, they were not allowed to conduct a search. At 5.30 p.m., two officers and 28 soldiers arrived from the Army School of Signals then located at Balcombe on the Mornington Peninsula. Their task was to provide a range of communications facilities.

By the time the Navy SAR vessel arrived at 5.45 p.m., another five Navy ships' divers from *Cerberus* had arrived. With the skilful use of lifelines, the Navy divers conducted a general survey of the foreshore in anticipation of the search continuing the next day. When they left the shallow water at 7 p.m., the eight members of the specialist Port Melbourne Team finally arrived. Lieutenant Commander Hawke recalls that, 'When we arrived at Cheviot Beach, we all had a look at the weather and sea conditions prevailing. We were all young, reasonably fit and experienced divers. We all agreed that none of us would have gone swimming for pleasure in those conditions'.[9] But by then it was too late to start a search of the deeper waters off Cheviot Beach. Had the Port Melbourne Team been despatched when they first contacted the Victoria Police, they could have conducted a search before nightfall. Just after 10 p.m., Clearance Diving Team 1 commanded by Lieutenant Michael Shotter RAN, who had just returned from active service in South Vietnam, arrived from the RAN's Diving Training School at HMAS *Rushcutter* in Sydney. They brought with them three tons of specialist equipment and enormous experience. Although Shotter's team was Permanent Navy and Hawke's Reserve personnel, the two officers agreed that Hawke would remain in overall command. Within twelve hours of Holt's disappearance there were more than 190 personnel and 24 organisations involved in the search but there was very little hope of Holt being found alive. There was a real sense of disbelief across the nation.

When they received police confirmation mid-afternoon that the Prime Minister was missing, Eggleton and Bailey agreed that Eggleton would arrange for a VIP aircraft to be available (the planes were usually on thirty minutes' Standby Notice) should Zara want to travel to Melbourne. Eggleton would travel to Melbourne, with or without her, to deal with the media. Bailey, who would remain in Canberra, would have to tell Zara that her husband was missing and ascertain her wishes. Bailey recalled that telephone call:

> 'I'm afraid I have some very bad news.' And I told her what we knew. She asked me a few questions which of course I couldn't answer because nobody knew anything at the time. It had only just come over the news. Then she said to me, 'Do you know if he was wearing his sandshoes or his flippers?' I said, 'It is my impression'—Tony had told me this—'that he had his sandshoes on.' And she said, 'Oh, he's gone!' I thought to myself, 'Oh God, how awful!' . . . So she knew, I think, that he had no hope; of course she hoped but she knew deep down he was gone.[10]

Coppin drove Zara to RAAF Base Fairbairn in the prime ministerial Bentley, collecting Tony Eggleton along the way. They boarded a RAAF Mystere aircraft and proceeded to Essendon Airport. Arriving at 4.25 p.m., Zara was then given a police escort to Portsea. Eggleton recalled: 'On the beach road down to Portsea, holidaymakers who had heard the news of the PM's disappearance and of Mrs Holt's dash to Portsea, stood in curious, silent groups. A big crowd was on the road outside Weeroona Estate, as we turned into the PM's holiday house'.[11]

The Deputy Prime Minister, John McEwen, was at his Stanhope farm when he received a telephone call from the wife of his friend Sir Reginald Ansett. Had he heard the radio news that Holt was missing? He had not. McEwen was then officially informed by departmental staff and made his way to Canberra where he met with Doug Anthony and Peter Lawler, the Acting Secretary of the Prime Minister's Department. (Bunting was on leave.) It was clear to all that Deputy Prime Minister McEwen considered himself in charge. That evening, as the search was being wound down for the night, he went to Yarralumla to confer with the Governor-General. By this time, it was all but certain that Holt was dead but, under Victorian law, he could not be declared so without his body being recovered. Casey was advised that McEwen could act in Holt's place should the need to do so arise. Although there was no constitutional requirement for a new Prime Minister to be sworn-in immediately, for his own reasons the Governor-General had already initiated certain actions:

> Casey, at once in close contact with John Bunting [who returned from leave] and the Victorian police, moved very quickly to have his letter about McMahon retrieved from Holt's briefcase at Portsea, though a journalist, Alan Reid, either saw the letter, or a copy or a summary of it, and published an account of it ('reasonably correctly' as Casey admitted) in his book, *The Power Struggle*.[12]

McEwen put it to Casey that he should be commissioned to form an interim Government with himself as Prime Minister, until the Liberal Party had elected Holt's successor. McEwen was prepared to give an undertaking that he would resign when the Liberals had made their choice. After all, he was still tired and unwell and had been thinking of retiring from politics, possibly in 1968 or by the 1969 election at the latest. His sole reason for remaining in Parliament had been to preserve the good health of the Coalition.[13] There was, however, one crucial point he wanted to stress. Neither he nor the Country Party would serve with McMahon should he be elected the new Liberal leader. The Coalition would be terminated. This created a problem for the Liberal Party as there was no obvious heir apparent to Holt and McMahon had already contacted the Victorian Premier, Sir Henry Bolte, asking for his support as Holt's successor.

McEwen told Casey that both McMahon and the Liberal Party would be informed of his resolution. In effect, the Liberals could have whomever they wanted as leader, as long as it was not McMahon. As the Liberals fell just short of a majority in the House of Representatives (notwithstanding rumours that Country Party Minister Iain Sinclair might have been persuaded to join the Liberal Party), they needed the Country Party members in order to govern. There is no record of Casey's response to McEwen's ultimatum. A response was probably not needed. Although McMahon was the Deputy Leader of the Liberal Party, it was unlikely that he could gather sufficient support to be elected leader. In a subsequent defence of his actions, McEwen said his assumption of the leadership also denied a 'temporary' Leader gaining 'an absolutely unfair advantage in a leadership election'. In any event, by the time McEwen had made his pitch at Yarralumla, Casey had already taken advice from the Attorney-General, Nigel Bowen, and the Chief Justice of the High Court, Sir Garfield Barwick. They concurred with Casey's thinking which was to wait a decent interval—no more than a few days—and then commission McEwen to form a Government on the understanding he would vacate the prime ministership when the new Liberal leader was elected. But there were some, including Jim Killen, who felt that Casey's actions were wrong.

> One of the decisive tests of the grant of a commission to form a Government is an assurance that the holder of the commission can face Parliament and get legislation through it. McEwen as Leader of the minority party could give no such assurance. McMahon as the Deputy Leader of the [majority party] could have stood in far greater prospect of giving such an assurance.[14]

The question of the succession was not, however, one that Casey wanted to debate. He was of the view that as Holt had endorsed McEwen as Acting Prime Minister during his frequent absences overseas, the Liberals would have been content to have McEwen as an interim Prime Minister. On the two previous occasions in which a Prime Minister had died in office (Joseph Lyons in 1939 and John Curtin in 1945), the Deputy Prime Minister was commissioned until the party leadership was settled.

Within nine hours of Holt's disappearance, his immediate successor as Prime Minister was almost settled. Attention now turned to his replacement as Liberal Party leader. The Country Party was committed to finding a Liberal leader with whom it could work. After a short conference with McEwen, Doug Anthony went to speak with Senator John Gorton at his home in the Canberra suburb of Narrabundah. Earlier in the evening Gorton had dined with the New Zealand High Commissioner, Luke Hazlett, at his official residence. Hasluck and Sir James Plimsoll, Secretary of the Department of External Affairs, were also present. Robert Macklin claims that McEwen much preferred Hasluck to Gorton.[15] McEwen had telephoned Hasluck at 7.20 p.m. to be told that he would resign if McMahon were elected. Hasluck also advised Casey that he too would not serve under McMahon. His reasons were similar to those of McEwen: 'I did not trust or respect him, had a deep contempt for his political methods, and, far from expecting even the minimum of loyalty from him, had learnt from experience to expect disloyalty and betrayal from him to his colleagues'.[16]

Dudley Erwin and Malcolm Fraser also arranged to meet Gorton. Malcolm Scott, the Liberal Party Whip in the Senate, joined them, along with Erwin's secretary, Ainsley Gotto. They were a rather curious cabal. As Hasluck notes:

> Erwin, Scott and Gotto were the minions of Gorton, not his promoters. They were tools, not planners. They did not have to persuade Gorton to stand. He had longstanding ambitions of his own. Fraser was a different case as he was after his own ministerial advancement and his association, if any, with Erwin and Scott would have been temporary and opportunistic. He was more intelligent and of a higher grade than they were.[17]

Don Chipp claims 'there were moves before Harold Holt drowned for [Gorton] to take over as Prime Minister. I know that Gorton was not a party to any conspiracy'.[18] It was simply a case of believing that Gorton was a potential leader should Holt need to be replaced. Gorton's prospects were, in any event, slight. As Alan Reid points out: 'But for the unusual circumstances then existing, Gorton would certainly have lived out his political life in the comfortable obscurity of the Senate'.[19] No Senator had ever become Prime Minister, so Gorton would first need to enter the House of Representatives. The next morning, Gorton met with the Clerk of the Senate and author of *Australian Senate Practice*, James Rowland

Odgers, to discuss the constitutional ramifications of a Senator becoming Prime Minister. Gorton explained his understanding of the situation: were he to be elected Liberal leader he would need to move to the House of Representatives via a by-election that would first necessitate his resignation from the Senate. This meant Gorton would be Prime Minister but, for a short period, without a seat in either House. Odgers pointed out that there was no constitutional impediment to his proposal, as section 64 of the Constitution allowed a person to be a Minister of State for up to three months without being a member of either House. Gorton would, however, have to win a by-election: an achievement that had consistently eluded Holt as Prime Minister. The obvious seat for Gorton to contest was Holt's now vacant—and safe—seat of Higgins, but this would require the goodwill of the local branch of the Liberal Party.

There had also been rumours that Wilfred Kent Hughes might be induced to retire from his seat of Chisholm to make way for Gorton. But Kent Hughes was outraged by the suggestion and struck back with the claim that 'Dudley Erwin started gathering a pro-Gorton party because he anticipated Holt's inability to continue' on the grounds of ill-health.[20] In mid-1967 Holt had collapsed in Parliament House suffering from what was later diagnosed as a vitamin deficiency but at the time was widely thought to be a heart attack. Although one can excuse Erwin for being overly diligent in wanting to find a replacement for Holt if necessary, Gorton was always an unlikely choice. And yet, Gorton's actions during the VIP airline scandal were interpreted by some as indicating at least a willingness to imperil Holt's leadership. Was Gorton an active conspirator? Political commentator Don Whitington concluded that there was:

> little doubt [Gorton's] action contributed to the Holt Government's loss of support at the 1967 Senate election and reinforced the movement against Holt which began in the Parliamentary Liberal Party at the time. It has been said that this was merely one of Gorton's impetuosities, characteristic of his 'shoot from the hip' behaviour, his impatience with red tape and the need to proceed through orthodox channels; that may be a perfectly valid explanation. For anyone seeking evidence that Gorton was prepared to embarrass his leader in order to deprecate further his leader's standing within the Liberal Party, and to advance his own claims as a man capable of dealing swiftly and ruthlessly with any situation he encountered, this was a classic example.[21]

Gorton reacted angrily to Alan Reid's *The Gorton Experiment*, in which he was accused of being party to a plot to remove Holt, stating, 'I would not only not be in it, but would tell him of it and do my best to defeat it'. He described Holt as 'an idealist, a good man and a friend'.[22] In a 1975 interview Gorton again denied that he ever tried to undermine Holt. In an interview conducted in 1990, Gorton stated emphatically that he was 'never approached by anyone before Mr Holt's death with any suggestion that I should work against him or stand against him . . . I was never thinking of moving against Holt. Ever'.[23] But why, then, did Erwin include Gorton in the very small group of parliamentarians shown a draft of the letter he later sent to Holt concerning his leadership? The most obvious answer was that Gorton was Government Leader in the Senate and they had both served in the wartime RAAF and were friends.

Hasluck was initially suspicious of the company Gorton kept. In 1968 he wrote: 'I am now informed credibly . . . that [Gorton's] link with Wentworth had been formed before Harold Holt's death and that a scheme had been prepared while Holt was still alive to promote Gorton as a rival candidate to Holt for the leadership of the Liberal Party and the prime ministership'.[24] He doubted 'whether this scheme had reached the stage of being an active plot' but thought that Gorton was party to it in some way given how smoothly the problems he faced were solved when he was drafted into the leadership.[25] Gorton's biographer, Ian Hancock, argues that Hasluck's 'use of coincidence and innuendo and gossip made the case look damning. Yet, in the absence of any solid or verifiable evidence of an actual plot which included himself, Gorton's emphatic denial remains credible'.[26] After considering all of the evidence and interviewing most of the key players myself, Hancock's conclusion is the most compelling.

Gorton counterclaimed that McMahon was trying to undermine Holt and he may have told Holt that McMahon would challenge for the leadership. This might account for the conversation overheard by Lawless on the weekend of Holt's death. It is also consistent with Hasluck's recollection of a conversation he had with Holt after a meeting of senior ministers in mid-1967. The Prime Minister 'spoke feelingly about the disloyalty of McMahon to him. He said it was all very well for McEwen to complain of McMahon but he [Holt] had just as much cause'. Holt also told Hasluck that Bob Menzies used to grizzle about McMahon but he did nothing about him. 'If only Bob had done something about it we all would have been saved a lot of trouble'.[27] There was, in fact, little that Holt could have done about McMahon given the extent of his backbench support. McMahon also enjoyed the backing of the Packer press. Holt could do nothing but endure McMahon's subversive activities in the hope that an alternative candidate might eventually emerge and challenge for the post of Deputy Leader.

Malcolm Fraser has also steadfastly denied that there were 'any pro-Gorton discussions of any kind between him and either Erwin and Scott, at any stage prior to Holt's disappearance'.[28] He does not deny that discussions took place but is adamant that he was not party to them. In fact, Fraser says he was first approached by Gorton himself and that 'the pro-Gorton machine of Erwin, Scott and Fraser has been grossly overrated'.[29] It is worth noting that Jim Killen does not mention a plot against Holt as he was one of the backbenchers whose support for an alternative leader would have been sought.

> Erwin was astute in many ways and he could be most disingenuous, but he did enjoy embroidering a story. I do not know if Erwin informed Holt that there was unrest in the party and, if so, what description he gave to the unrest. I certainly was not aware of unrest which would have justified the Whip saying to the Prime Minister that parliamentary Members were concerned to the stage that a move against him was afoot. Harold Holt had run into turbulence, but that is usually the case with all Governments . . . I saw no evidence of Harold Holt being undermined and no member of the parliamentary party asked me to participate in a move to oust him.[30]

Of course, the leadership contest could easily have been more complicated. As Marr points out, 'If Barwick had still been in Parliament the leadership might possibly have been his'.[31] But most commentators believed that Gorton was probably the best placed to follow Holt in that:

> he appeared to possess qualities for lack of which Holt was increasingly, in the months before his death, coming under criticism in the Liberal parliamentary party. Where Holt was vague, imprecise, Gorton was laconic, definite and direct. Where Holt was nice to the point that his essential decency was viewed as weakness, Gorton had the air of being prepared to be rough, tough and nasty if he had to be.[32]

As Holt's would-be successors as Liberal Leader began to emerge, Zara arrived at Cheviot Beach and was immediately given a briefing on the search by the Victoria Police and the Army Liaison Officer, Lieutenant Colonel John Bennett. All of the organisations participating in the search were summoned to a planning meeting held at Badcoe Hall in the Officer Cadet School, where a strategy for the next day was outlined, agreed, and announced at a press conference convened at 9 p.m. Eggleton told the gathered media that there was still a slim hope that Holt might be alive while Mrs Holt, he reported, was composed and very brave. During the night, heavy rain fell along the coast and strong seas pounded the beach. The search for Holt resumed at first light—4.52 a.m. Despite continuing strong winds, occasional rain and heavy seas, the helicopters took off and around 50 divers were prepared to enter the water. The weather impeded their every effort. At 5 a.m. the divers were sent into the rock pools and around the ledges where the Prime Minister was last seen. Lieutenant Commander Hawke recalled:

> The first direction I gave was that, given the conditions, no breathing apparatus was to be used. Essentially, on either side of the point where Mr Holt had disappeared, there was a sheer underwater cliff with a drop to about 20 feet. The water at the base of that cliff was in turmoil and the likelihood of a diver, with diving gear, being able to get down there and carry out a search was very slight. More importantly, he was likely to be caught in an upsurge and thrown onto the top of the cliff face. If he had diving gear on, he could be seriously injured. So we dived in wet suit, fins, a diving mask and a deep breath. That did not stop the injuries and a number of us, including myself, lost not only a goodly part of a wet suit but also of skin, as a result of being thrown onto the top of the cliff face.[33]

When the tide turned at 8 a.m., the divers withdrew from the water. The divers would be unable to go back in until after 2.30 p.m. when the tide ebbed again. Eggleton convened a second press conference at 9 a.m. Inspector Newell told the large media gathering that more than 340 personnel were committed to the search operation. He said a shark had been seen two miles from Cheviot Beach, but he would 'let that circumstance speak for itself'. (A large shark was caught shortly afterwards by a local fisherman. It was cut open but no sign of human remains were found.) The huge headline in Sydney's *Sun* newspaper summed up the prevailing sentiment: 'Dawn—and all hope is gone'. The front-page story began: 'At dawn today the truth sank home—the Prime Minister, Mr Harold Holt, is dead'.

With the mid-morning press conference over, Commodore John Dowson and Commander Mike Hudson from HMAS *Cerberus* arrived at Portsea for a conference with Newell. Dowson, the senior naval officer in Victoria, believed a larger Navy ship was required and asked Fleet Headquarters to despatch the Ton Class minesweeper HMAS *Snipe* from Sydney. After surveying the coastline and foreshore Commander Hudson, the training commander at *Cerberus*, concluded that Holt would have been swept in a north-easterly direction towards Point Nepean had he been caught in the inshore current.

At 2 p.m., Eggleton held a third press conference. Zara returned to Cheviot Beach at 4 p.m. Her husband had been missing now for more than 28 hours. She thanked those involved in the operation and suggested two areas that ought to be closely searched. They had already been searched thoroughly but within 15 minutes of her request, they were searched again to no avail.

The drama of the succession was still being played out in Canberra. Earlier in the day, as the 'Gorton' camp attempted to gather support, McEwen asked McMahon to see him. In a very short interview, McEwen told McMahon that neither he nor the Country Party was prepared to serve under him as Prime Minister. He later remarked:

> The prospect of having McMahon as prime minister troubled me to say the least. McMahon was an able and hard-working minister but during his time in Cabinet he and I had often had very serious policy differences. While the policy differences were not in themselves sufficient to make McMahon unacceptable to the Country Party as a Prime Minister, he had on occasions handled our policy differences in a way that, let me say, I could not condone.
>
> I can remember that when there were discussions lasting longer than a single Cabinet meeting, and when McMahon and I were on opposite sides of the fence, the press would often get slanted versions of my policy which had been leaked to discredit my views. McMahon consistently used his influence as Treasurer to oppose my policies. I thought on a number of occasions that he was attacking particular proposals simply because I was putting them forward and not on their merits. There were also incidents that aimed to sabotage me as Leader of the Country Party and they seemed to be directed at me personally rather than at the Country Party as such.[34]

McMahon did not respond to McEwen's remarks, but left the room. Fuming, he went back to Sydney a few days later and decided to issue a statement containing a compendium of his differences with McEwen. His press officer, Peter Kelly, managed to dissuade him: it would gain him nothing but put him at risk of losing both the position of Deputy Leader of the Liberal Party and the Treasury portfolio.[35]

Although Holt was yet to be officially declared dead, Casey issued a statement.

> I have today asked the Right Honourable John McEwen to assume the office of Prime Minister of Australia. We are all aware of the tragic circumstances in which the Prime Minister, the Right Honourable Harold Holt, disappeared off Portsea . . . In these circumstances I have consulted my ministers. Their advice is that it is necessary to determine his commission as Prime Minister so that a successor can be appointed. In the light of this tragic sequence of events I have decided that I must take this course to enable the government of the Commonwealth to continue without uncertainties which could otherwise exist. I have therefore asked Mr McEwen to accept my commission as Prime Minister . . . Mr McEwen has agreed to accept the commission. He has told me that he would intend to retain the office of Prime Minister until the Government parties assemble to consider their position and to decide by proper processes to appoint a new Leader . . . I intend to swear McEwen as Prime Minister on the afternoon of Tuesday 19 December and the other Ministers on the following day.[36]

Casey had already telephoned Zara to inform her personally of the arrangements that he had made. Harold Holt had become the third Australian prime minister to die in office.

By this time, the Victoria Police had launched a formal investigation headed by Inspector Jack Ford, a former homicide detective. He was assisted by Inspector (First Class) Aubrey Jackson of the Commonwealth Police. Ford and Jackson arrived at Portsea at 2.30 p.m. and started to gather evidence and to confirm initial witness statements. In a secure office made available at the Officer Cadet School, the two detectives spoke with Marjorie and Vyner Gillespie, Alan Stewart and Robert Simpson while their recollections were still fresh. Other than a brief respite at 9 p.m. when the fourth press conference was held, those searching worked until midnight. The divers were still unable to find any trace of the Prime Minister.

The search was resumed at 7 a.m. on Tuesday 19 December. The weather was atrocious. The Navy SAR vessel was damaged by more floating timber beams. Rough seas on the eastern seaboard delayed *Snipe's* arrival. The Navy's divers were being criticised by some media commentators for failing to find the Prime Minister's body. Lieutenant Commander Hawke believed this was unfair. 'Any chance of finding the Prime Minister was lost by the Sunday night and that situation arose because of the delay in getting the *Lonsdale* team to the site. It is my understanding and belief that that delay was caused by the [Victoria] Police.' At 9 a.m. on Tuesday morning, a fifth press conference was held. There was little new to report. Later in the morning, there was a re-enactment of the events immediately before the Prime Minister disappeared in the surf. Later still, Eggleton was called back to the Holt beach house to take an urgent telephone call. After identifying himself to a woman with an American accent, there were several clicks and a voice said: 'Tony, this is LBJ. I am very distressed about Harold. I would like to come to his memorial service. Would this be okay?'.[37] Eggleton provided a description of the previous days' events. Johnson, who was about to go to bed on Saturday night when he was informed of Holt's disappearance, said he would make immediate preparations to fly to Australia and asked Eggleton to inform the necessary Australian authorities. Eggleton contacted Bunting and planning began for the second Presidential visit in fourteen months. By that afternoon, obituaries started appearing in the major Australian newspapers. A sixth and final press conference was held at Cheviot Beach at 9 p.m. Shortly after it began, Alan Stewart was seriously injured in a motor vehicle accident, not far from Cheviot Beach. The nation needed a new leader if only to help it mourn.

— ▬

While McEwen was at Government House the next day being sworn-in by Casey as Prime Minister, McMahon met with Hasluck, Gorton, Hulme, Fairhall, Fairbairn and Bury in his Parliament House office. Noting Casey's reference to the Government *parties* deciding on a leader, McMahon was concerned that some within the Liberal Party, such as Bill Kent Hughes, were hinting at their preparedness to have McEwen remain as Prime Minister for 'twelve to eighteen months' after the Liberals had elected a new leader.[38] Kent Hughes believed that Allen Fairhall was the best candidate among the Liberals but Fairhall was in poor health and unwilling to stand. Kent Hughes' next preference was McEwen and he lobbied on his behalf. In wanting to refute the suggestion that the Liberals lacked leadership ability within their parliamentary ranks, the meeting concluded with an agreement that the Liberal leadership would not be decided in the Joint Party Room. The Liberals would meet alone and choose their leader. There was deep philosophical opposition to McEwen within the Liberal Party. Senior figures such as Sir William Anderson felt that McEwen and his party was a 'Federal enlargement of Dunstanism—a sectional demanding force that had to be tolerated in the Government coalition'.[39] For his part, McEwen was taking steps to remove McMahon from the leadership race. His actions bordered on vindictiveness.

Shortly after being sworn-in as Prime Minister, McEwen contacted ASIO's Director General, Brigadier Charles Spry. McEwen had always been suspicious of McMahon's relationship with Maxwell Newton, despite Holt's insistence that there was to be no further contact between the two men. Now McEwen could employ ASIO to pursue the matter. During a meeting in his Melbourne office, McEwen asked Spry whether ASIO had any information of security significance on Maxwell Newton. In his record of their conversation, Spry replied:

> I had, in that I had a report from [name deleted] to the effect this man had removed, without authority, several documents from a table during the conference of Commonwealth Finance Ministers which had been held in Jamaica. Further, that Newton had entered the area without accreditation or a pass. His removal of the documents had been noted by members of the [name deleted] who had followed and spoken to Newton just as he was about to enter a taxi-cab. The documents had been removed from his possession and returned to the conference. I informed Mr McEwen I had asked for a report in detail, but this had not arrived. Mr McEwen said he would like to be kept informed when the material came to hand.[40]

After detailed inquiries, the most that Spry could say was that Newton's conduct was 'unbecoming' but that he had not committed any offence under Australian law. ASIO had not been of much help to McEwen's political vendetta.

As he continued to search for any information he could use to discredit McMahon, McEwen made his first prime ministerial statement on 20 December.

> Mr Holt, as you all know, was a typical Australian, I think any one of us would be happy to be so described. He was at home with his fellows here in Australia and undoubtedly he was an equal with his contemporaries when he was overseas. He was a good man. He was a brave man. And he was a devoted man to his country. We have all suffered a great loss . . . As I have already made clear, it is my intention to hold the office of prime minister only until the major party in the Coalition, the Liberal Party, shall have chosen for itself a new leader.[41]

In the ensuing press conference, McEwen confirmed his personal unwillingness and that of his Party to serve under McMahon. When asked for an explanation, McEwen would not elaborate. 'I decided firmly in my mind that what I have done is the correct course; that is, not to allow the Liberals to go to an election ignorant of the attitude of myself and my Country Party colleagues'.[42] McMahon was realistically out of the race.

National attention could now turn to a farewell for Holt. Australians were still shocked that their Prime Minister could disappear in such incredible circumstances. The *Bulletin*'s editor, Donald Horne, thought that 'if we are to treat our national leaders with such disdain that we do not pay people to look after them night and day, how can we take ourselves seriously as a people worth preserving?'. If Holt had a bodyguard with him, would he have been allowed to enter the surf at all? In what was a rather backhanded swipe at Australian personal protection measures, President Johnson assured American reporters that this could not happen to the President of the United States. The security detail that surrounded the President, especially after John F. Kennedy's assassination in 1963, was enormous. Most Australians believed their country was different.

> Like Deakin travelling to work in a cable tram sixty years before, or Chifley standing in the queue for 'Rusty Bugles' twenty years earlier, an Australian Prime Minister still had relatively little need to guard against physical assault or assassination by even his bitterest domestic political opponents, and he could still live his own private life when off duty.[43]

But Kocan's assassination attempt on Calwell and Holt's disappearance demanded that there be changes in the provision of prime ministerial security. Of course, for Harold Holt it was all too late.

The weather at Cheviot Beach finally improved on Wednesday 20 December. The wind dropped, the seas abated and visibility was almost perfect. They were now searching for a body. HMAS *Snipe* arrived at 6 p.m. and was brought into the search the following day. By Thursday afternoon, the search was being scaled down and by dusk most personnel were withdrawn permanently. Zara left the Portsea beach house and was driven back to St Georges Road, where she discussed arrangements for Holt's memorial service with the Anglican Archbishop of Melbourne, the Most Reverend Frank Woods. The search continued officially until Friday 5 January 1968 when, and with Zara's agreement, it was terminated by formal decision of Cabinet on advice from the Commissioner of Police in Victoria.[44] By that stage it was limited to a daily beach survey and an aircraft transit in the faint hope that Holt's remains might be washed ashore.

As Christmas was drawing near, Casey announced that a memorial service for the late Prime Minister would be held at noon in St Paul's Anglican Cathedral in Melbourne on Friday 22 December. It was the most significant gathering of international leaders in Australian history. The Queen had been advised on Sunday morning of Holt's presumed death and quickly informed Prince Charles. Prince Charles knew the Holt family and had spent two terms at Geelong Grammar's Timbertop School in 1966 so was considered the most suitable representative of the Royal Family to attend. Prime Minister Harold Wilson and the Leader of the Opposition, Edward Heath, would accompany him. President Johnson had already decided to attend. He would be joined by the President and Foreign Minister of South Vietnam, Nguyen Van Thieu and Tran Van Do, President Chung Hee Park of South Korea, President Ferdinand Marcos of the Philippines, Prime Minister Keith Holyoake of New Zealand, Deputy Prime Minister Tun Abdul Razak of Malaysia, Premier Thanom Kittikachorn of Thailand, Prime Minister C.K. Yen of Taiwan, the Vice-President of the Japanese Democratic Party, Shojiro Kawashima, Prime Minister Lee Kuan Yew of Singapore, Prime Minister Mataafa of Western Samoa, Chief Minister Ratu Mara of Fiji, Foreign Minister Adam Malik from Indonesia, Foreign Minister Sisouk Champassak of Laos and External Affairs Minister B.R. Bhagat from India. The *Washington Post* noted that 'the only notable official absence at the memorial service . . . was France—for whom Australian soldiers died in two world wars . . . France, as firm an opponent of the Vietnam war as Australia is a supporter, did not even send its ambassador'.[45]

As Prime Minister, McEwen insisted on meeting all of the visiting dignitaries who arrived in Canberra and then travelled on to Melbourne. President Johnson and Field Marshal Kittikachorn both called on the Holt family at Toorak on the morning of the memorial service to express their sympathies. Johnson later disclosed that he and Zara had cried together. The *Boston Globe* explained to its readers that Holt 'was one of a handful of world leaders who were on a first name basis with Lyndon Johnson. The two men were temperamentally alike, and there was a kind of symbolism in their relationship'.[46]

Holt's death had affected the Australian nation deeply. People who showed little interest in the living politician felt a genuine sadness at the death of a decent man. In anticipation of the huge crowds expected to gather and pay their respects, the streets around the Cathedral were closed and a public address system was installed with five broadcast points across the inner city. More than 2000 people were seated inside the Cathedral, another 10 000 thronged the streets. The service began at noon and was led by the Anglican Dean of Melbourne, the Very Reverend Thomas, assisted by the Cathedral staff.[47]

The Most Reverend Philip Strong, Primate of Australia and Anglican Archbishop of Brisbane, delivered the eulogy. In a long address, the Archbishop mentioned Holt's professional achievements and personal triumphs.

> We mourn today for a man who loved Australia, who lived for Australia, who gave his best for Australia. And as we commend him now into God's eternal keeping, we thank God for giving Harold Holt to us for a time, for what he was and for what he did.[48]

The Archbishop was perhaps being generous when he said that 'no scandal or intrigue ever marred his own reputation either before he became Prime Minister or since'. There were no other speeches or tributes. And as there were no mortal remains, the service did not end with the usual prayers of committal, an uneasy conclusion which reflected Holt's untimely death. His friend Simon Warrender remarked:

> Harold was an agnostic whose *raison d'être* was dedication to his career. His greatest source of inspiration was the Kipling poem 'If'. For Harold, this was a creed. In his soul-searching moments he always returned to its four short stanzas and used their sentiments as a guiding light in his political and private life.[49]

Despite the solemnity of the occasion, the jostling for political supremacy continued. Don Chipp remarked:

I can remember few occasions when I have felt more disgusted with politicians than at the Memorial Service. All the candidates for Leader were there, with their supporters. His former colleagues, from whom he could have at least expected this final show of respect, busily engaged themselves in much plotting, and lobbying, but little sympathy.[50]

Chipp's claim has, however, been disputed by others who were in attendance.

All could agree it was a sombre and moving occasion in which Holt's memory was properly honoured. Thirty newspaper reporters were given seats in the Cathedral, with the remainder situated on the first floor of a building overlooking the Cathedral west door. A handful of photographs were taken by an official photographer and the service was filmed from a static camera from the back of the building. It also provided the material for John Hamilton's Walkley award-winning 'best news story' for 1968. Hamilton worked for the *Age* and 'had been given a special pass to go inside the cathedral on the day of the memorial service but decided not to use it. He felt the ordinary man who came to pay their tributes in the streets would provide better copy than the celebrities'.[51] Hamilton rose at dawn and positioned himself on the tram tracks opposite the Cathedral to observe and record the reactions and emotions of ordinary Australians.

After the service, the principal mourners and the foreign dignitaries went to Government House in Melbourne for a formal reception. Johnson had earlier met with Cabinet. He recalled: 'It was a sad occasion, and I shared with the Cabinet members my memories of the sense of loss we Americans had experienced four years before with the death of President Kennedy. "I know where you are this morning," I told them. "In adversity, a family gets together. That's why I am here."'.[52] In Melbourne, Johnson said:

> I don't think I have ever known a man whom I trusted more or for whom I had more respect and affection. Mr Holt had the same qualities I had seen in the Australian people when I served there during the war—candour, friendship, honesty, courage, tenacity in doing what is right and staying with you if you are right, and never starting something if you are wrong.[53]

The *New York Post* commended the President for attending the memorial service as it meant that the United States would be 'in a solid position with whatever government succeeds the Holt Administration'.[54]

The occasion of Holt's memorial service also gave the President an opportunity to confer with the Asian leaders who had attended. On his way home, Johnson visited military bases in Thailand, then went to South Vietnam where he encouraged American troops before travelling to Rome where he had an audience with Pope Paul VI in the hope of achieving some progress on the release of American military prisoners in North Vietnam.[55] The President travelled for 112 hours and was home in time for Christmas. On his return to Washington, Johnson praised Holt's vision 'in trying to bring together a new regionalism for Asians led by Asians. There was no white superiority in Holt. I asked him to go into the brown countries'.[56] Holt's relationship with Johnson was such that he was one of only two world leaders to address Johnson by his given name (the other was British Prime Minister Harold Wilson). Zara would maintain a warm friendship with the Johnsons and visit them in 1968. Lady Bird Johnson enjoyed Zara's company and described her as 'a jolly, brisk, natural person, very refreshing'.[57] After thanking the official mourners, Zara returned to Portsea on Friday evening to contemplate a future without her beloved Harry.

With Holt publicly farewelled, Federal President Jock Pagan and Bob Southey invited Fred Osborne and a number of 'ex-Liberal parliamentarians' to a mid-afternoon meeting at Liberal Party headquarters in Melbourne. Osborne states that many in this group, whom he described as 'mainly organisation people', were keen to have McEwen as Prime Minister.[58] That evening, members of the Liberal Party Federal Executive were summoned to another meeting convened by Pagan at the old Menzies Hotel in Melbourne.

> With delegates sprawled over the bed and chairs, heated talks went on late into the night and early into the next morning to discuss the McEwen option which had significant support. A specific proposal put to the Executive detailed a proposed merger of the two parties which would have seen McEwen remain as leader . . . It was pressure from Victorian Liberals that effectively stymied the McEwen push, and at 2.30 am, as Executive members wearily emerged into Melbourne's deserted streets, McEwen's bid for supremacy was effectively ended, at least at an official level.[59]

McEwen himself was ambivalent about continuing in the office. Kent Hughes wrote an article for the Melbourne *Herald* on 29 December 1967, lauding McEwen's leadership. It received wide publicity the next day and became a leading news story when Kent Hughes claimed that McEwen was more popular with the public than the leading Liberal contenders.[60]

The 4 January 1968 edition of Rupert Murdoch's *Australian* newspaper, McEwen's staunchest advocate since first appearing in 1964, carried an article praising his abilities and aptitudes. It was accompanied by an editorial that made the proprietor's views very plain: 'The *Australian* believes that to deny a man with all Mr McEwen's qualities the leadership of the country because he belongs to the minority party in the Coalition would be contrary to the national interest'. Two days later, the front page of the same newspaper asked its readers for reasons why McEwen should not be allowed to remain Prime Minister. But the campaign lacked both the strength and momentum to succeed within the Liberal Party. McEwen was also reluctant to press his interests in a manner that might have damaged the future health of the Coalition. Notwithstanding the Country Party's veto on McMahon, the Liberals would not only choose their own leader—they would insist that he become Prime Minister.

At 2.30 p.m. on Tuesday 9 January 1968, the Liberals held their Party Room Meeting in Canberra. As Acting Leader, McMahon chaired the meeting and told his 80 colleagues that, in spite of the expectations of some, there would not be a spill of all positions. They had gathered solely to elect a new Party Leader. This meant his position as Deputy Leader remained secure. He then asked for nominations. Each had to stand and nominate themselves. There were four candidates: Leslie Bury, Billy Snedden, Paul Hasluck and Senator John Gorton. Both McEwen, and Menzies, who was influencing the process from the sidelines in Melbourne, strongly preferred Hasluck, who had also been encouraged to contest the leadership by Gordon Freeth and Robert Cotton. McEwen told Hasluck he had to work harder to secure the support of his colleagues. Snedden and Bury were quickly eliminated from the contest before Gorton achieved a substantial victory of 51 votes to 30 over Hasluck, who never appeared willing to pursue support actively among colleagues. Believing that Gorton was ill-suited to the office and work of Prime Minister, Hasluck's wife later remarked: 'I did not hesitate to make known my disgust with a party that was so bad a judge of men. I have had little faith in it ever since'.[61] McEwen resigned on 10 January and Casey commissioned Gorton as Prime Minister. Gorton resigned from the Senate on 1 February 1968 and was elected Member for Higgins on 28 February.

Gorton's first day in the House of Representatives was 12 March 1968. After he was introduced and he made the necessary oaths and declarations, the new Prime Minister moved a condolence motion. Gorton mentioned

Holt's 'physical and moral' courage, evidenced in his refusal to avoid criticism or accountability for the 1961 credit squeeze despite it being a collective responsibility of the Government. Gorton praised Holt's personal qualities rather than his professional achievements.

> He was known as a man of industry and of kindliness, one who was prepared to give of himself to each member who had brought to him some point of view which might have differed from that which he had suggested or proposed some course with which he did not agree. He showed clearly that he would always consider that point of view and would always take that course into his mind and test whether what he had intended to do was in his view right or not.[62]

Gorton also commented on the 'irony' that 'a man of peace, [Holt] should have presided over one of the greatest build-ups of military power that Australia has found itself engaged in'.

In what was considered by both sides to be a far superior tribute to the late Prime Minister, Gough Whitlam praised Holt as 'a great parliamentarian. He was at once the servant and the leader of this House. This is the place he knew best; this is the place where he was best known'.[63] Whitlam touched on the depth and breadth of Holt's experiences and qualifications, including his understanding of being in Opposition, and expressed his gratitude to Holt for the 'personal debt' he owed to him. In explaining his success as Minister for Immigration and Labour and National Service, Whitlam said the key to Holt's 'ability to establish relationships with men of different backgrounds, attitudes and interests was his essential decency. He was tolerant, humane and broadminded. His suavity of manner was no pose. It was the outward reflection of a truly civilised human being. He was in a very real sense a gentleman'.[64] Whatever history would make of Holt's achievements, Whitlam concluded, 'his place in the minds and memory of us, his colleagues, is secure, lasting and indelible'. McEwen likewise spoke of Holt's personal qualities. 'Harold Holt had great personal charm. He was one of the warmest and most friendly persons that one could possibly know. For all the greatness that came to him he was not a pretentious man. Great and important offices never took from him the modesty for which he was noted'. Arthur Calwell, who had known Holt since 1940, echoed this sentiment:

I learned to respect him for his honesty, integrity and loyalty to his leader and party. In all the vicissitudes of those times and in all the years in which the present government parties were in opposition in this parliament, he displayed the same humble loyalty and devotion to principle that were the characteristics of his life. I have always thought of Harold Holt as one of the best men I ever knew. He was a humane, charitable and generous man.

Senator Ken Anderson, the Minister for Supply and newly appointed Leader of the Government in the Senate, spoke in similar terms:

[Holt] was a man of uncomplicated warmth, a friendly human man who, in the words of Kipling, could 'walk with kings yet never lose the common touch'. I doubt whether there is an honourable senator or member who had not been touched at some time by his warm, open friendliness and courtesy. Nevertheless, in a political clash he would fight with all the forces at his command, but win or lose, after the encounter, he would revert to his same basic character as a cheerful, approachable and kindly man.[65]

Senator Vince Gair, the Leader of the DLP, declared his belief that 'Harold Holt's main aim in life, his goal in life, was to serve God and his country. He achieved that, I am sure. It must be conceded that he did it with a dignity and a friendship that won him the applause of all sections of our people'.[66]

The man who had known Holt longest, Bill McMahon, focused more on the positions Holt held in his public life. But he did touch on his 'great courage, both in his parliamentary life and in the way in which he approached the problems of life itself. I have never known anyone who showed greater courage than he did in the last few weeks of his life'. Was this a reference to Holt staring down McEwen over devaluation or an allusion to the struggle in which the two were engaged when Holt died? Whatever the outcome, Holt had now been assigned to history—Prime Minister of Australia for 692 days.

CHAPTER 15

Myths and mysteries?

1968–2005

'Waiting for Cronulla to win a [Rugby League] grand final
is like leaving the porch light on for Harold Holt.'[1]

On first glance there was nothing very unusual about Harold Holt's death. Hundreds of Australians around the continent drown each year in a range of leisure pursuits. Holt had 'cheated' death on more than one occasion after he was introduced to the sport of spear fishing in 1954. Although initially reluctant, he put his head under the water for the first time and said, 'It had me hooked'. He did not like oxygen tanks because he felt it was unsporting to spear fish and crustaceans while using breathing apparatus and always insisted on snorkelling. Very soon, he was skindiving all year round with the aid of a wet suit. His two favourite locations were Cheviot Beach because of its caves and limestone holes, and Bingil Bay. But he had almost drowned on two occasions earlier in 1967.

On 20 May 1967, Holt was diving at Cheviot Beach. He was wearing his customary black cotton skivvy with a v-neck jumper over the top of his bathers, together with his flippers, a lead belt, mask and snorkel. He was carrying his spear gun. After spearing four fish and five abalone during a dive of approximately 22 minutes, Holt became distressed and called for help. He was pulled ashore by his two diving companions, Eric McIllree (Managing Director of Avis Car Rental) and Diane Lett (a well-known model). Although conscious, Holt was a very bad colour by the time he reached the shore. He vomited seawater and was over-breathing. A leaking snorkel had caused him to ingest seawater and restricted the flow of oxygen to his lungs. When he had recovered his composure on shore, Holt exclaimed, 'That's the closest I have ever been to drowning in my life!' Three months later he was diving off Dunk Island in the Great Barrier Reef. It was his birthday and he was enjoying his first holiday at Bingil Bay since becoming Prime Minister. Holt had caught a large coral sea trout using a spear gun presented to him by President Johnson during his stay at Camp David. It was much heavier and more demanding to use than those he had owned previously and led Holt to wonder whether it should have been called a 'steer gun'. After fighting with the defiant fish for 25 minutes, Holt abandoned his catch but found he was very short of breath. Television celebrity Bob Dyer was in the launch boat. He said that Holt had been treading water for a long period but had remained calm.

Those who had dived with Holt over the years believed him to be an excellent spear fisherman with incredible powers of endurance underwater. The Prime Minister could hold his breath for phenomenal periods and often whiled away tedious parliamentary debates by seeing how long he could last on a single gasp of air. He maintained a high level of general fitness through tennis, golf and running. Although he spent a great deal of time in the sea and could tread water for hours, he did not like swimming and was not a strong surface swimmer. He also preferred to dive alone, relishing the solitary experience of being underwater which he thought must have been like 'travelling in space'. In an interview conducted with journalist Nigel Muir shortly before his disappearance, Holt did not underestimate the dangers of his favourite recreation: 'One mistake and you're gone. You just don't make that mistake. With time one's skill increases and one learns hunting tricks. With greater knowledge the dangers diminish'.[2] He also acknowledged that sharks were a cause of fear but felt they were rarely threatening. When Eggleton expressed the concerns shared by many about the dangers of spear fishing, he replied, 'Look Tony, what are the odds of a prime minister being drowned or taken by a shark?'. This did not obviate the need for Holt to act sensibly or for him to be protected, but such attention could not have extended to giving or withholding permission to go into the surf. He was not, of course, a child in need of parental supervision, but nor was he a young man in the prime of life.

Holt was approaching his sixtieth birthday—something he believed he would not live to see. His brother Cliff, eighteen months younger, had died in March 1967. Holt's father had also died before he reached his sixtieth birthday. Simon Warrender insisted that Holt was a fatalist and often quoted Marvell's verse: 'But at my back I hear, Time's winged chariot hurrying near'. Holt was, he said, 'not afraid of death, merely conscious of it'.[3] Holt's fatalism was also known to Liberal Party official Edgar Holt, who recalled:

> there is a story—and it may only be a story—that he once said: 'I'll never be sixty'. He was fifty-nine when he died. Perhaps he did have a premonition, because nobody could have crowded more into one life . . . the thought of old age and the infirmities of old age were repugnant; to be young in body and mind was a kind of Greek ideal in front of him.[4]

While the Prime Minister was in reasonably good health (he had always taken a range of pills), he suffered from a number of slight ailments. A shoulder injury he received while playing football as a young man troubled him for the rest of his life. In September 1967 Holt started to mention severe pain in his shoulder that he assumed was caused by over-exertion during tennis or swimming. He had treatment for muscle soreness in the shoulder and neck from Mr John Cloke, a Collins Street specialist in Melbourne. Further treatment had been delayed until after the November 1967 half-Senate election. He was given painkillers but rarely took them. He then started to complain of numbness in his hand which he tried to remedy by slapping the limb against his thigh. Eggleton recalled: 'On a flight from Adelaide to Perth he was in considerable agony, and took rather more pills than might have been desirable. I was very worried about him. He seemed light-headed, was unsteady on his feet and his speech was slightly slurred'.[5] Holt performed well at a press conference in Perth, although he did tell a group of Canberra correspondents that his shoulder was causing him problems but 'not to mention it because he did not want public sympathy'. The problem was a displaced bone pinching muscle tissue. After the election, Holt was admitted to the Freemasons Hospital in East Melbourne for manipulation treatment. This was followed by twice-weekly physiotherapy sessions at a Melbourne clinic. His personal physician, Dr Marcus Faunce, examined Holt briefly on Friday 15 December and considered him to be in good health although the Prime Minister complained to Pat de Lacy that his shoulder was still causing him considerable pain. Despite being advised by doctors to rest, Holt ignored their counsel and played tennis the day before his disappearance. He should not have entered the water the following day. His weakened shoulder would leave him at the mercy of the current.

Those familiar with Cheviot Beach and the local conditions were convinced that Holt had been knocked unconscious by a wave that flung his head on to rocks. He then drowned. They also believed that his body was either carried far out to sea in an easterly direction along the coast on the ebb tide or caught up in bull kelp and consumed by crayfish. Another possibility was that Holt might have been stung by venomous jellyfish which could have caused incapacitation.

In the early 1960s, three cray fisherman were lost from Rye ocean beach, about six miles from Cheviot Beach. Two of the bodies were carried in different directions while the third was never recovered. The Victorian Government's senior pathologist, Dr James McNamara, who specialised in the recovery of drowning victims, was allowed the final word in the police report into Holt's disappearance. He concluded that the Prime Minister's body could have been recovered presuming it was not trapped in kelp, attacked by crayfish, eaten by sharks or damaged by the propeller blades of passing vessels. If, however, his body were not free to rise and was subjected to attack by crayfish or sea lice, 'the body would have been reduced to a skeleton in a period as short as 24–48 hours'.[6] Within three to four weeks, the ligaments joining bones would be destroyed.

As with most unexplained or mysterious disappearances, there were a number of Australians who claimed to know the body's whereabouts. Typical was S.F. Baker, who wrote to McEwen on 30 December 1967:

> I am certain the body of the late Prime Minister is at present lying in the sea at a depth of 41 feet 6 inches and 2071 yards 1 feet 6 inches in the direction one point west of north from the place where he entered the water. I have arrived at this estimation of position by a method I have of divining which I have found on other occasions to be successful.[7]

The final police report issued on 5 January 1968 did not record a finding on how Harold Holt died or what became of his body. There was insufficient evidence for any firm conclusions on both matters. But this left plenty of room for speculation about why he entered the water and why his body was never recovered. The *News American* in Baltimore expressed its hope that 'the unusual circumstances of [Holt's] death will not explode in the sensational myth-making that still clouds the assassination of President Kennedy'.[8] As we shall see, this is exactly what happened.

There was (and is) no good reason to question or doubt the evidence of Alan Stewart or Marjorie Gillespie about Holt's actions or state of mind on the day he disappeared. The Prime Minister was hot and went for a swim to cool down—it was no more complicated than that. But the Australian edition of *Life* magazine was the first to suggest that Holt might have committed suicide. This provided a new angle on the tragedy. The thought that a national leader might kill himself was a novelty in the western world, which opened up many dramatic possibilities with a hint of scandal in the background. Where did these rumours originate? Political commentator Don Whitington observed that 'there have been stories circulating since [his death] that he wanted to die and chose his opportunity, but there is no evidence to support them'.[9] Ted St John was certainly one source. He believed that the Prime Minister was so overcome by attacks on his integrity and the declining fortunes of his Government that 'Holt's plunge into the stormy waters appeared to be an act of a man who either wanted to die or didn't much care whether he lived or died. But was it, rather, an act of bravado in front of a woman whom he was courting? It's still a bit of a mystery to me, as I think it is to most people'.[10] Former Labor Minister Clyde Cameron suggests another possible source.

> I asked Billy [McMahon] what was the real story behind Holt's disappearance. He told me he had been with Holt for several weeks before his death and had refused to discuss the matter, even with Sonia [his wife]. He spoke as though he knew what had happened to Holt, but looked and sounded quite mysterious about the whole matter . . . [McMahon] hinted that there was something deeper than even the [VIP airline scandal] which was responsible for causing him to disappear.[11]

But close colleagues were sceptical. Sir James Killen noted that:

> A number of political observers have contended that Harold Holt was so depressed that he just walked into the sea off Cheviot Beach to escape from his worries. I do not believe that contention at all. Concern and anxiety would have been keenly felt by Harold Holt because beneath that suave cheerfulness there was a marked sensitivity, but there was nothing I ever saw in his make-up which would give the slightest support to the view that he could become desperate and suicidal.[12]

Sir Alexander Downer remarked:

It is surprising how some people today consider this disaster a case of suicide. No one who really knew Holt would lightly come to such a conclusion. A gregarious man, with a zest for living, neither moody nor introspective, earthy in some of his tastes, happy in his marriage, interested in the welfare of his stepsons and their families, with an overriding love of politics and with his public career in full flight, Holt was not the sort of man who would sacrifice everything for the unknown. I do not know his innermost religious and philosophical beliefs: he always impressed me as one whose thoughts lay in this world, not the next.[13]

In a television documentary entitled *The Harold Holt Mystery* screened in 1985, Marjorie Gillespie commented rather enigmatically that Holt 'put himself in a situation where he was almost certain to die'. This is despite rejecting suicide as a possibility when she was interviewed in 1968. She also revealed in 1988 that she was 'Harold Holt's lover', a claim repeated in several magazines and newspapers. Simon Warrender had previously questioned Marjorie Gillespie about her relationship with Holt.

I referred to constant rumours since the Cheviot tragedy that she and Harold were having an affair. Impudently, she did not deny the rumours. 'Of course, Simon', she said, 'what is your interpretation of an affair?'. I told her. She said that there were various types of affairs—intimate affairs and sordid affairs and emotional affairs. Hers with Harold, she said, was an emotional affair based on 'mutual intellectual admiration and respect'.[14]

She also said she had 'written a book, which will not be published for twenty years, about Harold'. Nearly 40 years on, the book has yet to appear.

On the tenth anniversary of Holt's disappearance, Zara said that her third husband, Jefferson Bate, Liberal Member for the New South Wales seat of Macarthur (1949–72), was the only person who 'said to her face' that Holt had committed suicide.[15] In an interview on the thirtieth anniversary, Inspector Laurie Newell said: 'I can't discount the idea that it might have been suicide. I have no proof that that didn't actually happen ... [although] my opinion is that it is unlikely'.[16] Newell's 1968 Police Report dismissed suicide in noting that 'an ordinary domestic pattern was disclosed from the time Mr Holt departed on Friday 15 December 1967 [from Canberra]'.

There were other explanations for his disappearance. Melbourne's *Sunday Observer* claimed in 1968 in a front-page story that the United

States' Central Intelligence Agency (CIA) assassinated him. Other would-be assailants included disgruntled European refugees and North Vietnamese covert operatives using a delayed-action nerve agent. There was also suspicion that the police investigation could have been tainted. Inspector (Grade 2) Jack Ford and another detective, Jack Matthews, were later charged with extorting bribes from a Melbourne illegal bookmaker and backyard abortionist, Charlie Wyatt. Melbourne's *Truth* reported the story which led to the subsequent imprisonment of both men. *Smith's Weekly* added to the rumours and innuendoes when it asked a series of questions that could have been quickly and readily answered:

> Was a bag of top-secret Vietnam War papers in the PM's car left unguarded? . . . Did the PM's death prove Australia could not be trusted to guard secret American war information? . . . Why did the first official announcement say Mr Alan Stewart was a Commonwealth Quarantine official and close companion of the PM? Who told Mr John McEwen to announce to the world on that fateful Sunday night that Holt was only with Mr Stewart, and not Mrs Gillespie? When Mr Holt was in the Sorrento fish shop before his death, was his unlocked private car robbed of secret papers and, if so, was this covered up?

Holt did not take any papers relating to the Vietnam War to Portsea. The contents of his briefcase were listed on a manifest produced by the Commonwealth Police. The Prime Minister's car was not robbed or even tampered with. There was never any suggestion that Australia was unable to preserve the confidentiality of information relating to defence or diplomatic matters. As for the description of Alan Stewart and Holt's companions during that last weekend, the official statements in the first few hours following his disappearance were confused and contradictory, but this represented the relaying of inaccurate information rather than anything more sinister. In a feature article published in 1977, the *Weekend Australian* referred to 'wild speculation about a rendezvous with a Russian submarine'.[17] Six years later, this rumour would resurface, albeit with an important twist.

— ● ●—

In May 1983 British novelist Anthony Grey received an anonymous call from a man claiming to have established conclusively the fate of Harold

Holt. The man's decision to speak with Grey was not altogether random. As a young journalist, Grey had been sent to China by the Reuters News Agency to report on the Cultural Revolution during the mid-1960s. He was kept under arrest in Beijing by the Chinese Government for more than two years and became part of the news he was sent to report. On being freed, Grey was appointed an Officer of the British Empire (OBE). After making his mark in journalism, Grey moved on to write a number of successful novels including *Saigon, Peking* and *Tokyo Bay*. He also worked as a presenter for the BBC World Service, produced television documentaries and joined the Raelian Movement which asserts that all life forms on Earth were genetically engineered by an advanced extraterrestrial civilisation. At the conclusion of a three-part radio documentary series entitled 'UFOs: Fact, Fiction or Fantasy', broadcast by the BBC in 1997, Grey claimed that the evidence for craft from other civilisations visiting the Earth was overwhelming.

Grey's anonymous caller wanted his help in publishing a manuscript he had produced on Holt's disappearance. Several days later they met at Grey's London club where the hopeful author explained that he was a 'former naval officer' whose manuscript had been rejected by a number of publishers. His name was Ronald Titcombe. Grey accepted a copy of the manuscript and asked his literary agent for an opinion. This was a prudent step given the scandal of the bogus 'Hitler diaries' which had badly damaged the reputation and credibility of the German magazine *Stern* in April 1983.[18] Sceptical but intrigued, Grey analysed the story in minute detail with Titcombe between June and July 1983. Titcombe claimed that 'he'd had enough of covert naval operations to give him a clear understanding of the world of international intelligence, and had been on duty at Australia's naval headquarters in Canberra on the day Harold Holt disappeared'.[19] He became suspicious of the 'official' explanation of Holt's death because of 'some seeming inconsistencies in confidential reports passing across his desk. But it was not until six years later that he stumbled by chance on a hint that started him questioning'.[20]

After he left the Navy, Titcombe pursued various business interests. In Iraq during July 1973, an Iraqi civil servant mentioned to him a 'high Australian government official' whom he believed had sought asylum abroad. When Titcombe sought more information he was given the name of a Chinese Government representative in Baghdad. Between 1976 and 1983, Titcombe claimed to have 'gradually pieced together a more comprehensive story [of Holt's disappearance] from a series of meetings with several different Chinese government officials'.[21] After several interviews, Grey 'gradually came to feel confident that the man I was listening to was telling the truth'. They agreed that Grey 'should set down the whole remarkable story' while Titcombe would remain anonymous. The 'whole remarkable story' was told in *The Prime Minister Was a Spy*, which claimed to be 'a true account of what lay behind Harold Holt's mysterious disappearance' although, Grey conceded, 'I can't *guarantee* that it is true' (original emphasis retained).

> I cannot point to any incontrovertible documentary evidence or produce any tangible physical object like a rabbit out of a hat to prove beyond the last doubt that the story is true in every detail . . . In the last resort reliance has to be placed essentially on detailed verbal information provided in Asia, Australia and Europe by different Chinese informants.[22]

In effect, he is saying that there was no corroborative evidence. The story rests entirely on what Titcombe told Grey and his assessment of Titcombe's truthfulness and honesty.

Grey's 'true account' began in 1929 when Holt allegedly visited the Chinese Consul General to obtain information for a paper he was preparing for a debate at Queen's College, Melbourne University. At this stage, the recognised Chinese Government was dominated by the Nationalist Party (Kuomintang) led by Chiang Kai-shek. The Chinese Consul General, Sung Fa-Tsiang, obtained a copy of Holt's paper (how and why is not explained) and asked to speak with its author. Holt was then allegedly given a substantial sum of money by a 'Mr Chen who has a small publishing business dealing with commercial news'.[23] Holt was asked to sign a receipt for £50. Titcombe was shown a photocopy of this document. It carried the name 'Harold Holt' and was dated 1929. There were apparently six other receipts signed by Holt for amounts ranging between £50 to £100. While Grey concedes that Holt must have been aware that these payments were probably part of an effort by the Chinese to recruit him as some sort of agent, Grey cannot account for Holt's willingness to sign receipts and create evidence that linked him to the Chinese Government other than an overwhelmingly strong desire for money.

Sung was recalled in 1931 for disciplinary reasons—he had failed to recruit sufficient numbers of Australian agents—and replaced by Li Hung, a diplomat with intelligence training who continued to pay Holt for his articles on China. None of these articles, or even their preliminary drafts, survives or can be found. At the end of the year, Li told Holt that the Kuomintang's intelligence service had been infiltrated and that Chiang Kai-shek wanted a new group to report directly to him. Holt was to be this group's representative in Australia. Apparently Holt was flattered by the app-roach and agreed to give the matter serious consideration. As the Chinese Consulate in Melbourne was being closed down, Holt would be 'run' by Sung Ting-hua in the Consulate General's office in Sydney. By this time Holt had accepted Li's offer 'to help China's cause'.

Holt continued to meet with Sung 'at a house in Domain Street, South Yarra'. His particular task was to 'help open up trade lines between China and Australia and convince men of influence of the need to create a greater freedom between the two countries'. But was this spying or political lobbying? Perhaps the latter would be a more accurate description. Li Hung was then suspected of being a Communist and was replaced by Wang Kung-fang. At this point Grey remarks that both the Nationalists and the Communists were trying to recruit Holt although their reasons are not clear.[24] But certainly the Nationalists were delighted when Holt was elected to the Federal Parliament in 1935. This prompted a plan to turn Holt into a fully fledged spy with the code-name 'H.K. Bors'. During parliamentary recesses, Holt apparently met with Wang in Melbourne's Botanical Gardens, during which he was 'primed with seemingly innocent questions that he could ask publicly in the House of Representatives'. Grey continued:

> as Holt had already shown himself to be susceptible to flattery and appeared to have need of praise and admiration, Wang was to tell him in detail about outstanding Europeans of the past who had made great contributions to China's history; gradually over a period he should be encouraged to see himself growing into a similar role.[25]

By May 1936, Holt had completed his 'training' and was to become a 'sleeper'—a non-active agent. Grey claims that in mid-1936 Holt spent three weeks at the Consulate General in Sydney while supposed to be on holiday at Mornington. But others within the Chinese intelligence community believed that Holt was too valuable to be a sleeper and ought to be used 'at every opportunity'. His new controller was Hsu Mo. The nature of any information passed by Holt to the Chinese in 1938–39 was not made clear although presumably it had to do with the Japanese, who had invaded Manchuria in 1931 and central China in 1937. In 1940, however, Holt was allegedly copying Cabinet papers and passing them to the Chinese in despatches marked for the attention of 'Mr Trafford' at a London address. Other papers were left 'under the azalea bushes to the right' of the driveway entrance to Holt's residence in Toorak. Although the Chinese decried Holt's decision to join the Army after being dropped from the Ministry, his loyalty was apparently never questioned. When the Government lost office in 1941, Holt continued to provide information to the Chinese, who were at the time Australia's allies.

In 1948, Holt was told to cease reporting as the Kuomintang were losing the Chinese civil war. Holt became a 'sleeper' again. With the Korean War under way, the newly appointed Minister for Labour and National Service was contacted in March 1952 by D.R. Wong on behalf of the Nationalist regime in Taiwan. D.R. Wong was, apparently, an alias for Y.M. Liu, a Communist defector who believed that Holt was no longer under effective Kuomintang control. Holt is alleged to have told Liu that the Americans were contemplating use of the atomic bomb against China to hasten an end to the Korean War, 'intelligence' which brought the North Koreans and Chinese to the negotiating table at Panmunjom. Chinese Premier Zhou En-lai and Li Tao, Director of the Operational Department of the Peoples' Revolutionary Military Council, conferred over the possibility of reactivating Holt. Zhou agreed to Holt's reactivation in the hope of Australia's immigration policies relaxing so that mainland Chinese would have 'opportunities for gaining access to important industrial and technological intelligence'.[26] To facilitate this, the Chinese Communist Party allegedly paid Holt £30 000. This was a phenomenal sum of money that was never reflected in either Holt's lifestyle or his personal assets. Holt's frequent overseas trips apparently made him a superb source of detailed and varied information which he communicated to his Chinese controllers through the travel diaries sent to a very long distribution list in Australia. Holt also met D.R. Wong regularly in a small house in the Melbourne suburb of Carlton. To substantiate these incredible claims, Titcombe was shown four documents relating to the Korean War, an assessment of two rival Pakistani politicians that Holt had met in 1952, a 1954 assessment of Cambodia's future, and documents outlining Australia's attitude to the Communist uprising in the French colony of Vietnam. In fact, Holt had apparently become so successful and so enthusiastic that Wong suggested that he limit spying for fear of ASIO monitoring his movements and activities.

In October 1954, Holt is supposed to have told Wong that he could no longer serve the Nationalist cause as the government in Taiwan did not represent the people of the mainland. He claimed some sympathy for Mao Tse-tung and Zhou En-lai and remarked that Communism was an appropriate path for the mainland to take, given that China did not have a history of democracy. A special conference was held in Beijing to discuss Holt's change of heart. Although he was vehemently anti-Communist in his approach to Australia's domestic affairs, he was not anti-Communist when it came to Australian foreign policy. Holt was effectively 'self-deactivated' from 1954 to 1956. Apparently Wong met with Premier Zhou to discuss Holt's future and returned in May 1956 hoping to influence Holt's internal confusion over the progress being achieved by Communism within China and the threat Communism posed to Australia and its external interests. By this stage, Holt had apparently initiated inquiries into the status of D.R. Wong. He was able to do this without arousing suspicion because he was the Immigration Minister. Finding that such a person had not been cleared for entry into Australia, Holt realised Y.M. Liu was the only Chinese official whose accreditation matched Wong's. There was also a photo of Liu. Holt confronted 'Wong' and asked to see him on Monday 16 April 1957. Wong then revealed that the same Mr Chen who had expressed interest in Holt's papers on China was actually Chen Yi, who would shortly become China's Foreign Minister. Holt was apparently told of the Sino–Soviet split before it took place and was asked to support the PRC's admission to the United Nations. Holt was also told he could defect to China at any time should he wish. Strangely, Holt did not object to being deceived by Wong for more than five years.

In return for his continuing services, Holt apparently demanded three things. First, that Chen Yi would be appointed Foreign Minister; second, that Beijing's national newspaper would announce that China did not embrace Russian-style Communism; and, third, Mao was to affirm that although he was 'anti-rightist' he was not 'anti-intellectual'. When these conditions were met, Holt allegedly said, 'you will have a loyal ally in me—providing that the policies of China—mainland China—do not conflict with the interests of my country'.[27] Thereafter, Holt met with Wong in his Collins Street office. But in 1961, Wong reported that Holt was becoming agitated. When Wong also reported his fear that Holt might confess to spying, Zhou ordered a submarine to be deployed to waters off Sydney in the event that Holt needed to leave Australia. A Chinese submarine allegedly spent eight days off the New South Wales coast in January 1962 waiting to evacuate the Federal Treasurer. The boat was not needed as Holt did not 'crack'.

By this time the Chinese had concluded that Holt would be the next Prime Minister and that he needed to be left in place if at all possible. Grey claims that Holt engaged in some effective spying between 1962 and November 1964 when another submarine was despatched to Darwin in the event that Wong and Holt needed to be evacuated. During its passage to Australia, the submarine tracked an Indonesian flotilla near Sarawak before colliding with the Panamanian freighter *Capella*. By this time, the Chinese thought that the marriage between Harold and Zara had apparently become stale and they were living largely separate lives. This explained Holt's willingness to leave Zara and his life in Australia. Holt again returned to a 'more stable frame of mind' and the submarine was not needed.

When Holt became Prime Minister, the Chinese monitored his every move and allegedly claimed that Wong was 'the only person with whom Holt felt he could discuss the finer points of international diplomacy'.[28] In June 1966 while in San Francisco, Holt apparently met 'a senior Chinese official' and was again offered an escape route should it ever be needed. After Kocan attempted to kill Calwell in June 1966, Holt was obliged to accept the presence of a bodyguard. Around the same time ASIO had decided that 'no sensitive material should . . . be passed to the Prime Minister'. In May 1967, Holt called for an ASIO file and read that an important link in the Soviet intelligence network was a man named 'H.K. Bors'—Holt's code-name. Grey pondered: 'Was it an oblique and complex ploy by ASIO to indicate to him that they knew about his secret life?'[29] Holt rang Wong in a state of distress. He thought ASIO were now aware of his activities and asked to be taken out of Australia. He no longer wanted to be Prime Minister. He said: 'I want to get out'.

By July, Holt said he was having second thoughts. By October he was again adamant about leaving. Two dates for his defection were proposed, the first of which was Sunday 17 December 1967. Wong travelled to Portsea to supervise the operation and used a VHF radio to contact the submarine deployed off Cheviot Beach. Holt was to be picked up after the high tide turned at 11.32 a.m. The submarine, located four cables (800 yards) south-west of Cheviot Hill, deployed two divers in an underwater vehicle, supplied with oxygen. Holt was told to enter the water at precisely 12.15 p.m. Apparently Holt took a deep breath and was dragged down by the ankles while the Chinese 'gently guided Holt towards the conning tower of the long, grey submarine's . . . escape chamber which made up the conning tower's upper section'. Holt was then guided to the 'inner compartment'. In a moment of high drama and great relief for Australia's seventeenth prime minister, 'a mature-looking Chinese approached from among the young crew and said, according to the informant, "I am the captain and Chen Yi asked me to greet you on his behalf. Welcome to China, Mr Holt"'.[30] Grey claims that Holt was one of the highest-ranking Communist spies of all time, providing China with information that was 'most damaging to Australia's interests'. In what way the information was damaging Grey did not explain. But he claims that various reports of a submarine sighting were allegedly removed from naval operations and police files because 'ASIO knew something of Holt's past' and probably wanted to hide all evidence of a defection because they had failed to apprehend him. Holt was landed by the submarine in China where he lived until his death. Grey could not say when Holt died but he told me in October 2000 that his grave was in Beijing.

While the story contained in Grey's book seems far-fetched, implausible and unlikely, these are not sufficient grounds for concluding that it did not happen. Even those parts of the story which are factually incorrect or which can be challenged on some circumstantial grounds, such as the purported distance of the Chinese submarine from the coast, could be explained in other ways. By way of example, Grey states that the submarine sent to evacuate Holt was positioned 800 yards off Cheviot Beach. He confirmed that this was the distance in 2000. I asked the Commander of the Australian Submarine Squadron, Captain Rick Shalders RAN, to comment on the possibility that a Chinese submarine could bottom so close to the shore.

The position you quoted [800 yards off Cheviot Beach] should be about 38° 20' S 144° 40' E. The water depth off that beach is 10 metres to about three cables (600 yards) and 20 metres about 1.5 nautical miles off. It shelves slowly until 3 nautical miles [off the coast] where it is still only 30 metres in depth! Some maths to assist: submarine height (keel to fin top) is about 40 feet (old Romeo/Foxtrot) = periscope depth of 45–50 feet. This then means at a minimum about 10–15 feet is needed below for safety and excursion—thus depth of 55–65 feet (17–20 metres).

We [the Royal Australian Navy] do NOT have a bottoming area in that position and would not practise that procedure unless the area was adequately surveyed by the Hydrographer. From our operational experience we would have to surface in that depth of water. While it is possible with an *Oberon* or older conventional submarine to stay submerged in that depth it is dangerous and allows no margin for safety or 'ducking' any vessels. If a submarine chanced to bottom there then it would be taking a great risk and then not know what was above as its masts, etc., would be below the surface. A diver entering a submerged submarine is a highly dangerous activity practised by very few around the world: our SAS and British SBS and USN Seals. The procedures are only now being done with separate air tanks and supplies.

As far as Chinese submarines are concerned: it would be an absolute first if it came this far unnoticed and I doubt their capability in the 1960s. In summary, I would find it highly unlikely for another country to bottom a submarine in that area without great risk. The water depth does not allow even the older submarines to get closer than about 2 nautical miles submerged.[31]

It would have been impossible to navigate a submersible vehicle into the ditch in which Holt was last seen. Furthermore, the existence of planks in the water was a serious hazard for submarine operations.

While the impossibility of a submarine manoeuvring within two nautical miles of the coast (a nautical mile is 2035 yards; a land mile is 1760 yards) would appear to discredit Grey's claim that it was 800 yards, quite apart from the extreme difficulty of executing the evolution in any event, he could make the counterclaim that an error or a misunderstanding could have been made in relaying this particular detail of the story. For instance, it could have been 8000 yards (4 miles) rather than 800. The difficulty for Grey is that this possible 'inaccuracy' is but one of countless other defects in Titcombe's account.

There is also the implausibility of the claim that Holt was not just a spy, but that he was actively and enthusiastically engaging in espionage for Communist China and that he was motivated by more than just personal financial greed. But here Grey overlooks Holt's long-standing and vigorous anti-Communism and some of his more surprising policy decisions, such as establishing an Australian embassy in Taiwan. Notwithstanding the positive relationship that existed between Australia and 'Nationalist China' (Taiwan) during the 1950s and the recognition of a Taiwanese diplomat in Canberra, Australia was not formally represented by an ambassador in Taipei. During a debate in the House of Representatives on 28 April 1966, Hasluck stated that the question of representation would not be resolved in the short-term. Seven weeks later a joint communiqué was issued by Holt and his Taiwanese counterpart, Wei Tao-ming, announcing that Australia would establish an embassy in

Taipei.[32] Holt's former colleague, Percy Spender, by now a member of the International Court of Justice at The Hague, had thought Holt to be impulsive at times. In relation to this particular decision Spender said that 'according to my information, agreement to appointing an Australian Ambassador to Taiwan was made by him personally at a dinner party and without prior consultation with the Foreign Office or, apparently, his Cabinet'.[33] Official records appear to confirm that Holt had indeed acted entirely on his own initiative and without consulting Hasluck, Cabinet or the Department of External Affairs after he was personally lobbied by the Taiwanese ambassador to Australia, Chen Chi-Mai, and charmed by his attractive wife.[34]

The Government's decision was widely criticised for being unnecessary and in conflict with American and British attitudes. The United States was moving diplomatically towards China even as it remained distant from Taiwan while the British had formal representation in Beijing. The decision was described by one senior Australian diplomat, Walter Crocker, as a 'foolish and naïve off-the-cuff decision . . . [by] an amiable man . . . who knew almost nothing about foreign affairs'.[35] The decision naturally delighted Bill Kent Hughes, who had been lobbying Holt hard to make the decision.[36] T.B. Millar thought it was a 'strange decision', seeing it as a gesture more designed to support Taiwanese independence than an encouragement to Chiang Kai-shek to invade the mainland.[37] Holt later remarked that the appointment of an ambassador to Taipei would help to gather information on mainland China[38] although the Americans regarded Taiwan as an unreliable intelligence source and were gaining their information from Hong Kong.[39]

＊＊＊

An analysis of Holt's parliamentary speeches over 30 years does suggest some sympathy towards China. On 27 November 1935, he asked the Minister for External Affairs, Senator George Pearce, whether 'the League of Nations has received a protest from the Chinese Government against the action of Japanese forces in North China'.[40] But this was less to do with China and more an indication of Holt's commitment to multilateralism. However, his decision to appoint an ambassador to Taiwan is a curious decision because it seemed so out of character. Holt usually took important matters of this kind to Cabinet after seeking departmental advice. He was under no real political or diplomatic pressure but this decision would

create a problem for subsequent administrations when Australia began to
shift its policy on recognising the Communist Government in Beijing.
He may have acted as he did to obtain intelligence on Taiwan for trans-
mission to China, but a much more plausible explanation is his desire
to align Australia more overtly with anti-Communist Asian nations.
Richard Woolcott remembers Holt's meeting with Chiang Kai-shek in
March 1967:

> I had the impression that in stressing Taiwan's stability and progress Holt was
> implying that Taiwan, as 'a going concern', need not press its unsustainable
> claim to the government of the whole of China. At that time Taiwan also
> claimed Outer Mongolia and Taiwanese senior officials were irritated by
> Australia's recent [February 1967] diplomatic recognition [only the second
> Communist state Australia had recognised] of Mongolia as an independent
> state. I do not, however, recall Chiang raising this with Holt.[41]

He defended continuing trade with China which by 1967 had become the
country's fifth largest export market on the basis that the commodities
exported to China were in free supply on world markets and that Australia
was profiting from the trade and should go on doing so.[42]

But *why* would Holt spy for Communist China? And does Anthony
Grey really believe that Holt could simply have walked away from Zara,
Marjorie Gillespie, his stepsons and their partners and children? There is
ample evidence that the Holt marriage was no union of convenience.
Holt could not have turned his back on family and friends without giving
any indication that he was speaking with them for the last time. If he did,
he had greater composure than he ever showed in private or in public at
any other time. And why did Holt take the virtually unilateral step of
establishing an Australian embassy in Taipei? It is hard to imagine this
strange decision having any positive consequences for Beijing. And why
did the Chinese intelligence services tell Titcombe of their exploits,
but not until 1983? Why withhold all physical evidence that might
support the story? Grey argues that evidence does exist, in the form of
Holt's travel diaries:

> although ostensibly 'round robin' letters to family and friends they had been
> devised specifically to pass political information to Chinese contacts both in
> open form and in encrypted form . . . to check the likelihood of coded
> messages in them I employed a cryptanalyst (codebreaker) formerly of

GCHQ Cheltenham to analyse these diaries and in a report so far unpublished he satisfied himself that he had identified the code systems and possible information conveyed by them. Since Mr Holt was a Privy Counsellor I offered a sight of these travel diaries to the British Government via the British Cabinet Office in 1984. After a long delay they were returned with a note saying they were not of interest.[43]

Of course, Grey might have published the report he had commissioned on the diaries to substantiate his claim. The difficulty in accepting that they contained code is the existence of the drafts which show the editorial work of more than one hand and the random inclusion of material recalled by Zara and Holt's travelling private secretary.

Ultimately, the story rests upon the veracity and reliability of Ronald Mervyn Titcombe. Born on 30 March 1930, Titcombe joined the RAN Specialist Reserve after service in the Merchant Navy. In 1950, as a midshipman he sought a transfer from the Reserve to the Permanent Naval Forces. Although he claimed to have a First Mate's Certificate, he could not produce any documents attesting to the fact. Inquiries made by the Navy revealed that no such certificate had ever been granted. In 1957 he travelled to Britain to undertake specialist training in anti-submarine warfare. He was not an apt student and was placed near the bottom of his class. On returning to Australia he became the first General Duties Officer to become a Clearance Diver and was awarded the MBE for his service on 11 June 1960. In March 1961 he led a diving team that removed construction debris from deep and bitterly cold water near a diversion tunnel in an inlet tower regulating the flow of water from Lake Eucumbene in the Snowy Mountains. He later served as Executive Officer (Second-in-Command) of the *Daring* Class destroyer HMAS *Vampire* and was attached to the Directorate of Tactics and Weapon Policy in 1967. Titcombe claimed to have been on duty at Navy Office in Canberra the day that Holt drowned although this claim cannot be verified as the records have not survived. After being discharged from the Navy shortly after Holt's disappearance, Titcombe travelled the world. While his movements and activities over the next fifteen years cannot be ascertained with any precision, it is possible to piece together aspects of his life.

Titcombe lived for some time in Beirut (where he claimed to have made his first million dollars) before taking up residency in the Channel Islands until his assets were seized for non-payment of debts. He published the *Handbook for Professional Divers* in 1973. In the years that followed, he purchased and rejuvenated the Norton Motorbike Company before establishing a company based at Peterhead in Scotland providing logistic support and shore services to North Sea gas and oil platforms. He leased a substantial country residence at Aboyne, fifteen miles downstream from Balmoral Castle on the River Dee, and enjoyed a lavish lifestyle. His friends and associates included the Australian High Commissioner to London, Sir Gordon Freeth, with whom he stayed when in London. Titcombe claimed to have sold his business to British Oxygen for £40 million. There is no evidence of such a sale or the whereabouts of such a considerable sum of money. When Titcombe returned to Australia in 1981 and established two shipping companies, he used borrowed money. The first of the companies, Kapal Pacifico, existed to charter ships from Australia to South America. It secured one cargo from a Melbourne firm but several disruptions to loading meant little profit was made. The second, Ultra Marine, sought to moor a large oil tanker in waters off northern Papua New Guinea for the purpose of on-selling its cargo. The PNG Government was not convinced of the project's merit and would not give approval. Titcome then tried his hand at other work.

Following the retirement of G.W. Palamountain as secretary of the prestigious Melbourne Club, Titcombe was appointed as his successor on 6 October 1982. The author of the Club's commissioned history, Major General Ronald McNicoll, commented that:

> Titcombe was a very different kind of person from his predecessor. He was formal, precise, and was known to have been a competent executive officer in at least one ship. He had retired from the Navy in 1968, and had since followed commercial pursuits . . . Late in November, the Committee was informed of legal proceedings in Sydney against R.M. Titcombe, who was the subject of a petition for bankruptcy. A shipping company of which he was a director was in difficulties. Taxed with this, he admitted to financial troubles in the Channel Islands. The club's solicitors, Moules, were able to point to various matters that Titcombe should have disclosed before appointment. The committee was acutely embarrassed. It seemed likely that the club's reputation would suffer if Titcombe served out his probationary period, so agreement was reached with him, at some cost, that he would resign without delay.[44]

He then went to live at Mount Macedon where he leased a house that was almost completely devoid of furniture. Details about Titcombe's

290

subsequent activities and business dealings are even more difficult to obtain. He was the principal of Rainbow Oil Company Investments registered in Mauritius. The company was dissolved on 16 February 1999. One of the company directors was arrested in relation to a cheque payable to Rainbow. From the late 1990s, Titcombe lived in the south of England in a Council house in conditions approaching dire poverty. He died in January 2001 from cancer in a Chichester hospital and was buried from Boxgrove Priory in West Sussex on 10 February.

Those who knew Titcombe cannot attest to his reliability and veracity as a source of historical information. At the time of Holt's disappearance, Lieutenant Michael Shotter, the Commanding Officer of Clearance Diving Team 1, had recently returned from active service in South Vietnam. Titcombe was then the RAN's senior clearance diver and something of a legend in the diving community. Shotter thought Cheviot Beach a most unlikely place to bottom a submarine and was adamant that Holt would have needed tanks to have reached a bottomed submarine. He also felt these would have made movement under the water extremely difficult.

Shotter saw Titcombe as a 'Walter Mitty' type character. He was on the fringe of naval intelligence and liked people to believe he was more involved in intelligence activity than he really was. In 1968, Shotter and Titcombe were sent to train in counter-insurgency work at Swan Island. Titcombe subsequently told a woman with whom he was having an affair that he was involved with the Australian Secret Intelligence Service (ASIS) and left a briefcase of classified documents at her flat. When he tried to end their affair, she approached naval authorities with information about Titcombe's claims and his habit of carrying a gun. Titcombe tried to implicate Shotter, who was then sent to the United States while Titcombe was directed to resign from the Royal Australian Navy or face a court martial. This he did, abandoning his wife and two daughters for a new life abroad. Shotter, thought Titcombe was capable of exaggeration, and that he was prepared to lie in his own interests—such as when he nominated Shotter as the source of the alleged ASIS leak. Although the two later discussed Holt's death, Shotter never heard Titcombe speak of the story that later appeared in Grey's book. Another of Titcombe's colleagues described him as:

A person of boundless energy, full of ideas, a great raconteur, very self-confident and a true Walter Mitty. He liked to give the impression that, as a clearance diver, he had been involved in a number of covert activities, including some form of association with ASIS. Whether this was true or not I don't really know. I always felt he was a bit of a showman looking for a stage and what he was angling for was an audience to impress. Hence, I tried to avoid giving him the opportunity. Not only that, I felt he was indiscreet and his subject matter was not something I was prepared to talk about in the open. He was always a bit of a shadowy figure. I didn't trust him and he was not one of my confidantes.

A former naval colleague who worked with him briefly in 1982 said simply: 'he was a friend but also a professional con man'.

Despite all the objections to his narrative and doubts about Titcombe's veracity, Grey told me on 8 September 1999: 'There is a great deal to say about the Harold Holt book still because I am as convinced as ever that it contains the truth'. While I am sure that Anthony Grey sincerely believes in the truth of Titcombe's story, there is insufficient evidence on which to make such a judgment. In fact, as Grey readily concedes, there is absolutely no material evidence. It should have been so simple for Grey and Titcombe to provide some corroborative evidence, such as the receipts signed by Holt in 1929, but none has ever been offered. Having spoken to Titcombe myself, I believe the story is a complete fabrication.

Grey's account has fascinated and inspired other writers. In *The Chinese Secret Service*, Roger Faligot and Remi Kauffer state that on the day of his disappearance, Holt

> was holding a small outdoor party at his cottage at Portsea. The weather was magnificent. There was not a ripple on the water. The crystal-clear sound of laughter hung in the air, along with the aroma of grilled meat being barbequed on the beach. Harold Holt, in an athletic mood, said he was going to take a dip in order to work up an appetite. What could be more natural? His friends watched the Prime Minister swimming towards the horizon. But suddenly he disappeared. There was panic: and yet he was such a good swimmer![45]

Nearly every detail in this account, other than that it was daylight, is wrong. This work repeated Grey's claims and asserted that Holt 'was one of the greatest successes of Chinese espionage'.[46] But then the authors ask, 'Why had the extremely efficient Australian counter-intelligence service not uncovered the betrayal of this exceptional mole sooner?'.[47] And was there a link between Holt and the alleged 'Fifth Man' of the British Cambridge spy ring? By directing Australia's newly formed secret services on to the wrong track, did Roger Hollis of MI5 cover up the recruitment by the Chinese Communists of the future Prime Minister Harold Holt?'[48] There was more to come.

Ross Coulthart, a reporter with the Nine Network's *Sunday* television program, was trawling on the Internet for 'really hot info' in 1998.[49] He claims that:

> A colleague tells me of how he recently heard a classic Holt conspiracy yarn: While travelling in far North Australia he bumped into a man who claimed to be a former spook for the Australian Government who had helped Holt return to Australia several times since his death. Holt travelled incognito from a home in France. It appears the PM had swum around to the next bay, hopped in a car driven by a lover, and slipped out of the country. The spook claimed Holt had later died of a heart attack on the French South Coast sometime during the 1980s. The conspiracy theory has it that many people know about this, including one very senior Liberal Party figure. Just when we were trying to laugh away this theory, one former very senior Labor Minister told us he had 'the astounding truth' about Holt buried in his confidential files—only to be released in the event of his and his informant's death.[50]

Coulthart wrongly states that the public was not told that Mrs Gillespie was on the beach and repeats many of the more fanciful rumours and theories.

In his 2003 book, *Blood, Money and Power: How LBJ killed JFK*, Barr McClellan claimed that the American ambassador to Australia, Ed Clark, had earlier arranged for President John F. Kennedy to be killed to allow Lyndon Johnson to become president.[51] McClellan had worked alongside Clark in a Texas legal firm from 1968 to 1982. A review of the book by Gerard Noonan concluded: 'Now if only Clark had told McClellan he knew something about a Chinese submarine which was positioned off Portsea that fateful afternoon just before Christmas in 1967 when Holt went missing . . .'.[52] But perhaps the most bizarre story was published in the *Aussie Post* by Reg A. Watson in 1999. It featured 'respected Tasmanian spiritual medium Michael Cartwright' and 'George Eldred—a world renowned clairvoyant from Melbourne'. Both had contacted Harold Holt, who was adamant that he did not commit suicide. In a final statement from the spirit world, Holt apparently told the two men:

It's true that at the time of my death I was depressed and tired. I was under great pressure at the time. I just wanted to get away from people, hence I decided to go swimming. I did not want anyone around me. While I was in the water, I was knocked off my feet by the strength of the wave from the undertow. It dragged me under and I was turned over and over like I was in a washer. I soon lost consciousness. My body could not be found because in that very rocky area there was a large rock shelf, and my body was pinned under the shelf. This is why my body was never found. I want the truth to be known, as it had been bandied around that there was something wrong with me emotionally.[53]

On 25 August 2003, the Victorian Coroner Graeme Johnstone announced that he was considering holding an inquest into Holt's death.[54] The Coroner instructed his staff to gather information of Holt's disappearance. Sam Holt told the *Sydney Morning Herald* that an inquest would dispel many of the rumours and confirm that 'he drowned by accident and that was the beginning and end of it'.[55] At the time of writing, the Coroner had received all relevant information from the Victoria Police although there was no 'fresh' evidence to consider.[56] (The Coroner's findings were to be released in June 2005.)

The reports produced in 1968 by the Commonwealth and Victoria Police were competently produced and have stood up to scrutiny. There has never been any serious allegation that they were either a whitewash or failed to consider a compelling alternative explanation. The only questions that have been raised are why the case was not allocated to more senior officers and why the Government or even a parliamentary committee declined to conduct an inquiry of its own. In answer to the first, the circumstances surrounding Holt's disappearance were nothing out of the ordinary. There was never any suggestion of foul play. Other than the fact that the case involved the Prime Minister, it did not justify the involvement of more senior police officers. In any event, that the investigation was conducted by an inspector and a sergeant was a departure from usual procedure in which only one officer would be made available. On the second question, Parliament did not believe it could add anything useful to the police report. While the Government might have wanted to avoid the contents of Holt's briefcase being made public, there never was any suggestion that it contained a suicide note and the only item of real concern was

Casey's private letter to Holt about McMahon. This was hastily retrieved but easily could have been withheld from any public inquiry. A number of parliamentarians also wanted to avoid the personal distress an inquiry might have caused Zara. The Holt family did not want an additional inquiry, so there was no impetus to have one conducted. Although any future inquest conducted would almost certainly deliver an 'open finding', it might reassure a sceptical public and end much of the mischievous speculation that has led to claims of a cover-up or mystery when neither exists.

In an essay on Australian national identity, sociologist John Carroll claimed that Holt's death is 'fit to become a national myth' and that it conveyed something important about the relationship of the Australian people to the continent.[57] However, his description of the sea state and the search for Holt's body on 17 December 1967 is inaccurate, he is mistaken about Holt's aquatic abilities and wrong about what he did on entering the water. But this is to quibble. In a flurry of purple prose, Carroll claims that Holt 'felt a need for the cleansing power of the surf, for being alone in the vast cavern of the ocean deep, and the mercy of, in harmony with, the eternal swell of nature'. How does this provide the material for a national myth?

> Presumably he felt the need to take the risk. There was a certain celebration in this act, the greatest of all tributes: the last sight of him was of his silver hair in the broken water as he appeared swimming strongly with the current . . . In the martyrology of our country—and martyrs are always the leading heroes—Harold Holt has a far more important place than the squalid, unoriginal, irrelevant Ned Kelly, and not the less for his having been, as Prime Minister, an amiable and undistinguished figure.[58]

Really? As Ian Hancock rightly concludes, 'the obvious explanations were not sufficiently momentous to match the gravity of the event'.[59]

Despite the absence of a body and the wild speculation, there could never realistically be much doubt that Harold Holt drowned. There is certainly no evidence that he was suicidal. He was not assassinated, nor did he defect to China, the Soviet Union or anywhere else. He was, simply, one of the number of ordinary Australians who drown each year through poor judgment or bad luck. In Holt's case, it was probably both. He should not have entered the water when there was every chance of the strong current sweeping him out to sea. Holt's friend, and President of the Portsea Surf Life Saving Club, Milton Napthine, said: 'He knew damn well that the surf was too high. God only knows why he went in for a swim'. Indeed.

CHAPTER 16

The legacy

IN 2001, THE *Australian Financial Review* gathered a panel of six historians[1] to rate Australia's best and worst Prime Ministers as part of a series of retrospectives commemorating the Centenary of Federation.[2] Although each historian was asked to nominate five incumbents in each category, the range of opinion reflected their own political leanings. Only Alfred Deakin featured in each historian's 'best' list while Sir William McMahon appeared in five of six 'worst' lists. Holt did not appear in any of the 'best' lists but was nominated twice in the 'worst' list—those of Stuart Macintyre and Clem Lloyd. Both are well-known for their Left-leaning political sympathies. After Deakin, who was easily ahead of other contenders, were Sir Robert Menzies, John Curtin, Ben Chifley and Gough Whitlam. Behind McMahon were James Scullin, George Reid and Joseph Cook with Harold Holt ranking alongside Stanley Melbourne Bruce. Their reasons for placing Holt on the 'worst' list were not canvassed.

When he disappeared, the *Sydney Morning Herald* remarked: 'At least he will be remembered as one of the most likeable of Australian prime ministers'.[3] This was certainly the view of his colleagues. Jim Killen thought he was 'basically a friendly man, and would give encouragement to those around him ... His dress was precise, matching, it seemed, his manners. There was an urbanity about him that by contemporary standards would be looked upon as literally old-fashioned'.[4] Howard Beale described Harold as a 'comforter' ... 'because he was—well, he was Harold Holt'.[5] Sir Arthur Fadden said he was one of 'the kindest men I knew in politics'.[6] Sir Alexander Downer thought he was:

an unusually rounded personality. His warm nature, his liking for, and interest in, people, combined with infectious personal charm, soon made him one of the most popular members of the Australian Parliament. He quickly communicated these same qualities to all sections of Australians; whether they shared his politics or not, they admired his integrity, his passionate enthusiasm for our country and his belief in its future greatness.[7]

Characteristically, Hasluck succeeded in damning him with faint praise.

His greatest asset was his buoyancy, reassuring himself with his own optimism. And his optimism had some of the qualities of a faith—a belief that we were moving towards something good, that the better was sure to come and that our lot on earth was to bring it. He believed in progress without questioning what progress was—a sort of religious fundamentalist of politics.[8]

His political detractors consistently cite the same grounds. Bill Hayden thought that:

Holt's problem was that he has been under Menzies' shadow for so long that the authentic Harold Holt never emerged. On one occasion a senior Hansard reporter whispered to me as he was exiting from his shift in the House of Representatives, where he had covered Holt in a major debate, 'For Holt read Menzies'.[9]

This was simply not the case. The 'always a bridesmaid and never a bride' syndrome was cited by several commentators, such as W.F. Mandle, to explain his allegedly poor leadership.

Holt, if not an extension of Menzies, was an Anthony Eden to Winston Churchill, a crown prince long kept waiting for the throne, but a favourite son for all that. Holt, it is suggested, was finally given office, as was Eden, when political waters seemed calm, the weather set fair.[10]

John Molony thought his long 'apprenticeship' under Menzies may have 'bred a streak of inferiority in him'.[11]

Robert Johnson felt that while Holt was 'under the wing of the much stronger Menzies, his political success seemed assured. But once he became leader and had to stand on his own Holt discovered that charm and sociability did not guarantee success'.[12] What was worse, according to political scientist James Walter, was that 'the succession of Liberal Party leaders after Menzies' retirement in 1966 indicated one thing: that in reinforcing his own pre-eminence, Menzies had over the years deposed all potential crown princes, to leave only the untried and the second rate'.[13] The view that Menzies disposed of his rivals cannot be supported by the facts nor with Holt's many successes in 1966. Who were Menzies' genuine rivals and why and when would they have moved against him? Harrison, Spender, White and Casey were never serious threats to Menzies' position and he and they both knew that. Even when the Party might have moved against Menzies following the 1961 election, they remained loyal. In the end, Menzies outlasted all his would-be successors but the youngest and the most loyal, Harold Holt. In any event, the lack of good parliamentary 'stock' is not just a matter for the leader but also for the Party and its organisation. This applied to Labor, which also struggled to find a new generation of leaders after Curtin and Chifley.

Any explanation as to why Holt will never be numbered among the great Australian prime ministers must start with his inability to manage power and to deal with opposition—both within and beyond his own Party. The effective use of power and the efficient exercise of leadership require particular character traits and a cause or purpose to which they are directed. The absence of these vital traits or specific goals meant that greatness would always elude Harold Holt. As Edgar Holt observed, Harold saw:

> all people through rose-tinted spectacles. He seemed quite incapable of saying an unkind word about anybody. In the whole of Canberra it would be difficult to discover a man who ever recalled hearing Holt say anything personally hurtful. This, in itself, made him unique.[14]

His dislike of acrimony and his desire for affection meant he was 'the nicest man Australia had as a Prime Minister, but his very niceness was a major factor in his political failure . . . Holt was too unsure of himself, too lacking in the intellectual qualities needed for the making of major decisions, ever to be more than a good "departmental" man'.[15] 'Nugget' Coombs, who had the advantage of working with many prime ministers, said he was:

> not, even potentially, a great prime minister. He was, in a sense, too nice a person to exercise power effectively . . . He had been a successful Minister for Labour and National Service where his friendliness and human sympathy

made him welcome in trade union circles . . . his association with Roland Wilson was a great source of strength for him and when they came together again at the Treasury it ensured a continuance of that strength. As Prime Minister, however, he had to deal with restless, and often ruthless, strivings of ambitious colleagues, to resist the pressures of powerful outside interests and to control an over-large backbench majority.[16]

Malcolm Fraser thought that Holt was 'over loyal to his subordinates', taking their problems on his own shoulders where 'somebody else might have washed his hands and said "Well, sorry, you made the mess. You get yourself out of it"'.[17] Holt was probably too caring and possibly too compassionate for political life. He once chided a parliamentary colleague whose entire political career was spent on the Government benches for taunting the Opposition, saying, 'You don't know what it's like being in Opposition. There is no need to make it worse'. When Government Members such as Reg Wright and Harry Turner refused to accept Party discipline, Holt should have made an example of them both by seeking their disendorsement as Liberal candidates. Instead, he appealed to their sense of fair play. They survived but Holt's leadership suffered. But should this be seen as a mark of weakness? In other areas Holt showed that he had reserves of great strength. Rather it revealed a regard for other human beings that was seen by many as a political liability rather than an asset.

This raises some vexing questions. What kind of parliamentary leader did the Liberal Party require and the Coalition demand? Is it possible for a decent, honest and kind man to lead a nation? Do Australians expect their prime minister to be calculating, ruthless and brutal? Harold Holt could not be that kind of man, nor was he prepared to *become* that sort of person even for the sake of the prime ministership. On this point historian Manning Clark was right.

> [Holt] was sustained in his private life by a commendable vision of all men being brothers, and in his public life by the dream of educating Australians to the need for closer association with the peoples of Southeast Asia . . . [Holt] had lived through the terrible anguish of wanting men to be nice to each other only to find that he had come into his own in a time of hardening hearts.[18]

With a party accustomed to paternalistic leadership and autocratic rule, Harold Holt was frequently unable either to control or manage his inheritance. After the November 1966 election he was given a perfect opportunity to select a new leadership team and deal with the unfulfilled ambitions of his very large backbench. This would first, of course, require several of his more senior Ministers to return to the backbench and those whom he could not persuade to relinquish their ministerial duties voluntarily might have become bitter and difficult if they were left out. They might even have resigned and caused a by-election. But these sentiments would probably have been easier to contain than those arising from unfulfilled ambition. Lacking the nerve he showed at the racetrack, Holt avoided speculation of this kind. His preference for safety and stability meant the same old faces with most of the same old ideas remained. Holt was probably the most daring within the Cabinet. Creativity and initiative were not promoted as the critical characteristics of a minister in the Holt Government. And because he did not have the towering intellect or the personal prestige of his predecessors, some among his backbench were prepared to challenge his authority and question his judgment. On more than one occasion he failed to lead his own Party and his national standing suffered as a result.

——— ◆ ———

Holt once remarked that his two heroes were Sir Walter Raleigh (1552–1618) and Sir Robert Walpole (1676–1745). They are an interesting contrast. Raleigh became a favourite of Queen Elizabeth after several naval actions against the Spanish but was brought down by his enemies who colluded against him and eventually had him executed. Walpole was elected to the House of Commons at the age of 25 and, after some years as First Lord of the Treasury, became the leader of the Whigs and effectively Britain's first Prime Minister from 1721 to 1742. Both Raleigh and Walpole were persistent characters who more than once returned from apparent political oblivion to achieve greatness. But neither managed their opponents very effectively and both were brought down by conspiracies designed to diminish their power. Holt seemed unable to learn from either of his heroes.

But this explains only in part why greatness eluded him. He did not have an inspiring or sustaining vision of what Australia might become under his leadership. While Holt recognised that the country had changed and that the times demanded a new kind of political leadership, his conventionality and comfort prevented him from thinking creatively or expansively about what the country could become. In November 1966 the electorate appeared to want the same of what they had enjoyed under Menzies, but by the latter part of 1967 it was plain that the mood of the electorate had changed. Holt could not rely on politics being 'business as usual'. The 'forgotten people', the moral middle class, were being transformed into what Judith Brett has referred to as the 'chattering classes and the chardonnay set, self-interested minorities and cosmopolitan elites'. They were moving from being concerned Liberal voters to the progressive Left.[19] Holt no longer appealed to them. He had started to sound tired and even conservative, something that he had once despised in the ethos of the old UAP.

Perhaps he had spent too many years creating something that he was now unwilling to dismantle. Wedded in many ways to the past and apprehensive about the future, Holt frequently had little of substance to say. When he tried to be profound, he came across as banal. He never seemed to find his own voice or to settle on his own views. While it was unreasonable to expect him to answer every question or to provide exciting, fresh and new ideas every day, he could have directed the Party organisation to gather a team of creative and innovative thinkers to review and revise a Liberal Party Platform which had not been amended since 1960. He may not have been a young man, but he was far from being an old man. Although he identified with younger people and held a liberal outlook on life, he continued to mouth Cold War rhetoric and the tenets of 1950s suburban respectability. This caused a residual tension between what he embodied and the message he communicated. To some, it was not clear whether he was, in the idiom of the day, 'with it' or a 'square'. To say, as many did, that he had 'bohemian' tastes in the arts and in his recreational pursuits, only makes the picture more complicated.

Holt's disappearance marked a change in the Liberal Party's image and the conduct of its affairs. As sociologist Sol Encel observed: 'In retrospect, Holt's untimely death appears as the interregnum in which the friendly personality of the man acted as a restraint on the violent passions of his fellow ministers'.[20] This was conceded by the Liberal Party's Federal President in a statement issued shortly after the Government's electoral defeat in 1972: 'The personal ambitions and feuds inside the Parliamentary Liberal Party since the death of Mr Holt have been deadly and destructive'.[21] Don Aitkin has pointed out:

> The joint effect of the decline of Menzies as a symbol and the transfer of power from the neutral Holt to the controversial Gorton transformed the

perceived quality of Liberal leaders—the Party's strongest asset in 1967—to a distinct liability . . . [Holt's] difficulties as a manager of men and as a speaker were more sharply observed than those of his predecessor.[22]

Harold Holt was elected unopposed to the leadership of the Liberal Party in January 1966 as the best choice from the front rank of a political party that had exhausted much of its energy and many of its ideas. The next generation of leaders had not yet emerged and, other than Malcolm Fraser, remained in the background. It was not until 1975 that the Liberals found in Malcolm Fraser a leader who could deal with the dissidents of a party whose philosophy was becoming more disparate. Holt's disappearance effectively destabilised the Liberal Party for the next seven years.

What, then, were Holt's achievements? In his 22 months as Prime Minister he worked to strengthen Australia's alliance with the United States; preserve as much as possible of the British presence east of Suez; emphasise the importance of Asia in both the pace of global development and in the maintenance of international stability; and sustain a healthy domestic economy with high levels of foreign investment. He also attempted to prompt and guide some responses to Australia's changing social climate. In this respect, Holt was nearer to Gough Whitlam than many imagine although he did not face the full bloom of the Whitlamite vision in 1966–67. Holt was beginning to open Australia to the world and the world to Australia. He was not as forthright or as proactive as Whitlam would be, but he was adamant that Australia ought not to fear the world but rather to engage with it. Australia was much more than just a British outpost in the Pacific.

Holt was the link between the 'old' Australia and the 'new', between Menzies and Calwell and Whitlam and Barnard, between the British dominion and a nation edging closer to the United States. Alan Ramsey has noted that 'Holt wasn't racist, and he recognised that Australia, at least by law if not by habit and cultural inclination, couldn't continue to behave like a racist nation'.[23] The 1967 Aboriginal referendum and ending the White Australia Policy were hugely significant but there was no grand design, nothing to parallel the 'New Deal', the 'Great Society' or the 'New Jerusalem'. Holt was a pragmatist, always ready to compromise. He did not set himself long-term goals. He would be Prime Minister probably until

1972 if the electorate allowed and then he would retire. He would have been aged 64, the same age as Chifley when he was defeated at the 1949 election. Menzies retired at 71. John Howard is only the second Prime Minister in Australian history to serve beyond the statutory retiring age of 65 years.

Holt was not a complicated man. He was never troubled by existential despair or religious doubt. He enjoyed and savoured the things of this world. They brought him stability and security. Without any family traditions to uphold or property to maintain, Holt could make whatever he wanted of his life. He could embark on any vocation that appealed to him. After settling on a life in politics, he pursued his political aspirations with single-minded determination. Almost everything in his life was made a servant to this cause. From the day he entered Federal Parliament in 1935, Holt was encouraged to believe that one day he would be Prime Minister. For the next thirty years he pursued that destiny, but he worked so hard and so long to reach the political summit that in persevering with the journey he seemed to lose sight of the importance of the destination.

The real tragedy is that Holt spent almost all of his adult life pursuing a job that did not bring him satisfaction. When I asked Sir John Bunting to contrast Menzies and Holt as political leaders, he reflected for a few moments before saying: 'Robert Menzies wanted to be at the centre of the stage; Harold Holt just wanted to be at the front'.[24] The boy who felt so alone at Wesley College on Speech Night in 1924 went through life craving encouragement, affirmation, popularity, affection and love. He thought he would find it in politics. In part, he did. But when politics turned nasty or colleagues let him down he found himself drawn to his few family members, such as his brother Cliff, and his close friends for the unconditional support he needed. Holt could not do without a circle of people to whom he could be kind when the world was cruel. He remained steadfastly loyal to Menzies because he was so distressed by the way his friend was treated in 1941. He was grieved by his part, albeit small, in Menzies' fall from power and the indignity he suffered. Even if Menzies had stayed in power until he was 80, Holt would never have challenged for the Liberal leadership. When he succeeded Menzies, Holt expected that his example would not be lost on his possible successors. He had learned that if you live by the sword, you will die by the sword. Of course, you can also be an innocent victim of it. Had he not performed well in the 1969 election, he might have felt pressure from his colleagues to retire earlier rather than later.

It would appear that Holt also sought comfort in the arms of women other than his wife. There is no doubt that women were drawn to him and enjoyed his company. For a man who was starved of feminine company throughout his childhood and adolescence, he appears to have understood women very well. The number and names of the women with whom he had intimate relationships remains unclear. Zara's outburst that her husband had scores of women over the years was probably designed to humiliate Marjorie Gillespie and her assertion that she was special, more than anything else. It seems that these relationships were largely therapeutic. He explained to one Cabinet colleague that he had someone to whom he was very close in Canberra because it made parliamentary sittings easier to endure. He was not, however, attempting to excuse infidelity. Holt appeared to regard whatever was necessary for sustaining his parliamentary duties in a utilitarian rather than an ethical framework. When he went back to Melbourne, he went back to Zara. We don't know how much she really knew of these other women, or wanted to find out. And yet, by all accounts they loved and cared deeply for each other. This is more to Zara's credit than to Holt's. She was a loyal and, in many ways, a long-suffering political wife. Before they were married Holt had made it quite clear that she was neither to obstruct nor thwart his political career. She complied with his wishes and her reward was a lifestyle that, for the greatest part, she enjoyed.

Harold Holt was not a wealthy man although he might have been. He had probably punted more than was wise. Although his body was never recovered from the sea, he left a will and probate was granted. He had shares valued at $60 044 in a number of companies including BHP, CSR, Hammersley Mining, Myer and Riotinto Zinc London. He also had a part share in several commercial properties and a bank account containing $5119. The Melbourne *Herald* told its readers that Holt left $90 841 to Zara and $2000 to his late brother Cliff.[25] All of his property went to Zara as 'Joint Tenant'. Unsurprisingly there was a great deal of sympathy for Zara, both throughout the country and across the world. The Liberal Party was grateful for her support and many contributions over the years. On 8 June 1968 she was created a Dame of the British Empire (DBE).

Dame Zara married the Federal Liberal (later Independent) backbencher, Jefferson Bate, in 1969. They 'retired' to his New South Wales south coast property at Tilba Tilba in 1976. It was not a conventional marriage, as Zara moved to Surfers Paradise in 1980. She never left Jeff Bate, preferring to live separately and having occasional contact. This led

Zara to speak of the 'constant joys of reunion'. Bate died on 15 April 1984 from a perforated ulcer that was probably exacerbated by excessive consumption of alcohol. Unfortunately, Zara's last years were marked by personal bitterness. In early 1988, she launched an attack on Marjorie Gillespie in the *Sydney Morning Herald* after Gillespie claimed that Harold was planning to leave Zara for her. This led Zara to reveal that Holt had a number of lovers around Australia and overseas. She said: 'There were dozens of women in the woodwork . . . It was going on all the time . . . [Once] I walked past the door of the upstairs bedroom of the house we were visiting for a barbeque. It was ajar. I looked in and then rushed off liked a scalded cat'.[26] Diane Langmore has offered the best tribute to Zara (although the accusations against Harold are overstated):

> She was the only one of the prime ministers' wives to have been a successful businesswoman. No intellectual, and not particularly introspective, she had common sense and a lack of pretension which endeared her to many. Beneath her buoyant façade there was a sense of the vulnerability of the young girl who had dreamed of being tall and slim rather than short and dumpy. The tragedies of life did not make her bitter or cynical; she retained an openness and warmth until her death. Although her decision to stay with her chronically unfaithful and somewhat exploitative husband was not one that all women would make or applaud, it revealed a hard-headed realism and a tenacity behind the 'zany' exterior. In the light of her revelations about Holt's affairs and his relationship with her, it is possible to see, in her performance as prime minister's wife, a courage and dignity which transcended her bungles, her occasional silliness or aberrations of taste. She schooled herself to be a charming, well-groomed and gracious partner to her husband's approval, no matter what the cost.[27]

Zara died peacefully in her sleep at the age of 80 on 14 June 1989. Andrew Peacock delivered the eulogy at her funeral. She was buried in the family plot at Sorrento. A memorial plaque was placed in the Melbourne Cemetery after her death.

Holt
Harold Edward
1908–1967

Zara Kate (Holt) Bate
1909–1989

He loved the Sea

Holt was a loving husband and a devoted father. Nick and Sam became lawyers although not in their father's firm. Holt had withdrawn from his partnership in Holt, Graham & Newman in December 1963 after he and Jack Graham had a serious disagreement in late 1962 over the firm's fees in relation to a particular property sale. There was also disagreement over dispersal of profits and ownership of office furniture. When the firm Holt, Newman & Holt merged with Rigby and Fielding in July 1966, Holt announced that he was retiring from practising law although he had not been an active partner since 1949.[28] Andrew developed a creative advertising consultancy. Only one of the boys attempted to follow in their father's political footsteps: Sam was narrowly defeated by Phillip Lynch for Liberal preselection in the safe seat of Flinders in 1966. He was also unsuccessful in a preselection ballot for the seat of La Trobe in 1972. Andrew and Paulette were separated at the time of Holt's death. Sam's marriage was 'teetering' and finally ended in 1970. But Harold was very close to his two grandchildren Sophie and Christopher. Christopher called his grandfather 'Harry' while Sophie played with him on the lawn at Portsea the morning he disappeared. Two other grandchildren were born after his death. Nick married Suzie and had one daughter, Pippa. Sam later married Fiona and had one son, Robert Harold Holt, born in 1971. Robbie became a management consultant and married Natasha. Their son, James Harold Holt, was born at London in 2003.

James Fell retired to England after his service in the Indian Army and saw Nicholas once in the 1960s and again in the 1970s. He subsequently married an English actress and they had one daughter, Jennifer. Zara sold Magg Boutique in 1976 but kept the Bingil Bay property until 1986. The Portsea beach house was sold in 1992. Zara moved out of the family home at St Georges Road, Toorak after she married Jeff Bate. It was later sold and demolished in August 1995.[29]

There are a number of memorials to Harold Holt within Australia and abroad. A White House staffer, Sam Latimer, suggested in a memo to President Johnson headed 'Honouring the Memory of Harold Holt' and dated 28 March 1968 that the North West Cape Naval Communications Facility be named in his memory together with a US Navy warship. The keel for USS *Harold E. Holt* (a *Knox* Class destroyer escort DE-1074) was laid on 11 May 1968. Two days later, President Johnson conveyed his congratulations to the Secretary of the Navy on the keel laying: 'This fine ship will bear the name of a wise and courageous man whose love for the sea and devotion to the cause of freedom were both boundless'. This was the first time an American naval combatant had been named after a foreign leader. Zara launched the destroyer at Todd Shipyards on the Port of Los Angeles on 3 May 1969.

At Cheviot Beach, a plaque was bolted to the rock floor near where he had disappeared. It read: 'In memory of Harold Holt, Prime Minister of Australia, who loved the sea and disappeared hereabouts on 17 December 1967'. There was a new wing for boarders at Wesley College,[30] the naming of a Canberra suburb in his honour,[31] a sundial and garden in the Fitzroy Gardens,[32] a marine reserve on the southern shore of Port Phillip Bay, and a Federal electorate (initially a marginal Liberal seat but later a safe Labor seat) in 1969. The best known memorial is one that many have thought to be either in bad taste or ironic: the Harold Holt Memorial Swimming Baths in the Melbourne suburb of Malvern. Unlike his distinguished predecessor, within the Party he served for so long Harold Holt is remembered largely for the wrong reasons: 'Unlike Labor, the Liberals do not place much emphasis on honouring past leaders—except for Robert Menzies. These days, Harold Holt is all but forgotten. There is no memorial lecture, no biography, no statue or bust, no library'.[33] At least one omission has been dealt with in the publication of this book.

Sadly, Harold Holt's death now overshadows his life. But Australia's seventeenth Prime Minister ought to be remembered for encouraging the country towards a greater sense of social self-awareness, economic independence, national maturity and international pride.

Exaltavit Humiles
('He hath exalted the humble')

Appendix 1

Milestones in Harold Holt's career

1931	Admitted to the Bar in Victoria
1934	Unsuccessfully contested the Federal seat of Yarra against James Scullin
	Unsuccessful in attempt to enter Victorian State Parliament
17 August 1935	Elected to the House of Representatives as member for Fawkner
1937	Re-elected to the House of Representatives
26 April 1939– 14 March 1940	Minister without Portfolio assisting the Minister for Supply and Development
26 October 1939– 14 March 1940	Minister in Charge of Scientific and Industrial Research
29 October 1940– 7 October 1941	Minister in Charge of Scientific and Industrial Research
November–December 1939	Acting Minister for Air and Civil Aviation
1940	Re-elected to House of Representatives (Fawkner)
22 May 1940– 20 October 1940	Gunner, 2nd Australian Imperial Force
23 February 1940– 7 October 1940	Minister without Portfolio assisting the Minister for Trade and Customs

29 October 1940– 7 October 1941	Minister for Labour and National Service
1941	Member, Economic and Industrial Committee of Cabinet
1943	Re-elected to House of Representatives (Fawkner)
14 October 1943– 16 August 1946	Member, Parliamentary Joint Committee on War Expenditure
1946	Re-elected to House of Representatives (Fawkner)
5 July 1946– 31 October 1949	Member, Joint Committee on Broadcasting of Parliamentary Proceedings
October 1948	Member, Australian delegation to Empire Parliamentary Association Conference, London
1949	Re-elected to House of Representatives (Higgins)
19 December 1949– 10 December 1958	Minister for Labour and National Service
19 December 1949– 24 October 1956	Minister for Immigration
1950	Leader, Australian delegation to the Commonwealth Parliamentary Association Conference, Wellington (NZ)
1950–55	Member, General Council of the Commonwealth Parliamentary Association (Chairman from 1952–55)
1951	Re-elected to House of Representatives (Higgins)
July–October 1952	Discussions with British Government on immigration matters Leader, Australian delegation to the Commonwealth Parliamentary Association Conference, Ottawa
1953	Appointed Privy Councillor

May 1953	Member, Commonwealth Parliamentary Association delegation to the Coronation of Queen Elizabeth II
1954	Re-elected to House of Representatives (Higgins)
August 1954	Leader, Australian delegation to the Commonwealth Parliamentary Association Conference, Nairobi
1955	Re-elected to House of Representatives (Higgins)
January–March 1955	Acting Minister for Air and Civil Aviation
1956–66	Leader of the Government in the House of Representatives Deputy Leader, Parliamentary Liberal Party
26 September 1956–19 December 1967	Member, Parliamentary Standing Orders Committee
1957	Leader, Australian delegation to the 40th Session of the International Labour Conference, Geneva Elected President of the Conference
1958	Re-elected to House of Representatives (Higgins)
10 December 1958–26 January 1966	Treasurer
1959	Conference of Commonwealth Finance Ministers, London Leader, Australian delegation to the Commonwealth Parliamentary Association Conference, Nairobi
1960	Conference of Commonwealth Finance Ministers, London
1961	Re-elected to House of Representatives (Higgins)
1961	Conference of Commonwealth Finance Ministers, Accra

1963	Re-elected to House of Representatives (Higgins)
1963	Conference of Commonwealth Finance Ministers, London
1965	Leader, Australian delegation to the Conference of Commonwealth Finance Ministers, Kingston
1966	Re-elected to House of Representatives (Higgins)
26 January 1966– 19 December 1967	Prime Minister of Australia, Leader of Parliamentary Liberal Party
September 1966	Conference of the Commonwealth Prime Ministers, London
16 September– 8 October 1966	Acting Treasurer
October 1966	Manila Conference on Vietnam
14 June 1967	Appointed a Companion of Honour (CH)
4–10 July 1967	Acting Minister for External Affairs
28 September– 19 December 1967	Member, Joint Select Committee on the New and Permanent Parliament House

Appendix 2

Holt ministries

21 January 1966 to 14 December 1966

Cabinet

Holt, Rt Hon Harold	Prime Minister
McEwen, Rt Hon John	Minister for Trade and Industry (CP)
McMahon, Hon William	Treasurer
Hasluck, Rt Hon Paul	Minister for External Affairs
Adermann, Hon Charles	Minister for Primary Industry (CP)
Fairhall, Hon Allen	Minister for Defence
Henty, Senator Hon Denham	Minister for Supply
Hulme, Hon Alan	Postmaster-General, Vice-President of the Executive Council
Fairbairn, Hon David	Minister for National Development
Barnes, Hon Charles	Minister for Territories (CP)
Gorton, Senator Hon John	Minister for Works, Minister in Charge of Commonwealth Activities in Education & Research under the Prime Minister

Bury, Hon Leslie	Minister for Labour and National Service

Junior ministry

Freeth, Hon Gordon	Minister for Shipping and Transport
Swartz, Hon Reginald	Minister for Civil Aviation
Opperman, Hon Hubert	Minister for Immigration
Snedden, Hon Billy, QC	Attorney-General
Forbes, Hon Dr James	Minister for Health
Anthony, Hon Doug	Minister for the Interior
Chaney, Hon Frederick	Minister for the Navy
Howson, Hon Peter	Minister for Air, Minister assisting the Treasurer
Anderson, Senator Hon Kenneth	Minister for Customs and Excise
McKellar, Senator Hon Gerald	Minister for Repatriation (CP)
Sinclair, Hon Ian	Minister for Social Services
Rankin, Senator Hon Dame Annabelle	Minister for Housing
Fraser, Hon Malcolm	Minister for the Army

14 December 1966 to 19 December 1967

Cabinet

Holt, Rt Hon Harold, CH	Prime Minister
McEwen, Rt Hon John	Minister for Trade and Industry (CP)
McMahon, Rt Hon William	Treasurer
Hasluck, Rt Hon Paul	Minister for External Affairs
Adermann, Rt Hon Charles	Minister for Primary Industry (CP) (to 16 October 1967)
Fairhall, Hon Allen	Minister for Defence
Henty, Senator Hon Denham	Minister for Supply
Hulme, Hon Alan	Postmaster-General,

	Vice-President of the Executive Council
Fairbairn, Hon David	Minister for National Development
Gorton, Senator Hon John	Minister for Works (to 28 February 1967) Minister for Education and Science
Bury, Hon Leslie	Minister for Labour and National Service
Anthony, Hon Doug	Minister for the Interior (to 16 October 1967) Minister for Primary Industry (from 16 October 1967) (CP)
Sinclair, Hon Ian	Minister for Social Services Minister assisting the Minister for Trade and Industry (in Cabinet from 10 October 1967) (CP)

Junior ministry

Barnes, Hon Charles	Minister for Territories (CP)
Freeth, Hon Gordon	Minister for Shipping and Transport
Swartz, Hon Reginald	Minister for Civil Aviation
Snedden, Hon Billy, QC	Minister for Immigration
Forbes, Hon Dr James	Minister for Health
Howson, Hon Peter	Minister for Air Minister assisting the Treasurer
Anderson, Senator Hon Kenneth	Minister for Customs and Excise
McKellar, Senator Hon Gerald	Minister for Repatriation (CP)
Rankin, Senator Hon Dame Annabelle	Minister for Housing
Fraser, Hon Malcolm	Minister for the Army
Bowen, Hon Nigel, QC	Attorney-General
Chipp, Hon Donald	Minister for the Navy Minister in Charge of Tourist Activities

Kelly, Hon Bert	Minister for Works (from 28 February 1967)
Nixon, Hon Peter	Minister for the Interior (from 16 October 1967) (CP)

Note on sources

MORE THAN 90 PER CENT of all primary source materials relating to the life and death of Harold Holt are held by the National Archives of Australia (NAA). Most items have been cleared for public access and therefore are available for examination by researchers. A number of documents have been withheld on privacy grounds as they were never intended for public citation or quotation. The majority of these items are in a body of records transferred to the NAA by the Holt family in 2002 (NAA: M4298, 1–5 and NAA: M1945, 1) and relate primarily to the financial and personal affairs of the late Prime Minister and his immediate family. I was fortunate to examine this entire consignment before its transfer. This included the Prime Minister's briefcase and its contents which were retrieved by the Commonwealth Police from the Holt's Portsea house shortly after his disappearance on 17 December 1967.

It would appear that after being directed to take custody of the Prime Minister's papers police officers hastily gathered up all of the official papers and documents they could find in the Portsea house before transporting them to Canberra in Holt's battered brown briefcase. The briefcase contained government correspondence and documents, along with personal papers and records such as Holt's school reports and bank statements. When the briefcase and its contents were returned to the Holt family in 1968, some of the official documents had been replaced with copies while, somewhat strangely, other originals remained. In sum, it is very difficult to identify the papers which were taken in the briefcase that weekend from those that were already at Portsea. The NAA has, however, a comprehensive list of all the papers contained in the briefcase when it was transferred in 2002.

Approximately fifteen items in the Lyndon Baines Johnson Presidential Archives were also closed. They relate almost entirely to the conduct of the war in South Vietnam and are withheld on the grounds of national security. I am confident that no significant body of papers was overlooked in preparing this biography.

Throughout this book, abbreviated citations of the NAA's collection have been used. Records held by the National Archives of Australia are prefixed 'NAA'. This is followed by the series and item numbers. For example, the citation 'NAA: A1728, 7' denotes item 7 in series A1728: the seventh volume in Harold Holt's press cutting books covering the period 1958–60. As there was no standard system for arranging or filing Holt's official and personal papers, many files did not carry specific titles or designations. However, most of the file numbers allocated by departmental officers have been retained. Pennie Pemberton's *Harold Holt: Guide to Archives of Australia's Prime Ministers*[1] provides an excellent introduction to the Holt collection in the NAA. It lists personal papers, departmental records and the most significant records held by other institutions. In the latter category, the 'special collections' relating to Harold Holt in the National Library of Australia are the most important as they include the personal papers of many of Holt's colleagues and friends, in addition to the official records of the Liberal Party of Australia.

Notes

INTRODUCTION—A life that should have overshadowed a death

1   Manning Clark, 'The years of unleavened bread, December 1949 to December 1972', *Meanjin*, vol. 32, no. 3, September 1973; republished in Manning Clark, *Occasional Writings and Speeches*, Fontana, Melbourne, 1980, p. 196.

2   Geoffrey Bolton, *The Oxford History of Australia*, Oxford University Press, Melbourne, 1990, p. 174.

3   Don Whitington, *Twelfth Man?*, Jacaranda, Brisbane, 1972, p. 118.

4   Craig McGregor, *The Australian People*, Hodder & Stoughton, Sydney, 1980, p. 207.

5   Ronald Conway, 'Land of the Long Weekend', *Sun*, Melbourne, 1978, p. 20.

6   Tom Frame, *Where Fate Calls: The HMAS Voyager Tragedy*, Hodder & Stoughton, Sydney, 1992. The thesis was substantially re-written to appear as *The Cruel Legacy: The Tragedy of HMAS Voyager*, Allen & Unwin, Sydney, 2005.

7   Dame Zara Holt, *My Life and Harry: An Autobiography*, Herald & Weekly Times, Melbourne, 1968.

8   Anthony Grey, *The Prime Minister Was a Spy*, Coronet, Sydney, 1983.

9   L. Broderick, 'Transition and Tragedy: The Prime Ministership of Harold Holt, 1966–67', BA (Hons) thesis, Macquarie University, 1989, photocopy held by author.

10 I. Hancock, 'Liberal Government, 1966–1972', in J.R. Nethercote (ed.), *Liberalism and the Australian Federation*, Federation Press, Sydney, 2001, pp. 196–213.

11 Ian Hancock, 'Harold Edward Holt', in Michelle Grattan (ed.), *Australian Prime Ministers*, New Holland, Sydney, 2000, pp. 271–84. Hancock quickly covers Holt's early life and foreshadows how some of these experiences shaped the man he would become. He tracks Holt's journey into parliament and describes his close association with Robert Menzies. After noting Holt's ministerial responsibilities and rise in the Liberal Party during the 1950s and early 1960s, Hancock explains the change of mood that marked the bloodless succession from Menzies to Holt.

His treatment of Holt's 22 months as Prime Minister is dominated by the war in Vietnam, the withdrawal of British forces east of Suez and the contrast between the electoral successes of 1966 and the political controversies of 1967. Holt is credited with important changes in social policy and initiatives in the arts. Hancock concludes with a personal portrait that reveals a genuine appreciation of Holt's character. Hancock also contributed the entry on Holt in the *Australian Dictionary of Biography*. During the last decade he has written extensively on the post-war Liberal Party with his commissioned history—*National and Permanent? The Federal Organisation of the Liberal Party of Australia, 1944–1965*—and his 'authorised' biography of Holt's successor—*John Gorton: He Did It His Way*. Both projects, and his monograph on the 1966–67 VIP airline scandal, involved treatments of Holt that Hancock brought together for Grattan's book.

12 Paul Hasluck (edited and introduced by Nicholas Hasluck), *The Chance of Politics*, Text, Melbourne, 1997.

13 Mrs A. Blamirer to Holt, 28 January 1966, National Archives of Australia (hereafter NAA): M2606, 87.

14 The only area where I have consciously decided against a thorough treatment is Holt's relationship with the Liberal Party organisation. This is for two reasons: first, it was neither close nor, in my view, especially significant in determining the shape, structure or direction of the organisation. Holt may have tried to reform the organisation after 1967 but there is nothing to indicate that he believed it was a priority. As the organisation had helped him secure a record majority at the end of 1966, he saw no reason to tamper with its structures or staff; and second, his dealings with the Party and its principal officials do not reveal an added dimension to his character or disclose another aspect to Holt's approach to national leadership. He attended more meetings than his predecessor and was more open to the organisation's participation in parliamentary affairs although in detail rather than direction.

15 Lord Bruce to Holt, 19 February 1966, NAA: M2606, 87.

ACKNOWLEDGMENTS

1 Malcolm Fraser to author, 19 October 2004.

CHAPTER 1—A lonely life

1 A summary of early Holt family history was contained in a letter from Cliff Holt to the Administrator, Museum and Art Gallery, Birmingham, 27 January 1966, NAA: M4295, 10.

2 The meeting of Tom and Olive Holt is described in a letter from Cliff Holt to Tony Eggleton, 12 October 1966, NAA: M2684, 121.

3 Alan Reid, 'Harold Holt: The gambler', *Bulletin*, 31 May 1961, p. 13.

4 Don Whitington, *Twelfth Man?*, Jacaranda, Brisbane, 1972, p. 120.

5 Zara Holt, *My Life and Harry: An Autobiography*, Herald & Weekly Times, Melbourne, 1968, p. 30.

6 Ibid., p. 38.

7 Ibid., p. 48.

8 Tom and Lola had a daughter, Frances, who succumbed to cancer in 1961, aged only 21. After Tom's death in 1945 Lola married Phillip Portus and had another daughter, Josephine. Lola died in 1971.

9 Tom's 359-acre share of 'Sunnyside' was then sold to Claude Bradford. The remainder of the property continued to be managed by his brothers Will and Jack. When Jack died in 1957, the farm passed to his son Lister. On his death in 1993, Terry and Geoffrey managed the property until it was sold in 2001 to Peter Bradford, whose grandfather had bought Tom Holt's share of the farm.

CHAPTER 2—The early years

1 Undated press clipping, NAA: A1728, 1.

2 Ibid.

3 UAP executive secretary to Holt, 19 September 1934, NAA: A1728, 1. (Letter was posted into Holt's scrapbook from this period.)

4 H.M. Cremean to Holt, 9 March 1935. NAA: A1728, 1 [Holt press clippings, vol. 1].

5 Dame Mabel Brookes, *Memoirs*, Macmillan, Melbourne, 1974, p. 189.

6 Holt's speeches were reported in the Melbourne newspapers. Holt's clippings frequently did not include the publication name or date. Those of this period are contained in NAA: A1728, 1.

7 *Commonwealth Parliamentary Debates*, House of Representatives [hereafter *CPD* (Reps)], 23 September 1935, p. 36.

8 *CPD* (Reps), 10 October 1935, pp. 1660–3.

9 Dame Enid Lyons, *Among the Carrion Crows*, Rigby, Adelaide, 1972, p. 24.

10 *Table Talk*, 22 April 1937, p. 11.

11 Unmarked press clipping, NAA: A1728, 1.

12 Ibid.

13 Reported in an unidentified press clipping, ibid.

14 *News Chronicle*, 24 April 1939, NAA: B3229, 5.

15 Archie Michaelis to Holt, 26 April 1939, NAA: B3229, 5.

16 Keith Allen to Holt, 1 May 1939, NAA: B3229, 5.

17 Holt to F.H. Buss, 5 May 1939, NAA: B3229, 5.

18 Holt to Lieutenant Colonel David Fraser, 4 May 1939, NAA: B3229, 5.

19 Richard Casey to Holt, 7 August 1939, NAA: B3229, 16.

20 L.A. Moroney (Private Secretary to Holt) to G. Lightfoot (Secretary, CSIR), 23 October 1939, NAA: B3229, 6.

21 Sir David Rivett to Holt, 30 January 1940, NAA: B3229, 6.

22 Holt to Sir Frederick Stewart, Minister for Supply and Development, 5 February 1940, NAA: B3229, 16.

23 Stewart to Menzies, 5 February 1940, NAA: B3229, 16.

24 Sir David Rivett to Holt, 15 December 1939, NAA: B3229, 16.

25 Sir Earle Page, *Truant Surgeon: The Inside Story of Forty Years of Australian Political Life*, Angus & Robertson, Sydney, 1963, p. 281.

CHAPTER 3—Laying the foundations

1 Chris Coulthard-Clark, *Soldiers in Politics: The Impact of the Military on Australian Political Life and Institutions*, Allen & Unwin, Sydney, 1996; especially Chapter 6 on Federal Parliament.

2 H. Gullett, *In Good Company: Henry 'Jo' Gullett*, University of Queensland Press, St Lucia, 1992, p. 122.

3 Holt to Casey, NAA: B3229, 16.

4 Unreferenced press clipping, NAA: A1728, 1.

5 *Daily Telegraph* (Sydney), 14 August 1940.

6 *CPD* (Reps), 14 August 1940, pp. 373–4.

7 Paul Hasluck, *Australia in the War of 1939–45*, Civil Series: The Government and the People 1939–41, Australian War Memorial, Canberra, 1952, p. 244.

8 Gullet, *In Good Company*, p. 122.

9 Unreferenced press clipping, NAA: A1728, 1.

10 Ibid.

11 L.F. Crisp, *Ben Chifley: A Biography*, Longmans, Melbourne, 1961, p. 123.

12 S.J. Butlin, *The War Economy 1939–42*, The Official History of Australia in the War of 1939–45, Australian War Memorial, Canberra, 1955, p. 250.

13 H.C. Coombs, *Trial Balance*, Macmillan, Melbourne, 1981, p. 23.

14 *CPD* (Reps), 10 December 1940, pp. 690–7.

15 Arthur Fadden, *They Call Me Artie*, Jacaranda, Brisbane, 1969, p. 149.

16 *CPD* (Reps), 27 March 1941, pp. 338–40.

17 *Australian Women's Weekly*, 15 March 1941.

18 *CPD* (Reps), 2 April 1941, p. 543.

19 A.W. Martin, *Robert Menzies: A Life, Vol. 1 1894–1943*, Melbourne University Press, Melbourne, 1993, pp. 381–2.

20 Martin, *Robert Menzies*, vol. 1, p. 383.

21 *Daily Mirror* (Sydney), 20 January 1966.

22 Howard Beale, *This Inch of Time*, Melbourne University Press, Melbourne, 1977, p. 108.

23 Kevin Perkins, *Menzies: Last of the Queen's Men*, Rigby, Adelaide, 1968, p. 185.

24 *CPD* (Reps), 3 October 1941, p. 711.

25 Alexander Downer, *Six Prime Ministers*, Hill of Content, Melbourne, 1982, p. 65.

26 Peter Aimer, 'Menzies and the birth of the Liberal Party', in Cameron Hazlehurst (ed.), *Australian Conservatism: Essays in Twentieth Century Political History*, ANU Press, Canberra, 1979, pp. 213–37.

27 Aimer, 'Menzies and the birth of the Liberal Party', p. 227.

28 Graeme Starr, Keith Richmond and Graham Maddox, *Political Parties in Australia*, Heinemann, Melbourne, 1978, p. 27.

29 Press report, unreferenced, NAA:A1728, 1.

30 *Telegraph* (Sydney), 8 August 1942.

31 This letter was pasted into Holt's press cuttings book, NAA:A1728, 1.

32 *Herald* (Melbourne), undated press clippings but certainly August 1943, NAA:A1728, 1.

33 Unreferenced press clipping, NAA:A1728, 1.

34 Holt, 'Causes of Industrial Unrest', opening lecture at the Winter Forum of Australian Institute of Political Science, Sydney, 3 July 1946, NAA:M2607, 1.

35 Draft of speech, NAA:M4299, 3.

36 *Mercury* (Hobart), 12 March 1945.

37 *Daily News* (Perth), Monday 30 July 1945.

38 Press clippings scrapbook, NAA:A1728, 1.

39 *Sunday Telegraph*, 31 March 1946.

40 Unreferenced press clipping, NAA:A1728, 1.

41 By this time Zara's parents had gone to live permanently in Sorrento. This had been part of a duplex (numbered 110 and 112) but was converted to a single dwelling identified as '112'.

42 Zara Holt, *My Life and Harry: An Autobiography*, Herald & Weekly Times, Melbourne, 1968, p. 81.

43 Holt, 'Causes of industrial unrest', NAA:M2607, 1.

44 NAA:M4299, 3.

45 *Sydney Morning Herald*, 15 September 1949.

46 *Age*, 4 October 1949.

47 *Daily Telegraph*, 10 February 1949.

48 *Herald* (Melbourne), 11 March 1949.

49 Address to the Higgins Electorate Dinner, 25 July 1966, NAA:M2606, 124.

50 *Herald* (Melbourne), 16 November 1949.

51 *Herald* (Melbourne), 19 November 1949.

52 *Sun* (Sydney), 12 November 1949.

53 *Herald* (Melbourne), 23 November 1949.

54 *Herald* (Melbourne), 6 December 1949.

55 Unreferenced press clipping, NAA:A1728, 2.

56 Bland's father, Professor F.A. Bland, was elected to the Federal Parliament in 1951 as the Liberal Member for Warringah.

57 *Smith's Weekly*, 7 January 1950.

58 *Herald* (Melbourne), 23 December 1949.

CHAPTER 4—Halcyon days

1 J. Kremta, 'Economic mobility of immigrants in Australia', *Economic Record*, 1961, quoted in Tony Griffiths, *Contemporary Australia*, Croom Helm, London, 1977, p. 50.

2 *Herald* (Melbourne), 16 April 1951.

3 'Suggested lines of Government policy', (undated but probably late October or early November 1952), in 'General internal financial and economic policy 1952', NAA: A571, 1952/1161 Part 2.

4 John Murphy, *Imagining the Fifties: Private Sentiment and Political Culture in Menzies' Australia*, UNSW Press, Sydney, 2000, p. 126.

5 B.A. Santamaria, *Against the Tide*, OUP, Melbourne, 1981, p. 122.

6 Dr Daniel Mannix to Holt, 7 January 1950.

7 *Herald* (Melbourne), 6 May 1950.

8 *CPD* (Reps), 9 May 1950, p. 2268.

9 *CPD* (Reps), 25 October 1950, p. 1391.

10 L.F. Crisp, *Ben Chifley: A Biography*, Longmans, Melbourne, 1951, p. 398.

11 *CPD* (Reps), 25 October 1950, p. 1393.

12 *Argus*, 27 October 1950.

13 Quoted in Sir Percy Joske, *Sir Robert Menzies 1894–1978*, Angus & Robertson, Sydney, 1978, p. 200.

14 *Herald* (Melbourne), 25 April 1951.

15 *Herald* (Melbourne), 18 September 1951.

16 *Newcastle Morning Herald*, 24 September 1951.

17 *Age*, 8 October 1951.

18 Unreferenced press clipping, NAA: A1728, 2.

19 Robert Murray, *The Split: Australian Labor in the Fifties*, Hale & Iremonger, Sydney, 1984 (first published in 1970 by F.W. Cheshire, Melbourne), p. 145.

20 Don Watson, *Brian Fitzpatrick: A Radical Life*, Hale & Iremonger, Sydney, 1979, p. 234.

21 Ministerial statement, NAA: M4299, 3.

22 Press report 4 June 1952, NAA: A1728, 2. See also *CPD* (Reps), 3 June 1952, pp. 1292–3.

23 *Herald* (Melbourne), 26 May 1954.

24 *Herald* (Melbourne), 28 May 1954.

25 For a succinct account of the activities of Industrial Groups and their consequences for the ALP see Robert Murray, 'The split', in Robert Manne (ed.), *The Australian Century: Political Struggle in the Building of a Nation*, Text, Melbourne, 1999, pp. 148–78.

26 *Herald* (Melbourne), 2 March 1955.

27 *Age*, 22 May 1955.

28 *Argus*, 13 January 1955. This reveals either the shallowness of Holt's political philosophy or the extent of the Government's role in social life. It was clear that the electorate was content as support for the Coalition steadily increased. Holt was able to devote a great deal of time to his considerable parliamentary and ministerial matters because he held a very safe Liberal seat, but such was his respect for participatory democracy he was not accused of ignoring the needs of

the electorate and its people during his first five years as a minister. In his first election as a minister, Holt faced a maverick independent in Mary Kent Hughes. She was a radiologist, a former Army Major and the sister of Holt's parliamentary colleague Wilfred Kent Hughes. In her campaign, she proposed something akin to an industrial organisation for housewives whom she believed were neglected by government and overburdened by social expectations. She was also an enthusiast for 'marriage for everybody if it can be arranged' and for the exclusion of German immigrants on the grounds that 'German stock . . . is sadistic, arrogant and alien to our way of life' ('People in the News', *Woman's Day and Home*, 23 April 1951, p. 19). At the 28 April 1951 poll, she drew votes from both major parties although securing only 1925 first preferences. Holt secured 64.4 per cent of the primary vote and on the distribution of preferences gained a swing of 1.4 per cent from Labor's Benjamin Nicholas. The Labor candidate (again Benjamin Nicholas) performed better at the next poll—a two-man contest on 29 May 1954—achieving a swing of 2.8 per cent although Holt increased his share of the primary vote.

29 *Sydney Morning Herald*, 3 December 1955.
30 *Sun* (Sydney), 17 November 1955.
31 *Herald* (Melbourne), 8 December 1955.

CHAPTER 5—Heir apparent

1 *Eastern Suburbs Advertiser* (Sydney) dated 21 June 1951.
2 *Adelaide News*, 20 August 1954.
3 'Canberra Diary', *Voice*, May 1956.
4 'Canberra Commentary', *Age*, 29 May 1956.
5 W.J. Hudson, *Casey*, Oxford University Press, Melbourne, 1986, p. 275.
6 Clyde Cameron, *The Cameron Diaries*, Allen & Unwin, Sydney, 1990, p. 543.
7 *Sydney Morning Herald*, 27 September 1956, p. 3.
8 *Canberra Times*, 27 September 1956.
9 *Sydney Morning Herald*, 27 September 1956.
10 Katharine West, *Power in the Liberal Party*, Melbourne, 1965, p. 225.
11 Don Whitington, *Ring the Bells: A Dictionary of Australian Federal Politics*, Georgian House, Melbourne, 1956, p. 69.
12 Iain Sinclair, 'Government, Parliament and administration', in J.R. Nethercote (ed.), *Parliament and Bureaucracy*, Hale & Iremonger, Sydney, 1982, p. 70.
13 Paul Hasluck (edited and introduced by Nicholas Hasluck), *The Chance of Politics*, Text, Melbourne, 1997, p. 63.
14 *Age*, 21 January 1966.
15 Sir James Killen, *Inside Australian Politics*, Methuen Hayes, Sydney, 1985, pp. 94–5.
16 *Age*, 19 October 1956.
17 *Age*, 25 May 1956.

18 *Sydney Morning Herald*, 26 October 1957.

19 Ministerial Statement, 29 April 1957, 'Basic wage decision', NAA: M4299, 5.

20 Press Release No. 187, 'Socialist objective of ALP', 15 March 1957, NAA: M4299, 5.

21 *Age*, 27 March 1957.

22 *Daily Telegraph*, 5 April 1957.

23 Holt to Eric Harrison, 10 October 1957, NAA: M2606, 133.

24 Ian Hancock, *National and Permanent? The Federal Organisation of the Liberal Party of Australia, 1944–64*, Melbourne University Press, Melbourne, 2000, p. 160.

25 Harold Holt, 'The political situation 4 February 1957', quoted in Hancock, *National and Permanent?*, p. 169.

26 John Murphy, *Imagining the Fifties: Private Sentiment and Political Culture in Menzies' Australia*, UNSW Press, Sydney, 2000, p. 196.

27 Ibid.

28 D.W. Rawson, *Australia Votes*, Melbourne, 1961, p. 122.

CHAPTER 6—Immigration

1 James Jupp, *From White Australia to Woomera: The Story of Australian Immigration*, Cambridge University Press, Melbourne, 2002, pp. 69–77.

2 Address to the Australian Citizenship Convention, Canberra, 24 January 1950, NAA: M2607, 29.

3 K. Colm, *Calwell*, Nelson, Melbourne, 1978, p. 158, n. 8.

4 Draft speech, 'Mankind and tomorrow', undated, 1952.

5 Address delivered at the Seventh Citizenship Convention, 1956, NAA: M2607, 35.

6 Address delivered at the Third Citizenship Convention, 1952, NAA: M2607, 31.

7 Address delivered at the Second Citizenship Convention, 1951, NAA: M2607, 30.

8 *Straits Times*, 22 January 1952.

9 *Argus*, 14 September 1950.

10 As reported in the *Herald* (Melbourne), 11 January 1950.

11 *Courier Mail*, 13 April 1953.

12 *Sydney Morning Herald*, 30 January 1952.

13 April 1952, Press Statement, 'Employment situation', NAA: M4299, 3.

14 *Sun* (Sydney), 12 October 1954.

15 Written message to summer school of the Institute of Political Science, sent in January 1953 but published in March 1953, NAA: M4299, 3.

16 *Tasmanian Truth*, 26 December 1953.

17 *Sydney Morning Herald*, 8 July 1954.

18 Reported in the *Age*, 7 June 1955, NAA: A1728, 4.

19 *Sydney Morning Herald*, 9 November 1955.

20 Address delivered at the Seventh Citizenship Convention, Canberra, 24–25 January 1956, NAA: M2607, 35.

21 Private letter from Noel Flanagan to family written in London, 3 September 1952. Copy held by author.

22 Holt had led the Australian delegation at the 1950 conference in Wellington, New Zealand and was elected Chairman of the Association's General Council from 1952 to 1955.

23 *Herald* (Melbourne), 6 October 1952. While in Europe, Holt had proposed a world 'master plan' for migration that was embraced by a full conference in Geneva of the Provisional Intergovernmental Committee for the Movement of Migrants from Europe in November 1952.

24 *Sun* (Sydney), 28 May 1953.

25 *Times* (London), 23 August 1954.

26 Ministerial Statement dated 3 August 1957, NAA: M4299, 5.

27 *CPD* (Reps), 21 August 1952.

28 Geoffrey Bolton, *The Oxford History of Australia*, Oxford University Press, Melbourne, 1990, p. 77.

29 Alan Watt, *The Evolution of Australian Foreign Policy*, Cambridge, 1968, p. 202.

30 H.I. London, *Non-white Immigration and the 'White Australia' Policy*, Sydney University Press, Sydney, 1970, pp. 17–18.

31 *The Good Neighbour*, September 1956.

CHAPTER 7—Labour and National Service

1 H. Gullett, *In Good Company: Henry 'Jo' Gullett*, University of Queensland Press, St Lucia, 1992, pp. 299–300.

2 Draft document headed 'Introduction', 7 February 1951, NAA: M4299, 3.

3 Monk was born in London in 1900. His family came to Australia when Albert was ten. His father had become a technical officer in a Maribyrnong cordite factory. After leaving school at fourteen, Monk was employed by the Transport Workers Union (1919–23) and the Victorian Trades Hall Council (1924–39). In 1933 he was elected ACTU President and served for two terms in the capacity (1934–43 and 1949–69), as well as being its full-time Secretary from 1943 to 1949. Monk was also President of the Victorian Trades Hall Council, President of the Victorian branch of the ALP, and President of the Federal Clerks Union. He was a member of the governing body of the International Labour Office and the World Federation of Trade Unions from 1945.

4 *Newcastle Morning Herald*, 24 July 1950.

5 Statement by Minister for Labour and National Service, 4 February 1951, NAA: M4299, 4.

6 Section 30J of the Act allowed the issue of a proclamation that a 'serious industrial disturbance' exists that threatened overseas or interstate trade and commerce.

7 Alan Reid, *Sun* (Sydney), 15 May 1951.

8 *Age*, 28 October 1952.

9 *Sydney Morning Herald*, 22 May 1951.

10 Margo Beasley, *Wharfies: A History of the Waterside Workers' Federation*, Halstead Press, Sydney, 1996, p. 152.

11 *Courier Mail*, 30 October 1951.

12 *Sun* (Sydney), 6 June 1952.

13 *CPD* (Reps), 22 May 1952, p. 772.

14 *Sun* (Sydney), 28 June 1952.

15 *West Australian*, 14 August 1953.

16 Beasley, *Wharfies*, p. 156.

17 *Sun* (Sydney), 3 September 1953.

18 The whole episode is covered in *CPD* (Reps), 3, 8 and 9 April 1954, pp. 155, 252–3.

19 The WWF had been given a statutory monopoly to recruit labour in 1947 on the understanding that it would achieve performance improvements and ensure the labour force was sufficient to meet present and future needs. The Government was now arguing that there were insufficient waterside workers and the WWF was not keeping its side of the bargain.

20 *CPD* (Reps), 3 November 1954, pp. 2540–2.

21 *Herald* (Melbourne), 5 November 1954.

22 *Age*, 5 November 1954. Of all stoppages in Australia, the waterfront accounted for 6 per cent in 1951, 7.4 per cent in 1952, 10.7 per cent in 1953 and 13.3 per cent in 1954.

23 Statement issued 9 November 1954, reproduced in the minutes of the Federal Council of the Waterside Workers Federation, 10 November 1954, quoted in Beasley, *Wharfies*, p. 172.

24 *Sydney Morning Herald*, 9 November 1954.

25 *Sydney Morning Herald*, 16 February 1955. The conference would be held on 17 February.

26 Ibid.

27 *Newcastle Morning Herald*, 18 February 1955.

28 *Daily Telegraph*, 18 February 1955.

29 *Argus*, 18 February 1955.

30 Tom Sheridan, 'Regulator *par excellence*: Sir Henry Bland and Industrial Relations 1950–1967', *Journal of Industrial Relations*, vol. 41, no. 2, June 1999, pp. 228–55, page 241 quoted.

31 Deputations on s.29 of the *Commonwealth Conciliation and Arbitration Act*, 22 July 1955, NAA: M4299, 4.

32 *Age*, 6 July 1955.

33 *Sydney Morning Herald*, 26 July 1955.

34 The number of employment vacancies on 30 June 1955 was 57 645 compared with 63 696 at the same time the previous year. The number of people receiving unemployment benefits fell from 3825 to 2690.

35 *Herald* (Melbourne), 12 August 1955.

36 *Sydney Morning Herald*, 9 September 1955.

37 *Advertiser* (Adelaide), 23 January 1956.

38 *Age*, 24 January 1956.

39 *Age*, 1 February 1956.

40 *Sydney Morning Herald*, 2 February 1956.

41 *Sydney Morning Herald*, 6 February 1956.

42 *Age*, 6 February 1956.

43 *Sydney Morning Herald*, 12 February 1956.

44 *The Queen v. Kirby, ex parte Boilermakers' Society* (1956), 94 *Commonwealth Law Review* (*CLR*) 254 (High Court), affirmed by the Privy Council under the name of *Attorney-General for Australia v. The Queen and the Boilermakers' Society* [1957] AC. 288, (95 *CLR* 529).

45 *Argus*, 11 May 1956.

46 *Age*, 24 May 1956.

47 *Age*, 12 June 1956.

48 *Sydney Morning Herald*, 12 June 1956.

49 *Herald* (Melbourne), 3 July 1956.

50 Annual Report of the President of Conciliation and Arbitration Commission, 16 October 1957. Ministerial Statement, NAA: M4299, 5. Improvements were also attributed to the new Court and the reconstituted Commission that the Government had established in the wake of the Boilermaker's case. Holt noted that the 'operation of the new machinery in the period to August 1957 has seen less time lost on account of disputes in Australia than in any other year since 1942 . . . difficulties which existed previously when the Arbitration Court and Conciliation Commissioners functioned as two separate entities are no longer evident'.

51 Tas Bull, *Life on the Waterfront: An Autobiography*, Harper Collins, Sydney, 1998, p. 85.

52 *Sydney Morning Herald*, 8 January 1954.

53 NAA: M4299, 2. Holt was also the first Australian Minister for Labour to take part in an ILO conference. He attended as a 'Visiting Minister' in 1953. Incidentally, the 1953 conference discussed the admission of the Republic of China's (Taiwan) admission. There were 115 votes in favour (including Australia), 29 against and 47 abstentions. Holt made no reference to the problem of representation in his address at the Plenary session. Two years later, Australia supported moves to allow Taiwan to vote. By the time of the 1957 conference, there were representatives from 73 countries and a total membership of 800 delegates and advisers.

54 Official record of the ILO Conference, NAA: M4299, 5.

55 Presidential Address, ILO Conference, 40th session proceedings, NAA: M4299, 5.

56 *Mercury* (Hobart), 6 June 1957.

57 *Courier Mail*, 7 June 1957.

58 ILO Conference Proceedings, Thursday 27 June 1957, NAA: M2608, 5; M2608, 16.

59 Gallup Polls, nos 537–46, August–September 1948; nos 579–89, March–April 1949; and nos 607–18, July–August 1949.

60 David Lowe, *Menzies and the 'Great World Struggle': Australia's Cold War 1948–1954*, UNSW Press, Sydney, 1999. National Servicemen were automatically assigned to the Army, although those wishing to do so could volunteer to do their training in either the Navy or the Air Force.

61 See J.M. Main (ed.), *Conscription: The Australian Debate, 1901–1970*, Cassell, North Melbourne, 1970, pp. 130–1.

62 *CPD* (Reps), 21 November 1950, pp. 2723–4, 2728.

63 Ministerial Statement on National Service, March 1951, NAA: M4299, 3.

64 *CPD* (Reps), 1 May 1957, pp. 950–2.

65 *Training in Industry and Commerce*, Proceedings of a One Day Conference, 24 June 1955, Australian Institute of Management, Adelaide Division. NAA: M4299, 4.

66 Don Whitington, *The Rulers: Fifteen Years of the Liberals*, revised edition, Cheshire-Lansdowne, Melbourne, 1965, p. 76.

67 *Age*, 8 July 1952.

68 *Sun*, 1 July 1954.

69 Keith Sinclair, personal letter quoted in L. Broderick, 'Transition and Tragedy: The Prime Ministership of Harold Holt, 1966–67', BA (Hons) thesis, Macquarie University, p. 8.

70 Blanche d'Alpuget, *Robert J. Hawke: A Biography*, Lansdowne, Melbourne, 1982, p. 189.

71 *Daily Mirror* (Sydney), 20 January 1966.

CHAPTER 8—Patience and persistence

1 Paul Hasluck (edited and introduced by Nicholas Hasluck), *The Chance of Politics*, Text, Melbourne, 1997, p. 129.

2 C.B. Schedvin, *In Reserve: Central Banking in Australia, 1945–75*, Allen & Unwin, Sydney, 1992, p. 296.

3 Holt to Menzies, 14 August 1959, NAA: M2606, 130.

4 The 1959 and 1960 meetings were held in London. When these became biennial events, following the 1961 meeting held in Ghana, Holt returned to London for the 1963 meeting. The 1965 meeting, renamed the Commonwealth Consultative Council, was held in Jamaica. These trips were usually of one month's duration.

5 Holt to Sir Hudson Fysh, 3 October 1962, NAA: M2606, 2.

6 For background information see L.F. Giblin, *The Growth of a Central Bank: The Development of the Commonwealth Bank of Australia*, Melbourne University Press, Melbourne, 1951.

7 Sol Encel, *Cabinet Government in Australia*, second edition, Melbourne University Press, Melbourne, 1974, p. 88.

8 *CPD* (Reps), vol. 196, 1948, pp. 1102–3. See also John Uhr, *Deliberative Democracy in Australia: The Changing Place of Parliament*, Cambridge University Press, Melbourne, 1998, p. 114.

9 *CPD* (Reps), 26 February 1959, pp. 378, 380–1.

10 Arthur Fadden, *They Call Me Artie*, Jacaranda, Brisbane, 1969, p. 147. Holt and Fadden had both entered the same Parliament, through by-elections.

11 *Sydney Morning Herald*, 3 February 1959; *Age*, 16 March 1959.

12 Quoted without reference in Tim Rowse, *Nugget Coombs: A Reforming Life*, Cambridge University Press, Melbourne, 2002, p. 250.

13 F. Howard, *Kent Hughes*, Macmillan, Melbourne, 1972, p. 200, n. 6.

14 Ibid., p. 200, n. 7.

15 Ibid.

16 Don Watson, *Brian Fitzpatrick: A Radical Life*, Hale & Iremonger, Sydney, 1979, p. 276.

17 Quoted in Watson, *Brian Fitzpatrick*, p. 277.

18 'Mr Holt talks on inflow of capital', *Australian Financial Review*, 15 October 1964. Press clipping, NAA: M2606, 114. He went on to speak of partnerships, conditions relating to ownership of assets and the location of equity, but also to maintaining the conditions that made foreign investment attractive.

19 Sir Roland Wilson to Holt, minute dated 18 February 1964, NAA: M2606, 114.

20 Holt to Allen Chase, 20 February 1964, NAA: M2606, 114.

21 Unsigned card, NAA: M2606, 130.

22 For a description of the role of the Prime Minister's Department see A.W. Martin, *Robert Menzies: A Life, Vol. 2 1944–1978*, Melbourne University Press, Melbourne, 1999, pp. 431–2.

23 A.M.C. Waterman, *Economic Fluctuations in Australia: 1948 to 1964*, ANU Press, Canberra, 1972, p. 180. This observation is all the more ironic given a speech Holt had given six years earlier in which he said:

> Political considerations can affect economic judgements. Governments have a law of survival to live to and what may be economically sound and prudent at a particular period may be politically disastrous. I don't need to go very far back beyond the 1951 budget, known by some as the 'Horror Budget', to illustrate the point to you. Drastic economic action was taken by the Government at that time which it believed to be necessary for the economic health of the nation. But the political results of it were quick and were, from our point of view, highly damaging; in fact it took the whole three years of the life of that parliament for us to establish in the minds of the public that what we had done had been wisely done, and even then we barely managed to scrape through the next election.
>
> (Address delivered to a one-day conference on 'Trading in Industry and Commerce', 24 June 1955, Australian Institute of Management, Adelaide Division, NAA: M4299, 4.)

24 Calwell, who had been deputy since 1951, had been elected Leader of the Opposition in 1960. This was expected. The surprise was the election of the 44-year-old member for Werriwa, Gough Whitlam, as the deputy over the Left-wing stalwart, Eddie Ward.

25   Arthur Calwell, *Be Just and Fear Not*, Lloyd O'Neil, Melbourne, 1972, p. 206.

26   Sir Frank Richardson to Holt, 19 June 1961, NAA: M2606, 129.

27   'The Credit Squeeze', speech notes, Victorian Chamber of Commerce meeting, Melbourne, 22 May 1961, NAA: M2607, 75.

28   *Courier Mail*, 29 November 1960.

29   Papers associated with this incident were in the personal possession of Mr Nicholas Holt and were examined by the author on 28 January 2001 before the documents were transferred to the NAA. See NAA: M4295, 15.

30   The text of the retraction appeared in the *Courier Mail*, 29 November 1960, NAA: M4295, 15.

31   'Notes on the economic situation' prepared by the Treasury, 8 April 1961, NAA: M2606, 130.

32   C.B. Schedvin, *In Reserve: Central Banking in Australia, 1945–75*, Allen & Unwin, Sydney, 1992, p. 320.

33   *Australian Financial Review*, 21 January 1966, pp. 2–3.

34   Peter Golding, *Black Jack McEwen: Political Gladiator*, Melbourne University Press, Melbourne, 1996, p. 204.

35   John McEwen to Holt, 21 July 1961, NAA: M2606, 2.

36   Most of the telegrams were sent on 15 and 16 August 1961 in response to his Budget speech, NAA: M2606, 46.

37   Frank Chamberlain, Transcript of Radio 3DB 'Commentary', 10 February 1961, NAA: M2606, 2.

38   Holt to Allen Fairhall, 12 April 1961, NAA: M2606, 46.

39   Material prepared for the Treasurer, 'Recent development in the economy', November 1961, NAA: M2606, 4.

40   Treasury Press Release No. 1191, 'Statement on the financing of the Labor Party's election program', 23 November 1961, NAA: M2606, 6.

41   '1961 Campaign Theme', Draft Federal Council document, undated, NAA: M2606, 6.

42   Alex Rosenblum to Holt, 9 January 1961, NAA: M2606, 1.

43   Holt to R.C. Cotton, Acting Federal President of the Liberal Party, 21 August 1961, NAA: M2606, 14.

44   Holt in a letter to Dame Ivy Knox of Toorak, 2 August 1961, NAA: M2606, 46.

45   R.C. Cotton to Holt, 28 July 1961, NAA: M2606, 14.

46   Holt to Hon Alexander Mair, 19 October 1961, NAA: M2606, 46.

47   Holt to K.C. Wilson, 21 November 1961, NAA: M2606, 46.

48   Holt to Menzies, 24 October 1961, NAA: M2606, 46.

49   Holt to Menzies, 24 October and Treasury Submission, November 1961, Liberal Party of Australia, National Library of Australia, 394.

50   Holt to John Orchard, 21 November 1961, NAA: M2606, 46.

51   See minute from John Stone to Sir Roland Wilson, NAA: M2606, 111.

52   Address to the Australian Institute of Management, 11 November 1965, NAA: A1724, 13.

53 Peter Samuel, *Canberra Times*, 13 November 1965, NAA: A1728, 13.

54 Holt to Roderick Miller, 23 November 1961, NAA: M2606, 46.

55 'People in the news', *Sunday Mirror*, 12 April 1959.

56 Lease Portion 40, County of Nares, Garners Beach, North Queensland.

57 Don Whitington, *The Rulers: Fifteen Years of the Liberals*, revised edition, Cheshire-Lansdowne, Melbourne, 1964, p. 77.

58 Holt to Menzies, 'Liberal Party Council meetings', November 1962, 15 November 1962, NAA: M6206, 120. See also Ian Hancock, 'The Liberal Party organisation, 1944–64', in Scott Prasser, John Nethercote & John Warhurst (eds), *The Menzies Era: A Reappraisal of Government, Politics and Policy*, Hale & Iremonger, Sydney, 1995, pp. 87–8.

59 *CPD* (Reps), vol. 36, p. 15.

60 Quoted in Cameron Hazlehurst, *Menzies Observed*, Allen & Unwin, Sydney, 1979, p. 375. Between 1963 and 1972 the Country Party wanted one of its Members to have the Interior portfolio because it contained the Electoral Office which had responsibility for boundary adjustments and the management of vote 'weighting' in rural electorates.

61 See the chapters 'McEwen and the Defence of Australian Trade' and 'Australia's Revision' in Stuart Ward, *Australia and the British Embrace: The Demise of the Imperial Ideal*, Melbourne University Press, Melbourne, 2001, pp. 120–44, 177–95.

62 The Liberals won 52 seats, the Country Party 20 and Labor 50. Six Coalition seats lost in the 1961 election were regained (Oxley and Wide Bay were not) and another two seats won from Labor. Holt enjoyed a swing back to the Liberals of 3.4 per cent in the seat of Higgins. The biggest loser in the electorate was the DLP's Celia Laird whose primary vote was down by 2.9 per cent. This was probably a result of DLP people not manning all booths because the Senate, its stronghold, was not being contested. The vote for Labor's Roger Kirby was virtually unchanged.

63 NAA: M2606, 130.

64 The letter is in NAA: M2602, 130. For a critique, see G.S. Reid and Martyn Forrest, *Australia's Commonwealth Parliament*, Melbourne University Press, Melbourne, 1989, pp. 157–62.

65 John Uhr, 'Prime Ministers and Parliament', in Patrick Weller (ed.), *Menzies to Keating: The Development of the Australian Prime Ministership*, Melbourne University Press, Melbourne, 1992, pp. 97–8.

66 Peter Howson, *The Life of Politics: The Howson Diaries* (edited by Don Aitkin), Viking, Melbourne, 1984. p. 93.

67 Ibid.

68 Shane Paltridge to Holt, 22 June 1964, NAA: M2606, 129.

69 Frank Browne, *Things I Hear*, no. 562, 30 January 1958.

70 *Sunday Telegraph*, 9 February 1958, p. 26.

71 David Marr, *Barwick*, revised edition, Allen & Unwin, Sydney, 1992, p. 137.

72   Sir Garfield Barwick, *A Radical Tory: Garfield Barwick's Reflections and Recollections*, Federation Press, Sydney, 1995, p. 141.

73   Barwick, *A Radical Tory*, p. 199.

74   Hazlehurst, *Menzies Observed*, p. 374.

75   Ibid.

76   *Sun* (Sydney), 18 December 1961.

77   For Fairfax management's involvement in Government matters, see Clem Lloyd, *Parliament and the Press*, Melbourne University Press, Melbourne, 1988, p. 194; Maxwell Newton, *Management Newsletter*, 9 March 1962, NAA: M2606, 133.

78   Gorton's biographer includes this statement, taken from an interview with the Victorian State President, Sir John Buchan. Ian Hancock, *John Gorton: He Did It His Way*, Hodder, Sydney, 2002, p. 83.

79   Cited in Marr, *Barwick*, p. 204, n. 34 and David McNicoll, *Luck's a Fortune: An Autobiography*, Wildcat Press, Sydney, 1979, p. 225.

80   Barwick, *A Radical Tory*, p. 209.

81   Maxwell Newton, *Management Newsletter*, 14 August 1964, NAA: M2606, 2.

82   Howson, *The Life of Politics*, p. 118.

83   Holt to Sir Eric Harrison (Australian High Commissioner in London), 18 August 1964, NAA: M4295, 15.

84   Brian Johns, 'A time for chances and change', *Australian*, 15 January 1965.

85   Personal letter from Holt to J.T. Larkin, 19 August 1965, copy held by author.

86   Holt to Sir Alexander Downer, 22 October 1965, NAA: M2606, 140 Part 1.

87   Golding, *Black Jack McEwen*, p. 8.

88   Alexander Downer, *Six Prime Ministers*, Hill of Content, Melbourne, 1982, p. 69.

89   'Name of the new decimal currency', Statement by the Treasurer, 18 September 1963, NAA: M2568, 1.

90   *CPD* (Reps), 17 October 1963, pp. 1927–9.

91   Holt to Rupert Gerard, 2 September 1963, NAA: M4295, 12.

92   Holt's public statements and official correspondence are contained in NAA: M2568, 127; M2568, 139.

93   NAA: M2606, 143.

CHAPTER 9—The bloodless succession

1   Cameron Hazlehurst, *Menzies Observed*, Allen & Unwin, Sydney, 1979, p. 381.

2   Kevin Perkins, *Last of the Queen's Men*, Rigby, Adelaide, 1968, p. 228.

3   Alexander Downer, *Six Prime Ministers*, Hill of Content, Melbourne, 1982, p. 21.

4   Paul Hasluck (edited and introduced by Nicholas Hasluck), *The Chance of Politics*, Text, Melbourne, 1997, p. 134.

5   Richard Woolcott, *The Hot Seat: Reflections on Diplomacy from Stalin's Death to the Bali Bombings*, Harper Collins, Sydney, 2003, p. 77.

6   Quoted in John Edwards, *Life Wasn't Meant to be Easy: A Political Profile of Malcolm Fraser*, Mayhem, Sydney, 1977, pp. 2–3.

7   *Advertiser* (Adelaide), 21 January 1966.

8   This excludes McEwen, briefly Prime Minister after Holt's death, who had been in Parliament for 33 years.

9   Harold Holt, 'The Liberal tradition in Australia—Alfred Deakin: His life and our times', 1967 Alfred Deakin Lecture, in Yvonne Thompson, George Brandis and Tom Harley (eds), *Australian Liberalism: The Continuing Vision*, Liberal Forum Publication, Melbourne, 1986, pp. 83–4.

10 Holt, quotation from a press conference, *Current Politics*, vol. 7, March 1966, p. 4.

11 *Age*, 21 January 1966.

12 Holt, 'Meet the Press', ABC Radio Archives, Sydney, Tape reference: POL 86.

13 Foreword by Harold Holt to Justice Percy Joske, *Australian Federal Government*, First edition, Butterworths, Sydney, 1967.

14 *Australian Financial Review*, 21 January 1966, pp. 2–3.

15 Dame Zara Holt, *My Life and Harry: An Autobiography*, Herald & Weekly Times, Melbourne, 1968, p. 176.

16 *Age*, 31 December 1965, NAA: A1728, 13.

17 In a letter to Allen Chase, 20 February 1964, Holt said Zara 'abhors horse-racing', NAA: M2606, 114.

18 Interview with Peter Kelly, 9 August 2004.

19 Sir John Bunting, *R. G. Menzies: A Portrait*, Allen & Unwin, Sydney, 1988, p. 22.

20 Alan Reid, *The Gorton Experiment*, Shakespeare Head, Sydney, 1971, p. 196.

21 *Australian*, 29 January 1966.

22 Edgar Holt, *Politics is People: The Men of the Menzies Era*, Angus & Robertson, Sydney, 1969, p. 135.

23 Downer, *Six Prime Ministers*, p. 68.

24 Interview with the Right Honourable Reg Withers, 4 April 2004.

25 Fairhall, unpublished letter, quoted in L. Broderick, 'Transition and Tragedy: The Prime Ministership of Harold Holt, 1966–67', BA (Hons) thesis, Macquarie University, 1989, p. 12.

26 W.J. Hudson, *Casey*, Oxford University Press, Melbourne, 1986, p. 309, n. 64. Casey had been appointed to the vice-regal office the previous year.

27 John McEwen to Holt, 20 January 1966, NAA: M2684, 131.

28 Holt to John McEwen, 21 January 1966, NAA: M2684, 131.

29 Arthur Fadden, *They Call Me Artie*, Jacaranda, Brisbane, 1969, pp. 149–50.

30 Peter Golding, *Black Jack McEwen: Political Gladiator*, Melbourne University Press, Melbourne, 1996, p. 229.

31 Hudson, *Casey*, p. 304.

32 See Editorial, 'Sir Robert's Way in Cabinet', *Nation*, 22 January 1966.

33 'Menzies, Holt and the Liberals', *Current Affairs Bulletin*, vol. 37, no. 9, 21 March 1966, p. 138.

34 Statement by the Right Honourable Harold Holt, Leader of the Liberal Party, 'Elected Ministry, 20 January 1966, Prime Ministerial statements 1966–67, NAA: M4295, 21.

35 *Age*, 18 October 1966.

36 It was also known that Holt had favoured Senator Reg Withers' candidacy (Withers had been a leading figure in the Western Australian Division) for the Federal Presidency in 1965 ahead of that of Jock Pagan, because he feared the prospect of the powerful New South Wales Division gaining ascendency within the organisation. Pagan was elected.

37 Edwards, *Life Wasn't Meant to be Easy*, p. 31.

38 Personal interview, Dr Jim Forbes, 15 August 1993. There is a slightly different version of this conversation in Gerard Henderson, *Menzies' Child: The Liberal Party of Australia 1944–1994*, Allen & Unwin, Sydney, 1994, p. 233.

39 Philip Ayres, *Malcolm Fraser*, Heinemann, Melbourne, 1987, p. 105.

40 Katharine West, *Power in the Liberal Party*, Cheshire, Melbourne, 1965, p. 224.

41 Holt, *Politics is People*, p. 137.

42 Colin A. Hughes, *Mr Prime Minister: Australian Prime Ministers 1901–1972*, Oxford University Press, Melbourne, 1976, p. 167.

43 Clem Lloyd and Gordon Reid, *Out of the Wilderness: The Return of Labor*, Cassell, Melbourne, 1974, pp. 12–13.

44 Interview with author, 8 October 1993.

45 Bunting, *R. G. Menzies*, pp. 82–3.

46 Murray Goot, 'Party dominance and partisan division, 1941–72', in Cameron Hazlehurst (ed.), *Australian Conservatism: Essays in Twentieth Century Political History*, ANU Press, Canberra, 1979, pp. 263–91, p. 266 quoted.

47 'Menzies, Holt and the Liberals', *Current Affairs Bulletin*, vol. 37, no. 9, 21 March 1966, p. 138.

48 Speech at a Liberal Party meeting in Box Hill, Victoria, 20 February 1966, NAA: M2606, 126.

49 Jock Pagan, 'New horizons in Liberal thinking', address to the Liberal Party Federal Council, 4 September 1967, NAA: M2606, 123.

50 K. Colm, *Calwell*, Nelson, Melbourne, 1978, p. 251.

51 Calwell to Lee Kuan Yew, 21 March 1966, Calwell Papers, NLA MS4738. Quoted in Colm, *Calwell*, p. 253.

52 Downer, *Six Prime Ministers*, p. 72.

53 *Sun* (Melbourne), 18 December 1967.

54 'Menzies, Holt and the Liberals', *Current Affairs Bulletin*, vol. 37, no. 9, 21 March 1966, p. 138.

55 Reid, *The Gorton Experiment*, p. 11.

56 Tom Colebatch, 'In hindsight our first modern leader', *Age*, 1 January 1998.

57 Clem Lloyd, 'Prime Ministers and the media', in Patrick Weller (ed.), *Menzies to Keating: The Development of the Australian Prime Ministership*, Melbourne University Press, Melbourne, 1992, p. 119.

58 Lloyd, 'Prime Ministers and the media', p. 124.

59 John Bennetts, 'Development of the Federal Parliamentary Press Gallery,

1901–68', MA Qualifying Course thesis, Department of Political Science, School of General Studies, Australian National University, 1968, pp. 57–8.

60   Interview with Robert Moore, 'The talking heads', *Men in Vogue*, September 1976, p. 13.

61   Paul Hasluck, *Diplomatic Witness: Australian Foreign Affairs 1941–1947*, Melbourne University Press, Melbourne, 1980, p. 293.

62   Wallace Brown, *Ten Prime Ministers, Life Among the Politicians*, Longueville Books, Sydney, 2002, p. 44.

63   Ibid., p. 38.

64   James Walter, 'Prime Ministers and their staff', in Weller (ed.), *Menzies to Keating*, p. 44.

65   Hasluck, *The Chance of Politics*, p. 146.

66   Tony Griffiths, *Contemporary Australia*, Croom Helm, London, 1977, p. 98.

67   Lenore Coltheart, 'An Ideal Home? A history of The Lodge, Canberra', unpublished report prepared for Peter Freeman and Partners, Canberra, 1999, p. 25.

68   *Australian Women's Weekly*, 20 April 1966.

69   Coltheart, 'An Ideal Home', p. 31.

70   NAA: M4295, 11.

CHAPTER 10—From good to better

1   Address to the Young Australian Convention, University of Melbourne, 11 March 1966.

2   Address to Royal Commonwealth Society Luncheon, London, 8 September 1966.

3   Eastern Suburbs Liberal Rally, Box Hill Town Hall, 20 February 1966, NAA: M2684, 125.

4   Ibid.

5   K. Rivett, *Australia and the Non-white Migrant*, Melbourne, 1975, pp. 25–9. Reference to the 'White Australia Policy' was removed from the Liberal Party platform in 1960 and Labor's platform in 1965.

6   *Sydney Morning Herald*, 21 February 1966.

7   Peter Heydon, diary entry for 2 April 1966, copy supplied by J.R. Nethercote.

8   *CPD* (Reps), 9 March 1966, pp. 68–70.

9   *CPD* (Reps), 8 March 1966, p. 34.

10   Quoted in Robert Cooksey, 'Foreign policy review', *Australian Quarterly*, June 1966, p. 117.

11   *Daily Telegraph*, 11 March 1966.

12   *The Hindu*, 13 March 1966.

13   *Advertiser* (Adelaide), 10 March 1966.

14   *CPD* (Reps), 13 June 1968, p. 2307.

15   Mr A. Wrenford to Holt, 11 November 1967, NAA: M2684, 100.

16   Alan Watt, *The Evolution of Australian Foreign Policy, 1938–1965*, Cambridge University Press, London, 1968, p. 204.

17 James Curran, *The Power of Speech: Australian Prime Ministers Defining the National Image*, Melbourne University Press, Melbourne, 2004, p. 41.

18 Prime Ministerial Statement 17/1966 dated 23 February 1967, NAA: M4295, 21; Prime Ministerial Statement 25/1966 dated 17 March 1966, NAA: M4295, 21.

19 *CPD* (Reps), 31 March 1966, p. 801.

20 Prime Ministerial Statement 41/1966 dated 18 May 1966, NAA: M4295, 21.

21 President Johnson to Holt, 15 October 1966, NAA: A1209, 1966/7423.

22 Johnson Archives, WHCF Name file, Box 373, memo dated 28 September 1966.

23 *Sydney Morning Herald*, 7 October 1966.

24 Holt to President Johnson, 7 October 1966, NAA: A7854, 1.

25 For a general description of Johnson's visit see Stephen Wilks, 'The capital city as theatre: Celebrated foreign visitors to Canberra, 1914–1966', *Canberra Historical Journal*, new series no. 51, March 2003, p. 23.

26 David Hickie, *The Prince and the Premier*, Angus & Robertson, Sydney, 1985, pp. 66–7.

27 Dame Zara Holt, *My Life with Harry: An Autobiography*, Herald & Weekly Times, Melbourne, 1968, p. 202.

28 President Johnson to Holt dated 23 October 1966, NAA: M4295, 21. Holt sent Ambassador Clark two films in November 1966 covering the President's visit to Australia with the request that they be forwarded to Johnson who was then recovering from a minor operation.

29 Colin Hughes, 'The Dawson by-election, 1966', *Australian Journal of Politics and History*, vol. 12, no. 1, 1966, p. 15.

30 *Courier Mail*, 17 February 1966. Patterson's vote had increased from 41.4 per cent in 1963 to 55.1 per cent in 1966 while the Country Party's vote declined from 51.8 per cent to 44.9 per cent.

31 *Courier Mail*, 19 February 1966; *Australian*, 18 February 1966.

32 Prime Ministerial Statement, 20/1966 dated 27 February 1967, NAA: M4295, 21.

33 Michelle Grattan, 'The Kooyong by-election 1966', *Politics*, Special Supplement, vol. 1, no. 2, 1966, p. 10.

34 *Sun* (Melbourne), 29 March 1966.

35 *Australian*, 4 April 1966; Prime Ministerial Statement 32/1966 dated 4 April 1966, NAA: M4295, 21.

36 'Minutes of the Meeting of the Federal Executive, 9 June 1966', NAA: M2606, 123.

37 *Sydney Morning Herald*, 24 November 1966.

38 Prime Ministerial Statement 51/1966 dated 8 June 1966, NAA: M4295, 21.

39 'Minutes of the Meeting of the Federal Executive, 9 June 1966', NAA: M2606, 123.

40 *Sydney Morning Herald*, 15 November 1966, press clipping, NAA: M2684, 134.

41 'Policy Speech, Federal Election 1966', 8 November 1966, NAA: M2606, 121.

42 *Australian Financial Review*, 11 November 1966, p. 1.

43 Holt to President Johnson, 29 August 1966, NAA: A7854, 1.

44 *Canberra Times*, 18 November 1966.

45 *Bulletin*, 26 November 1966, pp. 13–14.

46 Menzies to Holt, telegram 24 November 1966, NAA: M4295, 14.

47 Graham Freudenberg, *A Certain Grandeur: Gough Whitlam in Politics*, Macmillan, Melbourne, 1977, pp. 61–2.

48 Arthur Calwell, *Be Just and Fear Not*, Lloyd O'Neil, Melbourne, 1972, p. 233.

49 It became a requirement of the Constitution after a referendum in 1977. See Geoffrey Sawer, *The Australian Constitution*, AGPS, Canberra, 1975; and *The Australian Constitution*, pocket edition, Parliamentary Education Office, 1991, pp. 10–11.

50 After two recent High Court challenges (the first was in May 1962 in relation to a Senate election in New South Wales in 1961 and the second in Victoria in 1965) and the Court's opinion that the *Commonwealth Electoral Act* was deficient in several important respects, the Attorney-General's Department feared the ballot paper would inevitably be the subject of legal action initiated by the Labor Party.

51 *CPD* (Reps), 18 October 1966, p. 1873.

52 E.H. Cox, *Herald* (Melbourne), 21 January 1966, NAA: A1728, 13.

53 J.R. Odgers, *Australian Senate Practice*, fifth edition, Australian Government Publishing Service, Canberra, 1976, pp. 108–9.

54 J.R. Willoughby to Holt, 14 December 1966, NAA: M2606, 123.

55 Freudenberg, *A Certain Grandeur*, pp. 106–7.

56 Paul Hasluck to Holt, 13 February 1967, NAA: M2684, 130.

57 Cliff Holt to Harold Holt, 28 November 1966, NAA: M2684, 121.

CHAPTER 11—'All the way': External Affairs

1 Alan Reid, *Bulletin*, 16 July 1966, p. 15.

2 *CPD* (Reps), 12 April 1967, p. 1178.

3 Paul Hasluck (edited and introduced by Nicholas Hasluck), *The Chance of Politics*, Text, Melbourne, 1997, p. 135.

4 NAA: M2606, 133.

5 Alexander Downer, *Six Prime Ministers*, Hill of Content, Melbourne, 1982, p. 73.

6 Richard Casey to Holt, 23 August 1966, NAA: M4295, 5.

7 Quoted in Philip Darby, *British Defence Policy East of Suez, 1947–68*, Oxford University Press, Oxford, p. 240.

8 *Age*, 19 January 1966.

9 Prime Ministerial Statement 16/1966 dated 23 February 1966, NAA: M4295, 21.

10 After armed insurgency had overthrown French rule in 1954, the former colony was divided into two nations: communist North Vietnam and capitalist South Vietnam. Refusing to recognise the division of their country, North Vietnamese forces joined with communist guerrilla units in the South to wage an armed struggle aimed at destroying the government in Saigon headed by Ngo Dinh Diem. As part of its policy of containing communism, the United States sent military advisers to South Vietnam ahead of providing combat troops and offensive capabilities.

11 President Johnson to Holt, 30 January 1966, NAA: A7854, 1.

12 Prime Ministerial Statement 7/1966 dated 1 February 1966, NAA: M4295, 21.

13 President Johnson to Holt, 30 January 1966, NAA: A7854, 1.

14 Prime Ministerial Statement 13/1966 dated 16 February 1967, NAA: M4295, 21.

15 *Current Notes on International Affairs*, vol. 37, no. 2, 1966, pp. 82–90.

16 Prime Ministerial Statement, *CPD* (Reps), vol. 50, 8 March 1966, pp. 26–8.

17 President Johnson to Holt, 7 March 1966, NAA: A7854, 1.

18 Prime Ministerial Statement, *CPD* (Reps), vol. 50, 8 March 1966, pp. 26–8.

19 *CPD* (Reps), 15 March 1966, p. 240.

20 Holt to President Johnson, 11 March 1966, NAA: A7854, 1.

21 Prime Ministerial Statement 37/1966 dated 19 April 1966, NAA: M4295, 21.

22 Bob Breen, *First to Fight: Australian Diggers, NZ Kiwis and US Paratroopers in Vietnam, 1965–66,* Allen & Unwin, Sydney, 1988, p. 247.

23 Wallace Brown, *Ten Prime Ministers, Life Among the Politicians*, Longueville Books, Sydney, 2002, p. 42.

24 Menzies to Holt, telegram 2 May 1966, NAA: M4295, 14.

25 Prime Ministerial Statement 44/1966 dated 23 May 1966, NAA: M4295, 21.

26 Prime Ministerial Statement 45/1966 dated 25 May 1966, NAA: M4295, 21.

27 These figures were provided in a minute from Peter Bailey to Holt, 3 June 1966, NAA: M2606, 116.

28 Glen St John Barclay, 'Problems of Australian foreign policy, January–June 1966', *Australian Journal of Politics and History*, vol. 12, no. 3, p. 329.

29 *Current Notes on International Affairs*, vol. 37, no. 5, May 1966, p. 262.

30 Holt to Harold Wilson, 12 May 1966, NAA: A7854, 2.

31 Prime Ministerial Statement 54/1966 dated 17 June 1966, NAA: M4295, 21.

32 Details of the visit, including Holt's itinerary, were included in NAA: A1209, 1966/7380.

33 Reported in the *Bulletin*, 9 July 1966, p. 7.

34 The second half of Holt's speech, including the impromptu ending, is reproduced in full in Sally Warhaft (ed.), *Well May We Say . . . The Speeches that Made Australia*, Block, Melbourne, 2004, pp. 123–4.

35 Only the final few paragraphs have been reproduced (and with an incorrect date) by Sally Warhaft in *Well May We Say*, p. 124.

36 Inward Cablegram I.34223 dated 7 July 1966, NAA: A1209, 1966/7423.

37 Details of Holt's visit to London, including an itinerary, were included in NAA: A1209, 1966/7423.

38 Waller to Holt, Inward Cablegram I.34731, 8 July 1966, NAA: A1209, 1966/7423.

39 Notes of a Meeting between Prime Minister Holt and Prime Minister Wilson kept by E.J. Bunting, 11 July 1966, NAA: A1209, 1966/7423.

40 Alan Watt, 'Australians at war in Vietnam', *Round Table*, no. 224, October 1966, p. 359.

41 Outward Cablegram [a reference number does not appear on this file copy], 10 July 1966, NAA: A1209, 1966/7423.

42 E.G. Whitlam, interview with Lloyd Broderick, quoted in 'Transition and Tragedy: The Prime Ministership of Harold Holt, 1966–1967' BA (Hons) thesis, Macquarie University, 1989, p. 29.

43 Sir Keith Waller, unpublished letter, Broderick, 'Transition and Tragedy', p. 29.

44 Bruce Grant, *The Crisis of Loyalty: A Study of Australian Foreign Policy*, Angus & Robertson, Sydney, 1972, pp. 2, 16.

45 Bill Hayden, *Hayden: An Autobiography*, Harper Collins, Sydney, 1996, p. 141.

46 Quoted in J.A.C. Mackie (ed.), *Australia in the New World Order*, Nelson, Sydney, 1976, p. 39, n. 13.

47 *Current Notes on International Affairs*, vol. 37, no. 12, 1966, pp. 753–55.

48 Quoted in Brian Toohey and William Pinwill, *Oyster: The Story of the Australian Secret Intelligence Service*, Heinemann, Melbourne, 1989, p. 113.

49 Quoted in Downer, *Six Prime Ministers*, p. 79.

50 Holt to Rupert Gerard, 6 October 1966, NAA: M4295, 12.

51 Holt to Harold Wilson, 16 August 1966, NAA: A7854, 2.

52 *Current Notes on International Affairs*, vol. 37, no. 10, 1966, p. 596.

53 Hugh Sidey, *A Very Personal Presidency: Lyndon Johnson in the White House*, Andre Deutsch, New York, 1968, p. 143.

54 Stuart to Holt, NAA: A1209, 1966/7728.

55 A full set of papers generated before and after Holt's visit to Manila is contained in NAA: M2684, 75 Part 1; M2684, 75 Part 2.

56 NAA: A1664, 1.

57 NAA: M2684, 75 Part 2.

58 Hubert Opperman to Holt, 16 June 1966, NAA: M2684, 133.

59 For material on the 1966 election campaign see NAA: M2606, 116; NAA: M2606, 122.

60 Colin Hughes, 'Australian political chronicle, September–December 1966—The Commonwealth', *Australian Journal of Politics and History*, vol. 13, no. 1, 1967, pp. 95–107.

61 Sir James Killen, *Inside Australian Politics*, Methuen Haynes, Sydney, 1985, p. 107.

62 *CPD* (Reps), 15 March 1966, pp. 239–40.

63 *CPD* (Reps), 23 August 1966, p. 305.

64 *CPD* (Reps), 28 October 1966, p. 2383.

65 Paul Ormonde, *A Foolish Passionate Man*, Penguin, Melbourne, 1981, p. 86.

66 This was conveyed through the two DLP sympathetic publications—*Democrat*, March 1966 and September 1967; and *News Weekly*, 13 December 1967.

67 Quoted in Killen, *Inside Australian Politics*, p. 108.

68 Quoted in Prime Ministerial Statement 133a/1966 dated 28 November 1966, NAA: M4295, 21.

69 *CPD* (Reps), 2 November 1967, pp. 2684–5.

70 John Gorton to Holt, 16 December 1966, NAA: M2684, 130.

71 Prime Ministerial Statement 124/1966 dated 22 December 1966, NAA: M4295, 21.

72 'Australia's answer to the Vietnam Crisis: An Interview with the Rt Hon. Harold Holt, PM of Australia', *Reader's Digest*, December 1966.

73 Brian Toohey and William Pinwill, *Oyster: The Story of the Australian Secret Intelligence Service*, Heinemann, Melbourne, 1989, p. 114.

74 Robert Cooksey, 'Pine Gap', *Australian Quarterly*, vol. 40, no. 4, 1968, p. 12.

75 Richard Woolcott, *The Hot Seat: Reflections on Diplomacy from Stalin's Death to the Bali Bombings*, HarperCollins, Sydney, 2003, p. 78.

76 Colin Hughes, 'Australian political chronicle, January–April, 1967—The Commonwealth', *Australian Journal of Politics and History*, vol. 13, no. 2, August 1967, p. 254.

77 Richard Casey to Holt, 25 January 1967, NAA: M4295, 5.

78 Foreshadowed in Prime Ministerial Statement 10/1967 dated 26 January 1967, NAA: M4295, 21.

79 A.L. Burns, 'Problems of Australian foreign policy, July–December 1967', *Australian Journal of Politics and History*, vol. 14, no. 1, 1968, pp. 4–6.

80 *Current Notes on International Affairs*, vol. 38, no. 4, 1967, p. 131.

81 Holt to Harold Wilson, Cablegram O.21524, 21 April 1967, NAA: A7854, 2.

82 Harold Wilson to Holt, 21 April 1967, NAA: A7854, 2.

83 Cablegram from Holt to Tunku Abdul Rahman, 27 May 1967, NAA: A7854, 3.

84 Cabinet Minute (British East of Suez), Decision No. 357 (FAD), 25 May 1967, NAA: A5842, 283.

85 Reported by the British High Commission (Canberra) to the Commonwealth Office (UK), 26 May 1967, Foreign & Commonwealth Office, 24/53, Public Record Office, quoted in Stuart Ward, *Australia and the British Embrace: The Demise of the Imperial Ideal*, Melbourne University Press, Melbourne, 2001, p. 251.

86 Holt to Tunku Abdul Rahman, 4 May 1967, NAA: A7854, 3.

87 Holt to President Johnson, 3 May 1967, NAA: A7854, 1.

88 Prime Ministerial Statement 56/1967 dated 29 May 1967, NAA: M4295, 21, Part 2.

89 Quoted in Glen Barclay, 'Problems of Australian foreign policy, January–June 1966', *Australian Journal of Politics and History*, vol. 12, no. 3, 1966, pp. 321–9, p. 327 cited.

90 Quoted in Downer, *Six Prime Ministers*, p. 96.

91 Holt to Harold Wilson, 16 June 1967, Information Cablegram to Canberra, NAA: A7854, 2.

92 Downer, *Six Prime Ministers*, p. 98–9.

93 Harold Wilson to Holt, 13 July 1967, NAA: A7854, 2.

94 Cablegram from Holt to Harold Wilson, 14 July 1967, NAA: A7854, 2.

95 Harold Wilson to Holt, 16 July 1967, NAA: A7854, 2.

96 Prime Ministerial Statement 74/1967 dated 19 July 1967, NAA: M4295, 21, Part 2.

97 President Lyndon B. Johnson, *The Vantage Point: Perspectives of the Presidency*, Weidenfeld & Nicolson, London, 1972, p. 295.

98 Johnson Archives, Austin, Texas, WHCF Name File Box 146, Folio 5.

99 Holt to President Johnson, 3 July 1967, NAA: A7854, 1.

100 Prime Ministerial Statement 78/1967 dated 28 July 1967, NAA: M4295, 21, Part 2.

101 Holt to President Johnson, 3 July 1967, NAA: A7854, 1.

102 Clark Clifford, 'A Vietnam reappraisal', *Foreign Affairs*, vol. 47, no. 4, July 1969.

103 Holt to President Johnson, 3 August 1967, NAA: A7854, 1.

104 Gerard Henderson, 'How Holt is still haunting Portsea', *Sydney Morning Herald*, 'Good Weekend', 13–14 December 1997, p. 36.

105 *Current Notes on International Affairs*, vol. 38, no. 6, June 1967, p. 246.

106 *Sydney Morning Herald*, 18 July 1967.

107 Johnson Archives, Special Head of State Correspondence file, memo dated 13 June 1967.

108 President Johnson to Holt, 17 August 1967, NAA: A7854, 1.

109 Peter Howson, *The Life of Politics: The Howson Diaries*, (edited by Don Aitkin), Viking, Melbourne, 1984, p. 325.

110 Cablegram from Holt to President Johnson, 6 October 1967, NAA: A7854, 1.

111 Killen, *Inside Australian Politics*, p. 101.

112 Ibid., p. 102.

113 *CPD* (Reps), 2 November 1967, p. 2687.

114 Brown, *Ten Prime Ministers*, p. 51.

115 Holt to President Johnson, 5 December 1967, NAA: A7854, 1.

116 Christopher Forsyth, 'Australia (and Mr Holt) turn to Asia', *Australian*, 2 February 1967.

CHAPTER 12—From bad to worse

1   NAA: M2606, 121. Also, NAA: M4249, 1.

2   Robert Cooksey, 'Foreign policy review, November 1966–September 1967', *Australian Quarterly*, vol. 39, no. 4, 1967, p. 97; Colin Hughes, 'Australian political chronicle, January–April 1967', *Australian Journal of Politics and History*, vol. 13, no. 2, 1967, p. 253.

3   W.C. Wentworth to Holt, 25 February 1967, NAA: M2684, 135.

4   Don Aitkin, 'Political review', *Australian Quarterly*, vol. 39, no. 1, 1967, p. 87.

5   James Walter, *The Leader: A Political Biography of Gough Whitlam*, University of Queensland Press, St Lucia, 1980, p. 152.

6   Arthur Calwell to Holt, 21 February 1967, NAA: M2684, 134.

7   Press clipping from the *Wellington Post*, 6 February 1967, NAA: M4295, 14.

8   Holt to Henry Bolte, 24 May 1967, NAA: M2684, 78.

9   Death and Funeral Notices, *Sydney Morning Herald*, 27 March 1967.

10 NAA: M4295, 10.

11 On 10 February 1964, the RAN Flagship, the aircraft carrier HMAS *Melbourne*,

collided with the *Daring* Class destroyer HMAS *Voyager* during night exercises off Jervis Bay. *Voyager* was cut in two and 82 men lost their lives. It was then the greatest peacetime disaster in Australian history. Prime Minister Menzies established a royal commission to inquire into the circumstances of *Voyager*'s loss and to attribute responsibility. After 50 days of public hearings, Sir John Spicer found that *Voyager* was to blame for the collision but he criticised three officers on the carrier's bridge—Captain John Robertson, Commander Jim Kelly and Sub-Lieutenant Alex Bate. When Captain Robertson was not reappointed to command of *Melbourne* after the inquiry and was instead posted to the shore training establishment HMAS *Watson* in Sydney, he submitted his resignation. This meant he was ineligible for a pension. Two pieces of evidence tendered at the Commission did not receive much prominence. The first was testimony from Barry Hyland, a steward, who claimed he had served a triple brandy to *Voyager*'s commanding officer, Captain Duncan Stevens, ninety minutes before the collision. The second was forensic evidence: the three bodies recovered from *Voyager* all contained trace amounts of alcohol. The Royal Commissioner did not ascribe much significance to this evidence. As the Navy was preparing for possible combat operations against Indonesia and was the principal beneficiary of a major defence spending program announced on 10 November 1964, both the Government and the Naval Board hoped the *Voyager* tragedy would soon drift from view. It would not be that simple.

12 *Australian*, 5 May 1967.

13 S.P. Crosland (AJA General Secretary) to Holt, 16 May 1967, NAA: M2684, 100.

14 *CPD* (Reps), 16 May 1967, p. 2169.

15 *CPD* (Reps), 16 May 1967, p. 2259.

16 Graham Freudenberg, *A Certain Grandeur: Gough Whitlam in Politics*, Macmillan, Melbourne, 1977, p. 107.

17 One of Menzies' last political acts before retiring was to legislate for two referendums. This was a significant step for Menzies, who did not like referendums. He lost both he put to the people in 1937 and 1951. Holt was not as reticent.

18 James Killen to Holt, 2 February 1966, Killen papers. Copy supplied to author.

19 WA Branch of the Liberal Party to Holt, 6 February 1966, NAA: M2684, 116.

20 Wood and Wright had opposed and voted against sections of Holt's Budget of 1960.

21 Bill McMahon to Holt, 13 June 1967, NAA: M2684, 132.

22 Prime Ministerial Statement 14/1966 dated 15 February 1966, NAA: M4295, 21.

23 See Prime Minister's Department file, 'Constitution Alteration Bills—Procedure in Parliament and Referendum, 1965–1967', NAA: A463, 1965/5445.

24 *CPD* (Reps), 11 November 1965, p. 2639.

25 *CPD* (Reps), 23 November 1965, pp. 3072–4.

26 See Cabinet Secretariat (CA 3) file, 'Voting Rights for Aborigines—Policy, 1961–1962', NAA: A4940, C3496.

27 See Faith Bandler, *Turning the Tide: A Personal History of the FCAATSI*, Aboriginal Studies Press, Canberra, 1989, pp. 100–1.

28 Reported in the *Sydney Morning Herald*, 28 February 1967.

29 NAA: A5482, 1–2; *CPD* (Reps), 7 September 1967, pp. 972–5.

30 John Hirst, *Australia's Democracy: A Short History*, Allen & Unwin, Sydney, 2002, p. 185.

31 *CPD* (Reps), vol. 56, 7 September 1967, pp. 972–5.

32 Prime Ministerial Statement 54/1967 dated 26 May 1967, NAA: M4295, 22.

33 Prime Ministerial Statement 55/1967 dated 28 May 1967, NAA: M4295, 22.

34 *CPD* (Reps), 7 September 1967.

35 Barrie Dexter to author, 9 April 2001.

36 Quoted in F.S. Stevens (ed.), *Racism: The Australian Experience*, vol. 1, Sydney, 1971, p. 101.

37 Quoted in Margaret Ann Franklin, *Black and White Australians: An Inter-racial History, 1788–1975*, Heinemann, Melbourne, 1976, p. 189.

38 H.C. Coombs, *Trial Balance*, Macmillan, Melbourne, 1981, p. 269.

39 Bill Wentworth to Holt, 3 October 1967, NAA: M2684, 135.

40 *CPD* (Reps), 7 September 1967, p. 973.

41 Prime Ministerial Statement 125/1967 dated 24 November 1967, NAA: M4295, 22.

42 Coombs, *Trial Balance*, p. 270.

43 Bill Wentworth to Holt, 23 November 1967, NAA: M2684, 135.

44 Paul Hasluck, *Shades of Darkness: Aboriginal Affairs 1925–1965*, Melbourne University Press, Melbourne, 1988, pp. 123–34.

45 Dexter to author, 9 April 2001.

46 Coombs, *Trial Balance*, p. 270.

47 Minutes of the Meeting of the Federal Council of the Liberal Party, 4–5 September 1967, NAA: M2606, 123.

48 The other contact was when Holt and the Attorney-General, Nigel Bowen, met Barwick to discuss the location of the new High Court building in Canberra.

49 Holt to Harold Wilson, 24 August 1967, NAA: A7854, 2.

50 These actions are itemised in a minute from Bill McMahon to Holt, 30 March 1966, NAA: M2606, 116.

51 Prime Ministerial Statement 69/1967 dated 29 June 1967, NAA: M4295, 21.

52 Prime Ministerial Statement 75/1967 dated 19 July 1967, NAA: M4295, 21.

53 Prime Ministerial Statement 52/1967 dated 10 May 1967, NAA: M4295, 22.

54 Clem Lloyd and Gordon Reid, *Out of the Wilderness: The Return of Labor*, Cassell, Melbourne, 1974, p. 381.

55 Bunting to H. Williamson (Assistant Secretary, Dept of Immigration) 'PM's Residence at Bingil Bay, QLD—Arrangements', dated 13 September 1967, NAA: A1209, 1966/7552.

56 *Herald* (Melbourne), 23 July 1967.

57 Inspector J. Hamilton to the Commissioner of the Commonwealth Police, 3 August 1967, ref: 166/2, NAA: 1209, 39.

58 Note for File, P.J. Lawler, 'Arrangements for Bingil Bay', 28 July 1966, NAA: 1209, 39.

59 C.A. Hughes, 'Australian political chronicle, May–August 1967', *Australian Journal of Politics and History*, vol. 13, no. 3, December 1967, p. 406.

60 Robert Southey to Holt, 17 February 1967, NAA: M4295, 13.

61 Prime Ministerial Statement 72/1967 dated 13 July 1967, NAA: M4295, 22.

62 Hubert Opperman, 'Letter to the Editor' published in the *Geelong Advertiser*, 2 August 1967, NAA: M2684, 92.

63 Hubert Opperman to J.R. Willoughby, 17 April 1967, NAA: M2684, 133.

64 *Age*, 8 July 1967.

65 Don Aitkin, 'Political review', *Australian Quarterly*, vol. 39, no. 3, 1967, pp. 121–3.

66 *Australian*, 10 July 1967.

67 Hubert Opperman, *Pedals, Politics and People*, Haldane, Sydney, 1977, p. 423.

68 Holt to Hubert Opperman, 22 July 1967, NAA: M2684, 92.

69 Undated letter from Bill Wentworth to Holt, NAA: M2684, 135.

70 Kevin Cairns to Holt, 11 August 1967, NAA: M4295, 13.

71 Quoted in memo to Holt from Peter Bailey, 17 August 1967, NAA: M4295, 13.

72 V.L. Ockerby to Holt, 28 August 1967, NAA: M4295, 13.

73 Memo to Holt from Peter Bailey, 17 August 1967, NAA: M4295, 13.

74 *Sydney Morning Herald*, 5 September 1967; *News Weekly*, 13 September 1967.

75 Message from the Prime Minister, 23 August 1967, NAA: M4295, 21.

76 *Courier-Mail*, 5 September 1967.

77 Prime Ministerial Statement 95/1967 dated 1 October 1967, NAA: M4295, 21.

78 *Sydney Morning Herald*, 2 October 1967.

79 *Australian*, 2 October 1967.

80 Freudenberg, *A Certain Grandeur*, p. 111.

81 Laurie Oakes, *Whitlam PM: A Biography*, Angus & Robertson, Sydney, 1973, p. 162.

82 Bill McMahon to Holt, 23 August 1967, NAA: M2684, 132.

83 J. Hutchinson, 'Cabinet and the Prime Minister', in Henry Mayer and Helen Nelson (eds), *Australian Politics: A Third Reader*, Longman Cheshire, Melbourne, 1973, p. 541.

84 Don Chipp and John Larkin, *The Third Man*, Rigby, Melbourne 1968, pp. 58–9.

85 Quoted in David McNicoll, *Luck's a Fortune*, Sun Books, Melbourne, 1980, p. 217.

CHAPTER 13—Controversy and complaint

1 This poll was necessitated by Menzies' decision—made after consulting Holt on the present state and future prospects of the economy—to have an early House of Representatives election in November 1963. The effect was to put the House of Representatives and Senate elections out of phase.

2 *CPD* (Reps), 13 May 1966, pp. 1109, 1913.

3 See 'Rules for use of VIP aircraft', NAA: A4940, C4344.

4 *Daily Telegraph* (Sydney), 17 October 1967.

5 Prime Ministerial Statement 106/1967 dated 16 October 1967, NAA: M4295, 21.

6 It is noteworthy that Holt asked Howson on 8 March 1967 to have Addison retained as his 'personal pilot' in command at 34 Squadron 'at least for the duration of this Parliament' although it would affect Addison's promotion prospects. Howson tried to resist Holt's request but the Prime Minister was adamant. Bailey explained to the Secretary of Air, A.B. McFarlane, that 'it was important that Wing Commander Addison be eased as gently as possible, and with as much encouragement as may be, into the position of personal pilot but without administrative responsibility for the Squadron' (Peter Bailey to A.B. McFarlane, Secretary of Air, 19 May 1967, NAA: M2684, 110). Addison remained at 34 Squadron (Howson to Holt, 17 January 1967 and Holt's penscript, 8 March 1967, NAA: M2684, 130).

7 Holt told this story to Alan Reid, who reported it in 'Harold Holt: The gambler', *Bulletin*, 13 May 1961, p. 13.

8 J.I. Fajgenbaum and P. Hanks, *Australian Constitutional Law*, Butterworths, Melbourne, 1972, p. 105.

9 *CPD* (Senate), 25 October 1967, pp. 1665–9. There were actually seventeen passenger manifests tabled. These documents were retained in the Senate Library as Department of the Senate, Paper No. 1134, 25 October 1967, Flight Authorisation Book, March 1966–October 1966; Department of the Senate, Paper 1135, 25 October 1967, Flight Authorisation Book, October 1966–June 1967; and Department of the Senate Paper 1136, Flight Authorisation Book, 20 June 1967–14 October 1967, marked at the foot of the page in red felt marker, 'Book Closed 15 October 1967'. Department of the Senate Paper 1128, 25 October 1967, consisted of 25 duplicated A3 sheets recording the number of passengers, the name of the VIP ordering the flight, the number of crew and passengers but no names of either the flight crew or the passengers. Also included were passenger manifests (RAAF Form No. AAP 873) with some duplicates. Most are handwritten.

10 *CPD* (Senate), 25 October 1967, pp. 1634–5.

11 Ian Hancock, *The VIP Affair, 1966–67*, Australasian Study of Parliament Group, Canberra, 2004, p. 52.

12 Ainsley Gotto (now Carson) told the author that, to her knowledge, Gorton did not know the records existed until 25 October 1967. Email to author, 14 January 2005.

13 J.J. Spigelman, *Secrecy: Political Censorship in Australia*, Angus & Robertson, Sydney, 1972, p. 47.

14 Reported by Hancock in *The VIP Affair*.

15 Andrew Peacock, interview, with the author, 7 October 1993.

16 *Sydney Morning Herald*, 1 November 1967.

17 Peter Howson, interview, with the author, 23 November 1993.

18 Ian Hancock has written a substantial account of the controversy with which I disagree on certain points of interpretation. See Hancock, *The VIP Affair*.

19 'Comment by Mr Tony Eggleton on VIP allegations', issued as Prime Ministerial Statement 117/1967, dated 28 October 1967, NAA: M4295, 21.

20 *Age*, 21 January 1966.

21 *Sydney Morning Herald*, 9 November 1967.

22 Alan Reid, *The Power Struggle*, Shakespeare Head Press, Sydney, 1969, p. 16.

23 David Butler, 'When should a Minister resign?', *The Canberra Model: Essays on Australian Government*, Cheshire, Melbourne, 1973, p. 68.

24 *Sydney Morning Herald*, 9 November 1967.

25 *Australian*, 1 November 1967, p. 1.

26 Louise Overacker, *Australian Parties in a Changing Society: 1945–67*, Cheshire, Melbourne, 1968, p. 298.

27 Howson to Holt, 14 November 1967, NAA: M2684, 130.

28 *Age*, 10 November 1967.

29 *Australian*, 10 November 1967.

30 *Australian*, 2 November 1967.

31 *Sydney Morning Herald*, 10 November 1967.

32 'Opening Address, Senate Election 1967', delivered 9 November 1967, NAA: M2684, 59.

33 *Australian*, 14 November 1967.

34 Prime Ministerial Statement 126/1967 dated 24 November 1967, NAA: M4295, 21.

35 *Mercury* (Hobart), 27 November 1967.

36 Katharine West, 'The future of the Liberal Party in Federal Politics', *Current Affairs Bulletin*, vol. 50, no. 2, July 1973, p. 17.

37 Sir Richard Randall to Bill McMahon (with a copy to Holt), 1 June 1967, NAA: M2684, 132.

38 Bill McMahon to Holt, 15 May 1967, NAA: M2684, 132.

39 Peter Golding, *Black Jack McEwen: Political Gladiator*, Melbourne University Press, Melbourne, 1996, p. 242.

40 Quoted in Golding, *Black Jack McEwen*, p. 244, n. 29.

41 Ibid., p. 244.

42 Ibid., p. 255, n. 4.

43 Quoted in Alan Ramsey, 'How Black Jack set the Scorpion loose', *Sydney Morning Herald*, 23 September 2000, p. 30.

44 Ibid.

45 Maxwell Newton, 'Mr Holt's low standing', *Management Newsletter*, 10 October 1967, p. 3, NAA: M4299, 7.

46 Richard Hall, *The Secret State: Australia's Spy Industry*, Cassell, Stanmore, 1978, pp. 152–3. Hall quotes a December 1976 *Nation Review* article as his source of the information.

47   Golding, *Black Jack McEwen*, p. 263.

48   Harold Wilson to Holt, 23 November 1967, NAA: A7854, 2.

49   Prime Ministerial Statement 122/1967 dated 20 November 1967, NAA: M4295, 21.

50   *Current Notes on International Affairs*, vol. 38, no. 11, November 1967, pp. 485–7.

51   *Bulletin*, 25 November 1967, p. 16.

52   McEwen, quoted in Golding, *Black Jack McEwen*, p. 265. All the major metropolitan newspapers published the next day (12 December 1967) carried the text of McEwen's statement. The *Australian Financial Review* quoted the full text with a commentary by Max Walsh.

53   *Daily Telegraph* (Sydney), 17 October 1967.

54   Address to the Federal Council of the Country Party, 20 January 1968, cited in Golding, *Black Jack McEwen*, p. 266, n. 20.

55   Prime Ministerial Statement 133/1967, 'Devaluation: Re-affirmation of the Government's Decision', dated 12 December 1967, NAA: M4295, 21.

56   Graham Freudenberg, *A Certain Grandeur: Gough Whitlam in Politics*, Macmillan, Melbourne, 1977, p. 117.

57   W.J. Hudson, *Casey*, Oxford University Press, Melbourne, 1986, p. 308, n. 68. Also, Peter Kelly, former Press Secretary to William McMahon, to author, email, 1 November 2004.

58   Hudson, *Casey*, p. 306.

59   Contemporary diary note, Tony Eggleton, 'Disquiet over Holt's leadership—1967', copy supplied to author.

60   Ian Hancock, *John Gorton: He Did It His Way*, Hodder, Sydney, 2002, p. 134.

61   Peter Howson, *The Life of Politics: The Howson Diaries* (edited by Don Aitkin), Viking, Melbourne, 1984, p. 354.

62   Ibid., p. 355.

63   Paul Hasluck (edited and introduced by Nicholas Hasluck), *The Chance of Politics*, Text, Melbourne, 1977, p. 144.

64   Private memorandum to the Prime Minister entitled 'Future operations', Tony Eggleton, 30 November 1967, copy provided to the author.

CHAPTER 14—Fate and destiny

1   Prime Ministerial Statement 136/1967 dated 15 December 1967, NAA: M4295, 21.

2   Tony Eggleton, private papers, 8:30 a.m. telephone conversation with Harold Holt, Saturday 16 December 1967, copy supplied to author.

3   *Australian*, 16 December 1967, p. 1.

4   Peter J. Williams and Roderick Serle, *Shipwrecks at Port Phillip Heads, 1840–1963*, Maritime Historical Productions, Melbourne, 1963.

5   Bernadette Long (on Holt's behalf) to John Reed, Museum of Modern Art, 19 January 1960, NAA: M2606, 13.

6   He was appointed on 15 November 1961; Basil Turner to Holt, NAA: M2606, 46.

7 Holt to Arnold Glass, 17 October 1967, NAA: M4295, 17.

8 Extract supplied by Eggleton to author.

9 Email from Lieutenant Commander Phil Hawke RANR Ret'd to author, 17 March 2004.

10 Peter Bailey, as quoted by Peter Golding, *Black Jack McEwen: Political Gladiator*, Melbourne University Press, Melbourne, 1996, p. 268, n. 25.

11 Extract from Eggleton diary.

12 W.J. Hudson, *Casey*, Oxford University Press, Melbourne, 1986, p. 306.

13 Golding, *Black Jack McEwen*, p. 317.

14 Sir James Killen, *Inside Australian Politics*, Methuen Haynes, Sydney, 1985, p. 123.

15 According to Robert Macklin, cited in Golding, *Black Jack McEwen*, p. 270, n. 27.

16 Paul Hasluck (edited and introduced by Nicholas Hasluck), *The Chance of Politics*, Text, Melbourne, 1977, p. 147.

17 Paul Hasluck, *Light that Time has Made*, Goanna, Canberra, 1990, p. 147.

18 Don Chipp and John Larkin, *The Third Man*, Rigby, Melbourne, 1968, p. 86.

19 Alan Reid, *The Gorton Experiment*, Shakespeare Head Press, Sydney, 1971, p. 10.

20 Ibid., p. 28.

21 Don Whitington, *Twelfth Man?*, Jacaranda, Brisbane, 1972, pp. 137–8.

22 Quoted in Ian Hancock, *John Gorton: He Did It His Way*, Hodder, Sydney, 2002, p. 348.

23 Alan Ramsey, 'How Black Jack set the Scorpion loose', *Sydney Morning Herald*, 23 September 2000, p. 30.

24 Hasluck, *The Chance of Politics*, p. 158.

25 Hasluck, *Light that Time has Made*, pp. 151–2.

26 Ian Hancock, *John Gorton*, p. 135.

27 Hasluck, *Light that Time has Made*, p. 147.

28 Philip Ayres, *Malcolm Fraser*, Heinemann, Melbourne, 1987, p. 123.

29 Ayres, *Malcolm Fraser*, p. 124.

30 Killen, *Inside Australian Politics*, pp. 120–1.

31 David Marr, *Barwick*, revised edition, Allen & Unwin, 1992, p. 224.

32 R. Johnson, *Australian Prime Ministers*, Nelson, Sydney, 1976, p. 183.

33 Email from Lieutenant Commander Phil Hawke to author, 17 March 2004.

34 Cited in Golding, *Black Jack McEwen*, p. 270, n. 28.

35 Interview with Peter Kelly, 10 August 2004, and email to author, 12 August 2004.

36 The statement was reported in all the Australian newspapers the next day, 19 December 1967.

37 Eggleton diary extract held by the author.

38 Howard, *Kent Hughes*, Macmillan, Melbourne, 1972, p. 224.

39 Ibid., p. 225, see also n. 3 on same page. Sir Albert Dunstan, a one-time Country Party Premier of Victoria, had governed for more than eight years (1935–43) with Labor support.

40 'Notes of discussion: Prime Minister, Senator J.G. Gorton/Director General of

Security, on Thursday 1 February 1968, at 1140 hours, at Commonwealth Offices, Treasury Gardens, Melbourne', quoted in Ramsey, 'How Black Jack set the Scorpion loose', p. 30.

41 See Golding, *Black Jack McEwen*, p. 274, n. 32.

42 Ibid., p. 275, n. 34.

43 Russell Ward, *A Nation for a Continent: A History of Australia, 1901–1975*, Heinemann, Melbourne, 1977, p. 376.

44 Prime Ministerial Statement 2/1968, Cabinet EC Decision No. 770, 4 January 1968, NAA: A4940, C4711.

45 *Washington Post*, 23 December 1967.

46 *Boston Globe*, 19 December 1967.

47 The choir sang Brahms' anthem 'How lovely is thy dwelling place, O Lord of Hosts!' and the congregation sang 'Praise my soul, the King of Heaven' and 'O God our help in ages past'. Archbishop Woods read the lesson from 2 Corinthians: 'we look not at the things which are seen, but at the things that are not seen; for the things which are seen are temporal; but the things which are not seen are eternal'.

48 *Sun* (Sydney), 23 December 1967, p. 6.

49 Simon Warrender, *Score of Years*, Wren, Melbourne, 1973, p. 147.

50 Chipp, *The Third Man*, p. 62.

51 Hamilton to Hurst, 30 April 1985, in John Hurst, *The Walkley Awards: Australia's Best Journalists in Action*, John Kerr, Melbourne, 1988, p. 36.

52 President Lyndon B. Johnson, *The Vantage Point: Perspectives of the Presidency*, Weidenfeld & Nicolson, London, 1972, pp. 378–9.

53 Quoted in Warrender, *Score of Years*, pp. 150–1.

54 *New York Post*, 22 December 1967.

55 Jack Valenti, *A Very Human President*, Norton, New York, 1975, pp. 278–9.

56 Henry F. Graf, *The Tuesday Cabinet: Deliberation and Decision on Peace and War under Lyndon B. Johnson*, Prentice-Hall, New Jersey, 1970, p. 146.

57 Lady Bird Johnson, *A White House Diary*, Holt, Rinehart & Winston, New York, 1970, p. 432.

58 Interview with The Hon. F.M. Osborne, 5 October 1993.

59 Norman Abjorensen, 'Black Jack McEwen almost a Lib PM', *Canberra Times*, 13 September 1992, p. 1.

60 Howard, *Kent Hughes*, p. 224.

61 Alexandra Hasluck, *Portrait in a Mirror: An Autobiography*, OUP, Melbourne, 1981, p. 263.

62 *CPD* (Reps), 12 March 1968, p. 13.

63 Ibid.

64 Ibid.

65 *CPD* (Senate), 12 March 1968, p. 15.

66 Ibid., p. 17.

CHAPTER 15—Myths and mysteries?

1 Jack Gibson, *Played Strong, Done Fine*, Lester-Townsend, Sydney, 1988, p. 11.

2 *Daily Express* (London), 18 December 1967.

3 Simon Warrender, *Score of Years*, Wren, Melbourne, 1973, p. 160.

4 Edgar Holt, *Politics is People: The Men of the Menzies Era*, Angus & Robertson, Sydney, 1969, p. 139.

5 Personal note on the disappearance prepared by Tony Eggleton. Copy held by author.

6 John Silvester, 'Fresh inquiry on Harold Holt', *Age*, 25 August 2003.

7 S.F. Baker to McEwen, 30 December 1967, NAA: M2684, 78.

8 *News American* (Baltimore), 24 December 1967.

9 Don Whitington, *Twelfth Man?*, Jacaranda, Brisbane, 1972, p. 127.

10 Ted St John to author, 8 August 1993.

11 Clyde Cameron, *The Cameron Diaries*, Allen & Unwin, Sydney, 1990, pp. 541–2.

12 Sir James Killen, *Inside Australian Politics*, Methuen Haynes, Sydney, 1985, p. 121.

13 Alexander Downer, *Six Prime Ministers*, Hill of Content, Melbourne, 1982, p. 103.

14 Warrender, *Score of Years*, p. 164. *Who Weekly* magazine spoke with Lieutenant Colonel John Bennett in 1997. He said he was not 'convinced Holt was even at Cheviot that day' claiming that the Army sentry could not verify that it was the Prime Minister who entered the restricted military area. He was troubled that no effort was made to check whether 'the footprints on the beach matched Holt's' while he thought suicide was 'not beyond the realm of possibility'. (*Who Weekly*, 29 December 1997, pp. 40–1.) The fact that the footprints [Holt was wearing sandshoes] were lost in the rising tide and strong wind and obliterated by others walking across the sand after Holt disappeared was overlooked.

15 *Weekend Australian Magazine*, 17–18 December 1977.

16 *Weekend Australian*, 13–14 December 1997.

17 *Weekend Australian Magazine*, 17–18 December 1977.

18 For a full account of the hoax see Robert Harris, *Selling Hitler: the Story of the Hitler Diaries*, Faber and Faber, London, 1986.

19 Anthony Grey, *The Prime Minister Was a Spy*, Coronet, Sydney, 1983, p. 3.

20 Ibid., p. 3.

21 Ibid., p. 4.

22 Ibid., p. 5.

23 Ibid., p. 23.

24 Ibid., p. 43.

25 Ibid., p. 53.

26 Ibid., p. 103.

27 Ibid., p. 159.

28 Ibid., p. 187.

29 Ibid., p. 198.

30 Ibid., p. 211.

31 Captain Rick Shalders RAN, Commander, Australian Submarine Squadron, email to the author, 18 December 2000.

32 *Current Notes on International Affairs*, vol. 36, no. 6, 1966, p. 379.

33 Percy Spender, *Politics and a Man*, Halstead, Sydney, 1972, p. 29.

34 See Paul K. Rodan, 'Harold Holt's foreign policy 1966–67', *Australian Journal of Politics and History*, vol. 25. no. 3, 1979, p. 316.

35 W.R. Crocker, *Australian Ambassador*, Melbourne, 1972, p. 204.

36 Interview with the Hon. Andrew Peacock, 7 October 1993.

37 T.B. Millar, 'The Making of Australian foreign policy', in B.D. Beddie (ed.), *Advance Australia Where?*, Melbourne, 1975, pp. 146–7. See also T.B. Millar, *Australia in Peace and War*, Australian National University Press, Canberra, 1978, p. 51.

38 *CPD* (Reps), vol. 54, p. 1175.

39 Stephen Fitzgerald, *Australian*, 10 October 1966.

40 *CPD* (Reps), 2 November 1935, p. 2761.

41 Richard Woolcott, *The Hot Seat: Reflections on Diplomacy from Stalin's Death to the Bali Bombings*, HarperCollins, Sydney, 2003, p. 82.

42 *CPD* (Reps), 30 March 1966, p. 729.

43 Email to the author from Anthony Grey, 19 September 2000.

44 Ronald McNicoll, *Number 36 Collins Street: Melbourne Club 1838–1988*, Allen & Unwin, Sydney, 1988, p. 231.

45 Roger Faligot and Remi Kauffer, *The Chinese Secret Service*, Hodder, London, 1989, p. 364.

46 Ibid.

47 Ibid., p. 365.

48 Ibid.

49 Ross Coulthart, 'Sink or swim? Spy or suicide', Sleuth's Corner, www.ninemsn.com.au.

50 http://sunday.ninemsn.com.au/sunday/investigative/case5.asp.

51 Barr McClellan, *Blood, Money and Power: How LBJ Killed JFK*, Hanover House, 2003.

52 Gerard Noonan, 'Mr Ed and his role in killing Kennedy', *Sydney Morning Herald*, 29 September 2003.

53 Reg A. Watson, 'What happened to our Harry?', *Aussie Post*, 4 September 1999, p. 5.

54 In 1985 the Victorian *Coroner's Act* was changed to allow inquests to be held without a body and thus obliged the Coroner to investigate 'suspected' deaths including drowning. The Victoria Police identified 103 cases of suspected drownings where bodies were never recovered between 1961 and 1985.

55 Sam Holt, *Sydney Morning Herald*, 26 August 2003.

56 Rick Roberts, Principal Registrar, State Coroner's Office, email to author, 3 September 2004.

57 John Carroll, 'National identity', in John Carroll (ed.), *Intruders in the Bush, The Australian Quest for Identity*, Oxford University Press, Melbourne, 1982, p. 224.

58 Ibid., p. 225.
59 Ian Hancock, in 'Harold Edward Holt', Michelle Grattan (ed.), *Australian Prime Ministers*, New Holland, Sydney, 2000, pp. 271–84, p. 282 cited.

CHAPTER 16—The legacy

1 The panel consisted of Ian Hancock, Stuart Macintyre, Graeme Davison, Geoffrey Bolton, Humphrey McQueen and Clem Lloyd.
2 Tony Walker and Jason Koutsoukis, 'The good, the bad and the couldabeens', *Australian Financial Review*, 3 January 2001, pp. 28–9.
3 *Sydney Morning Herald*, 18 December 1967, p. 2.
4 Sir James Killen, *Inside Australian Politics*, Methuen Haynes, Sydney, 1985 pp. 93–4.
5 Howard Beale, *This Inch of Time: Memoirs of Politics and Diplomacy*, Melbourne University Press, Melbourne, 1977, p. 72.
6 Arthur Fadden, *They Call Me Artie*, Jacaranda, Brisbane, 1969, p. 150.
7 Alexander Downer, *Six Prime Ministers*, Hill of Content, Melbourne, 1982, p. 102.
8 Paul Hasluck (edited and introduced by Nicholas Hasluck), *The Chance of Politics*, Text, Melbourne, 1977, p. 138.
9 Bill Hayden, *Hayden: An Autobiography*, Harper Collins, Sydney, 1996, p. 141.
10 W.F. Mandle, *Going It Alone: Australia's National Identity in the Twentieth Century*, Penguin, Melbourne, 1978, p. 204.
11 John Molony, *The Penguin Bicentennial History of Australia*, Penguin, Victoria, 1987, p. 337.
12 Robert Johnson, *Australian Prime Ministers*, Nelson, Sydney, 1976, p. 85.
13 James Walter, *The Leader: A Political Biography of Gough Whitlam*, University of Queensland Press, St Lucia, 1980, p. 244.
14 Edgar Holt, *Politics is People: The Men of the Menzies Era*, Angus & Robertson, Sydney, 1969, p. 137.
15 Don Whitington, *Twelfth Man?*, Jacaranda, Brisbane, 1972, pp. 117–18.
16 H.C. Coombs, *Trial Balance*, Macmillan, Melbourne, 1981, p. 270.
17 Judith Brett, *Political Lives*, Allen & Unwin, Sydney, 1997, p. 59.
18 C.M.H. Clark, *A Short History of Australia*, second revised edition, Mentor, Chicago, 1980, pp. 266–7.
19 Judith Brett, *Australian Liberals and the Moral Middle Class: From Alfred Deakin to John Howard*, Cambridge University Press, Melbourne, 2003, pp. 210–11.
20 Sol Encel, *Cabinet Government in Australia*, second edition, Melbourne University Press, Melbourne, 1974, p. 99.
21 Liberal Party Federal Secretariat, Press Statement, 4 December 1972.
22 Don Aitkin, *Stability and Change in Australian Politics*, second edition, ANU Press, Canberra, 1982, pp. 237, 243. These opinions were based on comprehensive longitudinal survey data.
23 Aitkin, *Stability and Change in Australian Politics*, p. 243.
24 Interview with Sir John Bunting, Canberra, 17 August 1993.

25 *Herald* (Melbourne), 21 November 1968.

26 *Australian Women's Weekly*, April 1988, pp. 12–13.

27 Diane Langmore, *Prime Ministers' Wives: The Public and Private Lives of Ten Australian Women*, McPhee Gribble, Melbourne, 1992, pp. 224–5.

28 *Sydney Morning Herald*, 2 July 1966.

29 *Malvern-Prahan Leader*, 25 October 1995.

30 Reported in the *Age*, 22 March 1968.

31 Reported in the *Canberra Times*, 23 May 1968.

32 Reported in the *Age*, 29 October 1968.

33 Gerard Henderson, 'How Holt is still haunting Portsea', *Good Weekend*, 13 December 1997, p. 38.

NOTE ON SOURCES

1 Pennie Pemberton, *Harold Holt: Guide to Archives of Australia's Prime Ministers*, National Archives of Australia, Canberra, 2003.

Index

Aboriginal people
  Aboriginal Welfare Conference (July 1967) 214
  assimilation 213–14, 216
  Council for Aboriginal Affairs 215–16
  culture 214, 216
  discrimination against 213
  Federal Council for the Advancement of Aborigines and Torres Strait Islanders (FCAATSI) 212
  referendum 1967 211–14
  right to vote legislation (1962) 212
Accra 118
Addison, Wing Commander Warwick 229
Adermann, Charles 166, 228
Admiralty House 241
Advisory War Council 23, 24, 31
Aged Persons' Homes Bill 218
Air Disaster (1940) 21, 22
Air Force Association 64
Aitken, Don 301
All Party Joint Committee on Constitutional Review 172
Allen, Keith 17
Anderson, Ken 271
Anderson, Sir William 263
Andrews, Gordon 128
Ansett, Sir Reginald 253
Anthony, Doug 228, 239–40, 248, 253, 254
Anthony, H.L. 26
Arbitration Court see Court of Conciliation and Arbitration of Australia
Arts 216
  Australian Council for the Arts 217
  Australian Elizabethan Theatre Trust 217

  Museum of Modern Art (Melbourne) 249
Asia 186–7, 192, 195, 244, 302
  Asian Development Bank 180
  Colombo Plan 180
  Communism 178, 183, 190, 234
  Economic Commission for Asia and the Far East 180
  Holt's diplomacy 180, 183
  importance to Australia 179–80, 134, 202, 247
  South-east Asia 112
  SEATO 186–7
  West Papua 112
Askin, Robin 164, 223
  government 163
Associated Chambers of Commerce 64
Australia Day 1966 144, 157
Australia's Immigration Policy (pamphlet) 160
Australian and Overseas Transport Association 83
Australian Army 22
  1RAR 177, 179
  5RAR 178
  6RAR 178
  Citizen Military Forces (CMF) 95, 96
  South East Asian Deployments 177–8, 187, 200–1
  Training Team Vietnam (AATTV) 174, 177
Australian Association of Advertising Agencies 69
Australian Broadcasting Commission 31, 148, 208
Australian Council of Employers' Federation 64, 83
Australian Council of Trade Unions

(ACTU) 35, 39, 48, 51, 64, 78, 86–91, 97, 161
Waterside Workers Federation (WWF) 81–5
Australian Industry Development Corporation 236
'McEwen Bank' 236
Australian Institute of Political Science 69
forum 1950 78
Australian Legion of Ex-service Men and Women 64
Australian Labor Party (ALP) 10, 12, 22, 29, 30, 33, 39, 42, 50, 52, 60, 63, 84, 92, 102, 109, 113, 119, 145, 161, 166, 168, 170, 188–9, 201, 204, 218, 221–3, 225, 232, 234–5
1955 split 50, 51, 86
Anti-Communist (DLP) 50, 52
communist effects 44, 46, 48
Federal Conference '36 Faceless Men' 120, 145
Industrial Groups 50, 86
National Conference 1957 60
socialist program 35, 37–8, 60
Vietnam policy 201–2
Australian National Secretariat of Catholic Action 44
Australian National University 113, 215
Research School of Pacific Studies 113
Australian Peace Council 50
Australian Security Intelligence Organisation (ASIO) 206, 238, 263, 282, 284–5
Australian Security Intelligence Service (ASIS) 190, 291
Australian Tourist Commission 168
Australian War Memorial 163
Australian Wheat Board 103
Australian Women's National League 11, 29

Bailey, Peter 150–1, 240, 251–2
Baker, S.F. 275
Ball, Professor McMahon 66
Bandiana 68
Bank Nationalisation Act 1947 38
Bankers Refinance Corporation 222, 236
Barnard, Lance 205, 302
Barnes, Charles ('Ceb') 166, 216
Barwick, Sir Garfield 119, 122–5, 217, 254, 258
Basic Industries Group (BIG) 169, 236–7
Basic Wage Decision (1957) 60

Bass Strait 249
Bate, Jefferson 277, 304–6
Beale, Howard 27, 296
Beasley, Jack 61, 229
Bedarra Island 115
Bennett, Lieutenant Colonel John 259
Bennetts, John 55, 148
Bhagat, B.R. 265
Bingal Bay 115, 133, 149, 152, 218–19, 272–3, 306
Bland, (Sir Henry) Harry 39, 85
Bolte, Sir Henry 165, 206, 254
Bolton, Geoffrey xii
Bonegilla Migrant Camp 68
Bourke, William 38
Bowden, Herbert 191, 195
Bowen (electorate) 81
Bowen QC, Nigel 172, 208–9, 254
Bradfield (electorate) 136
Brett, Judith 301
Britain
  Asia 120, 184, 190, 192–3, 195
  Australia 13, 61, 65, 157, 175, 183, 191–3, 197, 240
  Commonwealth Brigade 196
  defence plan 192
  defence spending/cuts 191–3, 195, 203
  devaluing the pound 236, 239–40
  EEC 118, 182, 191, 194–5
  Europe 118–19
  France 191
  Hong Kong 192
  markets 110
  Nasser's blockade 197
  NATO 191
  overseas investment 175, 191
  Rhodesia 185–6
  Singapore/Malaysia defence 175, 177, 191–2, 196, 197
  United States 182
  Vietnam 177, 181, 201
  Wilson Government 175–6, 191–2
  withdrawal east of Suez 189, 191, 193–4, 196, 203, 217, 302
British Commonwealth 73, 118, 182, 191, 194–5
Broadby, Reg 64, 89
Broderick, Lloyd xiv
Brooke, Bernie 219
Brookes, Dame Mabel 10, 11
Brown, Coralie 33
Brown, George 192, 195

Brown, Rev Jeffrey 33
Brown, Peter 100
Brown, Wallace 179
Browne, Frank 122
    Things I Hear 122
Bruce, Lord (Stanley Melbourne) xvi, 55,
    57, 133, 296
Bryant, Gordon 212
Buchan, John 115
Buchanan, Alexander 140
Buckingham Palace Court Circular (27
    May 1953) 73
Bull, Tom 211
Bunting, Sir John 136, 144, 147, 150,
    215–16, 228–31, 253, 262, 303
Burton, John 24, 48
Bury, Les 118–19, 141, 243, 262, 269
Büsst, Alison 115, 256
Büsst, John 115, 218
Butler, David 232

Cabban, Peter 207
    statement 208
Cairns, Dr Jim 188, 205, 219
Cairns, Kevin 222
Callaghan, James 176, 194
Calwell, Arthur 39, 48, 63–4, 67, 74, 107,
    113, 120, 123–4, 146, 149, 166–70,
    179–80, 188–9, 191, 200, 205, 207, 210,
    222, 226, 235, 264, 270, 302
Cameron, Clyde 55, 61, 119, 276
Cameron, Donald 11–12
Capricornia (electorate) 222
    1967 by-election 222–3, 225, 244
Cariappa, General K.M. 70
Carrick, Sir John 243
Carroll, John 295
Cartwright, Michael 293
Casey, Lord (Richard) 9, 16, 21, 44, 55–6,
    133, 138–9, 176, 191, 237, 241–2,
    253–4, 261–2, 265, 269, 294, 298
Cerberus, HMAS 251–2, 260
Chalk, Gordon 222
Chamberlain, Frank 110, 181
Champassak, Sisouk 265
Chaney, Fred 121, 172
Charles, Prince of Wales 265
Chase, Allen 102, 105
Chen Chi-Mai 287
Chen Yi 283–4
Cheviot Beach 249–52, 259, 262, 264,
    272, 275–6, 284, 307

Cheviot, SS 249
Chiang Kai-shek 280–1, 287–8
Chifley, Ben 24, 33, 38, 45–7, 54, 103,
    133, 150, 264, 296, 298, 303
    government 35–64, 66, 95
    socialism 35
Child Endowment 25, 26, 33, 138
Child Endowment Act 26
China 186, 287
    anti-Chinese 48
    communists 281–3, 286, 288, 292
    import agencies 103
    markets 186
    Nationalist Party (Kuomintang) 280–2
    People's Bank of 104
    trade 288
    submarine 283–6, 293
Chipp, Don 172, 208, 224, 255, 266
Chung Hee Park 265
Churchill, Sir Winston 297
Civil Aviation and Air 18
Civil Supply Section 18
Clarey, Percy 51, 64
Clark, Ed 164
Clarke, Manning xii, 299
Clifford, Clark 199
Clifton Hill (Victorian state seat) 10
Cloke, John 274
Cockatoo Island Dockyard 89
Cockburn Sound 195
Coles, Arthur 27–8
Colonial Sugar Refining Co Ltd (CSR)
    113
Committee of Economic Inquiry
    (Vernon) 113
Commonwealth Bank 101, 105
    Bill 103
    Board 10
    central bank 102–3
    Corporation 103
    influence in Treasury 101
Commonwealth Employment Services
    (CES) 59, 82
Commonwealth Finance Ministers' AGM
    102, 118, 263
Commonwealth Industrial Court 90
Commonwealth Jubilee Citizens'
    Convention 68, 176
Commonwealth Manpower Committee
    24
Commonwealth Parliamentary Association
    37, 71–3, 229

Commonwealth Prime Minister's
Conference 73, 139, 162, 185
Commonwealth Public Works 36, 60, 65,
72, 244
infrastructure 42, 106, 158
Joint Public Works Committee 172
rail 59
roads 59
Snowy Mountains Scheme 62, 65, 158
water 42
Communist Party 34–5, 37–8, 44–6, 61
Dissolution Bill 45–8
referendum 47–8
Communists 21, 34, 48–50, 68, 97, 105,
112, 205, 222
conspiracy to disrupt industries 78–9
'Domino Theory' 166
in Asia 190
in South Vietnam 166, 181, 188, 203
influence on trade unions 77–8, 82, 86,
91–3
Tribune 82
Conciliation and Arbitration Act 76, 79,
85–7, 90
Conciliation and Arbitration Commission
90, 97
penal provisions 87
Connolly, Brian (Barney) 33
Constitution 76, 135, 210, 212–13
Conventions Concerning the Abolition of
Forced Labour (ILO) 94
Conway, Ronald xii
Cook, Joseph 296
Cooksey, Robert 190
Coombs, Dr H.C. (Nugget) 24, 101, 103,
105, 109, 214–16, 298
Cooper, William 166
Co-ordinating Council for Physical Fitness
15, 17
Cope, Jim 123
Coppin, Ray 151–2, 250–1, 253
Corio (electorate) 187, 220
1967 by-election 220–2, 244
Cotton, Bob 112, 269
Country Party 10, 12, 16, 19, 22, 33, 37,
39, 52, 99, 102, 106, 113, 124, 131,
138–9, 166, 241–2, 260
and William McMahon 254, 260, 264, 269
Federal Council 241
Independent Country Party 27
leadership 27, 242
'three-cornered' contests 167, 169, 222

withdrawal from Coalition 16–19
Court of Conciliation and Arbitration of
Australia 9, 28, 76, 79–81, 86–90, 93
Cox Brothers 108
Cox, E.H. (Harold) 87, 171, 181
Craig, Hazel 151
Crawford, Sir John 113
Cremean, John 10
Cremor, Brigadier William 29, 112
Crimes Act 79, 84, 123
Crisp, Fin 24
Crocker, Walter 287
Crosdale, Aircraftsman Charles 22
Crowley, C.J. 11
Cummings, Bob 102
Curtin, John 21, 26, 28, 32, 44, 202, 254,
296, 298
government 28, 30
Curtin, Pierce 24

Daly, Fred 226
Davidson, Charlie 106
Davis, Frank 126
Davis, H.O. 64
Dawes, Allan 22
Dawson (electorate)
by-election 165
Deakin, Alfred 134, 264, 296
Dedman, John 220
defence 62, 64, 210
Defence Act 95
policies 189
spending 96, 162, 176, 227
Three Year Defence Plan (1950) 95
de Lacy, Pat 151, 246, 274
de L'isle, Viscount 126
Democratic Labor Party (DLP) 50–1, 63,
92, 102, 113, 165, 170, 189, 210, 218,
221–2, 225–6, 235, 271
Department of
Air 226–7, 229
Attorney-General 171
Defence 200, 207
Education and Science 168, 209
External Affairs 132, 175, 190, 200, 255
Immigration 36, 39, 52, 55, 58, 74, 96, 213,
219–20, 270
Interior 228
Labour and National Service 23, 27, 39, 58,
68, 84, 97–8, 270, 298
Munitions 24
Navy 207–8, 224

Post-war Construction 214–15
Primary Industries 228, 248
Territories 216
Trade (and Industry) 18, 99, 109, 113–14, 118, 139, 236–9
Social Services 228
Supply and Development 16–17, 23
Devlin, Stuart 129
Dexter, Barrie 215–16
Dixon, Sir Owen 125
Dorrian, Phil 24
double dissolution 47, 79, 219
Downer, Sir Alexander 28, 128, 132, 175, 182, 193–4, 196, 276, 296
Dowson, Commodore John 260
drought 130, 162
farm loans 162
relief 162
Dunstan, Keith 146
Dyer, Bob 59, 273

economy 43, 63, 69, 76, 93, 103, 109, 110, 113, 126, 130, 161, 302
Edgar, Jonathan 248
education 42, 162, 168, 221–2, 234
schools and colleges 72, 168
Edward VIII, King 15
Edwards, Dr Bruce 247
Egerton, Jack (Sir John) 108–9
Eggleston, Sir Frederic 67
Eggleton, Tony 131–2, 147–8, 150–1, 179, 197, 202, 232, 242, 244, 247, 250–3, 259–60, 262, 273–4
Eldred, George 293
Electoral Commission 170
electricity 42
Elizabeth II, Queen 49, 182, 265
coronation (1953) 73
Elford, R.E. 21
elections
1940 21–2
1943 29
1946 33
1949 37, 44
1951 42, 47
1954 49–50
1955 51, 53
1958 63–4, 99, 103
1961 108–13, 124, 298
1963 119–20
1966 126, 142, 146, 149, 164–70, 187–9, 204, 207

1967 by-elections 220
1967 half-Senate 202, 205, 221–3, 225, 228, 234, 239, 244, 256, 274
1969 221, 225, 244, 253, 303
1972 173, 301
'Australia Unlimited' 63
'building for tomorrow' 111
communist fear 170, 205
'donkey' votes 225
policies 167
televised policy speech 167
South Vietnam 167, 187
violence 166
Emmerton, Alice Mabel Maud 10–1
Empire Air Training Scheme 19
employment 10, 49, 59, 76, 86–7, 107
Encel, Sol 301
Engelhard, Charles 102, 129
Erwin, Dudley 242–8
Essendon Airport 253
European Common Market 110, 112
European Economic Community (EEC) 118–19
Evatt, Dr H.V. 46–7, 50, 52, 60–1, 63, 106–7, 136, 144
anti-Chinese 48
DLP 51
Everingham, Dr Douglas 222–3
exports
National Export Convention (1960) 105
primary 42
ex-servicemen 142, 207

Fadden, Arthur 22, 25–7, 39, 42–3, 87, 99, 101–2, 106, 115–16, 138–9, 169, 296
government 27–8
Fairbairn, David 141, 243, 262
Fairbairn, James 18, 21–2
Fairhall, Allen 110, 137, 141, 200, 243, 262
Faligot, R. and Kauffer, R., *The Chinese Secret Service* 292
Farouk, ex-King of Egypt 74
Faunce, Dr Marcus 248, 274
Fawkner (electorate) 11–12, 16, 21, 29–30, 33, 38
Fell, Major James 7–8, 33, 306
finance 62
Firth, Gerald 24
Fitchett, Ian 115
Fitzgerald, John 53
Fitzgerald, Tom 236–7
Fitzpatrick, Brian 48, 105

Fitzroy Gardens 307
Flanagan, Noel 39, 71–2
Flinders (electorate) 65, 165, 306
Foggon, B. 78
Forbes, Dr Jim 141
Ford, Inspector Jack 261, 278
foreign affairs 62
  ANZUS 188
  Britain in South-east Asia 176–7, 183–4,
    191–6
  Cambodia 192
  diplomacy 174, 180, 185, 202
  Foreign Affairs and Defence Committee
    (Cabinet) 174
  foreign policy 174, 199, 234
  Indonesia 177, 183, 195
  Malaysia 193–5, 199
  Manila Conference 186–7, 202
  SEATO 186–7, 192
  Taiwan, embassy 286–8
  trade and tariff with the US 198
  Vietnam Policy 179, 187, 199, 201, 204, 234
  West Papua 112
foreign aid 118, 162
foreign investment 99, 105, 114, 302
Fordyce, John 165
'forgotten people' 158, 301
Fox, Max 207
Fraser, Allan 119
Fraser, Lieutenant Colonel David 16–17
Fraser, Malcolm 133, 141–3, 243, 255,
  258, 299, 302
Freemasons Hospital 274
Freeth, Gordon 169, 269, 290
Fremantle (electorate) 32
Freudenberg, Graham 170, 210, 223, 241
Funnell, William 39
Fysh, Sir Hudson 102

Gair, Vince 221, 226, 271
Garden Island Dockyard 86
Garners Beach 115
Geelong (electorate) 220
Gelber, H.G. 118
George V, King 217
  statue and memorial 217
Gerard, Rupert 129, 185
Gibson, F.J.R. 83, 91
Gillespie, Marjorie 246–8, 250, 261,
  276–7, 288, 293, 304–5
Gillespie, Vyner 248, 250, 261
Gillespie, Winton 246

Glass, Arnold 249
Glover, Rev Neil 50
Golding, Peter 128, 237
Gorton, John xiii, 126, 133, 141, 189, 209,
  228–34, 242–3, 254–8, 260, 262,
  269–70, 301
Gotto, Ainsley 243, 255
Graham, Jack 14
Grant, Bruce 183
Great Barrier Reef 218, 273
  Ellison Reef 219
  Beaver Cay 219
Greenwood, Betty 151
Grey, Anthony 278–80, 284–6, 288–9, 292
  The Prime Minister Was a Spy xiv, 280, 291
Grey, George 222
Griffiths, Tony 151
Groupers (Industrial) 50–1, 86
Gulf of Aqaba 197
Gullett, H.B.S. ('Jo') 23, 77
Gullett, Sir Henry 21

Hamer, Rupert 265
Hamilton, Inspector 219
Hamilton, John 267
Hammarskjöld, Dag 73
Hancock, Ian xv, 229–31, 257, 295
Hannaford, Clive 204
Harders, Clarrie 251
Harold E. Holt, USS 307
Harold Holt Memorial Swimming Baths,
  Malvern 307
Harold, Martin 4
Harriman, Averell 178
Harrison, Eric Fairweather 16
Harrison, Eric John 26, 31, 39, 54, 56–7,
  61, 126, 298
Hartwig, Dr 167
Hasluck, Sir Paul 37, 100, 126, 130, 132,
  137, 149–50, 172, 174–5, 183, 192,
  200–1, 216, 243, 254, 257, 262, 269,
  286–7, 297
  history of the war effort 22
  on Holt xv
Hawke, Bob xiii, 220
Hawke, Lieutenant Commander Phil
  251–2, 259, 262
Hay, Ronald 220
Hayden, Bill 183, 297
Haywood, John 250
Hazelhurst, Cameron 131
Hazlett, Luke 256

health 42, 221, 234
 hospitals 49, 72
Healy, Denis 175, 176, 195–6
Healy, Jim 78–80, 85, 91, 97
Heath, Edward 265
Heister, Gustave (Gus) 51–2
Henderson, Gerard 199
Henty (electorate) 28
Henty, Denham 122, 141–2, 226, 228
Hewitt, Joe 91
Hewitt, Lennox 100–1
Heydon, Naomi 159
Heydon, Peter 159
Heyes, Sir Tasman 39
Heyward, Dick 24
Higgins (electorate) 38, 53, 63, 111, 113,
 170, 256, 269
High Court
 appeal by WWF 80
 Arbitration Act's penal provisions 87
 'Boilermakers' Case' 90
 Chief Justice of the High Court 54, 125
 Communist Party Dissolution Bill 45–7
 Immigration Act 67
 imposition of levies by registered trade
  unions 92
 separate elections for Senate vacancies 171
 Wartime Refugees Removal Act 1949 67
Higinbotham (electorate)
 by-election 51, 221
Hilton, Conrad 102
Hirst, John 213
Hitchcock, Flight Lieutenant 22
Hollis, Roger 293
Hollway, Tom 28
Holt, Andrew 34, 115, 168, 306
Holt, Carol 206
Holt, Christopher 306
Holt, Cliff 4, 173, 206, 303–4
Holt, Edgar 137, 150, 274, 298
Holt, Harold E.
 achievements 302
 affairs xvii, 277, 304–5
 airline food 102
 All Party Nation Government 21, 27
 'All the Way' xiii, 181, 183–4
 and Aborigines 213–14, 216
 Army: xvi, 16–7, 20–3, 28
 'squibbed' out 188

Arts 216
Bors, H.K. (code-name) 281, 284

briefcase 253, 294
Cabinet 140–4, 174, 191, 200, 207, 232,
 237, 240–1, 246, 300
car accident (1955) 51–2
childhood xi, xvi, 4–6
coat of arms 3
Companion of Honour (CH) 217
Coronial Inquest 294
debating skills 58, 146
Deputy Liberal Leader 56–7, 75, 96, 99, 122,
 132
disappearancexiii, 250–3, 255, 259–61, 264,
 273, 275, 279, 294, 302
disappearance theories:
body 275
Chinese spy and submarine 280–5
CIA 277
clairvoyant conversation 293
conspiracy theory 293
knocked unconscious 275
link to MI5 'Fifth Man' 293
North Vietnamese 278
Russian submarine 278
suicide 276–7

Eden, Anthony comparison with 57, 297
elected to parliament 12
eulogy 266
Evatt, H.V. 46–7, 136
family memorabilia 206
father's death 7
foreign affairs:
diplomacy 180, 183, 185, 202
friendship with Lyndon Johnson 162, 175,
 198–9
Gala dinner 111
gambling 136, 304
network of contacts 102, 126, 174–5, 181
government:
'battleship' theory 232
consensus 135, 143
no confidence vote 231

hate mail 106, 110, 127, 160–1
health 256, 274
holidays 115, 136, 218–19, 246, 273
income 114, 153
Leader of the House 57–9, 75, 120, 123, 132
leadership 31, 33, 39–40, 52, 54–7, 59, 96,
 235, 241–3, 256, 299, 302–3
legal practice 9, 11, 14, 28, 33, 165, 306
legal studies 6
Liberalism 32, 38, 94

long wait xii;
loss of confidence in 207, 210, 218, 223–4, 233
marriage 33
memorial service 262, 264–7
memorials 306–7
Minister for Immigration 39, 48, 55, 58, 65, 74, 96, 99
Minister for Labour and National Service 23–5, 27, 39, 47, 58, 85, 90–1, 93, 95, 98–9
Minister for Melbourne Olympics 99
Minister in Charge of Scientific and Industrial Research 17
Minister without Portfolio 16
mother's death 5
nicknames 5
Opposition Spokesman on Immigration and Industrial Relations 34
paper, 'The political situation' 1957 61–3
parents' divorce 4
parliamentary life 13–14, 28, 58, 100, 120, 136
parliamentary procedures 58, 121, 209
parliamentary reforms 58–9
Party leadership 123, 137, 139, 245
personal security: 149, 206, 219
bodyguard 149, 219, 264, 284
personality: 145, 224, 245
aggression 121–2
charm xv, 15, 175
determination 144
honesty 27, 267, 271
integrity 229, 233–4, 271
loyalty 26, 55, 133, 140, 271, 303
'niceness' 123, 146, 258, 298–9
style 58, 103, 121–2, 136–7, 175, 179, 224, 258, 270, 301
temperament 125

political outlook 9, 12, 134–5, 158
politics 11
Prime Minister 123, 137–40, 142, 147, 157–8, 161, 174, 177, 224, 274
Privy Counsellor 73, 289
public profile 31, 40, 114, 125, 145, 217, 223
relationship with President Johnson 162, 175, 198–9
scholarship, Alexander Wawm 5
schools 4–5
scrapbook xvi, 7
search for: 250–2, 259–60, 265
Army School of Signals, Balcombe 251

divers 251–2
helicopters 251
Navy SAR vessel 251–2, 262
Port Melbourne Naval Diving Team 251
Snipe, HMAS 260, 262, 265
speeches: 244, 287
1949 38
1962 117
Alfred Deakin Lecture (31.7.67) 199
anti-communist (19.4.40) 44
Australia Day 1967 204
Australian Institute of Political Science, July 1950 78
Bien Hoa, April 1966 179
Budget 1960 106
Christmas 1949 40
election campaign 1943 29
Fremantle by-election 1945 32
half-Senate election (2.11.67) 202, 234
ILO Conference 1950 93–4
Liberal Party inaugural meeting 32
maiden speech 12
policy speech (8.11.66) 167–8
Press Club 184
Prime Ministers Broadcast (first) 158–9
'Report to the Nation' (8.3.66) 178
Summer School (1953) 69
White House, 'All the Way' (28.6.66) 181–3, 186

speechwriter 150
staff 100, 136, 150–2
successor 245, 254, 256–8, 259, 303
swimming/skindiving 136, 248–9, 272–3, 295
tennis 15, 39, 136, 247–8, 250, 274
travel diaries: 288
cryptanalyst report 288–9

Treasurer 100, 102, 108–9, 111, 116, 123, 126–7, 132, 137, 139, 176
tributes to 264, 267, 270–1
trips:
1948, August (Europe) 37
1957, May–August (Singapore, Geneva) 39, 59, 73
1951–52, December–January 71
1952, July (Singapore, Pakistan, Europe, US) 71–2
1953, May 73, 81
1954, August (Kenya) 73, 84–5
1966, April (South Vietnam) 162, 179
1966, June (US and Britain) 162, 181–4

1967, February (New Zealand) 205
1967, March (Cambodia, Laos, Taiwan) 192, 206
1967, May (US, Canada, London) 194–6

Wesley College 5, 113, 115, 227, 303, 307
will 304
women 15, 111, 304
writ for defamation (against Jack Egerton) 108–9
Holt, James Harold 306
Holt, Maura 206
Holt, Nick 7, 115, 168, 247, 306
Holt, Peter 206
Holt, Robert Harold 306
Holt, Sam 115, 168, 306
Holt, Sophie 306
Holt, Susan 206
Holt, Thomas 3–4
Holt, Tom xvi, 4, 6–7
Holt (Dickens, Fell), Zara Kate xvi, 6–8, 33–4, 37, 71–2, 114–15, 137, 151, 246, 248, 251, 253, 259, 261, 265–6, 268, 277, 284, 288–9, 295, 304–7
Dame of the British Empire (DBE) 304
demonstrators 164
disappearance and search 252, 259–60
dress shops 6, 34, 114, 306
'Harry' 136, 268
The Lodge 151–2
Holyoake, Keith 265
Home Savings Grant Scheme 120
Honeysuckle Creek 190
Horne, Donald 264
House of Representatives Practice 57
housing 10–1, 41–2, 49, 65, 72, 78, 138, 161, 222
Howard, John xiii, 133, 303
Howse, John 37
Howson, Peter 121–2, 126, 141, 200, 226–34, 242–3
Hsu Mo 281
Hudson, Commander Mike 260
Hudson, W.J. 55
Hughes, Andrew 53
Hughes, Billy 26, 28–31, 57
Hughes, Wilfred Kent 9, 104, 142, 207, 262–3, 256, 268, 287
Hulme, Alan 141, 243, 262
Humphrey, Hubert 178
Hursey, Denis 92
Hursey, Frank 92

Hurst, Herschel 130, 250–1
Hutchinson, William 20, 26, 30

Immigration 41–3, 57, 59, 62, 64–71, 72–3, 78, 106–7, 141, 158, 174, 220
Advisory Council 64, 159
Asian 187
Asilturk, Kemal 52
assimilation 65, 67
Australia's Immigration Policy (pamphlet) 160
citizenship 74, 160
citizenship conventions 68, 176
country of origin 15, 65, 70, 158
creating unemployment 67–8
deportations 36, 67
family reunions 159
German 66, 68
illegal 66
Migrant Citizenship Convention:
1950 67
1953 70
1954 69
1956 71

Nationality and Citizenship Act 160
'New Australians' 60, 66, 68
non-European 159
one millionth post-war immigrant 70–1
passports 49–50, 160
Planning Council 65
quotas 70
residential permits 67
refugees 67
screening tests 73
settlement 65
The Good Neighbour 74
White Australia Policy 36, 66–7, 74, 158, 160–1, 203, 302
industrial expansion 62
industrial relations 24, 41, 76, 93, 98
'Holt–Monk' axis 78, 87
Manufacturing Industries Advisory Council: 105
exports 14
mineral exploration 62
Miners' Federation 79
mining 77, 158
Ministry of Labour Advisory Council 96
Mount Newman Mine 161
Ord River Scheme 161
Secret Ballots Bill 92

shipping:
Australian Shipping Board 35
Australian Stevedoring Industrial Authority
(ASIA) 91–2
Australian Stevedoring Industrial
Board(ASIB) 78, 80–1, 84
Bill (1948) 35
Overseas Shipping Representatives
Association 78
shipowners 85–6, 89
stevedoring 77, 90
Stevedoring Industries Act 83–5, 90
strikes: 25, 34–5, 45, 49–50, 52, 76–77, 80,
86, 92
1928 Waterfront 84
1949 National Coal 77, 79
1967 Postal Unions 217
WWF against non-union labour recruiting
83
WWF pay and hours 88
WWF ship-loading rules 91

Tait Inquiry 90
use of military as a labour force 79, 82, 89
Waterfront reform 78, 91
Waterside labour supply 83–5, 91
industrial unrest 25, 86, 91
disputes 80–2
Innisfail 115
International Labour Conference
1950 93
1957 93–5
International Monetary Fund 101, 118
Bank for Reconstruction and Development
101
Finance Corporation 101

Jackson, Brigadier David 179
Jackson, Inspector (First Class) Aubrey
261
James, Betty 6
Japanese External Trade Organisation
(JETRO) 238–9
Jennings, Frank 151, 179
Jervis Bay 208
Jess, John 142, 207–8
Jodoin, Claude 93
Johns, Brian 126
Johnson, Lady Bird 268
Johnson, Lyndon B. 127, 162, 175, 177,
179, 181, 194, 197–200, 202–3, 262,
264–8, 273, 307

'All the Way' 183
Australian visit (1966) 163–4, 186
interfering in Australian politics 189
see also Holt, Harold E.
Johnson, Robert 297
Johnstone, Graeme 294
Joske, Percy 135
Australian Federal Government 135
Judd, Percy 24

Kawashima, Shojiro 265
Keating, Paul 133
Kelly, Peter 180, 216
Kennedy, John F. 149, 264, 267, 275, 293
Keon, Stan 48
Killen, Jim 58, 108, 142, 188, 201, 210,
254, 258, 276, 296
Kipling, Rudyard 266, 271
Kirby, Roger 113
Kirby, Sir Richard 90, 97
Kirribilli House 131, 152
Kittikachorn, Thanom 265
Knox, George 111
Kocan, Peter 149, 166, 264, 284
Koorine, SS 110
Kooyong (electorate) 11
by-election 165–6, 221
Korean War 45, 48, 50, 282
Korman & H.G. Palmer 108
Kosygin, Aleksei 197
Ky, Air Vice Marshall Nguyen Cao 183,
190–1

Laird, Celia 63, 113
Lang, Jack 9
Langmore, Diane 305
Larkin, Terry 100, 127
Latham (electorate) 57
Latimer, Sam 307
Latrobe (electorate) 221, 306
Law Council of Australia 83
Lawler, Peter 106, 179, 253
Lawless, Edith Mary 'Tiny' 34, 152, 246,
247–8, 251, 257
Lawson, James 18
League of Nations 13
Lee Kuan Yew 146, 265
Lett, Diane 272
Lewis, Essington 24
Liberal Party xv, 32, 34, 38, 51–2, 61–3,
74, 79, 111, 113, 120, 130–4, 137, 145,
166, 201, 217, 223, 235–6, 243–4, 253,

256, 261–2, 268–9, 293, 301
backbench 108, 116, 120, 125–6, 140, 142
Coalition strains 240
contesting rural seats 139, 166–7, 169, 222
discipline and solidarity 62, 207–9, 211, 236, 240
economic policy 99, 116
Federal executive 79, 116, 124
opposition 61, 70, 104, 121, 137, 206–7, 209, 224, 238, 242, 257–8
Liberal Party Council 32, 116–17, 217, 221, 268
Joint Party Meeting 119
Joint Standing Committee on Federal Policy 116
leadership 61, 133, 138, 253–60, 263, 267, 298, 302–3
organisational tensions 117, 120, 133, 166
party room 242, 269
philosophy 63
platform 66, 158
Reform Group 169
Victorian Party meeting 119
liberalism 32, 37–8, 54, 62, 65, 158, 160
Li Hung 280–1
Li Tao 282
Lillico, Alexander 211
Linklater, Art 102
Liu, Y.M. 282–3
Lloyd, Clem 143, 147, 296
Loan Council 101
Locsin, Aurelio 160
London's Royal Mint 128
Melbourne 128
Perth 128
Long, Bernadette ('Bernie') 151
Lonsdale, HMAS 251, 262
Looker, Cecil 26
Lowe, Justice Sir Charles 45
Lynch, Neville 250
Lynch, Phillip 306
Lyons, Dame Enid 14, 133, 141
Lyons, Joseph 15–16, 56, 135, 254
government 10–12, 18

Machin RA, Arnold 129
Macintyre, Stuart 296
Mackay, Rev Dr Malcolm 121–2, 207, 243
Macklin, Robert 255
Malik, Adam 265
Malony, Jim 297

Mandle, W.F. 297
Mannix, Dr Daniel 45
Mao Tse-tung 283
Marcos, President Ferdinand 86, 265
Marr, David 123, 125, 258
Martin, Harold 4, 5
Marvell 273
Mataafa 265
Matthews, Jack 278
Mattner, Edward 210
Maxwell, Bridges 243
Maxwell KC, George 11–12
McBride, Philip 22, 55–6
McCall, William 26
McClelland, Barr 293
McConnell, Jack 243
McEwen, John 26, 99–100, 106, 109–10, 113–14, 117–19, 124–6, 128, 130, 138–9, 165, 169, 224, 235–41, 244, 253–5, 257, 260–5, 268–71, 275, 278
McFarlane, A.B. 'Tich' 230
McGregor, Craig xii
McIllree, Eric 272
McIntosh, Hugh D. 4
McIntyre, Grant 219, 251
McKell, (Sir) William 39
McKellar, Colin 229
McMahon, Sonia 276
McMahon, William xiii, 4, 55, 63, 100, 119, 121–2, 131, 133, 137, 139, 141, 144, 161, 169, 174, 180, 200, 209, 211, 223, 235–9, 241–2, 244, 248, 253–5, 257–8, 260–4, 269, 271, 276, 294, 296
Deputy Party Leadership 137, 141
Treasurer 141, 161
McMahon–McEwen relationship 235, 237–8, 241–2, 244, 254, 260–1, 264
McManus, Frank 227
McMillan (electorate) 140
McNamara, Dr James 275
McNicoll, David 125
media 123–4, 143, 145–8, 158, 165, 167–8, 185, 187, 228, 247, 253, 259
current affairs programs 148, 208
Fairfax 124
The Harold Holt Mystery (documentary) 277
'Meet the Press' (NBC, US) 198
Murdoch 29, 124, 126, 269
Packer 123, 258
Parliamentary Press Gallery Committee 148
Parliamentary Proceedings Broadcasting Act 31
policy speech 167

political debates 63, 167
press 13–14, 16, 19, 22, 25, 29, 33, 37, 39, 49, 54, 59–60, 73, 85, 89, 102, 120, 123, 137, 141, 145, 148, 164, 167–8, 170, 184, 208, 221, 228, 232–3, 245, 267
press conferences 131, 147, 183, 197, 259–62
Press Gallery 115, 148–50, 202
radio 22, 31
television 59, 113, 143, 147, 167
This Day Tonight (ABC program) 148, 208
Melbourne Harbour Trust 249
Melbourne, HMAS 207, 209
Menzies, Dame Pattie 130, 227
Menzies, Sir Robert xvii, 5, 9, 11, 16, 18, 22, 33, 37, 43, 45, 52, 56–7, 68, 73, 92, 95, 100, 104–5, 111, 113, 115, 117–18, 121–5, 127–8, 131, 138, 144–5, 151, 158, 165, 174, 188, 205, 210–11, 227, 239, 245, 257, 269, 296–8, 302–3
Cabinet 23, 26, 44, 49, 54, 62, 82, 86, 88, 92, 99, 107, 119–20, 131, 140–1
Holt 30, 116, 122, 133, 146, 169, 180, 224
government (I) 18–22
government (II) 39, 41, 61–3, 77, 85, 105, 116
leadership tensions and succession 26–8, 55, 59, 117, 123, 132, 303
retirement 54
UAP transition to the Liberal Party 29–30, 131
Warden of the Cinque Ports 127
Wentworth, Bill 61
Michaelis, Archie 17
Millar, T.B. 287
Monk, Albert 39, 64, 78–80, 82–8, 97
Moore, David 163
Moore, Jan 151
Moore, Robert 148
Morgan, Private Peter 250
Muir, Nigel 273
Murdoch, Sir Keith 29, 112
Murphy, John 44
Murphy, Lionel 218, 230, 233
Murray-Smith, Stephen 48
Myer Store 114

Napthine, Milton 295
Nasser, Gamal Abdul 197
National Council of Women 64
National Farmers' Union 67
National Fitness Campaign 15, 17

National Service 15, 95, 167, 189
birthday ballots 96
cards 206
conscription 187, 188
National Register Act 18
National Service Bill 96
National Servicemen 95, 168, 178, 180
nationalising
banks 37, 50, 103
health service 37
Nazis 66, 68, 72
Nethercote, John
Liberalism and the Australian Federation xv
New Zealand 205
Limited Free Trade Agreement 205
Newcastle 97
Newell, Inspector Laurie 251, 259–60, 277
Newport, Mary 150
Newton, Maxwell 124, 126, 237–9, 242, 263
Management Newsletter 124, 238
Nixon, Peter 128, 228
Noack, Pte Errol 180
Noonan, Gerard 293
North West Cape (Joint naval communications facility) 120, 190, 307
Nubba 4–5

Oakes, Laurie 223
Odgers, James Rowland 255
O'Keefe, Annie 36, 67
Opperman, Hubert 159–60, 172, 187, 220–1
Oronsay, SS 70
Osborne, Fred 268
Overacker, Louise 233

Packer, Sir Frank 123
Pagan, Jock 243, 268
Page, Sir Earle 16, 23, 26, 55, 103
Palmer, Corporal John 22
Paltridge, Shane 122, 141–2, 144, 171–2
Parliamentary Joint Committee on
Broadcasting Parliamentary Proceedings 31
War Expenditure 31
Parramatta (electorate) 119, 122
Patterson, Dr Rex 165
Peacock, Andrew 165–6, 205, 305
Pearce, George 287
Pearce, Olive May 4, 5, 206
Pearce, Vera 5, 206

Pearson, Keith 100
Pearson, Lester 194
Perkins, Charles 215
Petrov, Vladimir 49–50, 123
Phayer, Bruce 170
Pine Gap 190
Pius XII, Pope 72
Plimsoll, Sir James 255
pneumoconiosis conference 93
Point Nepean 248, 260
Port Kembla 97
Portsea 114, 133, 149, 152, 241–2, 246,
    249–51, 253, 261, 265, 268, 278, 293,
    306
  backbeach 249
  Officer Cadet School 250, 260–1
Post Office 106
Postal Act 218
  postal charges 106, 218, 244
  Saturday services 217–18
Premiers' Conferences 101, 162, 205
Prime Minister's Department 18, 144,
    150–1, 197, 226, 229, 231, 253
  Civil Supply Section 18
  **Council for Scientific and Industrial
    Research (CSIR):** 17–18, 23
  National Oil Pty Ltd Agreement 18
  National Register Act 18
  North Australia Survey Act 18
  Office of Aboriginal Affairs 215
  Science & Industry Research Act 1920–1939
    17
  Standing Committee on Liquid Fuels 18
  vehicle 151, 253
Privy Council 73, 137, 205
  appeals 90, 217
proportional representation 52
Prowse, Edgar 211
public transport 42

Qantas 102, 141

Radnor 82
Rahman, Tunku Abdul 160, 193, 194
Raleigh, Sir Walter 300
Ramsay, Alan 302
Randall, Richard 100–1, 118, 141, 150,
    236
Rankin, Dame Annabelle 141
rationing 36–7
Ratu Mara 265
Razak, Tun Abdul 265

Reeve, Ada 4
Referendum 47, 210–11, 213
  Aborigines in census 211–12, 214, 216, 302
  Communist Party 47–8
  House and Senate size 'nexus' 210–11, 214,
    244
Reid, Alan 79, 86, 181, 232, 237, 255, 257
  The Gorton Experiment 257
Reid, George 296
Reid, Gordon 143
Reid, Murray 108
Reserve Bank of Australia 103, 106
  Bill 103
  currency issue 103, 128
  Rural Credits Department 104
  visits 104
Returned Sailors', Soldiers' and Airmen's
  Association 64
Rhodesia 185–6
Richardson, Sir Frank 108
Rivett, Sir David 17
Robertson, John 207, 209
Rockefeller, David (III) 102
Roman Catholic Social Studies
  Movement 50
Rose, Alec 248–9
Rosenblum, Alex 111
Royal Australian Air Force (RAAF) 22,
  71, 120
  34 Squadron 226–7, 229–30
  planes 120, 149, 210
  Vietnam deployments 177–8, 190
  VIP Fleet 149–50, 226–8, 246
Royal Australian Mint 128–9
Royal Australian Navy (RAN)
  Far East Strategic Reserve 198
  submarine 'bottoming' 285–6
  Vietnam deployments 190, 198
Royal Commission into
  Communist Party 45
  Soviet Espionage in Australia 49, 123
  HMAS *Voyager* (1964) 207
  HMAS *Voyager* (1967) 209, 244
Royal Empire Society 10
Royal visits
  1954 49
  Duke of Edinburgh 206
  Princess Alexandra 206
  Queen Mother (1966) 152
Rushcutter, HMAS 252
Russell, Charles Wilfred 169
Ryan, Rupert 29, 65

Salter, Dr Wilf 106
Samuel, Peter 114
Sandford, Charles 171
Santamaria, B.A. 44
Saunders, Ray 219
Schedvin, C.B. 109
Scholes, Gordon 221
Scott, Malcolm 255, 258
Scullin, James 9–10, 296
Selleck, Austin 100
Senate 143, 204, 210, 228–30
  Australian Senate Practice 255
  casual vacancies 171–2
  'House of Obstruction' 103, 234
  rejecting financial decisions 218, 244
  Senate Elections Act 1966 171
  Senator becoming PM, ramifications of 256
Seward, Harrie 90
Shalders, Capt Rick 285
Sharkey, L. 34
Shaw, George 165
Sherrington, Robert 171
Shiff, Alfred 63
Short, Jim 100, 151
Shortell, James 83, 91
Shotter, Lieutenant Michael 252, 291
Sim, Peter 172
Simpson, Robert 'Martin' 248, 250, 261
Sinclair, Iain 144, 205, 228, 239–40, 254
Sinclair, Keith 97, 150, 157
Six Day War 197
Skinner, Frederick 170
Smith, Ian 185
Snedden, Billy 133, 141, 220, 269
socialism 9, 35, 37–8, 60
Sorrento 246–7, 278, 305
Southey, Bob 268
Spender, Percy 30, 287, 298
Spicer, Sir John 9, 29, 80, 90, 209
Spooner, Bill 55–6, 119, 122, 171
Spooner, Eric 26, 56
Spry, Brigadier Charles 263
St John QC, Edward 208, 243, 276
  maiden speech 208–9
St Paul's Anglican Cathedral, Melbourne
  265–7
Stanley, Morgan 73
Stanner, Prof W.E.H. 'Bill' 215
State Electricity Commission (Victoria)
  71
Stevens, Capt Duncan 207–8

Stewart, Alan 248, 250, 261–2, 276, 278
Stewart, Sir Frederick 17
Stirling, HMAS 195
Street, Brigadier Geoffrey 21–2
Strong, Most Rev Philip 266
Stuart, Francis 187
Suez Crisis 54–6
Sung Fa-Tsiang 280
Sung Ting-hua 281
Sydney Stock Exchange 107
Sydney Trades and Labour Council 86

Tait QC, J.B. 83
  Inquiry 85, 90
Talbot, Wal 39
Tange, Arthur 24
Tangney, Dorothy 37
Taylor, General Maxwell 198
The Lodge 151–2, 163, 206, 250–1
Thieu, Nguyen Van 183, 265
Thomas, Very Rev T.W. 266
Thornton, Ernie 10, 34
Thornwaite, Lieutenant Colonel Francis
  21
Thring, Viola ('Lola') Margaret 7
Tidbinbilla 190
Titcombe, Lieutenant Commander
  Ronald xiv, 279–80, 282, 288–92
  reliability 291–2
Tivoli circuit 4–5
Townsville 115
Tran Van Do 265
Treasury 43–4, 101, 114, 118, 137, 139,
  144, 236, 261
  age pensions 49–50, 162
  Australian dollar 239, 240, 246, 271
  Banking Bill 31
  banking sector reform 102
  Budget:
  1959 106
  1960 106, 123; mini budget 107–9, 113
  1961 110
  1962 117–18; mini budget 117
  1963 119
  1964 119, 126
  1965 127

  cash deficit 117
  central bank 102–3, 111
  Committee of Economic Enquiry (Vernon)
  113
  Currency Bill 129

credit 'squeeze' 108, 110–11, 113–14, 116, 132
Decimal Currency 127–9
Decimal Currnecy Board 129
Decimal Currency Committee 127
deficit financing 117
devaluation compensation 241, 247
Development Bank 102
development strategy 101
economic policy 44, 71, 99, 101, 109
foreign aid and investment 99, 118
GDP 161
hire purchase 96, 108
industry protection 110, 169, 236
inflation 35, 42–3, 63, 68, 87–8, 107, 113, 117, 119, 146, 161, 187
interest rates 106–8
international reserves 106–7
Permanent Head (Wilson) 100
parliamentary salaries 13, 59, 114, 153
private banks 102, 105
recession 35, 42, 44, 69, 108
sterling devaluation 192, 236, 239–41
tariffs 240
tax deductibility 107
taxes 21, 36–7, 106–7, 109, 110–11, 117
trade boom 146
trade deficit 106
'Vernon Report' 113
wages 60, 76, 87–8, 93, 119, 161; average weekly earnings 60, 87
Treaty of Versailles 93
Turnbull, Reginald 5, 113, 227, 235
Turner, Harry 121, 136, 299

Underwater Skindivers and Fishermen's Association of Australia 249
unemployment 10–3, 42–3, 59, 62, 67–8, 87, 89, 107–9, 111, 113, 119, 146, 161
benefits 117
unions 23, 60, 67, 78, 87, 96, 299
Amalgamated Engineering Union 92–3
Australian Workers Union 48, 64, 83
communist leadership 29, 34, 37, 77–8, 82, 86, 92
compulsory unionism 93
immigration 67, 97
membership dues 92
Metal Trades union 86
postal unions 217
registration 77, 80, 84
trade union movement 34, 81–2, 87, 97

Trade unions 34–5, 37, 45, 48, 51, 127
Waterside Workers Federation (WWF): 35, 46, 78–9, 92
action against NZ shipping June 1951 79
communist influences 78, 82–3, 91
deregistration threat 80, 84–5
exclusion from bulk-loading terminals 91
'margins' dispute, January 1956 87–9
non-union labour in sugar cane areas, August 1953 81–2
overtime bans, May 1952 80
recruitment of waterside labour dispute, August 1954 83–5, 87
Tait Inquiry 90
wharfies 79–80, 82, 85, 89, 92
United Australia Party xvii, 9–10, 12, 16, 19, 22, 26–32, 111
party organisation 29–31
United Nations 37, 56, 61, 73, 95, 160, 283
China 186
Commission on Human Rights 160
Conference on Trade and Development 180
Middle East/Six Day War 197
Rhodesia 185
United States 72, 102
Australian relations 50, 61, 65, 179, 184, 189, 200–1, 302
Britain 182, 192, 195
Central Intelligence Agency 277
China 287
Information Service (USIS) 238
Pine Gap 190
Presidential visit 162–4, 262
request for troops 178, 199–200
satellite bases 190
trade talks 126–7, 198
Vietnam and South-east Asia 177, 185, 198
Vietnam and South-east Asia bombing campaign 177, 199–200, 234
Wool Tariff Interest Equalisation Act 198

Valenti, Jack 178
Vernon, Sir James 113
report 113–14
Verstak, Tania (Miss International 1966) 114
Victoria Police 250–1, 253, 259, 261–2, 265, 294
Victorian Cinematograph Exhibitors Association 9
Victorian Trades Hall Council 11, 21

Vietnam 150, 167, 186, 221–3, 225,
234–5, 252
anti-war protests 163–4, 188, 191
Australian commitment 178, 187, 189–90,
199
Battle of Long Tan 204
Dien Bien Phu 49
Holt's tour, April 1966 179
French 82, 183, 265
Manila conference 163–4, 186–7, 202
Prime Minister's visit to Australia 190–1
withdrawal from 168, 188
war 127, 161, 166, 168, 174, 186–9,
199–200, 203, 278
Vincent, Seddon 170, 172
VIP airline scandal 226–34, 244, 256, 276
Flight Authorisation Books 226, 229–31
Holt, answer to the house 226, 228–9, 232
Holt, family use of aircraft 228
passenger manifests 227–30
Prime Minister's Departmental reply 226
Senate 228–30
Voyager, HMAS xiii, 172, 207–8, 217, 225,
233, 244

Wade, Harry 171
Waller, Sir Keith 182–3
Walliker, Sergeant 219
Walpole, Sir Robert 300
Walsh, Max 181, 183
Wang Kung-fang 281
Ward, Eddie 28, 61, 74
Warrender, Simon 266, 273
Watson, Ron 55
Weeroona Estate 253
Weisner, Flight Lieutenant Richard 22
Wei Tao-Ming 286
Wentworth (electorate) 118
Wentworth, Bill 61, 123, 142, 205, 207,
215, 222, 243, 257
Werriwa (electorate) 120
West, Katharine 57, 235
Westerman, Sir Alan 238, 240
White, Lieutenant General Sir Brudenell
21
White, Tom 20
Whitington, Don xii, 57, 97, 256, 276

Whitlam, Gough 113, 120, 123, 133, 144,
150, 160, 166–8, 170–1, 173, 183,
200–1, 204–5, 210, 218–19, 221–6, 231,
234–5, 244, 270, 296, 302
government 161
Whitrod, Commissioner Ray 219
Wildlife Preservation Society of
Queensland 218
Wilkie, Douglas 181
Willesee, Mike 208
Williamstown Naval Dockyard 59, 86
Willoughby, J.R. 150, 172, 221, 243
Wilson, Alex 27
Wilson, Keith 20, 112
Wilson, Harold 175–6, 181–5, 192–7,
205, 217, 265, 268
government on sterling 192, 239
Wilson, Sir Roland 24, 100–1, 103, 109,
128, 141, 150, 236, 299
Wilton, Lieutenant General Sir John 179
Withers, Reg 137, 172
Wolfenden & Company 86
Wood, Ian 142, 210
Woodful, A.H. 11
Woods, Most Rev Frank 265
Woods, Corporal Neville 250
Woodward, Keith 85, 91
Woolcott, Richard 132, 190, 288
World Bank 118
World Peace Movement 50
World War II 64, 77
declaration of 18
Worner, Mary Ann 4
Wright, F.R. 115
Wright, Reg 90, 142, 211, 299
Wurth, Wallace 24
Wyatt, Charlie 278

Yarra (electorate) 9–10
Yeend, Geoffrey 229
Yen, C.K. 265
Young Australian Foundation 157
Young Nationalists 9

Zhou En-lai 282–3

Printed in Great Britain
by Amazon.co.uk, Ltd.,
Marston Gate.